STUDIES ON ETHNIC GROUPS IN CHINA
Stevan Harrell, Editor

Cultural Encounters on China's Ethnic Frontiers, edited by Stevan Harrell

Guest People: Hakka Identity in China and Abroad, edited by Nicole Constable

Familiar Strangers: A History of Muslims in Northwest China, by Jonathan N. Lipman

Lessons in Being Chinese: Minority Education and Ethnic Identity in Southwest China, by Mette Halskov Hansen

Manchus and Han: Ethnic Relations and Political Power in Late Qing and Early Republican China, 1861–1928, by Edward J. M. Rhoads

Ways of Being Ethnic in Southwest China, by Stevan Harrell

Governing China's Multiethnic Frontiers, edited by Morris Rossabi

On the Margins of Tibet: Cultural Survival on the Sino-Tibetan Frontier, by Åshild Kolås and Monika P. Thowsen

The Art of Ethnography: A Chinese "Miao Album," translation by David M. Deal and Laura Hostetler

Doing Business in Rural China: Liangshan's New Ethnic Entrepreneurs, by Thomas Heberer

Communist Multiculturalism: Ethnic Revival in Southwest China, by Susan K. McCarthy

Religious Revival in the Tibetan Borderlands: The Premi of Southwest China, by Koen Wellens

In the Land of the Eastern Queendom: The Politics of Gender and Ethnicity on the Sino-Tibetan Border, by Tenzin Jinba

Empire and Identity in Guizhou: Local Resistance to Qing Expansion, by Jodi L. Weinstein

China's New Socialist Countryside: Modernity Arrives in the Nu River Valley, by Russell Harwood

Mapping Shangrila: Contested Landscapes in the Sino-Tibetan Borderlands, edited by Emily T. Yeh and Chris Coggins

A Landscape of Travel: The Work of Tourism in Rural Ethnic China, by Jenny Chio

MAPPING SHANGRILA

• • •

CONTESTED LANDSCAPES *in the*
SINO-TIBETAN BORDERLANDS

Edited by

EMILY T. YEH

and

CHRIS COGGINS

UNIVERSITY OF WASHINGTON PRESS
Seattle and London

This publication was made possible in part by a grant
from the National Science Foundation

UNIVERSITY OF WASHINGTON PRESS
www.washington.edu/uwpress

LIBRARY OF CONGRESS CATALOGING-IN-PUBLICATION DATA
Mapping Shangrila : contested landscapes in the Sino-Tibetan borderlands /
edited by Emily T. Yeh and Chris Coggins.
   pages cm. — (Studies on ethnic groups in China)
Includes bibliographical references and index.
ISBN 978-0-295-99357-7 (hardback : alkaline paper) —
ISBN 978-0-295-99358-4 (paperback : alkaline paper)
1. China—Relations—China—Tibet Autonomous Region. 2. Tibet Autonomous
Region (China)—Relations—China. 3. Landscapes—Political aspects—China.
4. Landscapes—Political aspects—China—Tibet Autonomous Region. 5. Shangri-La
(Imaginary place) 6. Borderlands—China. 7. Borderlands—China—Tibet Autonomous
Region. 8. Geography—Political aspects—China. 9. China—Environmental conditions.
10. Tibet Autonomous Region (China)—Environmental conditions.
I. Yeh, Emily T. (Emily Ting) II. Coggins, Chris, 1963–
DS740.5.T5M37 2014   327.51051'5—dc23   2014004037

Contents

Foreword

Mapping Shangrila? The very title screams contradiction. The original Shangrila of James Hilton's *Lost Horizon* was unmappable—hidden away in a place no one had previously known about and no one could find except by accident. It was a place of the imagination. And now people are not just mapping it; they are visiting it, preserving it, developing it, and harvesting mushrooms from it for a world market. The imagined space that was really nowhere has become real (or at least the imagination of that space has been projected on a real place), while at the same time the real space of the Sino-Tibetan borderlands has been imagined—as a place of difference, a place of conservation, a place of abundant resources, a place of aesthetic pleasure.

In the introduction to this varied and stimulating collection, Chris Coggins tells the story of visiting Khawa Karpo and mentions that it is one of the eight *gnas ri*, or sacred mountains of Tibet. Recalling only Kailas out of that catalog, and curious what the other six might be, I searched online for *gnas ri* and found an entry for a country of that name at the *Nation States Encyclopedia*, a wiki site that consists of (as the editors inform us) more than forty-four thousand entries, all of them for totally fictitious countries and nations. Gnasri, according to the site, is "an isolated, landlocked country located north of Karenytenia and Purzkistan . . . at an average elevation of 4,500 meters." Several of the names associated with the geography and history of Gnasri are given *in Tibetan script*.

To most of us, the physical *gnas ri* Khawa Karpo is no more real than its eponymous kingdom next door to Purzkistan. And although the mountain is undeniably physically there, still, in the imaginations of people living nearby, it is, after all, a *gnas ri*, a "dwelling mountain" of a powerful god. The god, in fact, buried seventeen Chinese and Japanese mountaineers preparing to defile (i.e., climb) it in 1991, after which an unlikely coalition of local traditionalists and the Nature Conservancy successfully petitioned the State Council in 2000 to keep the real place imagined by not allowing anyone to go there, any more than they can go to Gnasri or could go to the original Shangrila.

But now people *can* go to Shangrila, because it is a real place, a county that used to be called Zhongdian in Chinese and is still called Gyalthang in Tibetan, easy to find on a real map north of Lijiang and south of Deqin in northwest Yunnan. And it is but one place in the Sino-Tibetan borderlands that is being not only reimagined but incorporated into the Chinese nation-state as a space of accessible wonder, friendly exotica, extraction opportunities, and conservation imperatives.

How the Sino-Tibetan borderlands are becoming legible—readable—is the topic of this book. And one can read the book as the history of any combination of a set of interlocking stories that make up a fascinating part of the real history of our time.

One can read *Mapping Shangrila* as a story of a real nation-state, or at least of a People's Republic of China that is trying hard to become one, by incorporating topographic, ecological, economic, and cultural differences into a proud, strong, united, modern nation that nevertheless preserves its local differences. Or one can read the book as the story of global capitalism and its penetration of previously inaccessible places in search of resources and profits, from lumber to minerals to mushrooms. In still another way, one can read the book as a story of the globalized reaction to this resource exploitation—of nongovernmental organizations, government agencies, and even private citizens working to preserve the landscapes, flora, fauna, and cultures of places that need to remain exotic both for their own sake and for the sake of people who want to visit them. Or again, one can read the book as a story of imagined places, or how imagined places become real and how real places become imagined from various vantage points.

My point is that the political, economic, conservationist, and imaginary projects are all part of a grand transformation, one we could not have foreseen when University of Washington Press editors and I conceived the Studies on Ethnic Groups in China series back in 1993. There are still ethnic groups in China, but their relationship to the state, the economy, and the rest of the populace, not to mention their relationship to the rest of the world, has been transformed beyond anything we could have imagined back then. We can no more return to the Zhongdian of 1993, or to the 1993 version of any of the places described in this book, than we can visit Hilton's Shangrila or the Gnasri kingdom of the role-player's imagination. But through the vision (dare I say "imagination"?) and editorial leadership of Emily Yeh and Chris

Coggins, along with the variegated and polyglot ethnographic sensibility of the chapter authors, this book has come together to make the nature of this transformation lucidly legible to readers. Read, then, and feast on the multiple contradictions of *Mapping Shangrila*.

STEVAN HARRELL
October 2013

Acknowledgments

Mapping Shangrila could not have been written without the many Tibetans in northwest Yunnan, Qinghai, the Tibet Autonomous Region (TAR), and beyond whose guidance, knowledge, and insights made this work possible. We thank them first and foremost.

We are very excited about this book's placement in the University of Washington Press's Studies on Ethnic Groups in China series. We thank series editor Stevan Harrell, two anonymous manuscript reviewers, and executive editor Lorri Hagman for their helpful suggestions and support. We are also grateful to editor Tim Zimmermann for his help throughout the publication process and to editor Mary Ribesky and copy editor Laura Iwasaki for their sharp eyes and detailed attention in seeing the manuscript through its final stages of production. Mark Henderson's cartographic skills significantly enhance *Mapping Shangrila*; we thank him for his maps. We thank Celia Braves for her index, which lends coherence to the volume. Publication was supported in part by a grant from the National Science Foundation (BCS 0847722).

Each and every one of the contributors to this volume was a delight to work with. We are very appreciative of their intellectual contributions, collegiality, timeliness, and patience. We are also deeply grateful to each other, for an exciting and truly collaborative exchange of ideas and for the hard work, wisdom, and energy put into this project.

Finally, we are both indebted to our families. Chris thanks Tanya, Aaron, and Noah for sharing in the journey with understanding, perseverance, and love. Emily thanks Kunga, Osel, and Seldron for their companionship and patience with her constant presence in front of a computer.

Note on Transliterations and Place-Names

Chinese terms and names are given in standard pinyin and are preceded by "Ch." if both Tibetan and Chinese terms are being used and there is a possibility of confusion within a chapter. For Tibetan, the dramatic differences in regional pronunciation, on the one hand, and the indecipherability of the Wylie transliteration system for those who do not read Tibetan, on the other, create difficulties. Upon first usage of a term, we generally give a simplified rendering of the Central Tibetan dialect pronunciation (preceded by "Tib.") followed by the Wylie transliteration (preceded by "Wyl."). Thus, for example, the term for "territorial deity generally abiding within mountains" is given as "Tib. *zhidak*" (the Central Tibetan pronunciation), even though the pronunciation is closer to *reda* in northwest Yunnan. In Wylie, it is written *gzhi bdag*.

For towns, counties, and prefectures, we use Chinese or Tibetan names depending on what is in more common use, for example, Zhongdian (the Chinese name) rather than Gyalthang (Tibetan), but Rebgong (Tibetan) rather than Tongren (Chinese).

Abbreviations and Foreign-Language Terms

CCP	Chinese Communist Party
CI	Conservation International
CITES	Convention on International Trade in Endangered Species of Wild Flora and Fauna
IUCN	International Union for Conservation of Nature
lhawa	Tibetan term, medium of a territorial deity (*zhidak*)
mu	Chinese measurement of area: 1/15th of a hectare
NGO	nongovernmental organization
PRC	People's Republic of China
TAR	Tibet Autonomous Region
TNC	The Nature Conservancy
tulku	Tibetan, incarnate lama
WWF	World Wide Fund for Nature
xiejiao	Chinese, heterodox or perverse cult
zhidak	Tibetan term, territorial deity commonly abiding within mountains

MAPPING

SHANGRILA

Introduction

• • •

PRODUCING SHANGRILAS

Chris Coggins and Emily T. Yeh

O<small>N</small> a clear, cool day in late October 2006, we are driving north along National Highway 214 near Deqin (Tib. Dechen) in Diqing Tibetan Autonomous Prefecture, in northwest Yunnan. After passing Feilai Temple and rounding a curve high above the upper Mekong River, we suddenly face Khawa Karpo,[1] a massive mountain looming beyond the deep gorge, guarded by a range of ice-clad peaks sparkling in the autumn sun; this is one of the most powerful deities in cultural Tibet. Ma Jianzhong, the director of the Nature Conservancy (TNC) office in Deqin, and the driver, Pema, whoop simultaneously, "Ohh lhaso lhaso lhaso! Lha rgyal lo! Wooo!" (Victory to the gods!). Although we are headed to northern Deqin County to conduct field research on *yullha* (Wyl. *yul lha*) and *zhidak* (Wyl. *gzhi bdag*), two types of local deities associated with lesser sacred mountains and depicted as warriors, ancestors, and ancestral divinities, there is time to stop the jeep and take a short break to behold this spectacle of supernature (Karmay 1994).[2] We gaze in wonder at the craggy features of the seven major horns, with their surrounding cirques, cols, and arêtes, and at the sacred Mingyong glacier, which descends in a hanging valley from a firn field bounded by a high head-wall. Like tens of thousands of tourists who visit each year, we also take photographs. I (Chris) have never seen Mount Everest (Wyl. Jo Mo Glang Ma), but I sense that Khawa Karpo is beyond compare. The summit of Everest rises 8,850 meters above sea level, 2,110 meters higher than Khawa Karpo's main peak (6,740 m), but scientific measurements operate within a different set of myths. Khawa Karpo is more than a common warrior god. It is one of the eight *neri* (Wyl. *gnas ri*), or "abode mountains," the holiest mountains in Tibetan Buddhism, and the name denotes both the god himself and the mountain where he resides. Originally a fierce *nyen* (Wyl. *gnyan*), or mountain demon, he was transformed into a protector of the Dharma by Padmasambhava in the eighth century.[3]

According to tradition, to climb to the peak would defile the deity, who would abandon the abode, and Khawa Karpo has never been climbed. Though Everest is also a sacred mountain, it is not one of the *neri*. Since Edmund Hillary reached the pinnacle of Everest in 1953, reputedly commenting to his colleague W. G. Lowe at base camp, "Well, George, we knocked the bastard off," more than 3,100 people have followed. This is not to say that alpine impulses have not been a serious threat to Khawa Karpo as well; between 1987 and 2000, many attempts on the peak were made by climbers from China, Japan, and the United States, but all without success. The best-known failure occurred in 1991, when a Sino-Japanese climbing team approached the peak on the second of January. When the team was all set to conquer the mountain the following morning, news of the final assault reached officials in the county seat of Deqin, and word spread quickly to people in the streets. Hundreds of Tibetans gathered at Feilai Temple to pray and to protest the god's submission to the climbers. Women reportedly yelled curses at Khawa Karpo and raised their skirts to insult the deity in protest while demanding an explanation for its submission. Lamas were deployed to pray for the mountain's well-being. The next morning, the entire team of seventeen climbers was wiped out by an avalanche that was observed by people in herding camps below. Supplicants later asked Khawa Karpo for forgiveness for their insulting behavior but thanked him for ending the assault on the mountain. There was concern about the lost corpses and how their spirits would be pacified. On the high slopes above Yubeng Village, a series of rituals was performed for the souls of the dead and the purity of the mountain (Litzinger 2004).

Scientific logic demands that the reader pay close attention here. Clearly those climbers died for reasons having nothing to do with mountain deities, the invocations of lamas, or the prayers and protests of lay believers. But the driver from Deqin who takes me to the foot of the Mingyong glacier, which lies along the 240-kilometer circumambulation (Tib. *korwa*; Wyl. *skor ba*) route, assures me that the connection is incontrovertible. Clear skies in the morning show that Khawa Karpo is happy and my visit is blessed. Clouds shrouding the mountain's head in the afternoon are Khawa Karpo's anger on display—Japanese tourists are visiting the glacier, and the driver makes it clear that the attempted assault on the peak is part of a longer history of Japanese atrocities perpetrated on China. Whether or not Khawa Karpo discriminates between heroes and villains in the Second Sino-Japanese War, the Dechenwa know that the mountain is ever vigilant over those who enter and exit its domain.

By the year 2000, TNC and Deqin County officials had successfully petitioned Beijing to ban mountaineering on Khawa Karpo and its neighboring peaks, and since then, no expeditions have been permitted. However, this did not solve the problem of contamination by exogenous forces and interlopers, and Yubeng villagers continued to voice concerns about the spiritual and environmental impact of both the climbing incident and the growing local tourist industry, despite the fact that the latter brought them unprecedented levels of income. In 2004, when global warming had been implicated in the glacier's dramatic retreat, a Yubeng Village leader named Ahnanzhu described his perceptions of the connection between the forces of globalization, global warming, and local environmental change.

> A little ways up above our village, up where the waterfall is, on the side of the river, there were large flat sections of ice that a plane could have landed on—I can remember this from when I was young. As I grew up, I saw that the glacier was receding year by year; . . . in the past [before tourism], our village didn't produce as much smoke [and ash;] . . . there wasn't much smoke and other forms of pollution, so the glacier was stable. Since then, there has been an increase in pollution year by year; smoke and dust increased year by year, and the glacier began to recede. . . . [The climbing accident] had a big impact on us [as well]. Throughout history there have never been such big impacts on the mountains. We have never had large-scale threats, sudden disturbances like deforestation, [and] the threat of road building. . . . People's lifespans have also shortened. In the past, people could live for over a hundred years; these days, people live to seventy or eighty at the most.

Similarly, in a participatory film made by several local Diqing intellectuals in 2002, Mingyong villagers discuss at length the causes of the melting of the Mingyong glacier. One states:

Especially after the year 2000 there are more people coming; the pollution is serious and now there's electricity. These three problems put together make the situation really bad. In the past, people couldn't even go up [the glacier]. Now even the cows can make it up. If there were no people going up, no littering, and no electricity use, the glacier could recover naturally. If the current situation continues, the glacier will continue to recede. Before, the Japanese ascent team was buried [under ice and snow]. Three years ago, they discovered their corpses on the glacier.[4]

Here again, glacial retreat is understood primarily as a local phenomenon that results from human violations of sacred space, rather than being seen through the lens of anthropogenic global climate change.

In each of these vignettes, one mountain massif is a congeries of narratives, beliefs, performances, and claims, many of which fail to conform neatly to the tidy ontological and epistemic categories of "nature" and "society" that are central to directives from the Chinese Communist Party (CCP) to build the "ecological state" (Ch. *shengtai lizhou* or *shengtai liguo*) and to establish a "harmonious society" (Ch. *hexie shehui*). However, it would be wrong to assume that these disconformities and hybrid ontologies are *not* products of the formal political orderings that emerge from governance. For TNC staff members mentioned above, Khawa Karpo is simultaneously a major Tibetan pilgrimage site—the domain of very powerful and idiosyncratic deities (whose beneficent, dangerous, and capricious qualities demand attention)—and the centerpiece for what is supposed to become an internationally prominent protected area, the Meili Snow Mountains National Park, the cultural and biophysical features of which they must assess with scientific precision. Thus the mountain stands at the center of their labors and provides grounding for their claims to professional expertise, while also animating a field of personal memories and meanings associated with the home place and home region. The driver speaks on behalf of Khawa Karpo's powers of surveillance and defense, as the mountain recollects dark atrocities in the form of menacing clouds high above our heads. Ahnanzhu gives voice to the anxiety that he and other residents of Yubeng Village experience vis-à-vis transnational conservation interest in the area and international environmental discourse on global warming (by this time, villagers have been interviewed on this subject by journalists from the *New York Times*, among others[5]); radical changes in household economies and internecine relations following a massive influx of trekking and horseback-riding tourists, both domestic and international; and the knowledge that the individual and collective health and fortune of village residents are contingent on a relationship of reciprocity with Khawa Karpo.

These scenarios reveal relationships between the shifting and competing *doxa* of religious and political ideologies and the *habitus* of everyday lives, relationships that are mutually constitutive with rapid infrastructural development, exponential growth in domestic and international tourism, and a wave of state and private environmental projects based on new forms of governmentality that prioritize "ecology" and "culture."[6] While these two terms assume the universality of Western secular, scientific discourse, they are, of necessity, grounded in particular landscapes, which are themselves material and symbolic, physical and ideational, and, in Tibetan contexts, quite capable of personal expression. While we do not conceptualize landscapes from a foundationalist or determinist perspective, each of the case studies in *Mapping Shangrila* explores ways in which landscapes are deployed—often as foundational evidence—in contests for epistemological authority. The cultural landscapes of the Sino-Tibetan borderlands are, as elsewhere, media for the social construction of territory, nature, and personhood. Our contributors adopt an interdisciplinary approach, examining the political ecology of changing landscapes and power relations in Tibetan communities during a period of unprecedented growth in the economic and political infrastructure of the People's Republic of China (PRC).

Although often relegated to the margins of "western China," "the Chinese frontiers," or "outer China," the Sino-Tibetan border regions historically have shaped and defined a vast peripheral zone between imperial polities, China and Tibet, whose expansions and contractions ensured a series of competing territorial claims by distant sovereigns supported or resisted by distinctive local and regional sociopolitical formations (Coleman 2002; Epstein 2002; Huber 2002; Peng 2002; van Spengen 2002). Despite their distance from the centers of political power and economic dynamism, the Sino-Tibetan borderlands are integral to understanding social and environmental change in the contemporary People's Republic of China. The margins are not a realm of exotic practices but rather "a necessary entailment of the state, much as the exception is a necessary component of the rule" (Das and Poole 2004, 4). Thus, a Beijing-centric or eastern-seaboard-centric view of China's rise is incomplete. Not only do Tibetan regions constitute roughly one quarter of PRC territory, but dynamics of middle-class subject formation, the creation of national geographic imaginaries, processes of state territorialization, and principles of ecological governance are worked out here, creating these places in relation to and mutually constitutive of the capitalist powerhouses of the east.

A necessarily imprecisely defined region, the Sino-Tibetan borderlands we refer to encompass much of the Tibetan cultural regions of Amdo and Kham. Despite our focus on Tibetan communities living in these border-lands, they were and are ethnically and linguistically complex and fluid. Indeed, part of our project is to investigate the multiple landscape and iden-tity effects of the marketing of these borderlands as reified representations of Tibetan culture that have accompanied the Great Western Development (Xibu Da Kaifa) strategy. The actual heteroglot nature of these borderlands, which is obscured by such development efforts, is particularly pronounced in the farming areas east of Xining, where Tibetan agriculturalists some-times live in the same villages as Han, Salar, Tu, and others, as well as north-west Yunnan, where Tibetans, Lisu, Han, Naxi, Yi, Bai, Hui, and others have long lived in proximity and sometimes in mixed communities. The Chinese government census taken in 2010 shows that in Diqing Tibetan Autono-mous Prefecture, Tibetans make up 32.36 percent, Lisu 26.72 percent, Han 18.34 percent, Naxi 11.60 percent, and Yi 4.16 percent of the population. In neighboring Ngawa (Ch. Aba) Tibetan and Qiang Autonomous Prefecture, in Sichuan, Tibetans compose 54 percent, Qiang 17.58 percent, and Han 24.55 percent of the population, with others making up the remaining 3.37 percent (China Statistical Bureau 2013).

In addition, these borderlands, where various ecological, cultural, and political zones intersect, were for many centuries organized into small chief-tainships and kingdoms with allegiance to neither the Chinese nor Central Tibetan empires. In the early twentieth century, Kham was an agglomera-tion of up to twenty-five independent or semi-independent polities, and a series of autonomy movements demanding "Khampa rule for Kham" arose in the 1930s (Peng 2002; Thargyal 2007, 183). In Amdo, the Golog deliberately sought to remain ungoverned by any state. Joseph Rock (1956, 127) recorded a Golog herder saying in 1908, "We Golog have . . . from time immemorial obeyed none but our own laws," and a folk song recorded in 1951 asserts, "Against the orders of the Dharma King of Tibet I rebel! Against China I rebel! . . . We make our own laws!" (N. Norbu 1997, 3).

These Sino-Tibetan borderlands experienced and reacted to multiple civ-ilizing projects, including not only those of distant imperial polities but also the "mandalization" of Tibetan nomadic communities by the major Gelug institution of Labrang Monastery (Makley 2007). The ethnic intermixtures, the historically weak, overlapping, and fragmented sovereignties of the Sino-Tibetan borderlands, and competing civilizing projects suggest that Zomia is a fruitful concept with which to approach them.[7] This is not a claim that the Sino-Tibetan borderlands are part of Zomia as a particular world area centered around highland Asia (cf. van Schendel 2002) or that they are perfectly described by Scott's (2009) observations of non-state spaces of Southeast Asia as characterized by mobility, religious heterodoxy, egalitarianism, and swidden agriculture. Instead, Zomia-thinking is useful for turning our attention to state effects on populations of the Sino-Tibetan borderlands.

These state effects were and are not uniform. While some of the social formations of the "shatter zones" of the Sino-Tibetan borderlands, particularly pastoral communities, intentionally chose to remain beyond the reach of taxation, conscription, and enslavement by central states, some of the larger chieftainships and kingdoms adopted many of these very same practices. As Michael Hathaway points out in chapter 6 in this volume, it is also likely that some groups were drawn to the region through "selective connections" to economic, religious, military, and governmental engagements in a border zone connected, internally and externally, by a web of highland trade and transport routes. Thus, we do not treat the borderlands as one monolithic region having one distinctive set of claims to Tibetan culture or national identity. Nor do we assume that the region is fully subordinated within post-Liberation techno-administrative boundaries or that incorporation into the People's Republic signifies an inevitable decline of cultural identity.

Since 1949, when far-western China fell within the range of the civilizing project of the high modern state, foreign observers and even many inhabitants of the borderlands have assumed that the territorial sovereignty of the People's Republic of China is an inexorable and accelerating process; to launch a substantive political challenge to the legitimacy of the state seems beyond the means of the many. The political fate of a region with an area greater than the national territories of more than two hundred of the world's countries now seems sealed within the techno-administrative signifiers and practices demarcating counties, prefectures, and provinces extending from northwest Yunnan and western Sichuan, through eastern Qinghai, and well into southwest Gansu (map 1).[8]

Despite the claim that Zomia "makes no sense" after 1950 (Scott 2009, 19), the framework retains currency in its attention to the ongoing process of how borderland groups are "simultaneously situating themselves to make

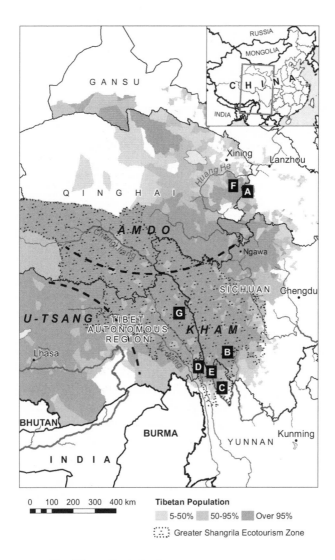

0   100   200   300   400 km   **Tibetan Population**
                                    5-50%   50-95%   Over 95%
                                    Greater Shangrila Ecotourism Zone

MAP 1. Sino-Tibetan Borderlands
Sino-Tibetan borderlands, with case study locations. Cartography by Mark Henderson.

A. Gannan Tibetan Autonomous Prefecture, Gansu
B. Yading Nature Reserve, Daocheng County, Ganzi (Tib. Kardze) Tibetan Autono-
    mous Prefecture, Sichuan
C. Shangrila (Ch. Xianggelila [formerly Zhongdian]) County, Diqing Tibetan Autono-
    mous Prefecture, Yunnan
D. Deqin County, Diqing Tibetan Autonomous Prefecture, Yunnan
E. Nature reserves in Diqing Tibetan Autonomous Prefecture, Yunnan
F. Rebgong (Ch. Tongren) County, Qinghai
G. Gonjo (Ch. Gongjue) County, Chamdo Prefecture, Tibet Autonomous Region

strategic and political claims vis-à-vis . . . nation-states, while also remaining deeply committed to the 'ungoverned' aspects of their identity" (Shneiderman 2010, 292). These strategic claims arise from the very projects used to manage and incorporate the borderlands in colonization efforts. Such projects are carefully orchestrated "mappings," the creation of territory itself as a political technology (Elden 2010) and its associated epistemological projects that enhance "legibility" for governance (Scott 1998). Rather than annihilating cultural others, these strategies reify new categories of culture and nature and give rise to new, often ungovernable realities.

In the Sino-Tibetan borderlands, a key mapping has been ethnolinguistic classification, which took place during the Republican era (1911–49) and especially during the first decade of the People's Republic, when the state enlisted ethnographers in a campaign to impose cultural legibility on all peripheral regions and marginal peoples. Based on rapid, systematic field assessments, this classification became the objective standard for the new taxonomy, leading to the radical simplification of cultural geographic complexity, particularly in the ethnically diverse borderlands.[9] The delineation of ethnic groups, based almost exclusively on linguistic evidence (and often eliding emic conceptions of heritage and ethnonational affiliation including traditional ethnonyms), has provided the foundation for a multi-ethnonational state in which fifty-five minority minzu (shaoshu minzu), form a constellation of subaltern peoples whose destinies revolve around the executive nation-within-the-nation—the approximately 92 percent of the population that constitutes the Han majority. The "fifty-six-minzu model" has in fact become "ethnotaxonomic orthodoxy" in official discourse and popular culture (Mullaney 2011, 117), an imagined community of "Chinese people" (Ch. Zhongguoren or Zhonghua minzu) representing a multiplicity of ethnicities, each of which receives official recognition in exchange for allegiance to, and incorporation within, a multiethnic China (Anderson 2005).

In light of this ineluctable regime of cultural absorption, containment, and control, one must keep in mind that civilizing projects often intensify ethnic consciousness among peripheral peoples, engendering ethnogenesis (including renewed and reconfigured ethnic and national identities) and simultaneously affecting values and perspectives of the "civilized self" and the "barbaric other" in colonial centers of political and economic power (Harrell 2000). More specifically, in the Sino-Tibetan borderlands, the project of PRC state incorporation has generated new forms of Tibetan unity and an affinity for a Tibetan nationalist project that did not previously exist

(Kolås 2008), as seen in the widespread geographical and social scope of the 2008 protests (Barnett 2009; Yeh 2009d).

Even with the *minzu* classification system established as an ontological condition of nationhood in China, ethnic identity in the borderlands continues to acquire new modes of expression in response to new forms of governmentality. Since the late 1990s, the official story of western China, including the Sino-Tibetan borderlands, has been one of state beneficence in the form of development. The Harmonious Society and ecological modernization have, in this civilizing narrative, enabled multiethnic cooperation in projects that enhance sustainable development. Citizens are expected to be grateful for favorable policy initiatives and the infusion of unprecedented levels of capital investment by the state, private corporations (domestic and multinational), and nongovernmental organizations (NGOs), particularly environmental NGOs. Development, in other words, has become a raison d'être of the state, the foundation of state legitimacy (Chatterjee 2006; Gidwani 2008; T. Li 2007; Ludden 1992; Wainwright 2008; Yeh 2013). This is true across postcolonial states the world over, but the dynamics of development as state incorporation are particularly pronounced in China's Sino-Tibetan borderlands, where landscapes, livelihoods, and worldviews have been dramatically transformed over the past several decades.

As a project of raising the standard of living and providing various forms of improvement and welfare, development targets specific populations, rather than operating at the level of the individual. In other words, it is a form of what Michel Foucault called "biopower," a science of government that aims to improve the condition of the population through calculation and the production of knowledge about the characteristics of a population as a whole, such as life expectancy and birth rates. In Foucault's words, the emergence of biopower as the right to "make live and let die" came to complement sovereign power as the right to "take life or let live" (Foucault 2003 [1976], 241). Unlike disciplinary mechanisms, which work by regulating individual bodies through surveillance and the organization of space and movement, the security mechanisms that characterize biopower work to optimize the population's state of life.

The emergence of the population as an object of calculation and knowledge enabled the art of government, or governmentality. In contrast to sovereignty, the purpose of government is not governing in and of itself but rather securing the welfare and the biological and economic condition of the population. This is accomplished by acting on the population through a set of calculated and rational ways of securing, or conducting, its conduct. Development can be understood as a form of government in that it deploys a variety of techniques and micropolitics that structure fields of action for its subjects; it is a set of practices that tries to accomplish rule by creating governable subjects and governable spaces.

With development operating as a form of governmentality aimed at fostering certain kinds of life, it is evident that state power in the Sino-Tibetan borderlands cannot be understood as sovereign power alone, though its application has become more pronounced since 2008 (discussed in detail in the introduction to part 3). Instead, it is a triad of "sovereignty-discipline-government" with different emphases and points of articulation between these modes of power operating at specific conjunctures (Foucault 1991,102; Moore 2005). In tracing the trajectory of development as well as environmental protection at work on the landscapes of the Sino-Tibetan borderlands, we can also trace specific ensembles of sovereignty, discipline, and government. These bear heavily on the landscape, practices of representation, and individual bodies. In the case of the latter, microtechniques of power are evident not only in specific punishments meted out to those perceived to challenge the prevailing order (see ch. 10 in this volume) but also in the wave of political resistance taking the form of more than 120 acts of self-immolation in the borderlands since 2009 (discussed in the introduction to part 3).

During the first decade of the twenty-first century, securing the welfare and the biological and economic conditions of the population of western China has required massive investments of China's surplus capital. In conjunction with increased access to the international market in cheap fossil fuel and abundant domestic coal supplies, in 2000, the state implemented a series of projects as part of its Great Western Development strategy. The aim of this program is to reduce the economic disparities between western interior regions, in which minority *minzu* predominate, and eastern coastal provinces, but it has also been interpreted as an effort to reconsolidate state power.[10] In addition to major expansion of the "hardware" of development—road and air travel networks, hydropower generation, and telecommunications systems—the Chinese Communist Party has worked diligently to increase its soft power in the region, encouraging transnational and local cooperation in the conservation and development of natural and cultural landscape resources. State-led efforts to capitalize on landscape amenities in the Sino-Tibetan borderlands have gone hand in hand with a turn away from some older strategies of resource extraction, particularly in forestry, while other forms, such as mining and hydropower development, intensify (Lafitte 2013). The exploitation of hydropower resources in the Sino-Tibetan borderlands remains critical for China's national strategy of energy development, and recent approval of a major dam-building project in the Nu River valley in Yunnan shows that what the state calls "green energy" flies in the face of research predicting a wide range of negative social and ecological impacts in southwest China and neighboring countries in Southeast Asia (Brown, Magee, and Xu 2008; Jacobs 2013).[11]

Such selective definitions of "green" are critical as CCP planners now contrast an older model of a "production power state" (Ch. *shengchan qiangzhou*) with a newer "ecological state" (Ch. *shengtai lizhou*, also *shengtai liguo*). The centrality of ecological construction projects in Yunnan, Sichuan, Gansu, Qinghai, and the Tibet Autonomous Region suggests that these cannot be understood merely as "minority issues," as might be suggested by a view of the borderlands as neglectable margins, but rather are essential elements in the central state's narrative of China's ecological modernization and the emergence of the ecological state. This is exemplified in the 1998 national logging ban in the upper Yangzi and Yellow River basins (the headwaters of both rivers are on the Tibetan Plateau) and the 1999 nationwide Sloping Land Conversion Program, which converts agricultural lands with greater than twenty-five-degree slopes to forest lands. Both of these policies forced rural communities in Yunnan, Sichuan, Qinghai, and Gansu to abandon some of their most important economic activities, especially logging. At the same time, the state has promoted a quasi-neoliberal development model for the Greater Shangrila Ecological Tourism Zone (described in part 1), in which border cultures and landscapes are viewed as renewable resources, available for endless reproduction and "subject to the laws of supply and demand" (Litzinger 2004, 489). Indigenous cultural landscapes and alpine ecosystems have thus become both marketable commodities and precious environmental resources in a global trade network that alternately (and sometimes simultaneously) commercializes, exploits, re-creates, and protects desirable landscapes while restructuring, to varying degrees, the spaces of everyday life and subjectivity. Since the establishment in 2001 of Shangrila County in Diqing Prefecture, Yunnan, the state, NGOs, and local people have become increasingly engaged in the physical and symbolic transformation of landscapes throughout the Sino-Tibetan borderlands.

Projects of the ecological state in the Sino-Tibetan borderlands also include the establishment of national- and international-level nature con-

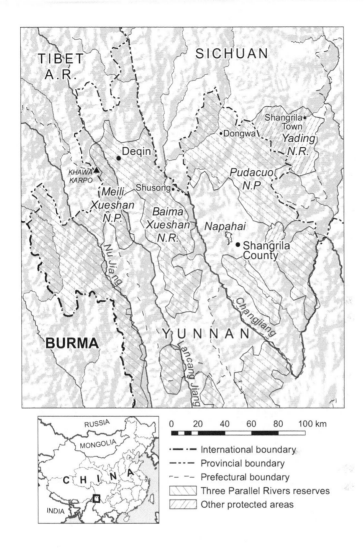

MAP 2. Nature Reserves
Nature reserves, national parks, and case study locations in northwest Yunnan and southwest Sichuan. Cartography by Mark Henderson

servation areas and support for ecological and ethnic tourism, both of which have undergone exponential growth (map 2). Taken as a whole, these rapid developments in governance, technology, and ideology have helped catalyze myriad local responses and innovations that are both manifested in and enabled by changes in rural and urban landscapes. Our case studies delve deeply into the relationship between landscape, ecology, subjectivity, geography, and power in this rapidly changing region, shedding light more broadly on the role of international and interregional dynamics driving social and environmental change in contemporary China.

The three main foci of this volume are examined in three parts. First, in exploring "shangrilazation," our contributors examine practices of governance and representation in Sino-Tibetan borderland areas where cultural economies are reconfigured for tourism-based development, and how these new mappings—processes of making legible and tractable "Shangrilas"— contradict and overlap with indigenous geographies, engendering spaces of convergence, tension, or outright resistance. Second, the volume examines the construction of the ecological state, analyzing new forms of state power as worked on and through nature conservation, and how these intersect with multi-scalar political ecologies of resource use, commodification, and trade. Third, the chapters that follow explore in greater depth the making of new identities, subjectivities, and notions of personhood among Tibetans as well as Han in relation to struggles over territory and sovereignty engendered by tourism, conservation, and statist development.

These dynamics are not unique to China. Beyond the Sino-Tibetan borderlands, in state peripheries across the postcolonial world, the power triad of sovereignty-discipline-government also increasingly assumes the form of capital investment in nature and culture treated as renewable, market resources. While the logics of the ecological state and tourism-based development are attractive to many parties across the political and theoretical spectrum, the cases presented in this volume provide an argument for careful scrutiny of how state practices and effects are manifest in landscapes, ecologies, and subjectivities. It is our hope that this volume will shed light on other geographies of shangrilazation around the world, and how they articulate with social movements even as they constitute new forms of utopian seduction.

INTRODUCTION

1   We use the spelling "Khawa Karpo" as a phonetically friendly alternative to the standard Wiley transliteration *Kha ba dkar po*. It is also seen in the literature as "Kawa Garbo" and "Kawagebo." In China and the West, this massif is most widely known as Meili Snow Mountains, or Meilixueshan. For discussions of the "Khawa Karpo" versus "Meili" naming issue, see J. Guo 2000b and Litzinger 2004. We

thank Robert Moseley and Renée Mullen for their notes on this important top-
onym.

2   Samten Karmay (1994) places the *yullha* (gods of the locale) and *zhidak* (territorial deities commonly abiding within mountains; literally "owners of the base")
at the center of the laic, secular "mountain cult" that constitutes the heart of
traditional Tibetan national identity and is still largely independent of Buddhist
and Bön doctrine. According to legend, the first Tibetan (Yarlung) king, Nyatri
Tsenpo (Wyl. gnya 'khri btsan po), is believed to have descended from the sky at
birth, suspended by a *mu* cord (Wyl. *dmu thag*), to the summit of Lhari Gyangto,
a sacred mountain in Kongpo, and to have ascended by the cord at death. This
became the way of Tibetan kings until the *mu* cord was severed, at which time
they became mortal. Local sacred mountains cults are, in a strong sense, reitera-
tions of this mythic pattern, serving as ritual centers in the "unwritten tradition of the laity" that demarcate both national identity and loyalty to local and
regional polities (see chs. 8 and 9 in this volume).

3   For the etymology and cultural history of *gnyan*, see J. Xie 2001 and Karmay 1996.
Both provide evidence that belief in these ubiquitous spirits evolved from the
ancient worship of argali (*Ovis ammon hodgsoni*). Karmay (1996, 66–67) notes, "In
popular rituals, it normally refers to the spirits that occupy the intermediate space
in the vertical axis of the universe: the lha in the heavens, the gnyan in the middle
and the klu on the ground. . . . [T]he gnyan are normally understood as being
the gzhi bdag as they are thought to dwell at high altitudes, such as mountain
tops. . . . The term gnyan is variously translated by Tibetologists." The word often
has a connotation of "awesome" or "feared."

4   *Glacier* (Bing Chuan*)* (Kunming: Yunnan Yinxiang Publishing House, 2002),
film. Camera, Zhaxi Nima; editors, Zhaxi Nima, Silang Norbu; producer, Guo
Jing, Team for Participatory Video Education, Baima Mountain Culture Center,
31 minutes.

5   Erik Eckholm, "A Holy Place in China Fights for Its Life, Body, and Soul," *New
York Times*, June 10, 2001.

6   For more on fields, *habitus*, and *doxa*, see Bourdieu 1990. We adopt these terms
with the objective of showing how they are mutually constitutive with and within
cultural landscapes that define the biopolitical regimes of the Tibetan borderlands
today.

7   Zomia is a region defined by Michaud (2010, 187–88; following van Schendel
2002) as extending from the highlands of Pakistan, Afghanistan, Tajikistan, and
Kyrgyzstan through the Himalayas, the Tibetan Plateau (including Qinghai), and
northwest China's Xinjiang region, and south to the lower end of the peninsu-
lar Southeast Asian highlands. James Scott's (2009) map of the region does not
extend northwest of northeastern India and the southern Himalayas or north
of southwest China, but his sociopolitical definition is hypothesized by many as
applicable to a broader region: "Zomia is the largest remaining region of the world
whose peoples have not yet been fully incorporated into nation-states. Its days are
numbered. Not so very long ago, however, such self-governing peoples were the

great majority of humankind. . . . I argue that hill peoples are best understood as runaway, fugitive, maroon communities who have, over the course of two millennia, been fleeing the oppressions of state-making projects in the valleys. . . . Most of the areas in which they reside may be aptly called shatter zones or zones of refuge" (Scott, 2009, ix).

8   We include here the Tibetan areas of Yunnan, Qinghai, Sichuan, and Gansu.

9   See Harrell 2000; Litzinger 2000; Mullaney 2011, 2010; and Schein 2000. Although the Beijing ethnographers charged with delineating ethnic groups in Yunnan during the classification (*shibie*) project of 1954 were expected to follow the four criteria of Stalin's *natsia* (nationality) model—common territory, common language, common mode of production, and common psychology or culture—Stalin theorized that these could be realized only in the capitalist mode of production. Peoples who had not entered the capitalist mode of production could not be "nations," but only "clans," "tribes," or "tribal federations." The ethnographers, who were not Party members, did not accept this mandate and instead developed the ethnonational classification (*minzu shibie*) system based on ethnolinguistic criteria and the "ethnic potential" of the many groups who sought recognition. The goal was not to describe already existing "imagined communities" but to "outline a set of plausible, or 'imaginable' minzu categories that it would be feasible for the state to actualize in the post-Classification world—categories that would be 'good enough for government use'" (Mullaney 2011, 16–17). In the process, hundreds of applicant groups were categorized within what became the state's fifty-six *minzu*, and these were inscribed, actualized, and "placed," in techno-administrative fashion, within the system of autonomous counties, prefectures, and regions.

10 The policy is aimed at six provinces (Yunnan, Sichuan, Qinghai, Gansu, Shaanxi, and Guizhou), which encompass the Sino-Tibetan borderlands, as well as Chongqing Municipality and five autonomous regions (Xinjiang, Ningxia, Inner Mongolia, Guangxi, and Tibet). The total target region comprises 71.4 percent of the area of China but only 28.8 percent of the population (Goodman 2002). From 2000 to 2009, average annual growth in gross domestic product (GDP) in the western region was 11.9 percent, higher than the national growth rate over the same period. According to the China Western Development Network, this accounted for an increase in the proportion of regional to national GDP from 17.1 percent to 18.5 percent; http://www.chinawest.gov.cn/web/index.asp (accessed October 31, 2013). See Goodman 2002, 2004a; Lai 2002, 2003; Oakes 2004, 2007; and Shih 2004.

11 With a total capacity of 145,070 megawatts, the six hydrobasins within or immediately downstream from the Sino-Tibetan borderlands represent roughly 64 percent of the energy potential found in China's twelve major hydrobasins (calculated from data in Brown, Magee, and Xu 2008).

PART I

SHANGRILAZATION

• • •

Tourism, Landscape, Identity

These old men [two seventy-five-year-olds in Hamugu Village] started hunting before Liberation because their families were poor—their living conditions were difficult, so they took up hunting. They hunted mostly musk deer and bears because of their high value, and this allowed them to make a go of it. At the age of sixty they stopped hunting. Now they regret having done it. Over the years their families and their livestock have suffered misfortunes of various kinds. Divinations at the monastery show that they've been punished for not respecting the zhidak [territorial gods commonly abiding within mountains] and sacred lakes. . . . [In similar fashion] government-organized timber-felling destroyed thousands of ancient trees—a serious misfortune. We now protect the forests and I am very happy; not destroying the sacred mountains and lakes is excellent. We Tibetans [believe] that wild animals living in the realm of the deity mountain have relationships with the zhidak, the ecology, the local people, and nature that is like the relationship between you and me. All are living beings. Conflicts between animals and people are like conflicts between people; if you violate someone they will take action against you. . . . The cable car system that is being built on the [primary local god] mountain is already having severe environmental impacts, and when droves of tourists ride up to the summit there will be destruction that takes forms not immediately visible to the eye. Already there are mudslides occurring in several nearby villages and the destruction is bound to increase. Only by protecting the ecology, the zhidak, and the sacred lakes can there be peace, and only after there is peace can there be prosperity.

—LAZONG RUIBA

WHEN Lazong Ruiba, an environmental activist from Hamugu Village, made these observations in 2005, Zhongdian County was still adjusting to its new life as "Shangrila." In 2001, China's State Council announced the "discovery of Shangrila" in an economically marginal region of southwest China internationally recognized for its high levels of biological and cultural diversity and its spectacular mountain scenery. On May 2, 2002, after a battle among neighboring provinces and prefectures lasting more than five years, Zhongdian County was officially renamed Shangrila (Ch. Xianggelila). Zhongdian's accession to Shangrila status occurred after a search party of more than forty scholars from Yunnan and other provinces "proved" that the setting for James Hilton's 1933 novel *Lost Horizon* (the source of the name) was based on descriptions of the Zhongdian basin in the writings of the early twentieth-century botanist and explorer Joseph Rock. Becoming the star attraction of the Greater Shangrila Ecological Tourism Zone, a region that includes the Sino-Tibetan border areas in Yunnan, Sichuan, and Qinghai, as well as the Tibet Autonomous Region (TAR), accelerated the transformation of the county into "a world tourism brand name" and global tourism hotspot and helped accelerate the development of tourism and other forms of commerce throughout the region.[1] A brief consideration of the shangrilazation process in Diqing Tibetan Autonomous Prefecture sheds light on how tourism development schemes shaped many towns and cities in the Sino-Tibetan borderlands in the late 1990s and early in the first decade of the 2000s.

In Diqing, a decade of explosive growth in the tourism industry has also seen the rapid extension of the transportation network and the transformation of urban and small-town landscapes. In 1999, when ground transport to Kunming, the provincial capital, was still limited to dirt roads, the Diqing airport was built among farmhouses and pastures just outside the Shangrila county seat, Zhongxin Town (known by Tibetans as Gyalthang, which is the source of another Chinese name for the town, Jiantang). Sections of the paved highway from Kunming were still under construction in 2004, but enhanced transport links arose in tandem with the architectural re-creation of a Tibetan sense of place in the town itself:

> Whereas in 1998 the town . . . was unassuming, dominated by the usual grey and unimaginative concrete blocks that could be seen in any Chinese town, in 2002, this was no longer the case. By then all the buildings lining the main street were being repainted with bright colors in "Tibetan"

FIGURE I.1 Young Chinese tourists exiting the maze of cobblestone streets and "Tibetan" shops, hostels, and restaurants that made up Dokar Dzong in 2011. Roughly two-thirds of Dokar Dzong was destroyed by a fire in January 2014. Photo by Chris Coggins.

designs, described by one visiting journalist as the creation of a "Tibetan toy town." Following this, elaborately decorated streetlamps were put up, and the sidewalks were repaved with stones. . . . Although the traffic in Zhongxin Town was still easy to navigate, the first traffic light appeared in 2003, while new hotels were emerging all over the town. In the Old Town of Zhongxin, Dokar Dzong [Dukezong], things were also happening. The streets were still squalid, as in the rest of the town's back streets, but this area was gradually developing a reputation as a backpacker zone with quaint little guesthouses and cafes opening up. (Kolås 2008, 4)

By 2004, there were several five-star hotels in and around Zhongxin, and even the "squalid," muddy streets that laced the Old Town, Dokar Dzong, were being carefully paved with cobbles, while more and more cafés, Tibetan souvenir shops, tea shops, guesthouses, and outdoor-gear stores sprang up all around. By 2005, the Old Town was the showcase of Shangrila—a simulacrum of a medieval Tibetan town—where cars were not allowed to penetrate into the winding, narrow lanes, and tourists, both Chinese and foreign, mingled with Tibetans before heading off on overland adventures into the wilds of rural Diqing, western Sichuan, or the TAR (fig. I.1). Each night, hundreds of local Tibetans and some adventurous travelers gathered in the newly rebuilt Culture Square to participate in folk dancing, moving clockwise in large, concentric circles in the fashion of a prayer wheel.

A critical reading of the restoration of Dokar Dzong could easily relegate the place to the likes of a Disneyfied Tibetan tourist trap (Llamas and Belk 2011), but that would require a static conception of the landscape, one that elides the involvement and agency of local people in making and remaking the Old Town to suit their own desires, interests, and values (Hillman 2010). An eye obsessed with signs of the ersatz is blind to the ways that Tibetan carpenters and woodcarvers hew the timbers, raise and fit the beams, and sculpt and paint the facades of the new stores using old techniques refined over generations of building farmhouses, shrine rooms, and temples across the region. Likewise, the work of Tibetan bureaucrats, entrepreneurs, academics, and others who are proud to promote "Shangrila" remains invisible or only dimly considered.

Perhaps more significantly, the invisible features of the landscape—attributes alluded to by Lazong Ruiba—become undecipherable, obscured by assumptions about the imposition of a new state-capitalist utopian order.[2] For the purposes at hand, it should be kept in mind that while landscapes appear to be solid, natural, and in a sense incontrovertibly "real," they are also both the products of visible and invisible sociocultural contests and the media through which form and meaning are continually instantiated. Furthermore, the practices that imbue a landscape with meaning and with a capacity for certain kinds of agency are not translatable without attention to the subject positions of those who live and work within them. We can conceptualize landscape as a *quasi-object*—a thing that humans act upon but that also has a certain degree of agency—with the capacity to structure social reality to a significant degree:

> [Landscape] represents to us our relationships to the land and to social formations. But it does so in an obfuscatory way. Apart from knowing the struggles that went into its making (along with the struggles to which it gives rise), one cannot know a landscape except at some ideal level, which has the effect of reproducing, rather than analyzing or challenging the relations of power that work to mask its function. (Mitchell 1996, 33)

Both conventional historical accounts and more critical analyses of economic development often *place* Shangrila within a telos in which a region deemed by the state as a "backward minority *minzu*" area, brutally restructured into communes, work brigades, and Maoist study groups for decades, is now being transfigured. Sanguine observers see empowerment, or at least its gradual emergence, while critics see a utopian diorama—a simulacrum of "Tibet"—and a remarkable exemplification of governmentality meant to produce a multiethnic and economically vibrant Chinese hinterland.[3] Politically astute and theoretically trenchant as such critiques may be, they miss the complex sociology of associations involving local and nonlocal actors in particular landscapes as both agentive subjects and objects of representation.[4] Border landscapes are constituted by associations of nature, culture, and capital that are constantly reworked in the production of multiple Shangrilas. The chapters in part 1 focus on several modalities of the shangrilazation process: literary representations of the landscape in fiction and nonfiction; the representation of Tibetan landscapes and cultures in official travel guides and in the act of travel itself; and travel, photography, and writing as means of representing embodied experiences of discovery that both map "new territory" and establish it within the common geography of the nation.

In chapter 1, Li-hua Ying addresses the contribution of literature to the shangrilazation of Sino-Tibetan border landscapes as well as the centrality of the borderlands for the construction of Han, Tibetan, and other ethnic identities. Contrasting and comparing the works of Wen Pulin, Fan Wen, Alai, Tashi Nyima, and Li Guiming, all of whom write about borderland areas of Sichuan and Yunnan, she shows how Han and Tibetan literary communities adopt different strategies to make distinctive claims on national identity, place, landscape, and nature. Ying focuses on the fluidity of identities in these ethnically complex areas but also on the ongoing dialectics of "insider" and "outsider" identities, showing how Sino-Tibetan border landscapes are represented as part of the constitution of self and other in what she calls the "vital margins." While travel literature is a catalyst for tourism, playing a critical role in the cultural economy of shangrilazation, the "frontier poetics" of Tibetan writers working in Chinese are a vehicle for reconstituting that which has been destroyed or obliterated—a means of challenging or dismantling the shangrilazation process. Ying demonstrates how contemporary literary renderings of life in the Sino-Tibetan borderlands articulate with a national discourse that places the region at the heart of a collective quest for spiritual renewal. She also shows how literary groups such as the Khawa Karpo Culture Society call for a return to indigenous roots, and how the success of Tibetan writers such as Alai and Tashi Dawa challenge the notion of the metropolitan center versus the cultural margins; literary renaissance thus becomes a form of reterritorialization that may counter the forces of shangrilazation.

Chapter 2, by Chris Vasantkumar, examines shangrilazation through a critical reading of two government-supported travel texts that depict Xiahe (Tib. Labrang) and Gannan Tibetan Autonomous Prefecture, in Gansu, as a touristic dreamworld of consumable Tibetan culture. Drawing on these texts as well as ethnographic observations, Vasantkumar highlights the complex politics at work in a place marketed as "little Tibet" but where local Han and Hui have long been important members of the community. He argues that Chinese domestic tourists' engagement with the landscape draws more on notions of the miniature than on Western landscape genealogies, and that the elision of the ethnic makeup of the area has been key to its shangrilazation as a miniaturizing method. At the same time, the two texts demonstrate the ambivalent and polyvocal nature of official tourist meanings. Chinese scenic spots are not necessarily hegemonic; instead, they are always in the making.

The final chapter in this section, by Travis Klingberg, also explores Chinese tourism in a Tibetan borderland area through a study of the transformation of the Yading Nature Reserve in southwest Sichuan, which has gone from a remote, rugged, and biologically diverse region visited by only the most determined explorers to a major destination that attracts tens of thousands of tourists annually. Packaged as "the Last Shangrila" and incorporated into the Greater Shangrila Ecotourism Zone, Yading is represented as a "nature destination" where tourism and biological diversity are seamlessly complementary. Like Vasantkumar, Klingberg challenges interpretations of hegemonic official tourist landscapes by focusing on the productive and influential role tourists themselves have had in the production of these landscapes through embodied practices of seeing and discovery. As the discovery of Yading becomes a shared routine for increasing numbers of Chinese tourists, even photography serves as a means of incorporating shared experience, of knowing and producing an exotic place within the national territory. Tracing three sets of explorations of the region—by Joseph Rock, Yin Kaipu and Lü Linglong, and the growing numbers of Chinese tourists, Klingberg demonstrates how Yading has become part of the national imagination and a remaking of Chinese national geography through tourists' inscribing and incorporating practices.

Each of these case studies reveals the power of inscription, travel, imagination, and embodied practice in the making of place, landscape, and identity in the Sino-Tibetan borderlands during the era of the Great Western Development strategy. Each author also raises questions, implicitly or explicitly, about the possibilities for a popular politics of the governed in a period of striking transformation (Chatterjee 2006). Where Han travel writers seek more authentic selves in the "vital margins," Tibetan writers forge a "frontier poetics" of recovery. Where the miniaturization practice is constitutive of a culture of landscape consumption that incorporates marginal places into the national imaginary, such works of imagineering do not endure unchanged for long. These chapters show that the landscape simulacra of shangrilazation are built of the visible and the invisible, of the remembered as well as the embodied. Therein lie struggles that are too easily obscured by reductive assumptions based solely on "reading" the landscape as text, productive as such readings can be. Above all, the work of landscape production is never finished. Thus, shangrilazation as material transformation and immaterial meaning-making is never hegemonic or complete but always in the process of formation, as a particular civilizing project of the Great Western Development strategy in the Sino-Tibetan borderlands. There is always more to the mountain than meets the eye.

PART 1. SHANGRILAZATION

Epigraph: Lazong Ruiba, personal communication, Hamugu Village, Shangrila County, Diqing Tibetan Autonomous Prefecture, 2005.

1   In 2004, *China Daily* (2004, 1) trumpeted the term "world tourism brand name" with pride, and tourism statistics indicate that it is not mere hyperbole. Diqing Tibetan Autonomous Prefecture has been open for tourism only since 1992, but the number of tourists increased from 42,300 arrivals in 1995 to more than 1.28 million in 2002 (Kolås 2008). By 2008, from 3 million to 3.8 million tourists visited Shangrila County (Jenkins, 2009; People's Daily 2008). The number of international tourists remains relatively small but continues to rise rapidly, with 80,000 in 2002 and between 300,000 and 400,000 in 2008 (Yunnan Tourism Bureau, personal communication, 2004; Jenkins 2009).

2   This is not to dismiss the idea out of hand. Karan's (1976) early and highly compelling study on the work of Chinese Communist ideology in reconfiguring space, landscapes, and everyday lives in the Tibet Autonomous Region is definitive of Maoist-era Sino-Tibetan spatial politics. More recent work by Hillman (2003),

Kolås (2008), and Yeh (2013) examines the complexity of Tibetan agency in the making of post-Reform landscapes. The degree to which "agency" constitutes *consent* is, of course, always open to contestation.

3   In this regard, it is important to contrast the analyses of Kolås (2008), Hillman (2010), and Llamas and Belks (2011). Whereas Kolås provides a robust account of Diqing Tibetan involvement in the making of Shangrila, and Hillman sees this as a model worthy of emulation throughout Tibetan regions, Llamas and Belk evince much more caution and skepticism regarding what they view as the "exoticization" and "marketization" of place and people.

4   The "sociology of associations," also known as actor-network-theory (ANT), is Bruno Latour's (2005, 3) formulation for a social science that surpasses the conventional "sociology of the social," which reifies "the social" as an ontologically extant causal force. In his words, social science of the second kind "posits the existence of a specific sort of phenomenon variously called 'society,' 'social order,' 'social practice,' 'social dimension,' or 'social structure. . . . [I]t has been important to distinguish this domain of reality from other domains such as economics, geography, biology, psychology, law, science, and politics." Negating the idea of the "social" as "the glue," Latour and other ANT practitioners seek to "reassemble" the many components previously not conceived as "social." Drawing on ANT, one can conceive of the landscape as a materio-ideational assemblage through which nature, culture, and subjectivity take form. The physical and discursive (in)stability of this assemblage determines the rate of what theorists once called "cultural change," a term that has been rendered meaningless, or at least nebulous, by post-structural and postcolonial theory. It should be understood that this use of landscape is heuristic, not ethnographic; there has been no equivalent ontological category for Tibetans until quite recently.

Vital Margins

• • •

FRONTIER POETICS AND

LANDSCAPES OF ETHNIC IDENTITY

Li-hua Ying

ROM the perspective of the Chinese imperial state, the regions that lay
beyond its grip were "lands outside civilization" (*hua wai zhi di*), a term
denoting not only their marginality and inferiority but also the wildness
and defiance of their inhabitants. The accounts left by early Han adventurers
allow a few glimpses into the frontier lands. Xu Xiake (1586–1641), China's
most celebrated travel writer, spent almost two years in Yunnan covering
fourteen prefectures, including Lijiang, which at the time had jurisdiction
over Zhongdian (Tib. Gyalthang) (see map 1, C). As a guest of the Naxi chief-
tain, Xu attempted to venture into the Tibetan town to see a large bronze
statue of Maitreya, only to be discouraged by his host, who intimated that
Zhongdian was filled with bandits and unruly Tibetan caravans (Xu Xiake
2004, 555). After the area was effectively incorporated into the Qing empire
(1644–1911), Yu Qingyuan, a less known traveler, was able to spend a year in
Weixi, an administrative entity that covered present-day Weixi, Deqin (Tib.
Dechen) (see map 1, D), and two other counties in Yunnan. In 1770, after
extensive interviews with the local inhabitants, he wrote *Weixi Notes* (Weixi
jianwen ji), about this far-flung land and its many peoples. He described the
climate of the White Horse Snow Mountain (Baimaxueshan) near Deqin
as so severe that even in the summer, "the wind swirled like water and it
was cold to the bone," and on top of the mountain, "if a voice was raised or
laughter heard, hailstones as big as fists would rain down continuously and

lots of people died as a result" (Deng and Bai 2012, 41). He painted the Lisu as a people who "loved to reside at steep cliffs and on mountaintops," "ran like crafty hares," and were "by nature vicious and loved to kill" (ibid., 96). In the Han literary imagination, the borderlands were a menacing landscape of high peaks and unpredictable weather, populated by wild ethnic tribes far removed from civilization.

No longer beyond the reach of state power and the pathways of ordinary travelers, as in the times of Xu and Yu, the Sino-Tibetan borderlands nowadays receive busloads of tourists daily. In advertisements produced by local governments and the tourist industry, they are touted as a better, gentler, and more beautiful alternative to the Tibet Autonomous Region (TAR). Pictures of snowcapped mountains, verdant valleys, crystal-clear lakes, virgin forests, lamas in crimson robes, and magnificent monasteries constitute "media-generated sets of signs" created solely for the consumption of domestic and international tourists (Urry 2002, 14). For better or for worse, globalization and tourism have opened up spaces for new modes of inquiry and identity formation. The once forbidding landscape of the Sino-Tibetan borderlands is now accessible by means of airports and modern roads, but it is still used to define the people who live there, the people who visit, and the relationship between border polities and the powers of the central state. As in the imperial context, writers play a key role in articulating these relationships, and they draw on specific features, both "natural" and "cultural," to compose border landscapes as particular kinds of claims on national and ethnic identity and belonging. In the postcolonial context and during a period of rapid globalization, these literary claims on the landscape are made by "insiders," "outsiders," and those who seek a world betwixt and between.

The writers examined in this chapter adopt different strategies for making claims on self, ethnic identity, and place in terms that both draw from and constitute particular kinds of landscape. Featured prominently in their writings is a vital connection between the natural environment and ethnic representation. Landscape, infused with vitality and spirit, is thus critical for the rediscovery of the self, as both the outsider and the insider see it as the living embodiment of cultural traditions and lifestyles. In their travel writings, Wen Pulin and Fan Wen, a Sinicized Manchu and a Han, both from metropolitan areas, view the borderlands as an enchanting landscape of dreams and minority culture as a mirror that reflects the deficiencies of urban existence. Their physical excursions are often portrayed as spiritual journeys that result in a deepened sense of self-awareness as well as an appreciation of ethnic and cultural differences.

While these outsiders focus on the individual self and on presenting a harmonious multiethnic society, the local writers examined here are more concerned with the survival of native cultures and of the specific ethnolinguistic groups that define ethnic identity in particular regions of the Sino-Tibetan borderlands. Increasingly aware of the importance of speaking for themselves, they express the sense of crisis facing their indigenous traditions. As they define place-based identities, they draw inspiration and solace from the mountains and rivers steeped in historical memories, to help negotiate the images outsiders have imposed on their cultural landscapes and practices. *Return* (Huigui), a Chinese- and Tibetan-language journal launched by the Khawa Karpo Culture Society, the first nongovernmental organization in Deqin, publishes folk songs collected and transcribed from live performances by villagers. As a platform for debating issues important to the survival of minority cultures and disseminating information about the society's activities, *Return* promotes what could be called "frontier poetics," a counterpart to metropolitan modes of poetic expression. Encouraged by a national discourse that sees China's frontiers as sites for the nation's spiritual renewal, the ethnic minority writers Li Guiming and Tashi Nyima respond by trying to shift the center of conversation away from the Han metropolis and toward the minority borderlands.

While Li and Tashi Nyima focus on preserving and revitalizing folk songs, which they believe shape the foundations of frontier poetics, Alai positions himself as a sort of intellectual tour guide of his native Gyarong, in Ngawa (Ch. Aba) Tibetan and Qiang Autonomous Prefecture, northern Sichuan (see map 1). His travelogue doubles as an introduction to Gyarong history and an intensely personal journey of remembrances. While recalling his childhood and youth in Ngawa, Alai takes himself and his readers back to the "childhood and youth" of Gyarong Tibet. As he climbs higher and higher on the Tibetan Plateau, he enters a process of what the postcolonial critic Homi Bhabha (1994, 90) calls "re-membering, a putting together of a dismembered past to make sense of the trauma of the present." The native son who left his homeland now returns to reclaim his ethnic identity by walking across what he calls "the earth's staircase," the gradually rising terrain from the Sichuan plains to the Tibetan Plateau, a landscape saturated in myths and legends of Tibetan military and cultural conquests as well as a recent history of political and natural devastations.

The fusion of the physical and spiritual in these writers' perceptual experiences makes the Sino-Tibetan borderlands a particularly appropriate locale for initiating an inquiry into the relationship between landscape and selfhood for both urban Chinese and frontier minority writers. Whether in the genre of travelogue or poetry, these place-specific writings treat landscape as a geo-cultural site and the borderlands as a serious contender for epistemological and moral authority. Indigenous literature or literature of the indigenous, which has risen in post-Mao China in the wake of globalization and mass tourism, is thus a dynamic form of landscape representation. While engaging in a national conversation about the "Chinese spirit" (*Zhonghua minzu de jingshen*) and "revitalization of the Chinese nation" (*Zhonghua minzu de fuxing*), this "regional" literature contributes, in some cases, to shangrilazation and, in others, to attempts to dismantle it.

WEN PULIN: EXOTIC LANDSCAPE AND THE SEARCH FOR SELF

The metropolitan self in search of the more authentic other in a rural or remote place is a common theme in travel writing, as it is in tourism, in which "othering is a key process of socially constructing and representing other places and peoples" (Mowforth and Munt 1998, 59). Travel naturally inspires comparisons, as it puts into prominent relief the differences between the metropolitan traveler and the subjects he or she encounters. While feasting on the exotic landscape, the traveler is simultaneously drawn to indigenous ways of life. Thus, "othering" becomes a vehicle through which metropolitan life comes to be seen as excessively materialistic and to be rejected in favor of a more virtuous, simple existence. In many ways, this pastoral sentiment is akin to "imperialist nostalgia," a longing for "more stable worlds, whether these reside in our past, in other cultures, or in the conflation of the two" (Rosaldo 1989, 107–8). While pastoralism is an old pursuit of Chinese scholar-officials, exemplified in the poetry of Tao Qian (365–427), finding the source of the pastoral in ethnic minorities is a relatively modern phenomenon, articulated first in the stories of Shen Congwen (1902–1988) in the 1930s but more prevalently in post-Mao literature, such as Bai Hua's *The Remote Country of Women* (Yuanfang you ge nü'er guo), Zhang Chengzhi's *Black Steed* (Hei junma), and Jiang Rong's *Wolf Totem* (Lang tuteng). In this ideologically fashioned structure, the less developed/civilized is expected to save the more developed/civilized, a reversal of the Hegelian Marxist stage evolutionary theory widely accepted in China. As objects of the metropolitan imagination and a mirror that reflects the morality of the city, the ethnic minorities living along China's frontiers are seen as representing the primitive innocence and vitality absent in the modern lives of Chinese urbanites. Due to their unique geography and religiosity, Tibetans in particular are the focus of this metropolitan fixation. As a result of the close encounter between the metropolitan self and the native other, the voyeuristic gaze, as depicted in the works of Wen and Fan, is invariably turned inward, leading to self-reflection and even self-transformation. Trips to the Sino-Tibetan borderlands, therefore, give Chinese urbanites opportunities to experience different cultures but, more importantly, as shown in the example of Wen, they represent inner journeys of self-discovery and possibly the reconstitution of self-identity (see chs. 2 and 3 in this volume).

Wen's travel writings cover a span of more than a decade, from 1989 to early in the first decade of the 2000s, when he took frequent trips to Tibet, often traveling on foot in the company of pilgrims, itinerants, and traders. This mode of transportation allowed him to come into close contact with ordinary Tibetans, who, he believes, are attuned to their natural environment. Wen thinks of nature as the source of salvation for modern metropolites alienated from the fundamentals of life. "We urbanites have been living far too long away from nature and land. [But] deep in our hearts we all have a yearning for them. Unfortunately, we have very little opportunity and very little luck to come into close contact with nature and land" (Wen 2003a, 278). The nature Wen speaks of is not just scenery or landscape; rather, it is the totality of a place, including its people and their way of life. The unsullied natural environment and the authentic minorities living in it go hand in hand. To Wen, Axu (in Dege County, Ganzi [Tib. Kardze] Tibetan Autonomous Prefecture), in northwest Sichuan, represents a cultural ecological paradise where man lives in perfect harmony with nature.[1] Wen describes his love for Axu as instantaneous. The moment he saw it, he writes, he knew he had found "the Shangrila of [his] dreams," "a flat prairie embraced by mountains on three sides, and the yellow grass bathed in the warm sun," a place that "existed as if in a dream or imagination" (Wen 2003b, 12). The landscape of Axu confirmed the scripted narratives of Tibet that Wen had read. He later organized a trip to Axu with a group of urbanites, which he calls "the last romantic journey at the end of the century," to witness the opening of a temple built with the funds he had helped raise. In his book, he recalls frequent squabbles among the group on the way to Axu, but at the end of the journey, they parted as bosom friends. "Cities have made men no longer able to cry! Axu made it possible for us to reclaim the long-lost emotions" (Wen 2003a, 277–78). As if by magic, Axu cleansed the soul of this traveler and brought out the best in him by returning him to the "lost" world of primitive innocence. "I'm not saying that everything here fits the image of Shangrila, but in comparison with city life, I feel much freer and happier. This land is closer to the sky and [therefore] closer to spiritual life" (Wen 2003b, 263). The equation of high altitude with spirituality is important to note, as geography is seen as a passage to the otherworldly realm. This portrayal of Axu as a place of freedom, spirituality, and natural beauty, everything Beijing is not, draws attention to the dichotomy of pastoral simplicity and metropolitan materialism. In the modern world, Wen needs to be emotionally and spiritually anchored in the fundamentals of life found in the unindustrialized frontiers. He confesses that "the string of my heart is attached to [Axu], which has become the source that sustains me in this corrupted world" (ibid.).

The sense of freedom Wen refers to often has to do with physical pleasures. To Wen, the endless open space in Tibet breeds an open sexual attitude. He admits to having some "unclean" thoughts about the place and its people when he first arrived in Tibet. "How charming were Tibetan women! The stench of butter coming from them, like incense in Tibetan [temples], sent us into fainting spells. They made me yearn for them. They were absolutely perfect and healthy, qualities that our girls in the interior lacked. Their cheeks were like ripe red apples or bread right out of an oven, rosy and milky" (Wen 2003b, 30–31). In mocking his earlier attitude, Wen shows that cultural stereotypes frequently inform perceptual experiences. Metropolitan Han men often see minority women as objects of sexual fantasies, portrayed as early as the 1980s in Bai Hua's *Remote Country of Women*, a novel in which a collision between the contrasting forces of sexual repression and freedom plays out between a Han man and a Mosuo woman. Wen shares this view to some extent, as he tells stories, in admiring tones, of Tibetan women exercising absolute liberty in choosing their sexual partners outside of marriage. In some ways, he still sees these women as noble savages, free from sexual constraints, who represent mankind's simple past and through whom his own hidden primitive desires can be awakened. Mythologizing the primitive other as "a body of pleasure" (Certeau 1988, 226–27), Wen discovers in Axu a "lost paradise" in which erotic innocence is on full display, tantalizing the traveler disenchanted with modernity and Confucian ethics. Here he is revealed to be a classic example of the metropolitan man attracted to the sensual native other.

In Wen's view, however, bodily enjoyment is on a par with spiritual well-being. Therefore, the search for the bodily authentic other is essentially a search for the "original" self, and in Axu, Wen has found the very source of energy that reconnects him to his primitive impulses. This cultural landscape that embodies the ideal of Shangrila, to which he returns for physical and spiritual renewal, becomes his second home, and his journey back to it is constructed as a personal allegory of finding the missing part of the self. With a newly acquired hyphenated identity, a Tibetan-Manchu-Axuwa-Beijinger, the self is finally complete and made whole. Furthermore, Axu is the site where he creates his identity as a writer. Wen yearns to go back to the days when he roamed its mountains and prairies, for travel is a context for re-creating the self. Without the outer journey, there is no inner journey toward greater self-awareness and self-creation. The metropolite needs his rural and ethnic Shangrila if he wishes to maintain equilibrium of the mind and body and continue to reinvent himself. Axu, as the counterpart to the metropolitan, serves as an agent of healing that repairs the damage done to the individual by industrialization and materialism. Landscape is thus granted the capacity to engender spiritual transformation, and the power it displays is most centrally located in the traveler's emotional response to the external stimuli found in ethnic minority communities.

FAN WEN: EPHEMERAL LANDSCAPE AND MULTICULTURAL HARMONY

In comparison with Wen Pulin, Fan Wen is more of an observer, a journalist on assignment who reports to his readers what he sees on the road, and less of a character in his own travel accounts. A man much more comfortable in his own skin, Fan prefers to deal with other people's issues of identity rather than his own. Cultural hybridity is a recurring theme in both his fictional and travel writings. By focusing on religious landscapes, such as churches, monasteries, and everyday acts of piety as indicators of the diverse cultural history and reality of the region, he treats the ephemerality of landscape as a metaphor for the temporality of cultural memory. He also looks at social habitus, ethnic composition, and family structures in order to underscore the interethnic relationships in the area.

Inhabited by many minorities and as reflected in their multilayered geography and ecology, the Sino-Tibetan borderlands of Yunnan and Sichuan are by definition a fusion of differences. In Diqing (see map 1, C, D) live

Tibetans, Lisu, Naxi, Bai, Hui, Yi, Miao, Pumi, and other groups, and among the many religions practiced in this area are Bön, Buddhism, Christianity, Daoism, Dongba, and Islam. Fan is interested in exploring how the locals view this mosaic of differences. His investigation reveals that the many ethnic groups in Diqing live in harmony, despite a turbulent history of ethnic and religious wars, which, he happily observes, have been put behind.

In these multiethnic borderlands, identities are fluid and even arbitrary. Often a person's ethnic designation depends on many factors, such as places of residence, career paths, and government policies. In the midst of all the apparent confusion, dual or hyphenated identities are frequently formed. Through many examples, Fan examines the complex and malleable politics of identity and self-identity in the area. The first person he met on the way to Shangrila was the owner of a small food stand selling Tibetan butter tea to tourists. Self-identified as Tibetan, this man had a Tibetan mother and a Naxi father, a common phenomenon in the area. Indeed, as Fan goes on to show, interethnic marriages, not just between Tibetans and Naxi, are a matter of everyday life in the region, and the children of such marriages have much flexibility in their ethnic self-identity, making many into "ethnic amphibians" (Scott 2009, 241).

The people in the area also exhibit a remarkable degree of tolerance and even casualness about their choice of religion, subverting some commonly held notions about ethnicity and religious beliefs. Fan cites Cizhong Village as a case in point. Paul Zhang, a retired government worker who had been baptized at the age of fifteen, was one of the elderly Catholics Fan interviewed. The son of a Naxi father and a Tibetan mother, Zhang was the embodiment of the diversity of Deqin. Having spent all his life in the county government, he spoke Tibetan, Naxi, Lisu, and standard Chinese (Mandarin) and felt completely at home in the predominantly Tibetan village. Zhang told Fan that church services had been conducted in Naxi, as most of the members were Naxi, but as more and more Tibetans joined, Tibetan replaced Naxi.

Given the violent history of religious conflicts in the area, Cizhong's peaceful environment and social harmony are striking, according to Fan. He writes of discovering that the Catholic Church, after decades of Communist suppression, is now the pride and joy of the locals. Even the vineyards and the wineries are making a strong comeback a century after they were brought to the area by Catholic priests from Europe. This church, nestled in the midst of Tibetan Buddhist monasteries and temples, is obviously a lonely site in this part of the world, but, Fan notes, "solitude itself is a kind of beauty," and he appreciates the resilience of the Catholic faith and the fact that it has survived in the least likely place, despite having been "a seed of religion unsuited to the native soil" (Fan 2000, 276, 265).

Fan cites many other examples of cultural fluidity and openness in this area: the Naxi man who is chosen to be a Tibetan *tulku* (an incarnate lama) while his brother has inherited the family mantle of Dongba priesthood; the holy land of the Dongba religion located not in Lijiang, the center of Naxi country, but in Zhongdian (Shangrila), the heart of Tibetan land in Yunnan; the Muslim-Tibetan family in Deqin whose mother is a devout Catholic; the Naxi men and women who believe in Tibetan Buddhism; and the Tibetan men and women in Cizhong and Yanjin who pledge their faith in Christianity. These examples foreground the predominant theme of his travel writings: landscapes of ethnic identity and religious affiliation in the borderlands debunk customary designations, and despite a history of conflicts, Diqing is a place of harmony, shared among all ethnicities and religions.

Highlighting what he calls the "peaceful coexistence" of all ethnicities in the region in the present day, Fan traces several bloody battles of the past between Tibetans and others. By remembering the turbulent past, he argues, one is able to better appreciate the present. He recalls his visit to Weixi, where a fortress built nearly five hundred years ago still stands, commenting:

> Just as Nature eventually turns into dust the fortresses and trenches
> imposed on its beautiful body, mankind will gradually erase the terrible
> traces of war from its memory as time goes on. The winners and losers who
> once upon a time were brave, moving, tragic, and magnificent or sad, lowly,
> and defeated are all gone, and their only value is the "historical lessons"
> they provide us. (Fan 2000, 166–67)

Fan embraces this historical view drawn from the landscape in order to show that the peace of the present is something that people ought to cherish. Landscape as a metaphor for cultural memory is seen to be evanescent, as no structure is permanent and nothing is preserved forever. Relating his interview of Kelsang Dawa, a Tibetan man who escaped to India in 1962 but returned in 1990, Fan laments:

> When the footsteps of history have gone far away and the back views of
> travelers have gone farther and farther from our sight and become more
> and more vague, can we still see their solitary eyes and hear their breathing
> under heavy loads? (Ibid., 292)

History is personified as a traveler always on the move. Once it is gone, there is very little trace left behind. The ephemeral nature of landscape demands that people follow the rules of nature and look beyond the past of their own ethnic or religious affiliations and prejudices. Fan takes comfort in the example of Kelsang Dawa and his fellow countrymen, including Deqin government officials, who managed to bury the bitter experience of the past. He sees Kelsang Dawa's story as an excellent illustration of not only the power of time but also the wisdom of men. Fan makes no mention of how Tibetans there really feel about the Tibetan revolts in the 1950s and the current standoff between Beijing and Dharamsala. He presents Diqing as a cultural melting pot, a place where group identity politics is not and should not be at the center of daily life. The picture of "interethnic unity" (*minzu tuanjie*), a policy the Chinese Communist Party inherited from Sun Yat-sen's Republican government,[2] seems to have been fully implemented in the borderlands. While there may be many other factors that contribute to this harmonious coexistence,[3] Fan, a poet at heart rather than an anthropologist or sociologist, chooses to concentrate on the link between the landscape and human behavior, avoiding altogether a discussion of the implementation and enforcement of CCP minority policies in the area.

Although Fan's work focuses on documenting the lives of the local residents, their stories have an obvious impact on him. Commenting on the relationship between the traveler and the native, he writes:

> The roles of the discoverer and the discovered can be switched, especially when the discovered is so full of attraction. My relationship to Tibet is probably like that. I took part in the cultural exploration trip sponsored by Yunnan People's Press to learn about the culture, history, customs, and the soul of Tibet, but in the process my own soul received a precious baptism in the Snow Land. (Fan 2000, 6)

He has certainly gained respect for religion, as he recognizes the difference between him and, for example, the Tibetan hermits who seek out suffering in order to reach enlightenment. In his view, the world of the monk and that of the ordinary man are two separate realms, and "we see each other as 'a different kind of people' and cannot find a common language" (Fan, 2000,189). He has also learned to not pass judgment but to only observe and learn. He notes that upon hearing that fasting Tibetan nuns were allowed only one meal every two days for three months, he dismissed his concern for their health by returning to the mantra he kept repeating to himself when his secular views clashed with Tibetans religious practices: "You cannot judge the behavior of the pious with the reasoning of a secular mind" (Fan 2000, 194). But he confesses that more than once, he has found it hard to watch passively from a distance.

On the way to Mangkang (Markam County, in the easternmost part of the TAR), Fan Wen met a Khampa who asked for too much money when Fan tried to hire his horse. Fan's first reaction was indignation, followed by understanding, and, finally, resignation.

> Khampas are known as smart businessmen. They have a tradition of doing business and therefore are better at adapting to the market economy than other Tibetans. What they do more or less ruins our beautiful impressions of Tibet. We wish they would be forever pure, kind, honest, pious, and simple, all of which form a kind of scenery and provide an example that would purify outsiders like us who have been corrupted by vulgar materialism. But is it fair to treat Tibet like this? . . . People living in one place should not stay unchanged for the benefit of the people living in another place so that the latter can satisfy their desire for pure cultural scenery. But whenever I have been ripped off, I would lament that the loss of moral values has reached even the pure Snow Land. I like the Tibetans who are kind, simple, and pious. To me, they represent tradition and the Tibet in my mind and in the minds of many other people. Those Tibetans who are smart businessmen only make me feel uncomfortable. (Fan 2000, 308)

Fan's conflicted feelings about the Khampas reflect the complex relationship between well-informed metropolitan travelers and Tibet. On the one hand, they condemn the objectification of the Tibetan landscape and culture; on the other, they continue to perpetuate that same practice. As much as outsiders wish to see a pure and pious Tibet, Tibetans, like any other people, are varied, and some are indeed materialistic and dishonest. But travelers who escape to Tibet with a scripted narrative and image of the place find it hard to accept the reality. Fan's reaction to the Khampa man reminds us of Wen Pulin's account of the Tibetan monk in Axu who reprimands an outsider when the latter expresses admiration for the "beautiful" and "charming" Tibetan culture and urges that it be preserved, "You Han people wish that we remain forever backward for you to look at" (Wen 2003b, 14–15). Fan readily acknowledges that the wish to preserve a "pure" tradition is self-serving and that there is a gulf between what is real and what is imagined. He himself is unquestionably opposed to treating minority cultures as objects of curiosity. About the future of the primitive salt fields of Yanjing in the TAR, he writes, "The salt fields should not become scenery for us. If possible, they should become part of history gloriously retired from service" (ibid., 394). He rejects the idea of preserving landscapes as sites of cultural memory for tourists. Conscious of his position as a Han from the city and the social and cultural implications of the boundary that separates him from the subjects he studies, he tries to avoid falling into the mind-set of a typical metropolitan tourist searching for primitive lifestyles. Nevertheless, the Tibet that he prefers is still something out of a picture book, a dreamlike image of Shangrila:

> Walking across the wilderness of Zhongdian is like wandering in a dream of warm and moist nature. The lakes are like women's moist eyes; the grassland is like watercolor paintings done playfully by children, with fairytale-like exaggeration and a romantic touch; on the other hand, the forests are like masterpieces of art, deep, profound, and multilayered; and the snowcapped mountains behind the forests even resemble the scenery of Europe on postcards. (Fan 2000, 198)

By comparing the landscape to seductive women, Fan assumes, perhaps unconsciously, the relationship between the viewer and the object he observes to be a gendered and hierarchical one. This gendered landscape is further reinforced by the references to "dream," "paintings," "fairytales," and "postcards," which emphasize the imaginary aspect of the borderlands. Instead of a real, lived space, Zhongdian is seen as a product of fantasies, to be gazed at by outsiders. And like a highly desired woman or a cherished artwork, it can fetch a good price. Indeed everywhere he went, Fan saw potential for tourism: "Zhongdian, unique for its forests, green vegetation, snowy mountains, and multiethnic and multicultural sites of human development (*ren wen jingguan*),[4] is like a lucky heir who has received a large inheritance, and therefore enjoys natural advantages in today's competitive market economy" (Fan 2000, 198). Here Zhongdian's landscape is measured on the global market of tourism, and its value is defined by the degree of interest it attracts from the outside. When Fan visited Cizhong's Catholic church, he imagined how the place would become a tourist attraction. With the eye of an outsider, he can't help but see the borderlands as a museum, a park, and a remote therapeutic site for urbanites fleeing materialism and modernity. His use of the phrase "multiethnic and multicultural sites of human development" indicates that, subconsciously, he regards the cultures of the minorities as "sites," like natural scenic sites, to be consumed by outsiders. The borderlands, in spite of the central role they play in his writings, remain no more and no less than an exotic place, a sanctuary and a place of escape. It is this land of natural beauty with its multiple ethnic groups living together in perfect harmony that he wishes to preserve and present, a portrayal that coincides with the message marketed by the local government and tourist industry as well as the project for a harmonious society that the central government in Beijing is promoting.

KHAWA KARPO CULTURE SOCIETY:
CENTERING FOLK SONGS AND FRONTIER POETRY

Contrary to the image of the borderlands as quaint and exotic places located on the margins of the nation, to their indigenous inhabitants, they are the center of their world. Once the midpoint of trade on the so-called Ancient Tea-Horse Road, connecting Tibet proper with tea-producing Pu'er County in Yunnan, Zhongdian was a vibrant town of commercial and strategic importance and an amalgamation of peoples. Although modern transportation has replaced horses, this notion of Zhongdian (meaning "Central Plain") remains in the subconscious and self-perception of the locals, who continue to use the old name even after its much more exotic replacement, Shangrila, was officially adopted. A group of young people, mostly Tibetans but also other ethnicities in the area, are giving Zhongdian a new definition, one based not on trade but on folk traditions. In essays published by *Return*, they propose a reconfiguration of the concept of center versus margin, replacing a criterion measured by political and economic strength with one defined by spiritual authority. These minority intellectuals use folk songs and poetry as a means of reversing or overturning geographic and sociocultural marginality imposed on the borderlands by Han metropolitan centers.

Their attempt at reterritorializing literary and cultural landscapes is predicated on a national discourse that centers on the assumption of the borderlands as a source of spiritual renewal for the nation as a whole. The trips taken and written about by Wen Pulin and Fan Wen reflect this metropolitan interest in the minorities. Faced with the excessive materialism that dominates urban societies, many Han writers have argued for a return to a world of innocence and vitality. Films and literature frequently explore the theme of nature versus culture. Jiang Rong's *Wolf Totem* calls for a metaphorical blood transfusion through which the Han absorb the Mongolian spirit embodied in the image of the wolf. In the movie *Sacrificed Youth* (Qingchun ji), the vibrant and "natural" Dai are to save the Han from wasting away, just as the Manchus and other non-Han groups saved the Han throughout Chinese history.

These and many other works demonstrate the Han metropolitan desire for primitive vitality, and the attempt to objectivize China's frontiers and the ethnic minorities who live there. The binary opposition between the "free" and "sensual" minorities versus the "restrained" and "emaciated" Han majority is built on essentialized qualities that highlight the differences between the two ideological constructs.[5]

When the metropolis longingly beseeches the borderlands, "Can you save us?" the editors of *Return* readily respond, "Yes, we can, with our landscapes and folk songs and the spirit embodied in them!" They offer northwest Yunnan as the place that has the answer for a nation looking for ways of cultural revitalization. Why northwest Yunnan? Li Guiming, a Lisu poet and a *Return* editor, attributes the reason to its "spiritual wisdom of survival," "reverence for the natural world," and relative isolation and "backwardness." The ambitious project proposed by Li and his colleagues is meant to challenge conventional concepts of space and authority, notions of inside and outside, center and margin. It is precisely because of its marginality, Li argues, that Yunnan has preserved "the solid fossils of twenty-six bones" (that is, the twenty-six ethnic minorities in the province) that have retained "historical patterns" (Li Guiming 2007b, 17, 19). Among the "fossils" unearthed are Tibetan and Lisu folk songs. The editors of *Return* see the oral traditions of minorities as an alternative to the vision of modernity shaped by globalization and Westernization. By turning their economic backwardness and their frontier status into an advantage, these minority writers wish to create a "Latin American effect."[6] In their view, the popularity of Latin American writers is a strong example of the Third World prevailing over the developed world, and the success of minority writers in China such as Alai and Tashi Dawa proves that the borderlands can replace the metropole as the center of a literary renaissance.

Their position might appear problematic at first glance. On the one hand, the idea that minorities are frozen in time is an essential part of Han fetishization of minorities, and in promoting this idea, Li seems to largely cede power to the Han to define the minorities. If minorities are indeed unchanged "fossils" from some primordial state of nature, does it mean that their lived history is effectively erased? If so, Li's willing acceptance of Han essentialism about minorities is unfortunate. On the other hand, it is presumptuous to assume that Li and his friends passively and naively buy into the metropolitan premise without much thought. One may argue that once adopted by minorities, these terminologies can acquire specific meanings as a result of conversations between "local and extra-local cultural systems."[7] Li's idea may be derivative, but it is hardly naive. Instead of being static and lifeless, his "fossils" are alive and pulsing with vitality. Preserved but not frozen, they are sung on the lips and danced by the feet of villagers. These "fossils" may come from a distant past but they are the very signs of a group's lived history. Kept not in museums but in life, they are now revealed to the outside world with a new role and a new set of implications. Indeed, tourism and globalization have not only given these ancient traditions a new audience; they empower the minorities, allowing them to represent themselves to the outside world with confidence. The borderlands are poised to take center stage, to speak directly and forcefully to the centers of power. As spatial representation is intimately connected to the politics of power, what Li and his colleagues attempt to do in mapping their own cultural landscape has the potential to change the dynamics of China's intellectual and literary conversation. The margins now not only speak to the center; they intend to become the center.

At the forefront of the Khawa Karpo Culture Society's undertaking is rescuing folk songs. *The Eye of the Snow Mountain*, by Tashi Nyima, a *Return* editor and Tibetan poet, is a collection of essays documenting the trips society members took to remote villages to record folk songs and dances and presents much evidence of the central role these songs play in village life. In their view, folk songs are the "childhood" of poetry and therefore the purest and most innocent. By naming their journal *Return*, the editors signal nostalgia for a lost or disappearing world, a world that is both physical and epistemological. Located in Tibetan or Lisu villages, minority folk traditions are regarded as receptacles of knowledge that the metropolitan centers lack. Rural northwest Yunnan is thus positioned to lead the nation to a spiritual and literary revival.

What is the essence of the poetic/cultural landscapes of northwest Yunnan? In Li's definition, it is the "lineage of freedom" (Li Guiming 2011). The freedom he refers to is not only a chosen lifestyle, such as the sexual practices admired by Wen, but also the courage of resistance characteristic of peoples living in the border areas. Indeed, borderland groups are seen to be "simulta-neously situating themselves to make strategic and political claims vis-à-vis multiple nation-states, while also remaining deeply committed to the 'ungov-erned' aspects of their identity" (Schneiderman 2010, 292). It is important to note that here Li uses the word "lineage" (*xuetong*) instead of the commonly used word "tradition" (*chuantong*), indicating that this concept of freedom is instilled in the genetic makeup of the many ethnic minorities inhabiting the area and passed down through blood—in other words, the umbilical cord that connects the landscape, the ethnic customs, and the poet has been established before birth. To be a poet of this tradition, one needs only to reach back and reconnect oneself to it through folk songs.

Folk songs are at the center of social and religious life in a village. For a people like the Lisu who do not have a written language, the songs also func-tion as historical records. For these reasons, folk songs play an important role in reconstructing the ethnic self. The following lines by Li Guiming give a clear indication of the relationship between landscape, folk songs, and self-identity:

> In this life, I've been circumambulating mountains and rivers
> In order to return to the homestead of folk ballads
> . . . .
> A folk song is a warm distance
> Safeguarding a solemn dusk
> Noble solitude
> Like the sorrows of swans
> Flying across the bloody red sky
> They are so white, so free
> The color of pride
> Telling me how far away from home I am (Li Guiming 2010, 186)

Successful, modern Lisu in China today are often unfamiliar with their eth-nic traditions. The higher they climb on the social and professional ladder, the further removed they are from their roots. The sense of guilt felt by Li's poetic persona is reflected in the accusing but loving words presumably com-ing from the ghosts of his ancestors. The gulf between him and his ancestors is immense, and the sorrow it creates in him is profound. Fortunately, this gulf can be bridged by a ballad, which guides him on his journey home:

On the forehead of my grandfather shine folk ballads
Brothers in front
Please bend down and take my hand
My right hand that has lost its way. (Li Guiming 2007b, 21)

Folk songs, to be rediscovered in the mountains, rivers, and "on the foreheads" of grandfathers, are conduits to ethnic roots and ethnic identity. Furthermore, they provide a model and an inspiration for the frontier poetry Li and his colleagues promote.

In their campaign to assert the centrality of frontier poetics, minority poets ascribe specific meanings to local landscape, which comes to embody their values and aesthetics. Tashi Nyima paints this picture:

Three cows
Stepping on the popping sounds of peach blossoms
Crossing the village paths
The sound of their bells falls on the asphalt pavement
Reverberated on the reflections of windows
A spot of green
A spot of red
A spot of tender yellow
At noon
Three cows
Standing on the slope in the upper village
Facing three directions
Recall past events. (Tashi Nyima 2007, 27)

In the smells, colors, and sounds of the earth and animals, in the heartbeats of village life, the poet roams freely in and out of the consciousness of the cows, epitomizing a harmonious relationship between humans and their environment. The pastoral scene forms the very substance of poetry. There is nothing that the poet needs to add; he simply appropriates these natural phenomena by turning them into poetic expressions. Tashi Nyima describes the village of Adong in Deqin:

Adong is like an open book, a book without words. But in the book are a
village, fields, irrigation canals, mountain paths, and countless trees. Birds
are flying about, insects are singing, cows and goats are grazing, pigs are

fattening, and people are bustling around, praying, experiencing sadness, celebrating the New Year, singing at the top of their lungs, and stamping on the ground in a group dance. How I wish I could keep Adong forever in that moment! (Tashi Nyima and Ma 2010, 115)

These descriptions foster a bucolic vision of a Tibetan village, possibly obscuring the realities of hardships that are bound to exist in rural communities in this area. They further define the essence of frontier poetics, the focal point of which asserts the primacy of the spatial experience as consequential to the epistemological and literary concerns. The birds, animals, and people give substance to the meaning of the "book," or the landscape, of Adong. Li's and Tashi Nyima's poems underscore the importance of landscape in defining frontier poetry, through which they hope to claim cultural authenticity and literary authority.

While trying to rescue folk songs and promoting "frontier poetics" through their own poetry, these minority writers are experiencing an ethnic awakening, as Li admits.

When I interact with poets from the interior, I always feel that I am a poet with an awkward identity. Why so? Because in the world of poetry written in Chinese, I am known as a Lisu poet. But I don't think I deserve that title. At most, I am an amateur poet who expresses himself in Chinese, and my ethnic identity is Lisu. Because I know very little of the knowledge passed down from my ancestors over a thousand years, I am faced with the impossible task of trying to communicate in Chinese those poignant passages existing within my native tongue that move me to tears. I think this dilemma is caused by the differences between the two languages and two cultures. (Li Guiming 2011)

Li finds himself in an awkward position that reflects the dilemmas of ethnic minorities in the borderlands. Nearly all contributions to *Return* are written in Chinese. Unlike the TAR, where Tibetans are the majority, the Sino-Tibetan borderlands are ethnically and linguistically diverse, and the Han presence is much more prominent. As a result, the Tibetans, Lisu, and others who live in the area are much more Sinicized. One of the consequences of assimilation is the disappearance of native languages. Sonam Norbu, a founding member of the Khawa Karpo Culture Society, shares a typical experience:

I began schooling at the age of six. The formal education I received was based on the national curriculum, all in Chinese. Till the day I graduated from the Yunnan School of Arts and began working for the government, I never learned Tibetan, knew nothing of my own cultural history, and had no interest in Tibetan Buddhism and Tibetan culture. While studying away from home, however, my lack of knowledge in my own culture put me in some embarrassing situations, which greatly changed my way of thinking. (Sonam Norbu 2009, 24)

This cultural awakening would later prompt Sonam Norbu to open Tibetan-language classes in Deqin and to rescue folk songs. Yet it is precisely because of their high level of Chinese-language proficiency that these minority intellectuals can effectively defend their culture against misrepresentations by the Han metropolitan center and can translate, though imperfectly, their poetic tradition into the language of the mainstream.

ALAI: THE "STAIRCASE" AND TIBETAN IDENTITY

While Li and his colleagues seem content to play the role of spiritual rescuers for lost urbanites, Alai, who is more familiar with postcolonial theories, does not want the Tibetan landscape to be a reference for the city. He writes,

In many books about the Tibetan Plateau and the Tibetans who live there, there is a tendency toward essentialism. When it comes to the Tibetan Plateau, to this unique cultural landscape, everything seems to be very simple. It is either good or bad, either civilized or barbaric. Even more troubling is that rural culture is completely turned into a reflection of the morality of the metropolis. Country life is not the paradise of Shangrila. On the ascending steps close to the Tibetan Plateau, there is much suffering, but the people who have been kept in the dark have not yet learned to express it in their own voices! (Alai 2000, 143)

Alai's distaste for popular representations of Tibetan culture as binary oppositions of good and evil reflects a critique of the long-standing image of Tibet as a pure landscape untouched by industrialization or as a backward culture known for its barbaric customs, images that plagued Tibet for decades. Alai rejects seeing Tibet in such simplistic terms; instead he wishes to present a "real" Tibet, in this case, his native Gyarong-Tibet, on the border of Amdo and Kham in counties spanning today's Aba and Ganzi Tibetan Autonomous Prefectures in Sichuan.

Sandwiched between two regional powers—Han China to the east and Tibet proper to the west—Gyarong historically maintained a delicate relationship with both of them. Depending on which direction the pendulum of power swung, Gyarong's allegiance fluctuated with the fortunes of its two mighty neighbors. Alai's novel *Red Poppies* (Chen'ai luoding) is an attempt to articulate this geopolitical position and Gyarong identity.[8] If self-identity in the novel is couched in the metaphor of idiocy, it is presented without the slightest ambiguity in Alai's travelogue, *The Earth's Staircase* (Dadi de jieti). The sense of belonging in this book is clear-cut and uncompromised. For Alai, his journey and writing represent a process of personal and collective remembrance, "every blade of grass and every tree triggering endless memories in my mind" (Alai 2000, 186). To search his native landscape for personal memories of his childhood and youth and collective memories of historical Gyarong is to come to terms with his own identity, to take stock of what makes Gyarong, and to defend Tibet and Tibetan culture against a history of misrepresentations. As an individual, Alai is reaffirming his Tibetanness, and as a self-designated spokesperson for his people, he is reconfirming Gyarong's Tibetan cultural territoriality. Here the personal and the collective become one shared experience.

Like Wen Pulin, Alai also plays a dual role in his writing: he educates his readers and reflects on his own relationship with the landscape. His authority as a teacher and proponent of Gyarong Tibetan culture is grounded in his identity as a Gyarong Tibetan, which is established through the act of "remembering," an emotional process of recalling the past and reuniting oneself with one's group. When the past is brought back to life, Alai writes, such as in the folk dance he witnessed, "I felt they [the dancers] were Gyarong men from a past era when Xiaojin was still called Tsanlha. . . . All of a sudden, the past was standing in front of my eyes" (ibid., 118). This memory of a bygone age is not the author's alone; it is shared by all Gyarong people. "I could see on the faces of those dancers, especially those men . . . that they were dancing their own dance and they were immersed in their own passion and the memories within that passion. . . . In this dance, they could return to the past, to an infinitely distant and expansive reservoir of memories" (Alai 2000, 120). Here the collective and personal memories, the present and the past, are collapsed in the moment of the dance, and a strong connection between the author and the dancers, between them and the Tibetan warriors the dance invoked, is established.

The old Gyarong in Alai's memory and imagination can still be seen, though rarely. Alai discovers a correlation between landscape and identity. As the land rises, "wheat turns to barley, and forests of maples, poplars, pines, grey-trunked spruces, and dark-barked hemlocks" (Alai 2000, 158) appear. Alai finds himself in the depths of old Gyarong, and the floodgates of childhood memories and memories of Tibetan culture suddenly opens. The lower he goes on the "staircase," the closer he comes to the Han interior and the more attenuated Tibetan culture becomes. It is this geographic and cultural "rise" and "fall" that is his focus in the travel account.

As the landscape changes, Alai notes sharp contrasts between the pure Tibetan Gyarong and the Sinicized Gyarong. Village names reflect changes in the political history of the region. The poetic name "Najue," meaning "a deep valley" and compatible with the environment, was changed to the nondescript "203 Lumbering Field" during the Cultural Revolution (1966–76), when large-scale logging turned the green valley into wasteland. In the mixed architecture in the area Alai notices a disparity between graceful traditional Gyarong houses, which "forever maintain a respectful silence and a sense of serenity in harmony with the mountains and rivers," and "the rough and arrogant cement boxes" typical of the Mao-era Chinese architecture, whose "open sewers filled with garbage become home for flies in the summer" (Alai 2000, 193–94). In the sharply contrasted and violently disconnected world of Tibetan beauty and Han dreadfulness, Alai's Tibetan identity is repeatedly and positively affirmed. Hence, Gyarong offers a site for the reassertion of the writer's sense of belonging, and his physical journey is framed as an interior mapping of his own attachment to the Gyarong cultural landscape.

This Gyarong cultural landscape, however, is a constructed entity, created through acts of remembering and imagining. To Alai, the true Gyarong is found in the past, kept alive in the myths and legends associated with the mountains and rivers. On the solitary journey that allows him uninterrupted meditative reveries, Alai indulges himself in a romantic nostalgic retreat into the past depicted in stories about the spread of Buddhism in Gyarong, and Tubo (Tibetan) military conquests. Intensely emotional in its self-location, Alai's travelogue expresses a longing for a Gyarong that was pure, unadulterated, elegant, and heroic. He is immensely proud of his ancestors, proud of his lineage: "I know that in my body flows the blood of my native Gyarong ancestors as well as the blood of the Tibetan warriors from Ngari" (Alai 2000, 35), not to mention the Hui blood that also courses through his veins. Throughout the book, however, it is his Tibetanness, not his other heritages, that he emphasizes.

In polyethnic Ngawa, hybridity has been a fact of life from the very beginning, when Tibetan soldiers appeared in the landscape. Originally settled by the Qiang, an ancient nomadic people, Gyarong was conquered by Tibetans in the seventh and eighth centuries, followed by Mongols, and later by the Qing empire, which brought Han and Hui soldiers from Sichuan and Shaanxi. Many of these newcomers settled in the area and married the local peoples. The Gyarong Tibetans, "as the colonizers yesterday, . . . were counter-colonized then and are recolonized today. Colonization is therefore never unidirectional, nor does it occur only once" (Choy 2008, 231). Although a pure and unadulterated Gyarong may never have existed, to Alai, the imagined past, embedded in the valleys and mountains of the landscape, was altogether whole and untainted. By reasserting Gyarong's Tibetanness, Alai embraces a Tibetan national identity distinct from the Chinese national identity, although his position is more cultural and aesthetic than political. As a repository of collective Tibetan consciousness, the Gyarong landscape evokes the legends of a glorious Tibet marked by beauty, religiosity, and political triumph. Compared with the writings of Tashi Nyima and Alai's own fictional work, *The Earth's Staircase* is an unapologetic affirmation of a Tibetan national identity at the expense of Gyarong's local and hybrid identity.

CONCLUSION

As China's economy grows, the Sino-Tibetan borderlands are becoming increasingly popular destinations for urbanites escaping congested cities and fast-paced lifestyles. Travel literature is both a product and a catalyst of this rush to the borders. It not only provides guidance on how landscapes should be viewed but also bears witness to the societies observed. What Wen Pulin, Fan Wen, and Alai have created, therefore, are textual spaces in which the encounter between the outsider and the indigenous takes place and issues of representing the landscape and its people are explored. The connection between travel/tourism and identity politics is well studied (Grenier 2005; R. Williams 2008). Although travel is essentially a process of finding the other, the intrusion of the traveler into the life of the native often has reverberating effects. While the outsider looks in, trying to uncover some unknown mysteries in the other, the insider, in response to the external gaze, looks back, searching the past for guidance in order to redefine himself or herself and defend indigenous tradition. Only in an imagined pure past, an untainted "childhood," with its own distinct cultural practices untouched by the project of "the Chinese nation" can minorities retrieve the bloodlines of their ethnicity. The Sino-Tibetan borderlands are thus fertile grounds for reimagining "the nation," be it a newly reconstructed Tibetan one, a reconfiguration of an older multiethnic People's Republic, or a completely new territory and polity.

Landscape features in the writings of both groups as a space in which meanings can be located. In the eyes of the outsider, landscape in the borderlands is constructed as a space that fulfills dreams and fantasies—a path to new kinds of selfhood. To indigenous authors, it is a repository for ethnic history and tradition, invested with memory and vitality and with the capacity to preserve knowledge and define self and group identity. For both groups, landscape serves as the primary location for interpretation of cultural differences, some of which manifest as differences in literary style and content. From this angle, landscape is not only a subject to be written about; it is an agent that can and does express itself historically and politically. Indeed, the travel writings and poems discussed in this chapter treat landscape as an entity that leverages ownership of moral, spiritual, and literary authority.

Fraught with questions related to history, tradition, and authenticity of representation, ethnic identity in the borderlands is always complex. The minorities living there straddle multiple allegiances and consider themselves as both part of and separate from the national culture. For Tibetans in the Sino-Tibetan borderlands, this means that PRC state incorporation and global tourism, which come together in shangrilazation, have generated new forms of Tibetan unity and an affinity for a Tibetan nationalist project that did not previously exist.[9] This tendency is most pronounced in Alai's travel writing, despite his professed disinterest in Tibetan politics. This is not to say that Tashi Nyima does not espouse a similar sentiment. However, the fact that the Khawa Karpo Culture Society and *Return* operate as a platform for all minorities in the region, not just for Tibetans, makes it hard, if not impossible, to advocate or express a particularly pan-Tibetan national identity, another indication of the hybridity of the cultural landscape of northwest Yunnan.

In the Sino-Tibetan borderlands, landscape plays an important role in imaginative constructions of identity. As each writer presents his own view of the region, the claims he makes on specific identities are contingent upon representations of the landscape. Landscape, therefore, is not just a physical space; it is a complex entity, codified and inscribed with meanings. As a cultural and political production, landscape is used to tell stories, teach historical lessons, set the terms for a literary form, and, most importantly, define self-identity and ethnic and national identity.

CHAPTER 1. VITAL MARGINS

1   Tibetans in this case are treated similarly as *Naturvölker*, defined as peoples who live close to nature, a concept proposed by the German psychologist and anthropologist Theodor Waitz (1821- 1864). See his seminal work *Die Anthropologie der Naturvölker* (Waitz 2012) and a critique of *Naturvölker* in Zimmerman 2001.

2   For a Chinese interpretation of Sun's minority policy and its implications in contemporary Chinese ethnic relations, see Hu 1995.

3   Emily T. Yeh's study of Lhasa neighborhoods in the pre- and post-1950s argues that a historical cosmopolitanism based on Buddhism in combination with a coercive state policy of national unity has facilitated smooth interactions among different ethnicities living in Lhasa (Yeh 2009c).

4   In China, tourist sites are divided into two categories: natural sites (*ziran jingguan*) and cultural or human development sites (*ren wen jingguan*).

5   For a discussion of how ethnic minorities are used to help define Chinese national identity, see Gladney 1994.

6   Li's use of this phrase reflects the Chinese view of the international recognition of Latin American writers, such as Gabriel García Márquez and Jorge Luis Borges, and the hope that their own "regionalism" could become mainstream as well.

7   In his study of China's politics of regionalism, Tim Oakes (1999, 2000) finds that ethnic minorities are represented and self-represent as "'living fossils' (huo huashi) of ancient China." The Miao people of Guizhou, the subject of his research, are portrayed as "the Chinese of the Tang dynasty" (618–907), and their Ground Opera is promoted as the exact form staged in the heartland of Chinese civilization up to the Ming dynasty (1368–1644). In the summer of 2002, I attended a concert of Naxi Ancient Music, which Xuan Ke, its famous spokesperson, claimed that the Naxi alone had preserved from the Han dynasty (206 BCE–220 CE).

8   Howard Y. F. Choy (2008, 224) argues, "Disoriented in the identity crisis between Chineseness and Tibetanness, the self of such a Chinese Tibetan as the writer Alai . . . is so confused that he can only present fictionally and fictitiously his identity in idiocy." Although I would not go so far as to equate the first-person narrator in *Red Poppies* with the author Alai, as Choy clearly does, I agree that in Gyarong, a "polyethnic gray area," self-identity is complex, shifting, and historically conditioned.

9   Tsering Topgyal's (2011) dissertation examines the cycles of (Chinese) state-building policies and strengthening of (Tibetan) identity and resistance and sees them as obstacles for solving the Tibet Question.

Dreamworld, Shambala, Gannan

• • •

THE SHANGRILAZATION
OF CHINA'S "LITTLE TIBET"

Chris Vasantkumar

IN the summer of 2009, I was sitting in Leisha's, a popular travelers' café in Langmusi, a small multiethnic (primarily Tibetan, Han, and Hui) village in southern Gannan Tibetan Autonomous Prefecture (see map 1, A), on the border of Gansu and Sichuan. Since my initial visit seven years before, a flurry of scarcely controlled tourist development had changed the village almost beyond recognition. Though it still huddled in a valley below mountains seemingly plucked from a Caspar David Friedrich painting, the narrow and winding dirt track running from the main road into town had been replaced by straight, well-graded asphalt. The small creek that once danced alongside the main street turning prayer wheels with its waters had been relegated to the backyards of the new hotels and restaurants. Leisha's, too, had changed, relocating from the small space across the river where the kitchen doubled as living quarters to a much bigger, purpose-built restaurant in the center of town. Clearly people were capitalizing on the town's inimitable location. And business was good.

The restaurant was crowded and noisy. Members of a boisterous contingent of Chinese tourists concluding a motorcycle tour of the province were hoisting a commemorative T-shirt bearing their autographs up to the rafters to hang alongside other similar garments (the older ones Western, the newer and more numerous ones Chinese) left by previous visitors. Others chatted animatedly, snapping innumerable pictures of the cards, notes, pieces of currency, and other bits of tourist detritus that covered the walls of the restaurant. As I ate my spaghetti, at one of the few empty tables in the house, two well-dressed Han backpackers asked if they could share my table. I agreed, and we soon struck up a conversation, at first in English and then in Chinese. "Greta" and "Bluse" ("Not 'Bruce'!") were very well traveled indeed. She hailed from Beijing via Shenzhen and was on vacation from her job running a small travelers' hostel near Sun Island in Lhasa. He was working in Kunming and had recently joined her on what would ultimately be a three-month trip (including a spell in Laos—his first time, but not hers). Her previous travels also included three trips to Nepal and one to India. Closer to home, she proclaimed herself to be "the expert" for a chapter on a nearby Tibetan region for the new Chinese-language edition of a famous Western guidebook company's volume on the People's Republic of China.

They noted that Leisha's itself had become something of a required stop for adventurous Chinese travelers. Having heard from many people that the food was quite good here but that the staff's attitude could be problematic (and that it was also a good place to experience both Tibetan and Western backpacker culture), they were a little concerned about what to expect. While they waited for their food to arrive, we chatted about traveling to "Tibetan" places. After discussing the merits of various destinations—"Lijiang isn't worth visiting: every other store is a tourist shop. Just go straight to Shangrila"—Greta commented, "In Tibetan places, you have to keep your expectations in check. The service here is like the service you would get in Nepal—you order your food and then you have time to walk around the neighborhood and come back and your food still might not be ready. Here it isn't like Guangdong or other eastern places with quick service. But if you just get used to it, it stops being a problem; it's just how things work. The higher you go [in terms of altitude], the lower your expectations [should get]!"

Bluse and, especially, Greta were both very (if rather ostentatiously) knowledgeable travelers, but both were still somewhat flummoxed by our host, Leisha, hot-tempered and voluble one moment, charming and expansive the next. While Langmusi was (and is) renowned as one of the most charming small Tibetan villages outside of Tibet,[1] and while Leisha's main calling card (after its [in]famous apple pie) was a hubcap-sized "burger" of that paradigmatically Tibetan meat, yak, Leisha also wore a hat that appeared to resemble the *haomao* commonly seen on the heads of female members of China's Hui Muslim population. Though her restaurant did bear the Chinese characters *qingzhen* marking it as serving halal Muslim cuisine, it did so in Tibetan as well. Thus, perhaps unsurprisingly, Bluse and Greta were of divided opinion on Leisha's *minzu*. While Greta suspected that the hat marked her as Muslim, Bluse argued just as forcefully that it had to be for hygienic purposes. After a couple minutes of debate that left them still at loggerheads, I had to settle the matter for them. I told them that I knew from previous visits that Leisha was in fact Hui. To mollify the slightly put-out-looking Bluse, I admitted that I, too, had initially thought her hat was for hygiene. Further, on my arrival in the region in 2002, I had been struck by how difficult it could be on casual inspection to tell Han from Hui from Tibetan, quickly learning that dress and linguistic ability in particular were unreliable indicators of an individual's ethnicity.

In addition to the general ambiguity of external ethnic markers in the region,[2] it seems likely that Leisha herself was complicit in such misunderstandings. The next day, with Bluse and Greta on their way to the source of the Yellow River, I witnessed a typically animated exchange in which she cajoled a family of prosperous-looking Henanese, a mother and father in fashionable windbreakers with expensive-looking cameras and bored seven-year-olds in tow, to try Tibetan tea and the characteristically Tibetan, barley-based dish of *tsampa*. When they looked skeptically at the unfamiliar concoctions, she became impatient, exhorting them to eat, concluding, in something approaching high dudgeon, "We Tibetans eat *tsampa*!" (Women zangzu chi zanba!). When I later asked her about this statement, her response was a mixture of humor and dismissiveness that signaled the malleability of *minzu* categories in her estimation: "You could be a Tibetan, too, no problem. You're Chinese, aren't you?"[3]

When I told a Tibetan businessman friend in town of this incident, he was incensed. "I don't know why she has to keep doing that!" he exclaimed. "Her business is good enough as it is." Elsewhere in the region, I found similar tensions between Tibetans and Hui (see Vasantkumar 2012). In particular, Tibetans and local Han often found common ground in a distrust of the Hui that stemmed from the latter's dominance of local commerce. In Xiahe (Tib. Labrang), for example, a strikingly high percentage of the stores on the high street (even those selling "Tibetan antiquities") were Hui-operated before the unrest that began in the spring of 2008.[4] Indeed, afterward, some locals expressed sentiments suggesting that some of the turmoil of that unhappy period was directed more against these Hui merchants than against the central government.

Tibetans (and many local Han) I met across the region spoke with grudging admiration of the "good brains" of the Hui (Vasantkumar 2013) that allowed them to succeed in business without formal education while also criticizing their perceived clannishness and questionable ethics. Leisha's reputation also preceded her in this respect. A Han bus driver familiar with Langmusi told me he had heard that she speaks "six or seven languages even though she is uncultured and illiterate." In response, echoing tropes I had heard many times before, I suggested, "But she's smart, she is good at business."

"Of course she's good at business," came the reply. "She's Hui! China's Hui are like the [rest of the] world's Jews."

Yet despite this vivid and oft-repeated analogy and the prominence of tension I observed between non-Muslim locals and the Hui during my time in Gannan, Hui and Han play little if any role in either popular or official depictions of the region for tourist consumption. This is unlikely to be a coincidence.

Though Greta and Bluse spoke of Leisha's as typical of a restaurant one would find in Tibetan areas, Leisha herself is not Tibetan. Moreover, though Leisha's is not actually a Tibetan restaurant, many of those who pass through, such as the Henanese family whose dining experience I had witnessed (and indeed many of the Westerners who attempted to conquer the yak burger back in the day), absolutely have experienced it as such. Such misapprehensions are made more likely, indeed, are even actively encouraged, by the particular ways in which Langmusi and other parts of the autonomous prefecture in which it is located have been zoned as locations of authentic Tibetan difference (as special ethnic zones, to put a new spin on the SEZ).

"LITTLE TIBETS" AND OTHER MINIATURES

This zoning is part and parcel of a series of official and quasi-official efforts over the past decade and a half that have fashioned the town of Xiahe, the prefectural capital of Gannan, and the prefecture as a whole as exemplary models of consumable Tibetan culture despite the multiethnic makeup of their populations. Whether casting the region as "China's 'Little Tibet,' Gansu's Back Flower Garden," as was the case from the late 1990s until the middle of the first decade of the 2000s, positioning Xiahe as the home of a unique but essentially Tibetan "Labrang Culture," or echoing the shangrilazation of Diqing by locating the Tibetan Buddhist Elysium of "nine-colored Shamb[h] ala" (Gongbao 2006, 1) in the prefecture, an attempt that has been ongoing since 2005, all have been aimed at harnessing local religious, cultural, architectural, and scenic resources for potential tourist development.[5]

The shangrilazation of the region has taken place against a backdrop of two important transitions as well as one perhaps unexpected continuity in Chinese tourist practices. First, in the past decade, as a result of China's internal turmoil since the spring of 2008 and the new mobility of its expanding urban middle class, the region has witnessed the almost wholesale replacement of Western backpackers with their nouveau riche Han doppelgängers. Second, this replacement of Western backpackers with their domestic counterparts has occurred in the context of a transition in the dominant modes of experiencing the ethnic diversity of the Chinese nation-state among urban Han easterners that can best be summed up as a move from the "theme park fever" (Nyíri 2006; Oakes 1998, 50) of the 1990s to what I term a "guidebook moment" in the burgeoning domestic tourism market. While both of these changes have significantly affected quotidian tourist encounters, the quasi-official representations of these places for tourist consumption and the experiences of the new crop of backpackers continue to be shaped by miniaturizing modes of producing "cultures of landscape" (Wylie 2007) that derive not from familiar Western genealogies but from older "Chinese" modes of spatial engagement.

The practices of spatial organization involved in shangrilazation and the zoning of multiethnic Gannan as a special ethnic zone of consumable Tibetanness are related to but not necessarily coextensive with European and American thought on the concept of landscape, which itself has a notably long and variegated history (see Wylie 2007 for a review). In its more recent incarnations, landscape has moved further and further afield from the "'Vidalian' landscape-as-essence and . . . 'Cosgrovian' landscape as 'way of seeing'" that lie at the heart of most Eurocentric approaches to contemporary tourism's fraught relationship to the concept (Minca 2007, 433). Recent reenvisionings of the term have moved it away from a focus on practices of seeing to conceptualizing it as alternately an amalgam of the material and the sensible *"with which* we see" (Wylie 2007, 152) or as simultaneously this "performative sensorium *and* site and source of cultural meaning and symbolism" (161).

While this expanded compass of theorizing around landscape has many salutary aspects, one worries that with this broad of a purview the term might slip off into the realm of words like "culture" (Trouillot 2003), "ontology" (Carrithers et al. 2010), and "modernity" (Ferguson 2006) that have arguably become too broadly applicable for their own good. Even if "landscape" can be seen as a term that binds together conceptual domains often kept at arm's length, allowing theorists to work, apparently effortlessly, across boundaries that separate the material and the ideological, scholars must still ask what things it *can't* do. What are the dangers of proposing "a productively diffracted vision of landscape [as] 'always already natural and cultural, deep and superficial . . . impossible to place on either side of a dualism of nature and culture, shuttling between fields of reference'" (Matless 2003, 231; quoted in Wylie 2007, 120)? Do such formulations conceal the degree to which landscape in contemporary geographic usage almost always proceeds via a particular Euro-American genealogy of concept and practice that might not be entirely appropriate for interpreting the hybrid "Chinese"-"Western" forms of tourist space in today's People's Republic?

This question of the appropriateness of Western concepts of landscape for "Chinese" materials might not be a very big deal if we could simply assume that Western and Chinese modes of tourism are basically one and the same. Yet such a belief has not been tenable since the publication in 2006 of Pál Nyíri's brief but important book *Scenic Spots*,[6] which argues that domestic tourism in China, however recent its dramatic efflorescence, draws on traditions of sojourning that date back to the journeys of sixteenth-century literati (Nyíri 2006, 7). A central focus of both these modes of travel and their contemporary analogues are a (now state-)codified set of "scenic spots" (*lüyou jingdian*) that serve as the preeminent nodes in the construction of tourist itineraries.

Where more familiar Euro-American models of travel are based on notions of discovery and of departing from the beaten track in order to access a realm of more immediate and authentic encounter, in contemporary China, domestic tourism is predominantly concerned with beating a path to state-sanctioned points of predefined interest. Western "journeys of discovery" are subordinated to journeys of "confirmation"[7] (Nyíri 2006, 93; following Ivy 1995). Ultimately, a preponderance of Chinese domestic tourists are not involved in a search for authenticity through a romanticizing tourist gaze tied to modes of landscape substantially consonant with inherited Western models;[8] these tourists are instead approaching their travels from an angle that is less about getting off the beaten track than about beating the track in the proper sequence (Nyíri 2006, 7, 78; also see Harrell 1995). Thus the tensions that many Eurocentric analysts see as fundamental to modern, Western tourists' engagement with landscape (e.g., Minca 2007) would seem to work rather differently in mainstream Chinese tourist circles.

Moreover, a scenic-spots-based mode of Chinese tourism appears to have much in common with older "Chinese" modes of interacting with space that draw more on notions of the miniature than on more usual landscape genealogies. In her 2011 essay "Miniatures of the Nation," which makes these arguments, Marizia Varutti takes from Bennett (2006) the notion of "museums as sites for the development of 'civic seeing'" whereby particular modes of displaying the material culture of China's ethnic minorities "can be understood as imparting a 'civic lesson' . . . on the unity [in] diversity' of the Chinese nation" (Varutti 2011, 1). She also draws from Lévi-Strauss (1966) the idea of miniatures defined not so much by "reduced scale as by the loss of some of the features of the original: details, volume, smell, colour, etc." (Varutti 2011, 3). This point about how figures, maps, and dioramas allow for cultural difference to be reduced and contained is applicable more broadly to the role official and unofficial miniaturizations play in shaping understandings of the terrain of social difference in contemporary China.

We must be attuned to the historical and cultural specificity of such forms. In particular, it should be noted that Chinese theme parks, as one of the "most recent interpretations of the concept of the miniature" in China, may have been drawn from a "tradition of reduced scale landscape architecture (Stanley 2002, 272), of which the Forbidden City may be taken as the most brilliant example" (Varutti 2011, 3–4).[9] This miniaturizing mode is potentially incommensurable with more familiar Western spatial sensibilities. Understanding the ways in which the two traditions diverge is essential for the proper experience of Chinese and Western theme parks:

> There is . . . a tradition in Chinese garden aesthetics of representing landscapes with architecture and even performance readily available for the modern constructor of theme parks. Indeed, many of the themes evident in contemporary Chinese theme parks are already present in traditional Chinese garden design: miniaturization, *shan-shui hua*, viewing pavilions, and performance. Even the business, the sudden changes of vista, the piling up of detail to the extent of creating disorientation in the viewer—all of these are present in the parks discussed below. This is not theming in the Western

sense of the term but the creation of a terrain that is specifically Chinese. There is no resorting to the easy visual cultural stereotypes of Epcot nor to the internationalist universalism to be found throughout Disney creations and copied assiduously in other Western parks. Chinese parks require work and recognition in both time and space. Viewers need to bring specific historical and topographic knowledge to their visit. (Stanley 2002, 272)

The overgeneralization of "Chinese"-ness in this passage is lamentable, but the larger point is worthy of consideration, given the links between China's "theme park fever" and contemporary Chinese tourist practices (Nyíri 2006).[10] The "theme park fever" of the 1990s was crucially important to the development of tourist modes of enacting, interacting with, and experiencing landscape in contemporary China. The two thousand–odd theme parks that opened during that decade became models for later tourist interactions, shaping the expectations of planners, visitors, and visited alike (Nyíri 2006). Prominent among these parks were a number devoted to the display of China's ethnic minority cultures in conveniently accessible less-than-full-scale form (see Ren 2007; Makley 2010). Before the massive expansion in domestic tourism of recent years, such parks were often the only way urbanites could experience the minority cultures of China's periphery.

Over the past decade, as Chinese tourism has moved from "theme park fever" to a "guidebook moment," the primary locus of miniaturizing models of ethnic difference has moved from the museum and the *minzu* park to the handbook, the Internet chatroom (Lim 2009), and the scenic spot. On the latter, Nyíri relates a conversation between a Chinese anthropologist and village officials in a Qiang village in Ngawa Tibetan and Qiang Autonomous Prefecture in Sichuan. "For these officials, 'developing' a tourist village meant undertaking what the leisure business terms 'theming': creating a 'tourist product' with a clear narrative of meaning, supported by a multitude of performative and interactive features—displays, shows and visitor activities" (Nyíri 2006, 50). Both theme park and scenic spot are marked by standardization of meaning and narrative. In both contexts, the ostensible point of tourism is not to make one's own meaning through novel or fortuitous encounters but to participate in a specific, state-sponsored structure (or, better, itinerary?) of feeling (78). Both instances, moreover, are "powerful illustration[s] of the argument that 'in the case of miniatures, in contrast to what happens when we try to understand an object or living creature of real dimensions, knowledge of the whole precedes knowledge of the parts'"

(Lévi-Strauss 1966, 23–24; quoted in Varutti 2011,10). Proper understanding of this whole is not instantaneous, however, but must be inculcated.

Miniature figures, whether mannequins, scenic spots, or "little" Tibets, work in part via "claims to the ability not only to reproduce variation and diversity in ethnic outfits' styles and materials, but also to reduce the complexity of ethnic minorities' physical, cultural and historical features" (Varutti 2011, 5).[11] As with mannequins, ethnic villages in *minzu* parks, and specific scenic spots, regional cultures undergoing shangrilazation also rely on "the loss of some of the features of the original: details, volume, smell, colour, etc." (3). Further, as with museological paraphernalia designed to impart a civics lesson about the "unity in diversity" of the Chinese nation-state (1), the scenic spots produced via the miniaturizing methods of Chinese tourist development do not invite their visitors to "look *into*" their particular detailed social worlds but rather attempt to "educate [them] to look *along* the relations that bind them" (10).[12] The kinds of relations tourists are being trained to look along are twofold. On the one hand, we see something akin to the relationships of common national unity familiar from museum contexts (cf. Varutti 2011). On the other hand, there is the sequence of proper movements involved in journeys of confirmation (cf. Nyíri 2006).

In the ethnic museum, the theme park, and the scenic spot under shangrilazation, the "visitor is given to see ethnic groups in terms of harmonious relations, docile character, laboriousness, dancing and musical skills, and folklore traditions. Conversely, what is concealed from view are the effects of modernization, hybridization and change, as well as inter-ethnic conflictual and hierarchical relations" (Varutti 2011, 13). Such reductions inform both everyday ethnic misunderstandings in tourist encounters and (quasi-) official government attempts to produce Gannan as China's "Little Tibet." The elision of particular (uncomfortable) ethnic details has been key to shangrilazation as a miniaturizing method. In many instances, the quasi-official formulations of the miniature have come to stand in for actual places in tourists' interactions. Tourists don't look into the messy quotidian ethnic mix of such places but look along them to larger narratives of national unity or cultural distinctiveness. Such instances also reveal the degree to which the miniaturization of ethnic groups renders them ahistorical. Scholars have tended to understand the miniature as "offer[ing] a world clearly limited in space but frozen and thereby both particularized and generalized in time" (Stewart 1984, 48). Yet, in contemporary China, something similar has also happened with regard to space—the Tibetannesses constructed for tourist consumption in various parts of China's Little Tibet are both particularized and generalized in space even as they are spatially circumscribed on Euclidean terrain.

MINIATURIZATION IN ACTION

Two recent publications sanctioned by both the county and prefectural governments and directed at tourists, both foreign and domestic, have sought to alternately recast the diverse, multiethnic town of Xiahe, Gansu, and Gannan Tibetan Autonomous Prefecture as exemplars of a distinctively local yet recognizably Tibetan culture primed for tourist consumption. Taken together, these attempts at shangrilazation illustrate both the miniaturizing method at the heart of Chinese tourist engagements with space and the degree to which earlier scholarly interpretations have overplayed the univocality of the meanings surrounding ethnic difference in Chinese tourist (and museological) practices (cf. Nyíri 2006; Varutti 2011). *Journey through Labrang Culture: Labrang English Handbook* (2005) and *A Dream World—Shambala, Gannan* (2006), published by Lanzhou University Press, were both edited by Gonbo Namjyal (Gongbao Nanjie),[13] a Tibetan. Although they predate the influx of Han tourists into the region after 2008, the hybrid Western-Chinese idiom they evince provides a particularly clear illustration of the degree to which miniaturizing modes of Chinese tourist promotion depart from familiar Western models of landscape even as Chinese and Western tourist practices increasingly converge.

Featuring parallel Chinese and English texts and almost identical in form, each book begins with a preface from the governor of the relevant political unit, the county for *Journey through Labrang Culture* and the autonomous prefecture for *A Dream World—Shambala, Gannan*. Each preface is followed by the editor's introduction to the region in question. *Journey* then turns to a list of tourist attractions within Xiahe County, while *A Dream World* features a county-by-county rundown of tourist attractions. In both books, the enumeration of tourist attractions is followed by nearly identical sections on "folk culture" and several advertisements for hotels and other "tourism service[s]." The volumes conclude with postscripts that, again, are identical save for the replacement of "Labrang" with "Gannan" in *A Dream World*.

Despite the formal similarity between these two works—which, in places, borders on plagiarism—on closer examination, subtle differences emerge. While *Journey through Labrang Culture* deals almost entirely with long-established tourist destinations and, perhaps as a result, hews very closely to its explicit theming of Labrang as a repository of timeless Tibetan culture, *A Dream World—Shambala, Gannan* is more composite and compelling. In *A Dream World*, the authors do not simply put a particularly Tibetan stamp on an already known tourist landscape; rather, they also attempt to bring new destinations onto the map of international tourism. Thus they write concerning the Zecha stone forest in Luqu County, "when tourists arrive here, they are often on the scoop. There are many other scenic spots to be developed in the area, [and] tourists can name them freely according to their imaginations" (Gongbao 2006, 64). In contrast to envisionings of the hegemony of state-sanctioned meaning at already established scenic spots (cf. Nyíri 2006), *A Dream World* instead shows state-sanctioned meanings that are not yet hegemonic—scenic spots in formation (also see ch. 3 in this volume, on incorporation and inscription).

Comparison of the two volumes also highlights small but important differences in the way each deals with ethnic diversity and Tibetanness. While both employ miniaturizing modes of representing the region's ethnic mix, they do so in divergent fashion. In brief, whereas *Journey through Labrang Culture* erases both interethnic and intra-Tibetan differences in the service of constructing Xiahe/Labrang as a distinctly local but recognizably Tibetan scenic spot, *A Dream World—Shambala, Gannan* simultaneously foregrounds and erases ethnic difference while emphasizing the local variability of Tibetan culture and the potential for tourists to bring new itineraries onto the map. *Journey* constructs Labrang as a locus of immanent Tibetanness posed as a worthy alternative to Lhasa and other famous locales of central Tibet ("See it here!"). By contrast, *A Dream World* is more ambivalent about the ultimate Tibetanness of the region it describes, incorporating not simply sites of Tibetan religious and folk significance but also tourist attractions linked to famous moments in both imperial and Communist history (Gongbao 2006, 115), while acknowledging the diverse ethnic makeup of the region. Further, the Tibetanness it elaborates is less unified and immanent than it is localized and diverse ("See them all!").

Journey through Labrang Culture sets up a bounded realm of locally specific but consumable culture. Cairang Danzhi, the head of Xiahe's People's Government, presents things this way in his preface: "When you enter into Labrang in Xiahe County, you will find that you arrive at the world of Tibetan culture and the garden full of primitive simplicity, original truth, goodness and heroism. It is a harmonious place between man and nature, and you will feel that it is *a completely different kingdom*—the world of Labrang culture" (Gonbo 2005, n.p.; emphasis added). In this passage, Cairang Danzhi (as the Tibetan name Tsering Dhonjub is rendered in pinyin), articulates both the separateness and the distinctiveness of the culture that the tourist will find and can find only in Labrang. The overall goal of the book is to expand the tourist visibility of "Labrang culture." The postscript to the guide makes this clear:

> In order to make the Labrang culture known worldwide, we dedicate *Journey through Labrang Culture* to the overseas tourists and travel agencies. Meanwhile, we set up a website in English so that the tourists will get to know the magical and charming Labrang culture as soon as possible. We hope this book can be widely accepted and provide the tourists [at] home and abroad with corresponding guidance and tour information. Besides we hope this book can provide the local tourism departments with some help. (Gonbo 2005, 101)

This is an interesting project given that Xiahe is already widely known among both foreign and domestic tourists.[14] Before the spring of 2008, when the unrest in the region began, Xiahe was firmly on the adventurous Western backpackers' route from Lanzhou in Gansu to Chengdu in Sichuan via the upland reaches of Amdo and Kham. Thus, it seems that the real purpose of this guide is less likely the popularization of a place that already figures highly on many tourists' itineraries than the production and promulgation of a particular vision of miniaturized, consumable Tibetan culture.

Interestingly, what this volume seeks to make known to the world is not "Tibetan culture" broadly construed, or even "Amdo Tibetan culture," but specifically "Labrang culture," a resource that can be found only in Xiahe and its environs.[15] The name Xiahe originated in an attempt to replace the authority of Labrang Monastery with that of the Republican government in the late 1920s.[16] For the past eighty years, government authorities have sought to deemphasize local structures of power and social organization, with the goal of integrating Xiahe more fully into the Chinese nation-state. In the context of this struggle, especially under the communists, the name Labrang, associated with the "feudal" social structure of the monastery, was virtually wiped from the maps of the nation. Yet in *Journey through Labrang Culture*, it returns to prominence precisely because of its associations with "traditional" Tibetan culture. In the introduction, the editor

Gonbo Namjyal describes the nomenclature in this fashion: "Xiahe is the name of this administrative region, while Labrang is the Tibetan historical name given to the monastery and surrounding region" (Gonbo 2005, 2). Here he is certainly reinscribing the difference between God and Caesar, but unlike past visions that sought to eradicate the influence and culture of the monastery, he constructs traditional, ecclesiastically informed but eminently consumable culture as precisely that which will draw visitors to the region.

In his preface, Cairang Danzhi presents the potential tourist with the panoply of experiences available for enjoyment. These run the gamut from the sacred, "When you enter Labrang you are able to appreciate the super-natural and reconditeness of Tibetan Buddhism, visit the relics with a long history, enjoy detachment and recitation of the sutra and find out thousands of monks, pilgrims, and learners in endless stream"; to the aesthetic, "When you arrive in Labrang you will be able to take beautiful pictures while you randomly press the shutter of your camera. As you walk the streets there is no shortage of photo opportunities"; to the transgressive, "You will find . . . the chance to enter into a Tibetan home or monk dormitory"; to the gusta-tory, "You will find the pure-hearted and brilliant smiles of the nomads and enjoy a cup of buttered tea with your newfound friends" (Gonbo 2005, n.p.).[17] Tourism here is less a set of predetermined sites and views (cf. Nyíri 2006) than a set of potentialities, of possible experiences. Tellingly, this panoply of consumption is framed in the second person, highlighting the openness of these itineraries to all potential visitors, inviting the reader to picture him-self or herself being welcomed by locals (though perhaps not by government officials) "holding white hada [Tib. *khatak*] scarves traditionally used to wel-come guests and eagerly awaiting your arrival" (Gonbo 2005, n.p.).

The last line of this preface is even more remarkable, highlighting pre-cisely the weird sort of alchemy that has gone into the production of "Labrang culture." The preface concludes with "Tashi delek!" a Tibetan greeting wish-ing the recipient happiness and luck (Gonbo 2005, n.p.).[18] This phrase is also printed in golden letters across a photograph of a bird's-eye view of the monastery that sprawls across two pages at the volume's end. While "tashi delek" is indeed a Tibetan greeting, it is not commonly used among residents of Amdo. Originally popularized in the refugee communities of northern India, the phrase later gained currency among speakers of the Lhasa dialect in central Tibet. The dialect spoken in Xiahe, by contrast, a topolect of the larger Amdo dialectical grouping, borders on being unintelligible to speakers of Lhasa Tibetan, and vice versa. The usual greeting in Xiahe is, thus, not "tashi delek" but "cho demo" (Wyl. *khyod bdemo*).

The use of "tashi delek" here could be seen as an instance of the miniaturizing method in action—here tourists are trained not to look *into* the ethnolinguistic details of Labrang as a particular historical location in contemporary Amdo but to look *along* the lines of relations that bind it to an ahistorical yet spatially generalized form of traditional (central) Tibetan culture, on the one hand, and to their next destination, on the other. The decision by the head of the People's Government to conclude his preface with the Chinese transliteration of the central Tibetan greeting instead of with its local equivalent points to the ways in which even as *Journey through Labrang Culture* argues for the distinctness and distinctiveness of Labrang regional culture, it also makes this culture into an instance of essential Tibetanness, a Tibetanness that is not shaped by place, region, or dialect but rather exists immanently, eminently available for consumption by all interested parties.

In this sense, China's "Little Tibet" is well positioned to serve as a substitute for "the real thing." In his essay "Labrang Culture" (Laboleng wenhua), Gonbo Namjyal writes, "At present, Labrang is a center focus of Tibetan culture after Lhasa in Tibet. Many say that Labrang has even retained its sense of Tibetan culture *more so* than Lhasa, the capital of the TAR" (Gonbo 2005, 2; emphasis added). Strangely, the latter sentence is missing in the parallel Chinese text. Gonbo Namjyal goes on to detail the richness, antiquity, and supernatural mystery of Tibetan culture in the region, noting that the Labrang monastery "is a symbol of the soul of the Tibetan culture" (2) that it is "now the largest Tibetology university in the world" as well as a "large Tibetan Buddhist museum filled with . . . relics from the past which tell a story of the history of the Tibetan nationality [Zangzu]" (3). Perhaps unconsciously, the author captures the ambivalence between Labrang as a seat of active religious learning and Labrang as reliquary by noting that it has been called the "'Eastern Vatican,' or 'Eastern Louvre'" (3), references that index very different relationships between cultural heritage, political power, and religious authority.

Gonbo Namjyal goes on to list in detail the monastery's holdings of sacred texts as well as the long line of eminent figures it has produced. Having established the "depth" and "breadth" of Labrang's contribution to Tibetan (*and* Chinese) culture, he then discusses the folk customs of the region, emphasizing their distinctiveness: "In the core of Labrang culture (Xiahe County), customs have a particular individuality by themselves. Its customs, etiquette, various clothes, food, religion and folk festivals are all different from those found in any other Tibetan regions." Yet despite this putative uniqueness, Labrang is also emphatically an embodiment of immanent Tibetanness to the extent that, because its culture is "so broad and deep," it is "sometimes called the 'second Tibet [di'er Xizang]'." Ultimately, Gonbo Namjyal hopes that the simultaneous Tibetanness and distinctiveness of Labrang will lead to its being "listed in the world cultural heritage because of its beauty, majestic appearance and rich cultural and historical background" (Gonbo 2005, 6).

While this is indeed a grand envisioning of Labrang's tourist potential, this vision is also freighted with a particular constellation of forgettings. First, the vision of Tibetanness with local characteristics that the book presents is premised on an essentialized and utopian vision of Tibetan culture that emerges from a process of shangrilazation. Second, the only hint in the book that there might be something other than Tibetanness going on in Labrang is a brief mention of the fact that "Xiahe county has 14 nationalities including Tibetan, Han, Hui, Salar, Dongxiang and Mongolian. . . . Tibetans account for 78% of the total population" (Gonbo 2005, 8). In a text that stretches to 103 glossy pages, this is the only mention of the non-Tibetan aspects of local society. Thus, this project of aligning local prospects with national imperatives of targeted development can be understood as employing a recognizably miniaturizing mode of creative metonymy for the purpose of making an idealized traditional Tibetan culture stand for the borderland region as a whole.

In the process of producing Xiahe as China's "Little Tibet," government rhetoric seeks to align itself with both the whims of trans-local financescapes and the influential terrains of tourist desire that locate purity and supernatural mystery in Tibetanness. By attempting to convert Xiahe from a heteroglot borderland into a commodified "minority area," an avatar of Tibetan spirituality or an art museum (they cannot quite decide), *Journey through Labrang Culture* seeks to place Labrang at a privileged intersection of development and ethnicity where reified ethnic difference itself provides the means of bringing the local into articulation with macro-scale economic and social phenomena. What is lost in the process of zoning Xiahe for consumable Tibetan culture are the quotidian diacritics of social difference that render the Han and Hui presence in "a Tibetan place" not only intelligible but integral. In such a vision, the *haomao* of the Hui can only be for hygiene.

Yet, though most English-language guidebooks divide Xiahe into the

Han and Hui part of town—which runs from the bus station southwest up the high street to the monastery, the monastery itself, and the "old Tibetan part of town" beyond—patterns of residence do not follow such ideological boundary lines. Tibetans live doors down from the mosque, Hui live up in the high valleys and take their sheep up the hills surrounding town in the mornings, and Han are sprinkled throughout. One of my Tibetan informants described growing up in a nearby pastoralist region alongside Hui who spoke the Amdo dialect "just like nomads." Others found community in an emergent multiethnic local market culture premised on the ability to speak the local dialect of Tibetan (see Vasantkumar 2012).

It is hard to find useful estimations of the relative makeup of the local population. Most estimates are either two decades out of date (e.g., 48 percent Han, 44.7 percent Tibetan, and 6 percent Hui [Hansen 2005, 28]) or likely distorted by ulterior motives (e.g., 78 percent Tibetan [Gonbo 2005]). What is certain is that there is great diversity. It is telling that one of the first anthropological works on the region, Robert Ekvall's (1939) oddly compelling, proto-structuralist *Cultural Relations on the Kansu-Tibet Border* (written largely from memory in 1938), took Han, Hui, and Tibetans (as well as subdivisions thereof) as its purview instead of focusing on some putatively distinctive Tibetan character to the region. It thus takes significant rhetorical and ideological work in a miniaturizing mode along with creative use of metonymy, all aided by the overarching architecture of the *minzu* classification scheme, to transform this hodge-podge into something emblematically Tibetan on either the macro-scale of the region as a whole or the micro-scale of neighborhoods in a town.

In descriptions of Xiahe on tourism-related websites, there is a marked ambivalence between stressing the attractions inherent in the diversity of the region and emphasizing the appeal of authentic Tibetan culture. The Xi'an-based website www.travelchinaguide.com presents things this way:

> Another reason for a visit to Xiahe is that it is a melting pot of Chinese, Middle Eastern, and nomadic cultures. In the villages outside Xiahe it is not unusual to see Muslims in white skullcaps hawking Tibetan jewelry. Tibetan nomads usually come from the grasslands to the nearby Hui trading cities. When you wander the streets of Xiahe you will see the flashes of bright maroon robes and have to dart between bicycles and taxis. Old monks meditate and pass prayerbeads through their hands at the street corner.

While the Han are absent from all but the first sentence, there is a real sense here not just of the hustle and bustle of the markets but of the texture of human difference. Interestingly, the cities are glossed as Hui rather than Han or Tibetan—signaling the commercial dominance of the former despite their relatively small numbers. Another website, ctrip.com, maps things rather differently:

> Xiahe is a tiny, bustling town centered in a valley of the Gannan Tibetan Autonomous Prefecture, southwest Gansu. . . . This rural haven hugs its neighbor Tibet."

The site overview refers to Xiahe as "the most famous of the Tibetan towns outside Tibet." The existence of such English-language versions of tourism-related websites is one clue to the source and utility of rhetoric that maps Xiahe as China's "Little Tibet." Charlene Makley has suggested that "one of the state's strategies to circumvent the 'Tibet Problem' [the unrest and crackdown in central Tibet in the late 1980s] and the obstacles it posed to the 'rigorous development of international tourism,' was to target Xiahe and its famous Buddhist monastery, geographically distant from the centre of Tibetan dissident activity in and around Lhasa as a 'little Tibet'" (1999, 352). In this formulation, far from "hugging" its Tibetan neighbors, Xiahe's very distance from the problems of central Tibet made it attractive to tourist development.

The events of March 2008 have made it clear that geographic distance is no longer an effective barrier to the spread of ethnic unrest. Indeed, after the turbulence of the Olympic spring, Xiahe was closed entirely to foreign tourists for more than a year and has been open to foreign tourism only intermittently in the intervening years. One side effect of these developments has been to highlight the prescience of the local authorities' attempts to articulate an alternative touristic theming of the autonomous prefecture in which Xiahe is located. A year after the publication of *Journey through Labrang Culture*, the same editorial board brought out the similar but geographically more ambitious *A Dream World—Shambala, Gannan*, which highlights the attempt of the Gannan prefectural government to emulate the successful theming of Zhongdian in Yunnan as Shangrila.

Whereas Shangrila is a fictional place plucked from the pages of James Hilton's eponymous novel and (re)located to Yunnan's northwest frontier, Shambala has historically been part of Tibetan mythology or, in the authors' words, has been "the Elysium in Tibetan Buddhism" (Gongbao 2006, 1). Yet

the guidebook makes no attempt to argue that Gannan is the original location of this mythical place. Instead it evokes Shambala as a placeless paradise of tourist consumption. As editor Gongbao Nanjie writes, "Shambala,
Gannan [is] the Pure Land for every tourist to realize his dream for travel"
(1). What is most compelling about this volume, however, is the subtle manner in which its treatment of the realities of human diversity on the ground
diverges from that of *Journey through Labrang Culture*. The volume's preface
is authored by the autonomous prefecture's Tibetan governor, who writes,
"Shambala, Gannan, is the paradise for Tibetans to live in, smile and revel; it
is also the Shangri-la of the world." Oddly, in the parallel Chinese text, this
last clause is rendered "it is also the last piece of blue sky in the world" (ye shi
shijie shang zui hou de yipian lantian) (n.p.). He also alludes to "Shambala"
as "a Tibetan world that one dreams of, inebriated and reluctant to leave."[19]

So far this is quite reminiscent of the rhetoric in *Journey through Labrang
Culture*, yet even in the preface, a few subtle differences start to creep in.
Where, in *Journey*, Gonbo Namjyal alludes to Labrang as "the wisdom of
Tibetans, [an important constituent part] of Chinese culture and . . . a bright
pearl in world culture" (Gonbo 2005, 6), Shabaicili, the prefectural governor,
writes in his preface to *A Dream World*, "Shambala, Gannan, is a world like
dreams—a treasury of snowfield culture, a place full of splendid Chinese
civilization and a dazzling pearl in the brilliant world culture" (Gongbao
2006, n.p.). Here "snowfield culture" (*xueyu wenhua*) replaces "Tibetan wisdom" (*zangzu zhihui*). The former is a geographic term, at least in principle
ethnically unmarked (even if the related and more usual term "snowland"
is commonly associated with Tibetan, or apparently Tibetan, commercial
establishments). And, indeed, Shabaicili notes, "hardworking and virtuous
people of Tibetan *and other* nationalities live in this wide land" (ibid.).

The editor's introduction also acknowledges Gannan's diverse human
terrain. It notes that while Tibetans compose 50.76 percent of the prefecture's total population of 678,900, Gannan is home to a total of "24 nationalities such as Han, Hui, Tu, Mongol, Manchu and others" (Gongbao 2006,
10). Further, apart from the chapter on heavily Han Hezuo City, each of the
chapters on tourist attractions gives details on the ethnic makeup of the
county in which they are found, from 88 percent Tibetan Maqu to 77 percent
Han Lintan. Yet the preface sets the tone for the volume in that even as the
multiethnic makeup of Gannan is acknowledged, its ultimate Tibetanness
(or the ultimate interestingness of its Tibetans) is reasserted. The governor's
preface concludes with these welcoming lines:

My dear friends, Shambala is singing! Singing and waiting for you to enter into the paradise of the Tibetan people—Shambala, Gannan.

My dear friends, Shambala is dancing! Dancing and waiting for you to enter into the world of *hada* [Tibetan scarves] flying—Shambala, Gannan. (Gongbao 2006, n.p.)

Readers are not summoned to enter a multiethnic paradise, nor are they hailed to dance in a world in which Muslim skullcaps and Han fashions fly alongside Tibetan scarves. No, the dreamworld that they enter is Tibetan. The guide devotes twelve pages to "folk culture" that deal exclusively with Tibetan traditions (Gongbao 2006, 138–50). Indeed, almost the entire section on folk culture is culled word for word from *Journey through Labrang Culture*, with Gannan merely substituted for Labrang. Yet just as the treatment of human diversity in *A Dream World* differs subtly from the treatment in *Journey through Labrang Culture*, so, too, does the consumable Tibetanness it seeks to construct.

A Dream World is very self-conscious about the marketability of Tibetan culture. In the chapter "Introduction to Gannan," the authors describe local resources for economic development. "The region has five advantageous resources, which are tourism attractions, pasturage, water and electricity, mines and Tibetan medicine and wild products in the mountains. Based on them five industries are developing vigorously" (Gongbao 2006, 12). Of the three main sets of tourist resources in Gannan, the guide explains that "first of all is the primitive and beautiful Tibetan Buddhism culture" (13). The authors note that Gannan has "not only static Buddhist architecture and invaluable cultural relics, but also dynamic Buddhist culture, art and various Buddhist activities" (13). "Second is the colorful Tibetan folk custom" (14), and "third is the wonderful scenery of vast prairie and dense forest" (15). Here we can see the manner in which the imperative to develop locally specific resources central to development schemes such as the Great Western Development (Xibu Da Kaifa) strategy of 2000 is productive of both the enhanced visibility of Tibetan culture and the invisibility, at least in the explicitly themed section of the text, of the traditions of other minorities (not to mention those of local Han).

Yet the manifold Tibetanness that *A Dream World* envisions as a tourist resource par excellence differs from the local but immanent Tibetan culture that *Journey through Labrang Culture* attempts to construct. "Although Tibetans in different areas belong to the same nation," the authors note, "they have differences in the folk customs of weddings, funerals, living, food and culture" (Gongbao 2006, 15). *A Dream World* emphasizes the effects of Gannan's varied environments upon Tibetanness. "As a result of different living conditions, Tibetans in Gannan have both common and different traditions compared with Tibetans in other areas. The customs of Tibetans in various areas of Gannan are dissimilar to each other too due to the environment" (14). The authors then contrast the customs of Tibetans living at altitudes above 3,000 meters (in places like Xiahe, Maqu, and Luqu) with those of Tibetans living at 2,000 meters or less in the mountains of Diebu or Zhouqu along the Bailong River. Whereas those at high altitude "mainly dwell in tents made of yak hair and cloth," those at lower altitudes "dwell in two-story houses made of soil and wood with rich characteristics of Qiang, Miao and Di [*sic*] minorities" (14). Clothing is also a critical vector for enumerating the differences between Tibetans in Gannan. In a passage absent from *Journey through Labrang Culture*, the section on folk culture clarifies, "There are 86 different kinds of Tibetan clothing in Gannan Prefecture. In Xiahe, Zhouqu, Diebu and Zhuoni counties, Tibetan clothing is completely different. . . . The most spectacular costumes are that of Wujihe (Tibetan gunmen) in Xiahe and Luqu counties" (148). In place of the internally unified, distinctly local, but recognizably Tibetan culture of *Journey through Labrang Culture*, here the potential tourist is confronted with dizzying variety and the corresponding necessity to venture into various corners of the prefecture to view local Tibetans and their diverse ways. Such tropes of plenitude and plurality appeal to the collector or the completist rather than to the romantic or the time-challenged. A further, not undesirable by-product of such miniaturizations for state purposes is a portrayal of Tibetans as disunified and culturally divergent. Where *Journey through Labrang Culture* casts its eponymous subject as an iteration of an immanent, apparently unitary, Tibetanness for which Labrang serves as a conveniently bite-size setting, *A Dream World* pluralizes Tibetanness, emphasizing environmentally influenced variation and the interpenetration of Tibetan customs and those of neighboring *minzu*.

CONCLUSION

Comparing *Journey through Labrang Culture* and *A Dream World* foregrounds the degree to which official tourist meanings in contemporary China can be ambivalent or multivocal, even if only in subtle ways. We can see the texts in question as marking a process of trial and error, of casting about for the proper formulation of tourist meanings. Once the latter are found, they may indeed take on hegemonic significance. Yet the power of official representations of scenic spots should not blind us to the contingent, sometimes fraught, processes of negotiation through which even official narratives are produced. Further, given both the recent instability of the region as well as the relatively unknown status of many of Gannan's scenic spots for foreign travelers, it would be premature to declare that the tourist geography of the prefecture is fully mapped or that current official representations of tourist sites will remain static or retain their hegemony.

Ethnic difference and distinctiveness have figured prominently if ambivalently in these attempts to cultivate tourism in the service of economic development since the beginning of the Great Western Development strategy in 2000. The striking contrasts in the treatment of ethnic differences in quasi-official texts promoting the region's tourist attractions and the everyday frictions, ambivalences, and resentments in what has historically been a polyglot and culturally multifarious multiethnic borderland highlight both the particularly "miniaturizing" (Varutti 2011) cast of the landscapes produced and negotiated in new tourist encounters and the extent to which visions of "tourist landscapes" as essentially monistic and "modern" in character (e.g., Minca 2007) may overlook specifically "Chinese" modes of tourist practice (Nyíri 2006; Stanley 2002). Ultimately, both processes of shangrilazation and their discontents need to be understood, not just in relation to largely Eurocentric work on the cultural landscapes of tourism but with attention paid to hybrid Chinese-Western modes of tourist and other miniaturizing practices that, despite surface similarities with Western forms, may operate in ways that are uncannily but distinctly unfamiliar.

CHAPTER 2. DREAMWORLD, SHAMBALA, GANNAN

1   I had heard Western backpackers speak of Langmusi in awed tones long before my first visit.

2   This ambiguity of external ethnic markers in the region is apparently of long historical standing. See Ekvall 1939 for a discussion of the then common process of the Tibetanization of in-migrant Han.

3   I am not Chinese, though I have been mistaken for a Uyghur on occasion.

4   Hui dominance of the local economic scene could be gauged by observing the number of closed storefronts on important Muslim holidays.

5   These attempts to harness local religious, cultural, architectural, and scenic

resources for potential tourist development duplicate to a certain extent similar processes of creative metonymy that have gone into producing tourist landscapes in minority areas of China more generally (cf. Schein 2000 on "internal Orientalism") and even further afield (e.g., D'Arcus 2000 on "Southwesternism" in New Mexico).

6   The brief account that follows draws on a more extended treatment in Vasantkumar 2009.

7   Marilyn Ivy notes of tourism in Japan before the 1970s that, "travel to [Mount Fuji, Lake Towada, etc.] was an exercise in confirmation: the sightseer . . . expected no unusual encounters, no solitary experience. The purpose of travel was to see what one was supposed to see, to view an already culturally valued scene, and to acquiesce to general opinion." (Ivy 1995, 44–45; quoted in Nyíri 2006, 93) Of course such approaches are not unique to the "East."

8   This is not to say that Chinese travelers are not in the process of becoming habituated to such Western modes of conceptualizing landscape. While not simply imitators of a Western model, China's new backpacking contingent has, at least in part, been motivated to travel not simply to find confirmation of received wisdom but to uncover novel landscapes and experiences. For an extended treatment of tourists' practices of "discovery," see chapter 3 in this volume.

9   Another, perhaps even more apropos example of this miniaturizing tradition might be the Qing-era royal retreat/ceremonial site at Chengde, north of the capital, where a series of grand models, slightly smaller than life-size, of famous Chinese, Tibetan, and Mongol sites were constructed between 1703 and 1792. James Hevia (2001) notes that the configuration of the complex "prefigured Splendid China [one of the theme parks Stanley discusses], incidentally" (225).

10   Stanley's argument also casts Coggins and Yeh's comment in the introduction to part 1 that "a critical reading of the restoration of Dokar Dzong could easily relegate the place to the likes of a Disneyfied Tibetan tourist trap, but that would require a static conception of the landscape, one that elides the involvement and agency of local people in making and remaking the Old Town to suit their own desires, interests, and values" in a slightly different light. Not only would such a reading require misreading landscape; it would also require a misreading (or at least ethnocentric reading) of the theme park. For an account of how even theme park spaces can be reworked by the "involvement and agency" of ethnic minority performers, see also Makley 2010.

11   One particularly noticeable aspect of the relationship between a miniaturizing method and the ability to construct the real as manifested in the process of shangrilazation is the trend in "Tibetan" areas in recent years to rebuild what had been anonymous "white tile" modern townscapes in faux Tibetan-style architecture.

12   The full quotation is "Chinese audiences are not invited to look into the figurines of ethnic minorities—in fact, museum displays make no claim as to their artistic, historical, cultural or scientific relevance—but they are being educated to look along the relations that bind them, that is their common Chinese identity."

13 For the second volume, *A Dream World*, Gonbo Namjyal uses the pinyin spelling "Gongbao Nanjie."

14 Locals are aware of Labrang's fame but are not precisely sure how it works. A hotel caretaker at an establishment popular with Western backpackers once remarked to me that the owners of the hotel at which he was then working "must have good advertising in the U.S.!"

15 It thus fits particularly well with recent calls to "develop locally specific economy."

16 For a historical and ethnographic account of Labrang's incorporation into the Chinese nation-state, see Makley 2007.

17 Gonbo Namjyal also emphasizes these sorts of pleasures in his introduction: "Some foods to try are Tibetan wine, milk tea, Tibetan dumplings, tsamba and Jiaoma rice. Travelers can experience true Labrang culture as they eat Tibetan food, live in Tibetan homes [which may not be legal], listen to Tibetan songs and dance with Tibetans" (2005, 6).

18 The Chinese version does without the parenthetical explanation.

19 There may also be resonances here with the dialectic between the real and the really real in traditional Chinese aesthetics that Emily Wilcox (2012) discusses in fascinating detail. Her analysis of the intended aesthetic impact of dance performance is reminiscent of the language used to frame tourist encounters as well: "The audience has become nearly intoxicated by the beauty of the piece, and he or she has been drawn into a dialectical experience of real and Real, represented here by 'reality' and 'a fairyland'" (109).

A Routine Discovery

• • •

THE PRACTICE OF PLACE AND THE OPENING
OF THE YADING NATURE RESERVE

Travis Klingberg

Should any outsider now venture into Konka land
he would be robbed and then slain.

—JOSEPH ROCK, "KONKA RISUMGONGBA,
HOLY MOUNTAIN OF THE OUTLAWS"

Here is the idealized heaven city dwellers seek,
the last pure land on the blue earth.

—*SHENGDI: DAOCHENG YADING*
(HOLY LAND: DAOCHENG YADING), YADING
NATURE RESERVE PROMOTIONAL VIDEO

WHEN I first visited Yading in 1999, I was neither robbed nor slain. On the contrary, when I set out from the trailhead, a man helped me into the saddle of his horse and placed his young child in front of me to hold until we arrived at his home, where he would deliver her before guiding me toward the sacred peaks of the Konka Risumgongba. In 1931, the American botanist Joseph Rock described this terrain as the domain of outlaw lamas and bandit pilgrims. Today, it is the centerpiece of the Yading Nature Reserve (Yading Ziran Baohuqu) (see map 1, B), a national reserve that has become a popular tourism destination. Yading remains a place of religious significance for local Tibetan residents and pilgrims, who annually circumambulate its mountain peaks. And since the mid-1990s, it has become a place of national significance, a place that has embodied the desires of a newly mobile nation in search of leisure.

Joseph Rock was by his own account the first foreigner to visit the Konka Risumgongba, a mountain range in southwestern Sichuan close to the border with Yunnan.[1] He called the area an unknown land, a claim that helped cultivate a new professional identity. Rock had come to consider himself an explorer and geographer; his lifelong work collecting botanical and zoological specimens was a side interest on this trip, while photography took on a central role. Rock wrote of the Konka Risumgongba, "[I]t is to the credit of [the National Geographic Society] that this terra incognita has become geographically known and its unsurpassed scenery pictured not only in black and white, but also in natural-color photographs" (1931, 4). Over the past twenty years, these photographs and the story of their making have been woven into the cultural history of Yading. Rock's legacy has been retained not only in the ways his writing and photographs have been utilized as a resource for tourism development but also in the ways his discovery of Yading is repeated through ongoing routines of tourism.

Each fall after a steady increase in tourism over the summer, Yading is crowded with tens of thousands of visitors, mostly Han from cities across the country arriving with cameras and the desire to view the scenery (kan fengjing). With eyes and optics trained again and again—year after year—on the peaks, it is tempting to interpret the tourism boom in Yading as the consumption of a place through the production and reproduction of photographic images. Interpreted in this way, Rock could be seen as an image-making pioneer (Balm and Holcomb 2003) whose photographs catalyzed the commercialization and commodification of Yading. However, Rock is not the only person to have discovered Yading. Other photographers and botanists discovered the area again decades later, and tourists visiting the reserve today repeat the discovery of Yading on an even larger scale. As Yading has been transformed into a nature destination—a protected area that is, or seeks to be, a star-rated tourism site[2]—increasing numbers of Chinese have discovered Yading through seeing, photographing, and walking the reserve, practices that mirror the ways Rock worked out his own tenuous place in the Konka Risumgongba.

Through increased tourism, Yading has been drawn into a national travel routine, a collectively shared set of practices that continually generates knowledge about the reserve. This knowledge is generated in part through inscribing practices (Connerton 1989, 73), ways that knowledge is codified in texts and images or even built into the landscape. Photography is a particularly powerful practice of inscription, especially in bringing distant and unfamiliar places close.[3] However, the tourist in Yading is engaged in more than the pursuit and creation of visual images. In negotiating mountain topography, weather, long travel distances, and a range of social interactions among local Tibetans, service industry staff, and other travelers, the tourist comes to know Yading in ways that remain embodied and uninscribed. Such knowledge about Yading is generated through incorporating practices, ways of knowing the world and our place in it that are remembered in the body itself (Casey 2000; Connerton 1989, 72).

As domestic tourism has grown, travel within China by Chinese has become a national routine, an ordinary activity that, when repeated on a national scale, has become a constitutive part of the production of geographic knowledge in China. While inscribing practices are often emphasized in studies of knowledge production, knowledge of place nearly always springs from bodily actions and from knowledge "sedimented" in the body (Connerton 1989, 78–79). Although the bodily practices that go into photography have been studied in the past (see Crang 1997; Yasue and Murakami 2011), the body has often been taken as a vehicle for the production of visual images (inscribed knowledge), while the ways the body itself comes to know place through picture-making practices (incorporated knowledge) have been ignored. Photography not only is a means of representing a place but is itself a bodily practice of knowing place.

In their desire to see a natural and unknown place, tourists enact ways of experiencing the Konka Risumgongba established long before Yading was planned and developed for tourism. Yading has been discovered repeatedly, many times over, through practices of photography that generate and sustain the knowledge of Yading as a shared experience. The following exploration stories show how the discovery of Yading has become routine, that its opening as a tourism destination is not simply the end stage in a process of commercialization and commodification but an ongoing practice of place, a socially binding experience that has been influential in remaking local and regional geographies. Indeed, the shangrilazation of the Sino-Tibetan borderlands has unfolded in this way, through both the representation and commodification of place and the sustained bodily practice of place. And as individual desires to explore have been repeated on a national scale, the collective practice of tourism has had an expanding role in remaking

China's national geography, especially as urban Chinese have discovered the nation on their own through independent tourism.[4] Yading's ten-year rise to national fame as one of China's most beautiful places could not have happened simply by its being represented and promoted as such. It required repeated discoveries, beginning with Rock and continuing through the explorations of growing numbers of Chinese tourists.

EXPLORATION I

[handwritten annotation: history of "exploration" & "discovery" of Yading]

In the winter of 1923, from a trail in the neighboring kingdom of Muli, Joseph Rock got his first view of the Konka Risumgongba. He looked directly west across Konkaling, the southern part of what is now Daocheng, a narrow, 160-kilometer-long county angled toward Yunnan that drops 2,700 meters in elevation between its northern extreme and its southern border (SDXBW 1997, 60). Rock waited five years for the opportunity to travel to the "far-away conglomeration of snow peaks" (1931, 3), and in late spring 1928, as he set out on his expedition, he took what could be the first image ever made of the range (fig. 3.1). From this vantage, the peaks rise on the horizon like the petals of a lotus, the geological incarnation of the Buddha's three protector bodhisattvas. From south to north, Rock saw Jambeyang (Manjusri), the bodhisattva of wisdom; Shenrezig (Avaloketisvara), the bodhisattva of compassion; and Chanadordje (Vajrapani), the bodhisattva of power.[5]

This unknown region was actually infamous. Konkaling's fame grew over the first decades of the twentieth century, beginning around the time the British asserted a geopolitically destabilizing presence in Tibet in 1904. It was known for its bandits and raiders, who had attacked major settlements in every direction, as far as Liangshan to the east, Lijiang to the south, Zhongdian to the west, and Ganzi to the north. The militarization of the area by the Qing precipitated the bloody siege of the Sangpiling monastery in nearby Xiangcheng by Zhao Erfeng in 1906; Konkaling's monastery was destroyed in the preceding months as Zhao's troops moved in from Litang (Sperling 1976, 17; van Spengen 2002, 12). Konkaling was cut off from what little trade passed through the area (see Booz 2011) and, in the aftermath of war, descended deeper into a lawless period, when "brigandage developed into larger-scale banditry . . . [after Qing forces] burned entire villages, crops, and livestock, and plundered, meaning starvation" (van Spengen 2002, 17). As inspiring as Rock's first panoramic glimpse of the Konka Risumgongba was, the place itself had been broken by war.

FIGURE 3.1 The found horizon: the Konka Risumgongba. From left, Jambeyang, Shenrezig, and Chanadordje. Photo by Joseph Rock. Courtesy of the National Geographic Society.

Rock finally made it to the mountains in 1928, setting out from Muli with the assurance that his party would not be harmed while circumambulating the peaks. As he entered Konkaling, his concerns turned to the practical. He had trouble developing photographic plates in the field and keeping his reluctant party pointed in the right direction. Rock also faced the challenges of high alpine travel:

> We crossed the Yaka Pass [below Chanadordje] under torrential downpours. There was no trail, and the ground was littered with slabs of schists over which the water rushed in torrents, depositing everywhere a slippery gray mud . . . difficult enough in good weather, but in a terrific hail and rain storm, with a howling gale driving the icy pellets into one's face and making one gasp for breath in this rarefied atmosphere, it [was] doubly disagreeable. (1931, 46–47)

The party camped at high elevations, "often disturbed by the thundering noise of falling blocks of ice, dropping and sliding from the heights above" (ibid., 50). Near the end of his circuit, Rock stayed at the Tsengu Gomba,[6] a small monastery at the meeting point of two glaciated valleys. The area provided good views of Shenrezig, but as for the monastery, Rock minced no words: "There was nothing beautiful whatever, only filth and evil smells. . . . [M]y nose and throat were irritated by ammonia-like odors from the surrounding stables" (ibid., 61). The place Rock felt so drawn to seemed, on one hand, disagreeable. But as he left the main valley, on one of his last mornings of the trip, he recorded one moment more precisely than any other: at 4:30 A.M. on June 26, 1928, at 4,815 meters and 4.4 degrees Celsius, he wrote, "I rose and stepped into the cold, gray morn. In a cloudless sky before me rose the peerless pyramid of Jambeyang, the finest mountain my eyes ever beheld" (ibid., 64). The climax of Rock's story comes at the end of sixty-five National Geographic pages in a moment of seeing that, while it seemed to transcend the difficulty, danger, and filth of the trip, had in actuality been born of them.

While it is tempting to read Rock's journey as an extension of a Western geopolitical gaze, akin to Halford Mackinder's views from Mount Kenya in 1899 (Ó Tuathail 1996) or Maxime du Camp's photographs of Egypt in the 1850s (Joan Schwartz 1996), Rock's written account of his trip reveals his deep engagement with—his implacement in (Casey 1996)—the social world of the Sino-Tibetan borderlands of Sichuan. An important account of Rock's explorations in the 1920s argues that his "archival practice . . . has much to teach us about how, as walking, mark-making, image-making human beings, we draw the earth into our social lives. . . . Seeing and being seen made Rock aware of his deep involvement in the flesh of the world—and its viscera, its filth" (Mueggler 2011, 152, 161). Throughout his travels, and as shown by his experience in Konkaling, Rock often put himself in visceral contact with the lives and circumstances of the southwestern frontier, a world he found both compelling and unbearable (ibid., 159). While Rock was unavoidably part of an American project of picturing the world (see Lutz and Collins 1993), his work as a botanist and a photographer also provided him a means of coming to terms with the world. The underlying subject of his 1931 article is not the "objective" facts about the mountains (Rock was a terrible surveyor and cartographer [see Mueggler 2011, 211]) but the social and political world of Konkaling, and Rock's ability to get in and out of there alive. In other words, what became geographically known about the Konka Risumgongba was deeply intertwined with the story of Rock's place in it.

I heard repeatedly from Yading reserve staff, village residents, and tourists that Rock "discovered" (*faxian*) Yading. This was also confirmed by a county-produced, Chinese-language guidebook for sale at the tourist center titled Discover Yading (Faxian Yading), an extended retelling of Rock's National Geographic article, including the account of his morning view of Jambeyang (Xiao 2006, 52–53). The narrative that Yading was discovered by Rock is compelling—it's a good story, after all. And yet to jump straight back to a single discovery in 1928 is to skip over the other ways Yading has been discovered and to miss entirely the ways that discovering Yading has become a routine today. While the establishment of Yading made strategic use of Rock's legacy of discovery, it would not have happened as it did, and become nationally significant when it did, without the travels of contemporary explorers, whose own embodied practices echo the ways Rock made his place in Konkaling.

EXPLORATION II

Konkaling's tumultuous early twentieth century had calmed by the 1940s (Qin 2007), when China was emerging from war with Japan and fighting a civil war that would put the Communists in power in 1949. However, life in Konkaling remained difficult. Nearly all major settlements in the region lie above 3,650 meters in elevation, and livelihoods based on animal husbandry and subsistence agriculture were often disrupted by hailstorms, droughts, earthquakes, and other natural disasters (SDXBW 1997, 7–26). Additionally, as the Communist Party asserted its presence in the area, it would precipitate new traumas, from early 1950s campaigns to collectivize agriculture (Shakya 1999, 138–40) to the Cultural Revolution campaigns that would lead once again to the destruction of the Konkaling monastery. Communism would be the third state project in less than fifty years to attempt to control the area, and it would persist in setting up a government infrastructure more extensive than that of its predecessors. The state's most transformative change would come many years later through economic reform, which would open Daocheng County to the outside world. The local state would eventually turn the area's hardship into cultural history and transform the Konka Risumgongba into the Yading Nature Reserve, the main attraction in a new tourism economy. These changes were aided by new botanical and photographic explorations of Konkaling, which would help stir national interest in seeing the area firsthand.

In 1973, Yin Kaipu, a botanist at the Chengdu Institute of Biology, traveled to Daocheng County to survey plant distributions in Yading.[7] Yin had been making botanical surveys in western Sichuan since 1961 and had studied the work of the English botanist Ernest Henry Wilson, who had worked in Sichuan at the turn of the twentieth century (see Glover 2011). Beginning in the late 1920s, more than two decades after Wilson's first explorations and contemporaneous with Rock, the Nationalist government undertook a national project to improve knowledge of China's frontiers (Chen Zhihong 2008). The spirit of this project would continue under the Communists, and teams of state-affiliated scientists began traveling the country's borderlands in the 1950s to survey and classify ethnic groups, topography, flora, and fauna. This was also a time when nature was exploited for national development, with forests being one of China's most important resources, economically valuable for raw materials and ecologically valuable for soil and water conservation (Harkness 1998). Extensive logging would be a consequence of industrialization throughout the country and would become pronounced in eastern Tibet in the 1970s. Yin made repeated trips to northern Sichuan's Jiuzhaigou valley in the 1970s and, having seen firsthand the impact of logging in the area, reported the problem to the central government in the summer of 1978. Within four months, Jiuzhaigou, with its extensive system of lakes and waterfalls, was designated a national nature reserve.

In 1982, Yin returned to Daocheng and heard that the area around Yading was also threatened by logging. His reaction to the news was similar to his response to the problem in Jiuzhaigou. At a scientific conference that fall, Yin proposed establishing a new nature reserve around the Little Gonggashan (Xiao Gonggashan), a reference to the Konka Risumgongba that called to mind the taller and better-known Gonggashan (Minya Konka) northeast of Daocheng. He suggested "Yading" as the name for the new reserve, a transliteration of the Tibetan name of the only village in the central Konka Risumgongba valley. The Yading Nature Reserve would become a part of Sichuan's conservation plans as early as 1985, though it would be ten more years before the reserve was formally established.

Inspired as it was by Wilson's work, Yin Kaipu's interest in establishing nature reserves was not simply born of his library and archival research. In his youth, Yin never imagined being a botanist and came to it only when assigned to a government position at the age of eighteen. He would travel widely in the foothills and ranges that a generation of foreign botanists had explored, walking long days over rough terrain and enduring food shortages. Of botany, he said, "[I]t was very boring work. We did the same thing day after day, month after month, year after year. Unless you loved botany and science, you wouldn't do it" (Morell and Wolkoff 2005). It was through this repetition, over decades of exploring Sichuan, that Yin worked out his own way of being in the world, finding his place in the mountains of Sichuan and in the history of botanical exploration. His work is, of course, embedded in and legitimated by a state geographic knowledge project, a positivist undertaking that has spanned the better part of a century, across two national governments, and had a significant impact on governance in China, from ethnic classification and the question of ethnic autonomy (Mullaney 2010) to conservation and the question of land use, in which Yin himself has been directly engaged. And yet, like Rock's before him, Yin's work required a bodily engagement in the world, a practice that, to borrow a phrase, drew the earth into his social life. "When I'm walking where Wilson walked," Yin said, "I have a great sense of peace" (Morell and Wolkoff 2005). It is unlikely that Yin would end up having a hand in the establishment of twenty nature reserves in Sichuan had he not first come to value those lands himself through his own practice of place.

Around the time Yin first surveyed Yading, Chengdu-born Lü Linglong had been sent down to work in Liangshan Prefecture, an autonomous ethnic region in southwestern Sichuan.[8] Through the 1970s, Lü worked as a blacksmith on railway construction projects in Chongqing and later in Xinjiang, but when China's higher education system resumed after the Cultural Revolution, he was able to participate in a short-term course in photography in Beijing. He began traveling more extensively on his own in remote parts of Sichuan in the 1980s, spurred by his interest in photography and his experience in the mountains among China's ethnic minorities. As Lü explored western Sichuan in 1982, he arrived in Daocheng unaware of the three sacred peaks 160 kilometers to the south; he departed vowing to return someday to see them but waited more than a decade for the chance.

In 1994, Yin Kaipu and the Chengdu Institute of Biology organized a survey of Daocheng with a team of Chinese, English, and American scientists. Their consultations with the local government would be part of a renewed plan to finally, and formally, establish a nature reserve. As part of the plan to open the reserve, the local government sought to promote the area by producing a photo book of the county's natural scenery. In 1995, the local government hosted Lü in Daocheng as the project's photographer. While Lü was not the only one to photograph Yading in this period, his early involvement with the local government, and his subsequent photographs of the reserve—published in Chinese National Geography magazine and elsewhere—would

稲城
—— 在那遥远的地方

DAO   CHENG   The Remote Land
稲   城   かのはるかに遠いところで
འདབ་བྱི།   རྒྱང་ཐག་རིང་པའི་ས་ཆ།

FIGURE 3.2   Shining with charm and enchantment: Shenrezig at dawn. Book cover of
Lü Linglong's *Daocheng: The Remote Land.*

become widely known and contribute to his fame as a photographer of China's western region.

Yin's interest in forest protection and Lü's photographic work were drawn
even more closely together in 1996. In March, the Daocheng County government officially established the Yading Nature Reserve, and in April, Lü's first
monograph, *Daocheng: The Remote Land*, was published (fig. 3.2). The Yading Nature Reserve covers roughly one-fifth of Daocheng County, about 1,350
square kilometers altogether (SDXBW 2009, 3, 30), well over twice the size
in total area of Jiuzhaigou (HBB 2009, 102–8). Rivaling Jiuzhaigou in natural
beauty, Yading rapidly gained the attention of higher government offices.
Within a year of its establishment, Yading was approved as a province-level
reserve, and in 2001 it was approved as a national-level reserve. Tourism and
conservation had converged on Yading simultaneously, and the opening

of the reserve would from its earliest moment be the opening of a nature destination. When proposing the reserve in 1982, Yin Kaipu had mentioned that the ecotourism development under way in Jiuzhaigou was a model for balancing conservation with poverty alleviation. With the coming boom in domestic tourism in the 1990s, the balance struck there between conservation and tourism development would become a model for other reserves and parks (see ch. 4 in this volume). By 1995, the Daocheng County government had already turned to tourism as a breakthrough point (*tupokou*) for local economic development (SDXBW 2009, 271). It was a small jump to connect the protected charismatic mountain scenery with the cultural economy of tourism booming in other parts of China (see Oakes 1998).

The county leaders who had invited Lü to Daocheng wrote the foreword to his book. While not explicitly writing in their official capacity, they began in an official style with the hard facts—latitude and longitude, elevation, and relative distances—and ended with a flourish: "Daocheng is a pretty country maiden who has been staying at her boudoir and unknown to the outside world. Its heavenly natural scenery, simple and unsophisticated customs, and mystical primitive human landscapes, having broken through the barriers of time and space, shine with charm and enchantment which have attracted photographers, whose artistic pictures present its beauty and charm before us" (Lü and Wang 1996, 4–5). This stretched metaphors of opening and discovery far beyond anything Rock wrote about the place, and yet it echoed the theme of seeing unknown territory. Lü's nature photography of Daocheng County was presented as both the debut of a new place and a call to action to protect nature by getting out to see it. The book was dedicated "To those who love the nature," and the facing page was printed with a map of southwest Sichuan showing roads and driving distances from major cities. The new Yading Nature Reserve appeared as prominently as the provincial capital, Chengdu, and the famed Emei Mountain, an early sign that Yading was being positioned in a new geography.

Lü's photos would be used alongside Rock's in official publications and promotional material. However, as with Rock's, there is more to Lü's photography than the production and circulation of the photographs themselves. When I asked Lü what he did during his sent-down years, he instinctively made the hammering motions of a blacksmith at a forge. His answer lay not only in his mind but also in the arms that carried their own memory of that labor. He spoke of the extreme conditions of those years as a personal "tempering." Lü had grown up in the city, and knew his place there, but his interest in the world outside (*chengshi yiwai*) grew from his time in the country-side. He said, "My whole life I've been interested in things I'm unfamiliar with, and photography has been my tool. Travel and photography are basically one and the same. . . . They are inseparable." At sixty, Lü continues to travel across western China photographing some of the world's most rugged terrain. His work has been important in representing western China as a region worth valuing, protecting, and exploring. It has also long been a way for him to make his own place in that world.

EXPLORATION III

When Yading was established in 1996, visiting the reserve involved a 24-kilometer trek that climbed more than 1.5 kilometers in elevation to its high lakes at 4,570 meters. Yading's rugged terrain is both its main attraction and its biggest obstacle to tourism development. This basic fact runs through Daocheng's first tourism master plan, created after a county-level decision in 1999 to speed tourism development. The plan referred to Yading as a scenic spot (*jingqu, jingdian*) (see Nyíri 2006), a reference to the part of the reserve to be developed for tourism, roughly matching the area that Rock had explored. The plan ranked the county's five main scenic areas on a standardized scale; Yading was given nine out of ten points for notoriety, ten of ten for uniqueness, and twenty-four of twenty-five for sightseeing value—a 90 percent score altogether, making it an AAAA tourism site in the planners' eyes.[9]

The tourism master plan referenced the need to protect Yading's natural environment, calling for the construction of boardwalks to minimize the trail damage from tourists (DZSL 2001, 76). This strategy, implemented in many nature destinations, found early, influential success in the Jiuzhaigou valley. The Yading plan also called for the closure of long sections of the pilgrimage route to horse trekking, a move that would in subsequent years threaten the tourism income for some local residents and cause at least one violent confrontation with the authorities.[10] While the plan acknowledged tourism's ability to help alleviate poverty, its concrete objectives targeted tourist bodies: how to increase the number of "person-visits," how to transport tourists to and through the reserve, how to house and feed them, how to manage their waste, and how to attend to their medical needs. The plan envisioned the tourist experience as a one-day visit for tour groups (90 percent of expected visitors) and a two-day visit for independent tourists, who could stay in one of the tent camps set up within the reserve. While the plan had projected 350,000 visitors annually by 2010, 92,000 made the trip that year, most traveling independently of a guided tour group. In the years following the introduction of the plan, even as mass tourism failed to take hold, the reserve continued to take steps to prepare for greater numbers. A 9.6-kilometer concrete road serviced by a fleet of gas-powered carts was built within the scenic area, and a thirty-two-kilometer improved road linked the tourist center to Yading Village.

I shared a ride into the reserve one day with Yinghua,[11] a young woman from Shanghai who had negotiated a few weeks' leave from work to travel. Along the high, winding road, we stopped at a turn that presents visitors with their first full view of Shenrezig and Chanadordje. It is a turn that usually resulted in a synchronized "Wah!" from bus passengers and a clamoring rush of bodies and cameras to one side of the vehicle. At peak times, the viewing platform along the road was crowded with vehicles and tourists. When Yinghua stepped to the edge of the turnout, she took a single photo with her phone and then quietly took in the view. It was a moment that stood out among the usual frenzy of group photos, individual photos, self-portraits, shots of jumping in the air or standing akimbo, and the occasional guttural yell into the valley by a male tourist announcing his presence. In being so easygoing about photography, Yinghua seemed out of place.

The following morning, I walked with Yinghua to the Tsengu Gomba—recently rebuilt for the first time since the Cultural Revolution—and then farther up the valley to a lakeside viewing platform positioned for iconic views of Shenrezig. She never seemed eager to photograph Yading, and at two spots where most tourists stopped to take photos, she put on headphones and sang softly to herself. Yinghua had already seen much of Sichuan, Tibet, and Xinjiang before her visit to Yading. In 2007, after the death of her father, she resigned from work and took a solo journey across China. She visited Lhasa, circumambulated Mount Kailash with Indian pilgrims, and continued on to Xinjiang. Once back at her desk job in Shanghai, Yinghua made a slideshow of her trip to share with friends titled "Walking alone in the world—2007 Sichuan travels." The slideshow began with a map of western China, with red stars marking "My footprints"; though she traveled without a camera, the presentation was full of photos collected from acquaintances she made along the way.

The fact that Yinghua was less concerned with taking photographs than many other tourists highlights the ways that many of the bodily practices that go into photography are the same practices required just to be there.

This is particularly clear in a place like Yading, where even with improved trails and motorized shuttles, visiting the reserve is an unavoidably physical event. I occasionally heard tourists say that they came to Yading to "taste a little bitterness" (*chi yidian ku*), to experience a manageable kind of difficulty typically absent from urban life. For most tourists, seeing the high lakes in Yading requires a hard uphill climb, nearly always over the same mud and schist that Rock described. Hail and rain are frequent, especially in the monsoon months. As with Rock's climactic view of Jambeyang, enduring a reasonable amount of hardship is often what makes a moment of seeing possible in Yading, be it the joy of seeing a mountain peak shining in the morning sun or the disappointment of seeing only rain and mist after traveling so far.

"Seeing" Yading is a practice of place, a bodily engagement with the physical and social world of a specific time and location, and Yinghua's experience highlights the ways that photography cannot be reduced to photographs. The growing popularity of photography and travel has made this fact even more apparent. As digital cameras have progressively become less expensive and put cameras close at hand for nearly everyone who can afford to travel in China, the practice of popular photography has changed. Full-color screens make photographs instantly available to tourists while they are still in the place being represented and still engaged with the people within the frame (Larsen 2008). This enables immediate social interaction, with photography taking on the role of a "collective technology, a resource for 'face-to-face' sociality" (Scifo 2005). The repetition of photography in Yading is not only about the individual search to capture an iconic image—the inscribing practice—but is also a socially embedded practice of incorporation. Photography is not only about the image itself but also about the range of social practices that travelers employ in making their own place (see Larsen 2006).

The high elevation, steep terrain, mercurial weather conditions, and long walking distances in Yading, on top of altitude-related disruptions to sleep and appetite, make it nearly impossible to essentialize the tourist in Yading as a picturing, gazing subject. The critique of the tourist gaze (Urry 2002) has been a recurring theme in tourism studies,[12] though the recent turn to embodiment (Crouch, Aronsson, and Wahlstrom 2001) raises questions of its own, such as what role representation continues to play if all practice is embodied, or how evanescent practices in place are related to enduring aspects of social and cultural life (Cresswell 2012). Many would likely agree that "geographical representations—in the form of maps, texts and pictorial images of various kinds—and the look of landscapes themselves are not merely traces or sources. . . . They are active, constitutive elements in shaping social and spatial practices and the environments we occupy" (Cosgrove 2008, 15). It is clear there is some kind of important relationship between representation and practice, but in what specific ways? Clarifying the relationship between inscribing and incorporating practices is a compelling way to frame an answer, since it asserts that what we know cognitively about place is nearly always connected in some way to our own or others' bodily practices in place. To focus only on the representational power of photography to inscribe knowledge of a place would be to ignore the ways that these representations are closely tied to shared bodily memories of being in place. As bodily encounters of Yading are repeated among a growing population of Chinese, photographs of Yading become more than abstract displays of beautiful scenery; they become full with the shared knowledge of being there.

KNOWING SHANGRILA, KNOWING THE NATION

The timing of Yading's opening was fortuitous. While the reserve rose in official status in the first few years after its establishment, little changed in the way of tourism. This changed with the county's plan to speed tourism development after the 1999 announcement of the Great Western Development strategy, which would begin affecting Daocheng almost immediately. Daocheng County was one of the last areas in China to open up to the outside world (*duiwai kaifang*) (Kang 2005), and while the Great Western Development strategy didn't explicitly focus on tourism development, once its demands were translated into action at the local level, tourism development often became a strategy for realizing project goals. The Daocheng County tourism plan made this link explicit (DZSL 2001, i). The Great Western Development strategy was an enormous undertaking, targeting a newly defined geographic region, well over half of China's total landmass. Coming at the end of a decade of socioeconomic change, the program both reflected and cued a new national interest in the west. The decade to follow would be a boom time in domestic tourism and would locate national desires out west. And the early years of the first decade of the 2000s would bring the boom to Yading, just in time for a socioeconomic tipping point in urban areas that would make tourism and photography a normal part of life.

There is perhaps no better indicator of the national desire to explore western China than the ways Shangrila became synonymous with tourism and development. In 2001, Yunnan would establish the first Shangrila, beginning with an administrative name change and subsequently with a place-making project that inscribed an "authentic" Tibetan culture in Zhongdian (Tib. Gyalthang) (Kolås 2008), a traditionally Tibetan town in the northwest of the province. Other areas in eastern Tibet would compete for the Shangrila name, Daocheng County among the most prominent. A few months after Shangrila was officially established in Yunnan, Sichuan approved the renaming of Riwa Township, where the Yading tourist center and management offices are located, to Shangrila Township.[13] The following years were a chaotic time, as the branding and placemaking of Shangrila proceeded in multiple sites at once (see map 2). But by 2003, Shangrila had been incorporated into a regional tourism and conservation project (see also ch. 4 in this volume) that targeted yet another Shangrila, the Greater Shangrila Ecotourism Zone (Da Xianggelila Shengtailüyou Qu) (see map 1), an interprovincial region focusing on tourism development that reflects an approach to regional development that echoes the Great Western Development strategy.

By turning much of eastern Tibet into Shangrila, the central government and participating provincial-level governments sidestepped the immediate concern of who could claim the Shangrila name. But Greater Shangrila also offered a chance to stimulate tourism and would be one of the main national tourism development priorities in China's Eleventh Five-Year Plan. Facing declining tourism in 2003 because of the SARS crisis, Sichuan held its first annual tourism development congress in late August,[14] which included a keynote address by the provincial party secretary, Zhang Xuezhong. Zhang said, "We must quicken the opening of a western tourism loop, extending China's Shangrila Ecotourism Zone to include Daocheng Yading, which will become one of Sichuan's tourism bright spots [liang dian]" (SDXBW 2009, 271). He added, "In the north there is Jiuzhaigou and Huanglong, in the center there is the Giant Panda, and in the south there is Daocheng Yading." Tourism growth in Yading began to accelerate after this point, as it was positioned as a more important tourism resource for Sichuan and a prime location at the heart of Greater Shangrila.

Joseph Rock's legacy became integral to Yading partly because his exploration of the area provided a direct connection to the Shangrila story. The Daocheng County annals explain that the English writer James Hilton created the Shangrila idea for his book *Lost Horizon* after consulting Rock's research in Tibetan areas (SDXBW 2009, 40). While a direct link between

Rock and Hilton has yet to be clearly established—and the Shangrila monastery in *Lost Horizon* could not be more different from the Tsengu Gomba of the 1920s—there are elements in the book that invite comparisons to Rock's work. Hilton's Shangrila was an enjoyable, though discomfiting, place that depended on the outside world for its luxuries even as it fought to maintain its distance. And there are moments when Hugh Conway, the main character, gazes at the sensational, pyramidal peak of Karakal, bringing to mind the climax of Rock's journey to Konkaling. Rock's explorations provided Daocheng County with a strategic heritage resource in its claim to be Shangrila, an "authentic" piece of Konkaling history that could be reinscribed as part of the new nature reserve and the new regional geography.

The ordering of China's southwestern geography by tourism, conservation, and the Shangrila brand unfolded through local and regional placemaking projects undertaken by state and private enterprises. The shangrilazation of eastern Tibet has made it increasingly governable (Rose 1999), as state thinking about culture, nature, and leisure has been territorialized through the establishment of Shangrila. However, the power of Shangrila as a placemaking strategy arose not simply from the state inscribing the name but rather from the fact that it could attract tourists whose bodily presence is the foundation of the tourism economy. Tourists, after all, are the desirable subjects of tourism development planning and are embedded in its grid of discipline (Certeau 1984, xiv), its techniques of encouraging and discouraging specific tourist behaviors. More generally, the Chinese state has worked to make domestic tourism an exemplary form of consumption (Klingberg and Oakes 2012), an increasingly ordinary part of social life, and a vital part of the economy. The success of many placemaking projects throughout southwestern China depends on keeping tourist bodies in motion.

The prospect of ever-greater numbers of tourists exploring the Sino-Tibetan borderlands recalls a classic argument about tourists as explorers: "Paradoxically, . . . [the explorer] serves as a spearhead of mass tourism; as he discovers new places of interest, he opens the way for more commercialized forms of tourism. . . . His experiences and opinions serve as indicators to other, less adventurous tourists to move into the area. As more and more of these move in, the tourist establishment gradually takes over. Thus, partly through the unwitting help of the explorer, the scope of the system expands" (Cohen 1972, 175). This perspective on the exploration of tourists tracks with the idea of a "first locator" in the photographic discovery of a place (Balm and Holcomb 2003, 160). These arguments portray exploration as a linear process, leading from unknown to known, and from an "authentic" state to a commercialized copy (see Oakes 2006). Many Chinese, already having experienced expert-organized group tourism, are seeking more out of travel than mass tourism can provide and turn to self-organized trips. There are many precipitating factors for this, ranging from higher disposable income, to private car ownership, to the large amount of up-to-date travel information available on the Internet. But the new interest in independent forms of tourism in China should not be mistaken as a kind of freedom from the institutional tourism industry. After all, the establishment of a mass domestic tourism industry beginning in the early 1990s made the boom in independent travel possible. Nor should independent tourism be mistaken as a politically unencumbered leisure practice, particularly in the contemporary context of the Sino-Tibetan borderlands. Instead, as domestic tourism—independent tourism in particular—has taken on elements of exploration in contemporary China, it must be taken as an important practice in itself instead of being reduced to a functional role in a larger system.

The repeated discovery of Yading by tourists is inevitably embedded in a placemaking project that commodifies nature, often to the detriment of local livelihoods and identity. The discovery of Yading is also embedded in the ecological state's national priorities of conservation, which have always been closely tied to other political, economic, and social goals. Conservation and tourism, for example, were never separate, or even necessarily conflicting, goals in Yading. And for protected areas established in China after the mid-1980s—that is, most of them—the example of tourism development in Jiuzhaigou looms large, as it was the first case of conservation becoming economically productive and profitable. Finally, the discovery of Yading is embedded in a global conservation project, as it was designated a United Nations Educational, Scientific and Cultural Organization (UNESCO) Man and Biosphere site in 2003.

While the state has up to now been the primary placemaking agent in Yading, it is the repeated explorations of domestic tourists—and the socially binding memory of those travels—that has fueled Yading's ten-year transformation from a relatively unknown nature reserve to an integral part of new regional, national, and international geographies. In traveling on their own across long distances, dealing with weather and elevation, and in seeing, photographing, and walking through Yading, tourists enact ways of knowing that came long before the reserve was built up for tourism. Yading Village became a center for tourist lodging because villagers opened their homes, not because a tourism master plan demanded it. The tent camps within the reserve were set up out of necessity, since without roads, a trek through the protected area would take days. The major trails in Yading follow the pilgrimage route that has been traveled for perhaps as long as three hundred years. The master tourism plan for the reserve begun in 1999 was in many ways a description of what already existed in the area.

Yading has been inscribed in new regional geographies, as Sichuan's Shangrila and as part of the Greater Shangrila Ecotourism Zone, though these new geographies have become powerful and permanent only to the extent that they are lived out and practiced. The notion of discovering and exploring Shangrila has not only provided the basis for a regional tourism economy but heightened domestic travel's role as a way of knowing China's geography. Mirroring the rural-to-urban movement of migrant labor, urban Chinese have become interested in rural and remote areas. And as urban—and industrial—China has been incorporated in rural migrant bodies over the past thirty years, so too has "the rest" of China begun to be incorporated into its urban bodies as domestic tourism has boomed.

The practice of place is always both to experience place according to plan and to make a place of one's own. Joseph Rock's exploration of Konkaling was both a part of a Western project to know China and a part of the way he found his own place in China. Yin Kaipu and Lü Linglong's surveys of Daocheng were integral parts of making that remote region known to the nation, just as they were important in working out each man's own place in Sichuan. Yinghua's travels to Daocheng and beyond were a part of the rising tide of tourism in China's remote west and a part of making her own social world. Over the years, the embodied practice of seeing Yading has become an ongoing social practice, repeated by Chinese tens of thousands of times a year. Yading has become a part of the national imagination because it has become a routine discovery, being geographically known not only through its representation but also through sustained bodily practices that layer new knowledge of a nation in the bodies of its travelers.

CHAPTER 3. A ROUTINE DISCOVERY

Epigraphs from Rock 1931, 14; and DXDZ 2004.

1   The area is known in Tibetan as "the Snow Mountains" (Wyl. *Gangs dkar ri bo*) and transliterated in Chinese as Gongga Ri'e. Rock acknowledged that other

foreigners had visited the lowland areas of Konkaling but maintained that he was the first to have explored the mountain range (1931, 30).

2   More than seven ministries manage China's protected areas; three out of four protected areas are managed by the Ministry of Forestry. National star ratings for tourism sites are regulated by the National Tourism Administration.

3   Examples of this power can be found in Schwartz 1996, Balm and Holcomb 2003 and Crang 1997.

4   Independent tourism has been called "informal" or "noninstitutional" tourism in English, though "independent" is closer to the Chinese term *zizhu lüyou*, which is more literally translated as "DIY (do-it-yourself) tourism."

5   The Tibetan names of the peaks are transliterated phonetically in Chinese as Yangmaiyong, Xiannairi, and Xianuoduoji. I retain Rock' s (1931) romanization for consistency.

6   Tsengu Gomba is usually transliterated in Chinese as Gongga Chonggu but is more commonly known as Chonggu Si.

7   This and what follows are from Yin 2010 and Yin 2003.

8   The following quotes are from interviews with the author in 2010 and 2012.

9   High ratings—up to five As—are valuable in attracting tourists as well as outside investment, though Yading has yet to be officially rated by the National Tourism Administration.

10   As this chapter went to press, road access into the main valley was extended to cover the last major horse trail in the park. The days of significant local income generation by horse guides (*mafu*) are coming to an end.

11   Yinghua is a pseudonym.

12   Larsen (2008), Crouch and Desforges (2003), and MacCannell (2001) each offer differing critiques of Urry (2002).

13   Shangrila in Yunnan is a county (*xian*). Shangrila in Sichuan was originally a township (*xiang*) and has recently been upgraded to a town (*zhen*).

14   See "Diyi miao sichuan lüyou fazhan dahui," http://www.ls666.com/html/ News_Center/LS_News/2008–02/16/082162225948K1GECKJ6AJJJKDGD48.html (accessed July 19, 2012).

PART II

CONSTRUCTING THE ECOLOGICAL STATE

• • •

Conservation, Commodification, and Resource Governance

Since at least the late 1990s, when international observers and the Chinese government itself began to publicly express concerns that the country's unprecedented economic growth was founded largely upon potentially disastrous levels of environmental degradation, ecological management and sustainable development have become critical aspects of the CCP's claim to political legitimacy. With the proliferation of environmental laws and environmental management projects, China has become, by the reckoning of its own government, an ecological state, one in which governmental logic is increasingly defined by the reduction of environmental hazards and, to a certain degree, calculated attempts to create a surplus of "ecological capital" (Escobar 1996). These initiatives are exemplified by CCP General Secretary Hu Jintao's exposition of his "new theory" of the "scientific outlook on development," which has "sustainable development [as] its basic requirement" (Xinhua 2007). Some Western observers have understood this as "ecological modernization," but in a different mode from that of Europe, where the concept was developed, and have read into the "greening" of China the growth of an increasingly robust civil society (Carter and Mol 2007; Mol 2006). This appears especially promising because of the rapid proliferation of environmental NGOs during the first decade of this century, and the assumption that, regardless of the state's original intention, these groups have a privileged role to play in the spatial politics of the environment and landscape management:

> These [environmental] NGOs represent far more than what Saich describes as "disgruntled workers in the northeast, rebellious farmers in the southwest and an uppity intellectual in Being"—groups that lack a common, bonding vision and might more correctly be described as "uncivil society."
> ... [Environmental] NGOs organize, inform, train and activate government officials and the public in an effort to protect environmental interests. . . . They reflect an important aspect of a nascent civil society and the potential direction of other expressions of Chinese civil society. (Jonathan Schwartz 2008, 70–71)

In this view, post-reform decentralization and the relaxation of administrative controls have left a very large space between state policy directives, on the one hand, and the regulation of everyday life, on the other. This space, which was formerly under the close surveillance and control of the state in a Maoist, disciplinary mode of governance, is open for collective negotiation and individual navigation. Environmental NGOs are believed to fill this space by providing information, services, monitoring, and collective initiative—"a common bonding vision"—to solve socio-environmental problems of many kinds (Carter and Mol 2007; Schwartz 2007). We view this assessment as insightful, but applicable only within a limited set of rather ideal conditions.

During most of the first decade of the 2000s, many Tibetan borderland communities were host to some radically new and fundamentally different international and interregional collaborations, and environmental NGOs working there were making exciting strides not only in identifying and seeking to mitigate socio-environmental problems but also in redefining them to include a reckoning of sociocultural factors, including economic disparities, ethnicity, spiritual values, and indigenous environmental knowledge. For example, in 2002, representatives of the Nature Conservancy (TNC), the World Wide Fund for Nature (WWF), Conservation International–China (CI-China), and more than eighty Chinese and foreign experts gathered to define conservation priorities for a newly declared biodiversity hotspot, the Mountains of Southwest China, a region of 262,400 square kilometers with an 80 percent overlap with what we call the Sino-Tibetan borderlands. The Sacred Lands Program, one of the new programs implemented in the hotspot by CI-China, was based on the premise that sacred landscapes have traditionally fostered "a harmonious relationship between Tibetans and their surrounding environment" and thus that maintaining these sacred landscapes would be "a particularly helpful cultural attribute in support of biodiversity conservation" in the hotspot (undated brochure). The organization began a number of different projects in the region, including surveys on biodiversity in sacred mountains, the formation of new nature reserves based on sacred mountain areas, and efforts to persuade Tibetan religious leaders to mobilize their cultural and religious authority in spreading environmental education.

Similarly, in northwest Yunnan, TNC began working together with the Kunming Institute of Botany and the Center for Biodiversity and Indigenous Knowledge to conduct research on ethnobotanical knowledge about the local flora. Western ethnobotanists began working with Chinese counterparts at the Kunming Institute of Botany to study local knowledge of the plants, particularly of Tibetan doctors. They argued for incorporating traditional ecological knowledge into conservation planning and including local Tibetans in conservation projects: "Tibetans have acted as environmental stewards for Khawa Karpo for millennia and the future should hold a sustained, empowered, and influential role for them and their traditions" (Salick, Yang, and Amend 2005, 322). As part of these efforts, TNC, the Kunming Institute of Botany, and the Center for Biodiversity and Indigenous Knowledge created an NGO in Deqin County for Tibetan doctors, the Tibetan Doctors Association, to build capacity for in situ medicinal plant conservation. The association was involved in working with Chinese and international scientists as well as preserving Tibetan culture for biodiversity conservation.

However, the conjuncture that had allowed these various projects to be implemented shifted dramatically with political and economic events of 2008. The combination of the global financial crisis and protests across the Tibetan Plateau led to the removal of state funding, logistical support, and approval for grassroots efforts as well as for translocal and transnational projects. The reassertion of state sovereignty in the wake of the Chinese nationalist backlash against the Tibetan protests was quite evident across the Tibetan Plateau. Numerous grassroots projects to revive Tibetan culture, protect the environment, and enhance livelihoods and development were shut down, either directly or indirectly through bans on receiving foreign money. In northwest Yunnan, the Tibetan Doctors Association lost all of its funding after 2008 and ceased to operate. Like other local NGOs, it was no longer allowed to receive funding from transnational organizations such as TNC. Although TNC's temporary economic limitations resulting from the financial crisis were generally given as a reason for the shift in priorities, residents of Diqing were firmly convinced that newly heightened political sensitivity was a driving factor, particularly given the Diqing area's association with Samdhong Rinpoche, until 2011 the prime minister of the Tibetan government-in-exile, despite the fact that no protests or unrest had taken place there.

Ethnobotanical discourse also shifted dramatically, away from an emphasis on the potential of traditional ecological knowledge and the importance of Tibetan culture and toward a new set of projects and plans in which Tibetan medicinal plants would be saved by being cultivated and commodified for new markets. Rather than empower Tibetans as traditional ecological knowledge holders, these new projects neoliberalize the management of Tibetan medicinal plants. The new projects that came to characterize transnational conservation's interaction with local people after 2008 were no longer designed to ensure Tibetans' positions as owners of cultural property. Instead, Tibetans were interpellated as "laborers for conservation purposes, cultivators of plants and new self-entrepreneurial subjects who are instructed to be motivated by the promise of development benefits but who are not actually granted any control or ownership over the means of production" (Dinaburg 2011). In these new schemes, Tibetan culture is no longer important for the protection of the environment. Instead, the development of new markets for newly commodified species promises to save nature by selling it.

Our contributors cover many aspects of these trends, using political ecology's analytical tools for grasping the political dimensions of human-environment interactions. As a conceptual and methodological approach, political ecology is particularly strong in analyzing the ways in which environmental governance, which often has roots in colonialism, may involve the expropriation of natural resources historically managed by local communities, through state enclosures as well as neoliberal forms of commodification. Our political ecology approach, which also draws on the Foucauldian analytic of governmentality, reckons closely with the market logics of ecological modernization, the emergence of new rationalities of rule (which modify and supplement sovereign power over life and death), and the production of environmental knowledge in the Sino-Tibetan borderlands. This approach also draws attention to how state-directed environmental projects produce environmental subjects. In other words, environmental governmentality gives rise to new forms of personhood, responsibility, and aspirations produced by a growing array of economic, political, and aesthetic connections to nature (Agrawal 2005). While these can lead to measurable positive social and environmental outcomes, the results are far from guaranteed.

Extending Foucault's concern with biopower to human-environment relationships also directs our attention to how forests, grasslands, and wetlands become objects of political and economic calculation in their designation as "nature" (Yeh 2009b). In this view, sustainability is a political project that creates the conditions for thinking about "nature" as resource *in potentia*. "Natural landscapes," if mapped, demarcated, and managed properly, will provide environmental services locally, regionally, and nationally. Natural biological organisms, if harvested sustainably, will give rise to new commodity networks that can promote economic stability in marginal regions while serving the demand for "natural products" in domestic and international urban markets (see chs. 6 and 7 in this volume).

Environmental governmentality and ecological modernity thus demand of states a thorough delineation of environmental services that are ultimately analyzed at the level of the landscape, mapped, and regulated within systems of environmental zonation. This process of internal territorialization is arguably a universal pattern among all modern states, which must "divide their territories into complex and overlapping political and economic zones, rearrange people and resources within these units, and create regulations delineating how and by whom these areas can be used" (Vandergeest and Peluso 1995, 387, 412)—in other words, the ecological state has requisite land classification systems that dictate, often with a high degree of specificity, which people have access to which resources in which times and places, and these regulations often have little to do with sociocultural patterns that have long-standing value for local and regional identities and livelihoods.

This spatial taxonomy works across scales. At the local level, post-Reform village land tenure systems are critical to contests over resources, development, and conservation. Many of the case studies allude to the fact that rural residents of the borderlands have a significant degree of agency over household and collective lands (*jiti de tudi*), but little or no authority over nearby nationally owned lands (*guoyou de tudi*). This land tenure system strongly shapes struggles over not only access to resources and the viability of locally generated forms of resource governance but also the status of sacred landscapes.

At the national scale, the process of internal territorialization is exemplified in a report from the Chinese Academy of Sciences:

> If all the above tasks [of systematic land use regulation] are fully accomplished, China's ecological modernization will reach the world's middle level in 2050. . . . About one-third of the national territory will be covered by forests (about 35 percent), one-third of the territory will be used for agricultural purpose (about 36 percent), . . . land for construction purpose will account for about 9 percent of the national territory and land for natural landscaping will account for 20 percent. (CAS 2007)

In this scenario, the west is the functional zone for forests and grasslands—a macrogeographic zone for the nation's watershed protection. One dramatic example of the technical implementation and monitoring of this process is in the Sanjiangyuan Nature Reserve in Qinghai, which is designed to protect the upper reaches of the Yangzi, Yellow, and Mekong Rivers, an area roughly the size of England and Wales combined. Establishment of the reserve has included plans for large-scale resettlement of pastoral communities from core areas through "ecological migration," grazing bans, fencing, tree plantations, and curtailment of logging and small-scale and uncontrolled mining (Foggin 2008; Harris 2008; Yeh 2005). The declaration of the Sanjiangyuan Nature Reserve exemplifies the state's view of the western borderland as an ecological zone: its function is to provide ecosystem services for downstream regions of capital accumulation and political power. In this way, a wide array of traditional and recently implemented local forestry and grassland resource utilization patterns becomes classified as forms of ecosystem degradation, and those who persist in practicing them are labeled backward and unscientific.

Concomitantly, those natural products that fall within the interstices of regulatory surveillance or those specifically targeted for sustainable harvest hold the potential to become crucial for the livelihoods of local people. The viability of such products depends on local articulation with regional and international commodity chains, as well as with state policies. The "tragedy of commoditization" is due not to market penetration alone but to the interplay of state policy and market forces, as well as other sociopolitical relations obscured by purely biological frameworks of resource management:

> Such policies are commonly driven by logics that are alien to the environment—such as the need to pay off foreign debts. In such political processes, local populations, who may have both a greater knowledge and a greater stake in particular environments, often have little voice in policy formulation. And, haplessly, even when governmental policies and regulations attempt to strike a balance between the conservation of natural resources and the economic interests of various competing groups, such efforts too frequently are either poorly coordinated or have contradictory effects on the environment. (Greenberg 2006,122)

The case studies in this section focus on the Sino-Tibetan borderlands as both a zone of watershed and biodiversity conservation and a region where specific non-timber forest products have mobilized networks of individuals, families, villages, state agencies, and both national and transnational corporations in commodity chains extending from the borderlands to other parts of East Asia and beyond. As a zone of nature conservation, the borderlands have become a zone of transnational cooperation but also one of significant institutional disharmonies and misunderstandings. In chapter 4, John Zinda offers an analytical perspective on the complexity of China's emergent ecological state and the role of transnational conservation in efforts to integrate environmental logics into governance. The chapter focuses on a succession of alliances that grew up around efforts to establish China's first national park in northwest Yunnan as a new model for managing protected areas. Demonstrating the importance of disaggregating the state in order to understand environmental governance, Zinda shows how local governments competing to expand tourism economies adopted the title "national park" for upgraded attractions but prioritized high-volume tourism and lagged on the active conservation management and resident involvement recommended in initial proposals. Zinda traces how, over time, TNC adjusted its proposals in response to changing situations, and different agencies worked with the organization when it suited their perceived interests. The chapter charts a shift in the focus of transnational conservation organizations as well as a relative decline in their capacity to influence local practices.

Chapter 5, by Robert Moseley and Renée Mullen, also discusses the role of TNC in northwest Yunnan, but from a very different perspective. As conservation professionals and organizers of TNC's Yunnan Great Rivers Project between 2000 and 2005, the authors are uniquely positioned to describe the environmental NGO's institutional conceptions of nature, standard operating procedures, and multi-scale conservation strategies. Their candid account is unprecedented in providing an insider's perspective on TNC's work in northwest Yunnan, focusing on a specific project in the Khawa Karpo region. It also offers an important invitation to dialogue from conservation scientists to their peers across the disciplinary divides that constitute "natural science" and "social science." As institutionally constructed networks of epistemological authority, these disciplines are kept separate— "purified," in the actor-network theory sense —through an array of tactical linguistic actions and discursive strategies. Moseley and Mullen argue that these walls must be breached in the interest of an applied, pragmatic science of conservation capable of working within what they recognize as the "complex socio-political-cultural milieu" found in places such as Shangrila. Of particular political import is their observation that in the first decade of the new millennium, sociocultural researchers (and their theories) lacked the support of the Chinese state and thus the capacity for agency that natural science projects were routinely granted.

In chapter 6, Michael Hathaway examines the ways in which the global commodification of the matsutake mushroom (*Tricholoma matsutake*) intersects with conservationist mandates to shape the landscapes and livelihoods of Tibetans in Diqing. Because of the high demand in Japanese markets, the matsutake mushroom has become Yunnan's most valuable agricultural export crop, its commodity chain linking villagers embedded in local resource tenure and management practices, to regional dealers and exporters, to Japanese consumers. Management of the matsutake as resource includes international laws regulating traffic in endangered species as well as efforts on the part of NGOs and villagers to reduce pesticide contamination, demonstrating the need to consider environmental governance at multiple scales and beyond the view of a bounded state. Moreover, these translocal networks of governance and trade may be new in form but constitute the reemergence of a long history of interregional and international connections that shed light on the applicability of the Zomia concept to the Sino-Tibetan borderlands.

Michelle Olsgard Stewart turns a more explicit political ecology lens on resource governance in chapter 7. She analyzes the landscapes and socio-ecological relationships that gather around another mushroom, the highly valued caterpillar fungus (*Ophiocordyceps sinensis*), which, like matsutake, has recently gained tremendous importance because of its high commodity value. The fungus grows as a parasite on moth larvae in high alpine grasslands from three thousand to five thousand meters in elevation across the Tibetan Plateau. For the tens of thousands of households across the Tibetan Plateau that gather *Ophiocordyceps sinensis*, this harvest accounts for 50–80 percent of annual income. Thus, the Tibetan harvesters are engaged in an array of local resource management systems that affect cultural landscapes and resource commons in diverse ways. Stewart compares two harvesting areas in Diqing Prefecture, highlighting the persistence of strong village-level governance arrangements in one site and their dissolution in another as a result of rapid tourism-related state development projects, particularly highway expansion. The chapter demonstrates the political nature of environmental governance, as well as the limits of conventional scientific frameworks of sustainable yield, given their elision of social, cultural, and political economic processes.

Each of these case studies shows that the ecological state is a modality of biopower involving transnational linkages and often high levels of participation by government agencies, NGOs, and individuals. They provide valuable lessons for scholars and activists interested in the power relations that guide and structure scientific knowledge production and environmental planning. The politics of ecological management in the time of the Great

Western Development strategy are manifest at scales ranging from house-hold contract lands to East Asian interregional trade zones and beyond, and these constitute spaces and places that are increasingly linked by the capital, commodities, and conservation policies that compose networks of environ-mental governmentality.

CHAPTER 4

Making National Parks
in Yunnan

• • •

SHIFTS AND STRUGGLES
WITHIN THE ECOLOGICAL STATE

John Aloysius Zinda

THE inauguration of Pudacuo National Park in 2007 added a jewel to Diqing Prefecture's Shangrila brand. Proclaiming it China's first national
park, promoters hailed Pudacuo as a new model joining tourism development to effective conservation and community involvement. The effort to set
up national parks in northwest Yunnan grew out of endeavors of the Nature
Conservancy (TNC) to encourage governments and other constituencies
to adopt new models for conserving the area's biodiverse landscapes. Yet,
when established, these parks emerged as mass tourism attractions that little
resemble TNC's proposals, while the process of creating them transformed
relationships among groups interested in northwest Yunnan's landscapes.

This story reveals a succession of alliances that grew up around efforts
to set up China's first national parks in Diqing Prefecture, Yunnan (see map
1, C, D, and E, and map 2). When TNC first arrived in China, it catalyzed
a remarkable coalition of local residents, religious figures, local governments, and conservation organizations determined to halt mountaineering
at the sacred peak Khawa Karpo (Litzinger 2004). By 2010, this coalition
had dissolved. Local governments assumed a more powerful role, employing
national parks to promote tourism but diluting provisions for resident participation and active conservation management. TNC retreated from direct

engagement with local governments and communities and sought new government counterparts as initial partners cooled on the national parks effort. The introduction of a new protected area category exploited ambiguities in laws and regulations concerning protected areas, leading provincial and national agencies to vie over the legitimacy of Yunnan's national parks. TNC increasingly watched from the sidelines as these parks became entangled in struggles within the state.

While proponents of national parks in Yunnan depict them as win-win ventures, national parks worldwide have multifarious relationships with local governments and communities. National parks provide employment opportunities and hubs for development but also constrain people's activities (Machlis and Field 2000; West and Brechin 1991). These constraints frequently fall hardest on rural residents, who find agriculture, hunting, and resource extraction restricted (Stevens 1997; West, Igoe, and Brockington 2006). At other times, extractive interests demand concessions within parks or changes to their boundaries (Naughton-Treves et al. 2006). Within China, protected areas have often burdened local populations, frequently on the basis of poorly substantiated claims about the impacts of residents' activities (Xu Jianchu and Melick 2007).[1] Simultaneously, poor implementation of zoning policies and lax oversight of tourism and resource exploitation impede conservation (Han and Zhuge 2001; Xie Hongyan, Wang, and Schei 2004). Major development projects often erode both biodiversity and resident livelihoods. Nonetheless, following two decades of co-management efforts, some reserves have made notable accomplishments working with residents to support rural livelihoods (Mei et al. 2010; Weckerle et al. 2010).

Nothing shows the joining of shangrilazation with the extension of the "ecological state" in China more tellingly than the transformations of protected area tourism attractions. Across the Tibetan Plateau and beyond, local governments have repackaged nature reserves and scenic areas in order to support high-volume tourism attractions. Concentrating management authority in state-affiliated enterprises, local governments have turned these parks into powerful revenue generators while extending state oversight of land use within. Diqing's national parks, dressed up in signifiers of Tibetanness—stone-faced visitor centers, cairns festooned with prayer flags, residents pasturing yaks—exemplify efforts to remake places to present a picture of a harmonious Shangrila. At the same time, the title "national park" has provided a way of distinguishing Diqing's scenic attractions in competition for tourists, in particular bolstering claims of cutting-edge conservation. Yet the mandate for active conservation management envisioned by the initial proponents of national parks, while central to local states' discourse, gets meager financial and institutional support. Meanwhile, extralocal agencies charged with resource management, competing to raise their profiles and expand or defend their jurisdictions, have vigorously disputed the status of Yunnan's national parks.

These conflicts suggest the need for careful consideration of what constitutes the ecological state. The "ecological construction" programs transforming western China's biophysical and social landscapes give an impression of massive and coordinated extension of state power directed toward managing resources (Yeh 2009b). But the history of Yunnan's national parks complicates this picture. Rather than the coherent expansion of a singular project of state building, these processes expose conflicts among state agencies and governments at different levels, contending over the meaning of green development and the control of the organizational machinery for directing conservation and tourism. Agencies link with one another and with non-state actors in ways that suit perceived organizational interests, building relationships that shape how those interests develop further. Whose efforts win out at any given juncture has major ramifications for how people and landscapes are governed. Developing an adequate picture of the ecological state in China requires taking a disaggregated view, examining how agencies with different purviews, support bases, and resources pursue varied goals (see Tilt 2010).

Given these considerations, that TNC's initial vision for national parks is only patchily incorporated into actual parks should be no surprise. Indeed, it exemplifies the friction through which engagement with local situations transforms transnational projects (Tsing 2005). In northwest Yunnan, rich not only in biodiversity but also in mineral deposits, hydropower potential, and tourism amenities, the national park initiative, with its aspirations to expand protected area coverage, empower protected area conservation agencies, and broaden residents' roles in management, aligned with some state projects but ran afoul of others. To understand how the ideas and resources TNC introduced into these engagements were transmuted in the making of the national parks requires delving into the changing configuration of a heterogeneous and conflicted ecological state.

This task necessitates methods that take into account the changing motives of and relationships among state agencies, enterprises, nongovernmental organizations (NGOs), and collectivities of citizens. Based on interviews and observations conducted between 2008 and 2011 with people in local and provincial government agencies, NGOs, national park administrative bureaus, tourism operators, and several villages in two national parks, as well as conservation scholars and tourism planners, this chapter examines key actors and arenas in the making of national parks. These observations, along with documents and policy statements from some of these actors, show how the stances and proposals of different actors changed over time. No picture can show all relevant perspectives or happenings, but these interleaved accounts from varied participants highlight patterns of engagement of various state agencies with other actors, sketching the changing shape of the ecological state in southwest China.

ORIGINS OF NATIONAL PARKS IN YUNNAN

When TNC's China program was initiated, its staff appealed to experts and policy makers to take part in the Yunnan Great Rivers Project, aiming first to demonstrate the importance of the region's resources and thus the necessity of setting up institutions to conserve them and second to compile a basis for systematic conservation planning. A process of consultation with scientists, cultural experts, and local governments and residents culminated in the "Conservation and Development Action Plan for Northwest Yunnan" (JPO 2001) (see also ch. 5 in this volume).

The "Action Plan" sets out a vision for turning northwest Yunnan's protected areas into centers of revenue generation and professionalized conservation through the adoption of a new protected area model, the national park, in a context of conservation-friendly institutions with broad stakeholder involvement. National parks are framed in six principles: enabling legislation for each park, a management agency with unified authority within park territory, broad participation of multiple stakeholders, separation of park oversight and business operations, systematic management according to International Union for Conservation of Nature (IUCN) guidelines, and coordination and benefit sharing with nearby communities, urban centers, and protected areas (JPO 2001, 25–26). The accompanying Ecoregional Assessment identifies five priority areas for conservation action: Lashi Lake, a wetland near Lijiang; Laojun Mountain, a region west of Lijiang, home to red sandstone outcrops, alpine lakes, and Yunnan golden monkeys; Shangrila Gorge, a swath of northern Shangrila County; the Meili Snow Mountains, an area along the Lancang River in Diqing Prefecture including Khawa

Karpo;[2] and the gorge of the Nu River west of Diqing (Great Rivers Planning Team 2001, 9). The "Action Plan" proposes that northwest Yunnan be designated a special conservation zone in the spirit of the special economic zones that have had a famous role in coastal China's economic ascent; this would complement its unofficial designation as a special ethnic zone, a location of authentic Tibetan difference (see ch. 2 in this volume). This special conservation zone would have several committees and councils dedicated to coordinating conservation and development, a comprehensive protected area management system, community-based co-management efforts, secure forest tenure, "green tourism" fostered through improved policies and capacity building, and efforts to constrain environmentally destructive industries (ibid., 25–34).

The "Action Plan" invokes international and domestic policies as sources of legitimacy. It calls for adopting internationally recognized forms and practices, citing the IUCN categorization of national parks and examples of national parks in the United States and elsewhere.[3] Simultaneously, the plan is presented as "a practical implementation blueprint" that seizes opportunities provided by the Great Western Development strategy (Great Rivers Planning Team 2001, 1) (also see the introduction to this volume). It invokes forest conservation under the Natural Forest Protection Program and Sloping Land Conversion Program; technological innovation to raise industrial energy efficiency and control pollution; consolidation of polluting industries in large, efficient enterprises; nature tourism development; and transportation infrastructure and urban construction. The authors justify their proposals by tying them to existing policies and aspirations to international model status.

The "Action Plan" gives conflicting pictures of residents. Residents were by default treated as threats to biodiversity in TNC's Conservation Action Planning standards, complicating the efforts of the organization's China program to combine conservation of biodiversity with that of culture. The predominant view in state circles of residents as profligate resource users compounded these difficulties. As a result, the "Action Plan," while asserting that residents should have a role in decision making, advocates changing their "crude production practices" in order to reduce dependence on natural resources rather than supporting resource use practices that do not harm ecological integrity and does not even ask residents what they would prefer to do. TNC's subsequent proposals validate resident-led resource conservation, but this narrative of destructive resource dependence would remain in later government pronouncements.

Although persuading Yunnan authorities to issue such a plan was a landmark achievement, building on the plan and the relationships it established would prove difficult. TNC was working with agencies that considered the conservation aims of the Yunnan Great Rivers Project as accessory to other goals. During the project, the organization's main government partner was the provincial Planning Commission (Jihua Weiyuanhui), renamed the Development and Reform Commission (Fazhan yu Gaige Weiyuanhui), in 2003. The Planning Commission refused to disburse promised funds for a subsequent project, creating difficulty for the partners TNC had recruited. One of these partners, a conservation scientist, attributes the Planning Commission's refusal to its preoccupation with economic growth and lack of genuine concern for conservation issues. TNC's next major collaboration took a similar trajectory. Between 2002 and 2003, it worked closely with the Yunnan Province World Heritage Office of the provincial Department of Housing and Urban-Rural Development (Zhufang he Chengxiang Jianshe Ting), providing assistance in the successful application for World Heritage Site status for the Three Parallel Rivers region. This partnership, too, was short-lived. Although national park proposals indicated the department as the central implementing agency as late as 2005, it was uninterested in that vision for protected area management and did not support the new category.

TNC was also intensifying its work with local governments. Representatives of numerous prefectural and county government agencies in northwest Yunnan had provided input for the Great Rivers Project. The organization set up several local offices that served as bases for field operations and enabled the organization to maintain a continual presence in local policy discussions.

Meanwhile, local governments were consolidating efforts around new development strategies. Since the late 1990s, the Diqing Prefecture government has mobilized around four "pillar industries"—mining, hydropower, biological products (farmed and wild products that can be gathered or cultivated for sale), and tourism—with the idea of "turning Diqing's resource advantage into economic advantage" (Li Yiming 2000; Diqing Prefecture Development and Reform Commission 2008). Tourism is central among local government priorities because, in contrast to mining and hydropower development, whose revenues are subject to requisitions from higher levels of government, tourism revenue potentially can remain entirely within the prefecture. Well before the 1998 logging ban, local leaders had begun urging a shift in development focus from forestry to tourism. The Diqing Prefecture government's resolution converting scenic and cultural resources into high-quality attractions meshed with TNC's wish to promote national parks. However, efforts to scale up biological products, hydropower, and, especially, mining would raise hurdles to achieving TNC's vision of conservation at an ecoregional scale.

PLANNING FOR NATURE TOURISM

Following the introduction of the "Action Plan," TNC facilitated further efforts to study and discuss the biological and cultural resources of northwest Yunnan. These projects focused on the Shangrila Gorge area, a rugged stretch of northern Shangrila County where fieldwork found high concentrations of vegetation, natural forest, and plant diversity targets (Great Rivers Planning Team 2001, 59). In 2002, the government of Shangrila County signed a memorandum of understanding with TNC on biodiversity conservation and sustainable development in Shangrila Gorge. With partners at research institutions in Yunnan, Conservancy staff undertook baseline surveys of geology, soils, vegetation, wildlife, and residents' resource use practices. The resulting feasibility report, like the "Action Plan," depicts a landscape of extraordinary biological value and entrenched poverty and urges in response the designation of Shangrila Gorge as a special ecological zone and the introduction of national parks (BCSD Program Team 2003).

This report further elaborates a vision in which national parks protect the environment, conserve biodiversity, support recreation that benefits the local economy, give rural residents a prominent role in decision-making bodies, and promote scientific research and environmental protection education. It makes specific suggestions for the organizational components of such a park, urging the establishment of a set of decision-making bodies, including "grass-roots local participatory management bodies" (BCSD Program Team, 27). This scheme has important offerings for governments at the county and, particularly, prefectural levels. First, while an administration agency would have overall authority over park affairs, local governments would have a stake in the park and the potential to obtain revenue from tourism operations. Second, "[t]he successful implementation of this program will mark a new phase of China's conservation cause," creating a model that might be imitated throughout the region, thus raising the profile of Diqing and its leaders (ibid., 18).

As TNC intensified its focus on Shangrila Gorge, while continuing efforts at Meili Snow Mountains and Laojun Mountain, changes were taking place within the organization. TNC expanded the Yunnan office into an official China Program in 2002. Also, the national parks project increasingly involved the organization with the Research Office of the Yunnan Provincial Government. This agency is charged with conducting research about a variety of topics, mainly concerning economic development, and providing the provincial government with reports that provide an empirical basis for policy decisions.

At the direction of provincial leaders, the Research Office worked with TNC to produce a report on the prospects for establishing national parks in Yunnan. The "Comprehensive Report on Establishing National Parks in Northwest Yunnan" (Dianxibei diqu jianshe guojiagongyuan zonghe baogao) (Research Office and The Nature Conservancy 2005a) follows the same narrative arc as the other documents reviewed here—great biological riches, underdevelopment, urgent threats, national parks as a win-win synergy of conservation and development—but reads very differently. The hand of the Research Office shows in the repeated invocation of policy formulas such as "scientific developmentalism" (*kexue fazhan guan*) and recent policy initiatives, including the "2004–2010 Action Plan for Redoubling Tourism in Yunnan." The "Comprehensive Report" also accentuates the eagerness of local governments to adopt the national park model and the potential of this model to make the region stand out in China and become a world-renowned tourism destination. More than the preceding reports, this one speaks to government agencies in their own terms and, by envisioning a national parks coordinating office staffed by multiple agencies, gives them each a stake. Working with the Research Office made TNC more able to articulate the national park project in language officials were ready to hear.

The "Comprehensive Report" was accompanied by specific proposals for five national park units. These proposals emphasize the separation of oversight from business operations, stakeholder participation, integration with the surrounding region including resident communities, and a national park administration bureau with overall authority to manage and oversee activities within each park. They also suggest a major support role in park management for TNC. The plans divide each park into a set of functional zones, including a special conservation zone limited to scientific research use; a special scenery zone for ecotourism, basic research, and "ecological experience"; a backcountry recreation zone including settlements where residents would run guesthouses; and a belt conservation zone containing a visitor center and other facilities. There is no mention of whether or how residents might continue their farming, herding, and gathering activities, though pasture sightseeing is to be one of the attractions. The main visitor facilities envisioned are hiking trails, visitors' centers, resident-run guesthouses, and service stations along the trails. The proposals provide for business operations as concessions granted by the administration bureau, subject to its oversight and paying a proportion of revenues to support conservation management (Research Office and The Nature Conservancy 2005b, 2005c).

In conjunction with these proposals and countless discussions, TNC also took officials on a fact-finding trip to Yellowstone National Park in the United States. By the end of 2005, senior officials in Yunnan had "endorsed plans to begin building a pilot national park system in northwest Yunnan" (TNC China Program 2007). The Research Office and TNC prepared a book of sixty questions and answers about national parks and distributed copies to various government agencies in Yunnan as part of a campaign for support.

While TNC was honing its proposals and winning support among provincial leaders, regional authorities were elaborating their vision of an upgraded tourism economy in northwest Yunnan. In January 2004, a committee of provincial Tourism Bureau personnel, tourism industry figures, and scholarly experts on tourism issued the "Development Plan for the Northwest Yunnan Shangrila Ecotourism Zone" (Dianxibei Xianggelila shengtailüyouqu fazhan guihua [gangyao]) as part of a broader initiative to reinvigorate Yunnan's tourism economy (Working Group on Drafting the Development Plan for the Northwest Yunnan Tourism Region 2004). Like the "Action Plan," this "Development Plan" represents an effort to coordinate on addressing a broad range of issues in northwest Yunnan. However, its emphases are quite different. The "Development Plan" pushes upgrading and coordinating tourism in an environment of competition with other regions. Whereas national park proposals situate northwest Yunnan in a biodiversity hotspot at the confluence of different ecological zones, the "Development Plan" emphasizes northwest Yunnan's location within the Greater Shangrila Ecotourism Zone, which also encompasses western Sichuan and eastern Tibet, in competition with these other areas to attract tourists.

The "Development Plan" expresses the mind-set of the tourism industry, speaking in terms of brands, products, routes, attractions, and accommodations. It calls for moving beyond sightseeing tourism to cultural, natural, and recreational products that would keep tourists in the region in order to raise northwest Yunnan's competitive profile and specifies attractions to be developed, including sites TNC had urged be set aside for national parks, as well as management agencies for them. Whereas TNC-facilitated national park proposals recognized unplanned or poorly managed tourism as a problem, the "Development Plan" specifies areas of management to be developed and ways of developing them. It is less specific, however, on environmental protection and resident involvement. While the "Development Plan" states emphatically that environmental protection measures need improvement and names nearly every proposed project a "conservation and development project," it does not indicate the conservation measures that will be undertaken. Meanwhile, it recommends increasing resident participation in the economic benefits of tourism, "thus raising their activeness and conscientiousness about protecting tourism resources and supporting the development of the ecotourism region" (Working Group on Drafting the Development Plan for the Northwest Yunnan Tourism Region 2004, 22). Resident participation is presented as a pecuniary exchange in an effort to induce cooperation in large-scale tourism development.

The "Development Plan" brings into view the intensification of tourism planners' involvement in national park initiatives. The governments of Diqing Prefecture and Shangrila County had been hiring tourism planning specialists since the end of the 1990s and tasked them with developing prospectuses for particular attractions and for the general sweep of tourism development in Diqing. These planners are usually organized as teams headed by professors from tourism management departments at universities or staff from planning consultancies.

Planners gather a broad array of information and synthesize it into workable plans that set what must, can, and cannot be done at a given location over a certain period of time. An overall plan for a protected area generally includes an introduction indicating the goals, scope, and justification of the plan; a description of the landscape and its geology, topography, and ecology; a catalog of conservation targets; a description of human settlements and the living conditions of their residents; an outline of conservation measures; a list of guidelines for the treatment of residents; a set of general prescriptions for tourism practices and their locations; directions for infrastructure; and instructions concerning a variety of other objects and issues. Planning teams consult with local authorities about intentions for the site. They ensure that plans accord with relevant laws and regulations. They conduct archival and field research on the biophysical and social contents of a project area. They survey residents to ascertain their skills and aspirations related to conservation and tourism and conduct market surveys that aid in assessing visitor demand. They compile maps and draw up tour routes and layouts for facilities. They research the construction and cost requirements of transport routes, built structures, and waste disposal systems. When a plan is drafted, it undergoes review by relevant local authorities and must be approved by the next-highest level of government, which, in the case of national parks overseen by prefecture governments, is the province.

The heads of planning teams hold the keys to getting plans composed and approved and thus are quite influential. A head planner is a licensed expert who contributes knowledge about tourism operations in other places and has the potential to bring in profitable elements that local authorities might not know about. Head planners are usually well connected; they have worked on a succession of projects across a region or province and are hired by local officials who are keenly interested in their work, which sets guidelines for what is intended to be major revenue-generating vehicles. Over the course of a year or more, through meetings, conversations, meals, and site tours, planners build working relationships with local leaders. Tourism planners are able to exercise discretion by drawing on their expert status and trust sedimented through past projects. They may insert elements in a plan that reflect their own interests, whether trends in tourism products, conservation measures, or ways of involving residents. Planners would play a key role in translating national park proposals into working attractions, although their ability to persuade local authorities to adopt conservation and participation measures would be limited.

In 2006, the Government of Yunnan commissioned the Research Office to draft a report addressing concerns about the impact of national parks on other industries. The "Summary Report from Research on Relationships between National Parks and Industrial Development in Northwest Yunnan" (Guanyu Dianxibei guojiagongyuan yu chanye fazhan xianghu guanxi yanjiu de huibao) (Research Office of the People's Government of Yunnan Province 2006) highlights the complicated relationships between national parks and the region's major industries, tourism, forestry, hydropower, and mining, as well as transportation infrastructure. It claims that insufficient management measures for tourism have caused unneeded environmental damage, while unclear division of responsibilities for tourism development causes suboptimal utilization of tourism resources. National parks, it follows, provide precisely the tools that would solve these problems, raising the quality of tourism and ensuring the protection of scenic resources—and establishing a new brand for tourism in northwest Yunnan. There would be little conflict between proposed national park boundaries and roads, rail, and reservoirs, although planned hydropower development might require zoning adjustments. National parks might even provide employment for people displaced by big dams. Finally, while some overlaps with mining might emerge in the area proposed for Shangrila Gorge, these would be minor and easily remedied.

The report concludes that, overall, national parks would have a synergetic relationship with infrastructure and industry; there are no irresolvable contradictions. It is hard to see how the report could conclude otherwise. It illustrates how efforts at promoting conservation have to contend with powerful interests that would benefit from resource exploitation. Provincial officials are under pressure to realize a vision of technological, industrial development. Conservation promoters had to do some apparently uncomfortable maneuvering in order to show how national parks might be reconciled with the project.

NATIONAL PARKS IN PRACTICE

These claims of accord notwithstanding, as governments prepared to turn proposals into actual parks, tensions surfaced. The first hint came with the appearance of an additional national park site, Bita Lake–Shudu Lake, in the "Comprehensive Report" and the "Development Plan." These alpine lakes are just over twenty kilometers east of the seat of Shangrila County. Both had been receiving visitors since the early 1990s. At Bita Lake, residents of surrounding villages gave visitors horse rides around the wetlands and sold them refreshments. In 2005, the prefectural government assumed control of the site. The newly formed Diqing Prefecture Tourism Development Investment Company, an investment platform that enabled the prefecture to leverage funds to invest in tourist attractions, assumed control of tourism operations. The prefectural government hired planners from the ecotourism faculty of Southwest Forestry College (Xinan Linxueyuan) in Kunming to draft a plan for the new attraction.[4] In summer 2006, the area reopened as Pudacuo National Park. Visitors to the park shuttle through a vast entrance hall and board buses painted green as a reminder that they meet stringent European Union emissions standards. On the buses, park employees with microphones recite facts and stories about the park's geography and the animals, plants, and humans that live there. At two points, visitors can leave the buses to travel on foot on raised wooden walkways along the wetlands, and at another, they can disembark to view residents pasturing yaks in an alpine meadow.[5]

Pudacuo National Park was an immediate commercial success. The new bus route configuration enabled thousands of tourists to cycle through the park daily. Between its 2006 opening and October 2008, the park sold 1.3 million tickets, taking in ¥236 million in revenue (Yunnan Province Government 2009, 7). While figures on internal expenditures are not publicly available, respondents in park management claim that more than half of these revenues were submitted to the prefectural government budget, and most of the remainder went to paying down loans for development projects, so one may infer that the proportion of revenues allocated to operating expenses is relatively small.

Pudacuo's performance did not go unnoticed. Xu Rongkai, then the governor of Yunnan, attended the official unveiling of Pudacuo National Park in June 2007, and further promotion of national parks was put on the provincial government's work agenda for 2008. The provincial government's blueprint for tourism development for 2008 to 2015 put national parks among five attraction types slated for concerted efforts (Yunnan Province Tourism Bureau and Yunnan Province Development and Reform Commission 2008). Diqing Prefecture surged ahead in promoting national parks, unveiling two more parks, Shangrila Yunnan Golden Monkey National Park and Meili Snow Mountains National Park, in late 2009.

The choice of this site was a disappointment for TNC staff. According to one former staff member, "The Nature Conservancy was trying to get protection where it didn't exist already, in order to extend protected area coverage to key biodiversity-rich areas, so we had not sought national park status for Bitahai, which was already a reserve. We pushed . . . to get Shangrila Gorge made into a national park. But the Diqing government had its own considerations" (interview, June 4, 2009). TNC's strategy for promoting national parks focused on expanding the region's portfolio of protected areas by securing conservation designations for new sites. As noted above, field research had found Shangrila Gorge to have one of the richest concentrations of biodiversity in northwest Yunnan. But the local government, intent on rapidly setting up a new tourism attraction, was moving in another direction. An official from the Pudacuo National Park Administration Bureau explained that Shangrila Gorge "is 102 kilometers out of Shangrila, and there was no infrastructure, so it would be really hard to set up tourism there. In terms of tourism amenities, it might be good for whitewater rafting and backpacking, but it's not well situated for mass tourism" (interview, July 1, 2009). Local authorities wanted to build a high-volume tourism operation. The vision of low-volume, backcountry tourism presented by TNC and the Research Office did not mesh with their priorities. The overlap of the proposed Shangrila Gorge National Park with a major copper seam gave the local government further reason to demur.

Pudacuo National Park looks quite different from the hiking trails and backcountry bed-and-breakfasts proposed by TNC and the Research Office, and the independent, unified oversight that they endorsed has not been instituted. Instead of going on backpacking treks, visitors ride buses. While the new park limited tourism use to less than 5 percent of its area, dedicated facilities for conservation have not been built. Local authorities have set up a separate administration bureau and tourism company, but staff at the bureau are unable to make effective claims on the company because the company, which was granted the same bureaucratic rank, has greater clout. Minimal funds from tourism revenues are directed to conservation activities, and the administration bureau's operating expenses come out of the prefecture's administrative budget. This set-up is very different from the concessions system envisioned in the "Comprehensive Report," in which an administration bureau would be empowered to define the scope of tourism operations and collect a proportion of revenues as a concession fee to be used for resource conservation. The Bita Lake Provincial Nature Reserve Administration Office continues to facilitate patrolling, monitoring, and research, without substantial added support. Multi-stakeholder decision-making committees are absent. While the national park has revolutionized tourism at the site and made it much more profitable, it is not clear that it has added anything to the practice of ecological protection or resident participation in decision making or conservation.

Although the realized park was far from TNC's vision, planners were able to moderate some of the local officials' plans. For example, while local leaders had wanted to construct a set of small dams along a wetland stream to replicate the cascades of Jiuzhaigou, an attraction in northern Sichuan, the head planner persuaded them that this would be an undue modification of the area's scenery (interview, July 24, 2011). Planners also drafted a two-stage plan, designating areas away from the bus route for the low-impact, backcountry tourism activities envisioned in TNC's proposals, to be developed once the mass tourism route was established.

Residents were incorporated into the new national parks as employees and also received compensation. In return for relinquishing the right to provide services directly to tourists, park authorities granted residents the opportunity to take jobs as sanitary workers and promised to provide each household with several thousand renminbi annually. At Meili Snow Mountains National Park, residents continued to give mule rides and provide refreshments and accommodations to visitors. Each park set up organizations to mediate with rural residents. Pudacuo National Park established a community affairs committee with representatives from villages around the park, local government offices, the tourism company, and the administration bureau. At Meili Snow Mountains, administration stations charged with regulating tourism services and conservation efforts have become points of contact between the park and communities. Some station personnel are drawn from those communities. These personnel attend village council meetings and relay concerns from communities to national park management and vice versa. In each place, residents continue to farm, graze, and gather forest products, fuelwood, and timber from collective forests, as in communities outside the parks. As the parks lack conservation management capacity, residents are by default the primary implementers of resource management. In some cases, as with the accelerating use of timber to build guesthouses in Yubeng, a village in Meili Snow Mountains National Park, residents raise concerns about tourism's impact on beliefs and institutions that had once constrained resource use—the very beliefs and institutions that TNC's initial efforts had aimed to nurture.

These changes have drawn varied responses. At Pudacuo National Park, residents were initially unhappy with losing their rights to provide horse rides and found the compensation offered by the park too meager. In 2008, the park raised the level of compensation, yet some discontent remained. Some residents see their share of the take from the national park, totaling less than 5 percent of annual revenues, as unfairly small. At Meili Snow Mountains, some residents complain that although the national park collects ticket fees from every visitor, it has not invested this income in beneficial infrastructure in the park. Others in both parks express faith that the national park management will make good in time, and some of these returns have already come to pass. By 2012, Pudacuo National Park had followed through on promises to provide running water to each household and to build a hotel that residents could take part in running.

With the commercial success of Pudacuo National Park, the prefectural government put national parks at the center of its tourism development plans. The chief of the Diqing Tourism Bureau declared, "Based on the successful experience of establishing Pudacuo National Park, Diqing will rapidly promote and boldly explore national park construction, management methods, and standards, as well as innovative tourism development and management methods, so that national parks become a key pillar of the Shangrila tourism brand" (Liu Juan 2009, 1). In the competitive market sketched out in the "Development Plan," local governments strive to make their localities' tourism attractions more visible. Seeing this potential in Pudacuo National Park, leaders in Diqing seized on national parks as a way of advancing the area's prospects.

RESPONDING TO NATIONAL PARK DEVELOPMENT

Pudacuo National Park created a challenge for TNC. Some staff members did not want to support an operation that departed so sharply from the organization's vision. In the end, TNC decided to provide support in order to try to push Pudacuo toward something more like that vision and to ensure that it could remain involved in further efforts around national parks. TNC provided assistance for training staff and developing interpretive materials. TNC staff worked with prefecture authorities on drafting legislation. Finally, the organization's staff and the ecotourism faculty of Southwest Forestry College conducted a participatory rural appraisal to identify residents' skills and needs in relation to providing tourism services in the park, including traditional handicrafts, performances, and accommodations. Park management did not adopt the resulting report's recommendations for enabling residents to comanage and directly provide tourism services (TNC China Program and International Ecotourism Research Center 2009).

A leadership transition in 2008 brought major changes to TNC's China program. Yunnan native Rose Niu, who had led TNC's efforts in China since their initiation in 1998, was replaced by Sean Zhang, a technical expert who had worked on policy projects based at TNC's China program Beijing office. This transition cemented a shift in focus away from Yunnan and toward regional and national projects. Following the 2008 economic downturn, the China program's funds fell by about half, and two-thirds of the Yunnan staff were cut, including several who had led place-based projects in northwest Yunnan. Several field offices in northwest Yunnan closed. People who had long-term relationships with TNC before the transition report that these relationships, especially those with local cultural experts and governments dating from the 1900s, were damaged by the departure of experienced staff.

TNC continued to promote national parks, shifting its efforts toward shaping incipient national parks at Meili Snow Mountains and Laojun Mountain and engaging provincial agencies on policy and oversight. In 2007, TNC obtained cofinancing from the European Union–China Biodiversity Programme for a project aimed at developing and implementing legislation for these two national parks, establishing functioning organizational structures, building management capacity, facilitating participation of local communities, and promoting awareness and advocacy for replicating the new model.

In Diqing, while national park development surged, policy lagged. The establishment of national parks brought into being administrative bureaus and business operators whose organizational interests conflicted with those of many other agencies. A staff member at the Pudacuo National Park Administration Bureau, interviewed on July 1, 2009, reported:

> Within the prefecture, forestry, tourism, land resources, and hydrology departments as well as the Tourism Development Investment Company all want a hand in what's going on [in the national park]. . . . Forest management is in the purview of the Forestry Bureau. So Forestry employees regularly go into the park to do their work. Tourism and other bureaus send special guests, demanding that they not be charged for tickets. But if there's an accident in the park—say, a tourist gets injured—everyone points their fingers at the National Park Administration Bureau. We need them to facilitate our work. Right now we have no power to fine people for infractions or get other departments to work along.

Staff at National Park Administration Bureaus struggled to play the roles that the founding statements of national parks prescribe. While local leaders boldly declared new national parks—ahead of approval from provincial agencies—they showed less eagerness to issue regulations that might constrain tourism and other endeavors.

Provincial agencies also contended over the new category. As of 2008, TNC had a new ally in advancing national parks, the Yunnan Province Forestry Department, which had previously been chary of the national park effort. The Forestry Department's about-face followed events in Beijing and Kunming. In 2007, the chief of the Yunnan Forestry Department was replaced, and when the new chief went on a fact-finding trip to Pudacuo, he was impressed (interview, May 9, 2010). In May 2008, TNC cosponsored the China Protected Area Leadership Alliance Project, aimed at building management capacity at model national nature reserves. Twenty-seven participants from across China, including seven from Yunnan, took part in classroom training at Tsinghua University, two weeks of field study in the mainland United States, including visits to several national parks, and a week of workshops at the University of Hawai'i. At that point, the Yunnan Forestry Department applied to the State Forestry Administration to allow Yunnan to pilot national parks. In June 2008, the State Forestry Administration issued the "Notice on Approving Designating Yunnan Province as a Pilot Province for Constructing National Parks," authorizing the Yunnan Forestry Department to undertake work on a national park model and to set up an office for that purpose (China State Forestry Administration 2008). Shortly thereafter, the Nature Reserve Administration Office of the Yunnan Forestry Department assumed the added title of National Park Administration Office. In July, Southwest Forestry College held a conference on national park development, with the Yunnan Forestry Department taking a central role. TNC, the Research Office, and tourism planners at Southwest Forestry College had helped garner substantial support from the State Forestry Administration and its subordinate agencies in Yunnan.

The National Park Administration Office began working with TNC, the Research Office, and tourism planners to build policy and management capacity for national parks. In 2009, the Yunnan Forestry Department released a long-term plan for developing national parks, emphasizing the importance of comprehensive management authority within parks for national park management agencies that would now be supervised by the national office. This plan set out an agenda for establishing twelve national parks across the province by 2020 (Yunnan Province Government 2009). By the end of 2009, plans for four, including a new plan for Pudacuo National Park, had been approved by the Yunnan provincial government. With assistance from TNC, the National Park Administration Office facilitated three training workshops and conferences for staff at current or planned national parks. These activities, which put the national office in repeated contact with current and prospective national parks administration bureaus as a management resource, worked to consolidate its role as the main agency in charge of national parks.

Local governments contest efforts by the National Park Administration Office to influence national parks. Having taken the initiative to establish national parks, they assert their prerogative to make decisions about park administration. Responding to these challenges, the National Park Administration Office has pushed to advance national park policy within the province and to become involved in the day-to-day affairs of each national park. The Yunnan Forestry Department and the Research Office issued a report in 2009 affirming the potential of national parks to mitigate conflicts between resource use and conservation. It identified problems related to overlap with nature reserves and scenic areas, disconnects in provincial agencies' oversight of local government agencies, national parks' inadequate provision for community development, tourism's contributions to meaningful conservation actions, and a lag in legislation that might resolve these issues (Yunnan Province Forestry Department and Research Office of the People's Government of Yunnan 2009; see also Research Office of the People's Government of Yunnan 2010a, 2010b). Provincial legislation faces hurdles similar to those impeding local legislation, as agencies balk at encroachment on their jurisdictions. The national office also commissioned four teams of attraction planners to draft technical standards for national parks, which required approval from a provincial bureau but did not need to pass through the legislature. With these standards, the National Park Administration Office asserted the authority to bestow or revoke the label "national park"; to require regular, science-based assessment of biological and cultural resources and how they are affected by activities within a park; and to stipulate where construction is allowed and how it must be approved.

The National Park Administration Office worked to get involved in the practical management of national parks through on-the-ground programming. Training sessions not only acquainted park personnel with a conservation-oriented vision of national parks but also drew them into continued interaction with the national office. Likewise, in 2010, the national office initiated biological surveys at several national parks. These surveys were intended to provide baseline data for longer-term monitoring of vegetation and wildlife. Through these actions, the Forestry Department has worked to demonstrate continual engagement with management agencies at national parks.

The Yunnan Forestry Department has pursued these efforts aggressively because the national parks initiative, as a new program with shaky legal foundations that could potentially affect various government agencies, is politically vulnerable. Efforts around national parks have met with resistance from other provincial agencies, whose staff members fear encroachment on their spheres of authority. In addition, the parks' lack of grounding in national law makes it difficult for park managers to make claims on other agencies. Park personnel avoid making strong statements about the administrative status of national parks, particularly any that would raise hackles with agencies that provide them with support. Asked about the possibility that the national park project might not survive, one participant asserted that even if the title "national park" were eliminated, the forestry department would have laid the foundation for stronger conservation management in these areas, which he says is important in itself.

Meanwhile, TNC retreated from on-the-ground work in northwest Yunnan. It closed its Shangrila office in 2009, and its last action at Pudacuo was the presentation of several flat-screen monitors to display the park's wonders in the entrance hall. After the departure of the head of the Deqin office, interns struggled with local political complications around removing trash from rural tourism sites and a short-lived project to enlist villagers to monitor wildlife and poaching. When provincial agencies commissioned a new "Action Plan for Biodiversity Conservation and Sustainable Development in Northwest Yunnan" (Yunnan Province Environmental Protection Department 2009) in late 2009, TNC did not participate.

CONCLUSION

The making of Yunnan's national parks illustrates how different state agencies mobilize around protected areas and how the roles of transnational organizations have changed over the past decade. These complications show the disunity within the ecological state, which shapes how state agencies engage with other actors on environmental issues. Because of the leverage local governments have in protected area management, their development priorities have been predominant in shaping national parks. Line agencies competing for funds, jurisdictional turf, and prestige have made scenic landscapes terrain for pursuing differing organizational goals. TNC's approach has changed as its proposals have met with obstacles and government actors have seen or dismissed a role for TNC in achieving their goals. Meanwhile, other participants in the coalition that TNC catalyzed early in the years 2000–2010, particularly local residents and religious figures, have had little say in major decisions about these landscapes.

National parks have become sites of contestation within the ecological state as government units with divergent mandates compete for prestige and control. Local governments control the practical management of protected areas, but, in competing to build high-profile attractions, they are not inclined to support active conservation or resident involvement. The Diqing government seized on the national park idea to build a distinctive brand while at the same time mimetically replicating the mass tourism operations of places like Jiuzhaigou and Zhangjiajie. While protecting nature is front and center in local state discourse in northwest Yunnan, action on behalf of this goal is subordinate to the priorities of tourism revenue and resource extraction. Meanwhile, line agencies, especially at the provincial level, compete to acquire and maintain organizational turf. Development-oriented agencies have resisted the constraints inherent in TNC's proposals, while the Yunnan Forestry Department has found in this new model a chance to expand its purview and produce visible accomplishments in protected area management. But the disconnect between its conservation goals and the aims of local governments has constrained the Forestry Department in strengthening park management. Local governments responding to pressures for tourism-led growth have become central actors in environmental management.

The establishment of national parks has recast the terms on which local residents and governments work with each other around landscapes. Whereas at the start of the period covered in this chapter, threats to the sacred landscape had brought these groups together to demand that activities accord with this sacredness, the growth of tourism changed the stakes. In the 1990s, local governments assisted communities in what would become Pudacuo and Meili Snow Mountains National Parks with setting up cooperative tourism services run by residents, who obtained the majority of benefits. With the advent of national parks, local governments found a revenue interest in channeling visitors into high-volume attractions, which is in tension with residents' interests. Because local authorities conceive of participation narrowly as economic benefit, they have incorporated residents through employment and compensation schemes. Park authorities may take residents' concerns into account, though they do so reactively, in response to complaints, rather than proactively, by offering involvement in decision making. Local governments have worked as much to cultivate and constrain residents' activities and wishes as to promote them, and relationships between residents and park management have become characterized by negotiation and, often, contention. At the same time, since local authorities have not invested in conservation management, residents have by default become, or continued to be, resource managers, but there have not been active efforts to understand and learn from their practices. In this context, TNC's proposals, while limited from the perspective of democratic participation, were groundbreaking—and for this reason did not get very far with the local state. The national parks project worked to divide these parties as much as it did to bring them together.

These changes in the ecological state have contributed to a shift in the focus of transnational conservation organizations and a relative decline in their capacity to influence local practices. As domestic capacity for development and research have grown, what TNC has to offer has changed. In the late 1990s, the scientific studies and rural development assistance brought by TNC met demands that local and provincial governments had difficulty meeting, while its planning programs fit in with the efforts of local governments and development-oriented agencies to identify natural and scenic resources. With these offerings, TNC worked to win favor for its vision of national parks. A decade later, as domestic financial, scientific, and planning capacity grew and local government tourism agendas solidified, it became harder for the organization to promote a conservation model that constrains economic activity. Nonetheless, TNC's resources for policy consultation, aided by ties to the Yunnan Provincial Research Office, appealed to a Forestry Department that was working to raise its profile in protected area management.

The course of TNC's involvement in Yunnan shows an organization learning about the ecological state, working across scales to promote a conservation agenda, and adjusting that agenda in response to changing signals from state agencies. As extractive interests in northwest Yunnan grew, TNC had to withdraw from a vision of coordinated, constrained development across an ecoregion and focus on specific national parks. Its vision for national parks, in turn, increasingly diverged from the aims of local government agendas, straining relationships with local governments. TNC staff adapted their visions to respond to changing situations at national park sites and appeal to different government counterparts. New partners adjusted the organization's proposals, bringing in elements reflecting their roles in mediating with other agencies. Still, TNC clung to several points, in particular, empowering administration bureaus to oversee parks, subjecting business operations to concessions policies, and securing the participation of residents in decision-making bodies, even when it became clear that local governments would not adopt them. Park planners incorporated elements of TNC's visions into designs that could satisfy local government authorities. The vision of the National Park Administration Office, building on foundations laid by TNC and the Research Office, reflects the role of national parks in efforts to build the power and influence of forestry agencies.

This unfolding of events raises important questions about transnational organizations. It has been amply documented that these organizations' projects often have perverse consequences due to the complications of on-the-ground engagement. Scholars often present such organizations as anti-politics machines that turn value-laden issues into technical problems that can be solved with their prefabricated tool kits (Ferguson 1994; T. Li 2007). TNC's application of such a tool kit and its struggles with local politics fit this picture in some ways, but the political implications of its efforts to prioritize active conservation management and resident involvement aroused local state resistance. Weak connections to the communities involved constrained TNC's capacity to advocate for them. While this account does not claim that TNC was entirely benign toward residents, the organization's staff were aware of power differentials and actively worked to expand the involvement and autonomy of rural residents. Meanwhile, its efforts to promote active conservation ran up against local state agendas, and its higher-level allies had little leverage to exercise in achieving this goal. In this narrative, we see the staff of an organization realizing, however incompletely, the political implications of their efforts, which collide with the countervailing projects of state actors, and the limitations of their ability to assist civil society stakeholders.

Given current trends, it is likely that professionalized conservation in southwestern China, which implies the cultivation of professionalized bureaucracy, has stronger chances for success than building resident participation and autonomy, which requires investing in capacity building and granting residents space in which to pursue opportunities that they value. On either of these fronts, though, the story is not over. In Yunnan, TNC has made a notable contribution in bringing ideas about active conservation management and community involvement into policy discussions and institution building. A variety of possible events might propel these efforts forward, such as funding from above conditioned on implementing professionalized conservation, changes in national or provincial legislation on protected areas, increased assertiveness on the part of national park administration bureaus and the National Park Administration Office, or perhaps even a change of heart or personnel in local governments (Zhou and Grumbine 2011). People who attempt to bring about such changes would have to address entrenched local state interests. Just what these wrangles will yield is hard to foresee.

4. MAKING NATIONAL PARKS IN YUNNAN

Interviews were conducted in confidentiality, and the names of interviewees are withheld by mutual agreement.

1   China's protected areas include more than 2,500 nature reserves, over 200 scenic areas, and more than 600 forest parks, not to mention a collection of areas in other categories (State Council of the People's Republic of China 2009; Ministry of Environmental Protection 2010). For discussions of the status and management of these protected areas, see Xie Yan, Wang, and Schei 2004 and Harris 2008.

2   "Meili Snow Mountains" is a translation of the commonly used standard Chinese name for the area around Khawa Karpo (Meili Xueshan). Government actors have promoted the use of this name, even though it does not correspond with local residents' conceptions of these places. For more on these names, see Litzinger 2004 and Guo 2009.

3   These versions of national parks have complicated relationships to one another. IUCN categories refer mainly to the types of land use allowed in a protected area, presuming management "through legal or other effective means" (Dudley 2008, 8). In this context, the U.S. national park "model" concerns organizational traits, in particular, unified oversight by an agency like the National Park Service, commercial operations subject to concessions policies, and outreach and negotiation with surrounding communities (Machlis and Field 2000; Sellars 2009). TNC and government agencies in Yunnan strategically draw on both IUCN and U.S. National Park Service rubrics for different purposes.

4   In 2010, Southwest Forestry College was renamed Southwest Forestry University (Xinan Linye Daxue).

5   For more sustained discussions of Pudacuo National Park, see Tian and Yang 2009 and Zinda 2012a, 2012b.

CHAPTER 5

The Nature Conservancy in Shangrila

• • •

TRANSNATIONAL CONSERVATION
AND ITS CRITIQUES

Robert K. Moseley and Renée B. Mullen

IN the past decade, two prominent articles criticized transnational conservation organizations, including the Nature Conservancy (TNC), for their preference for "virgin wilderness" at the expense of the culture and livelihoods of indigenous peoples in developing countries (Chapin 2004; Dowie 2005). At about the same time, a series of investigative articles about TNC in the *Washington Post* made just the opposite argument (Stephens and Ottoway 2003).[1] In its series, the newspaper implied that TNC programs that strive for some level of environmentally sustainable human use, be it with family farms or large forest product companies, are not compatible with nature conservation. While both sides clearly claim that big organizations are bad for conservation, their reasons for arriving at this conclusion are exactly the opposite. On the one hand, TNC is accused of creating "conservation refugees" by being culturally insensitive and excluding subsistence and commercial enterprise from conservation areas; on the other hand, it is criticized for allowing any economic activity on conservation land, the implication being that humans should be kept separate from nature. These divergent critiques squarely delimit extremes in the debate on the role of human communities in conserving the Earth's biological diversity.

We know firsthand that TNC is a big conservation organization. Both of us are conservation scientists who worked for TNC during its formative years in China,[2] when it was a major actor in the construction of the ecological state in northwest Yunnan. From our point of view, the debate over big versus small and local versus transnational organizations misses the point. That point is about effectiveness, fairness, respect, and human compassion in biodiversity conservation in an already globally connected world where most economic development models have little regard for native species and indigenous human communities. In no small measure, it is also about the multitude of scales at which humans interact with nature and are accommodated within conservation programs when proximate causes of local biocultural diversity loss are often driven by distal factors operating on national or global scales.

This critical review describes the Nature Conservancy's history vis-à-vis evolving institutional conceptions of nature-as-wilderness as the organization went from a federation of state-based programs in the United States to the large global organization it is today. We also provide a candid critique of TNC's work regionally in Yunnan and locally in the Khawa Karpo area, especially in regard to how conservation planning was adjusted to include social and cultural elements that were not well incorporated into TNC's methods at the time. We are blunt about how the organization's conservation work with local people was replete with cultural misunderstandings, successes and failures, lessons learned, and strategic innovations. This real-life example of institutional evolution leads into a review of the work of Western social scientists who studied how TNC engaged with and interacted across many levels of Chinese and Yunnanese society between 1999 and 2005. We examine these critiques from the vantage point of the ones being studied and explore some of the common thematic areas that emerge, focusing on the organization's attempts to integrate social elements into biodiversity conservation programs. Our objective here is to explore the possibilities for dialogue across the disciplinary, paradigmatic, and epistemological divides that separate academic social science from conservation practice. The communication barrier between these two disciplines is significant, but we think that the effort needed to bridge this gap is critical for the sake of the Earth's biosphere and its human occupants.

At its inception, TNC concentrated its core business locally, at places containing important biodiversity, where it made its greatest investments by far. But the organization's conservation goals, as well as the methods it employed, have broadened considerably during the past sixty years. Similar to most conservation movements born in the early twentieth century, TNC has its origins in the Western notion of "wilderness," where natural and human communities are considered separate (Cronon 1995). The organization can trace its origins back to the establishment of the Ecological Society of America in 1915, a professional organization founded by leading American natural scientists of the day (Smith and Mark 2009). Not satisfied solely with academic research, some of these scientists formed an activist wing that eventually split from the society in the 1940s, resolving to take "direct action" to save threatened natural areas, not just study their demise. This group incorporated as TNC in 1951.

For its direct action, TNC took full advantage of the dominant land tenure system in the United States, that of private property (Freyfogle 2010). This strategy was unique among U.S. conservation groups in those days. Before this, protected areas were established exclusively through government programs, although often under pressure from conservation activists through political processes. The organization purchased private tracts of undeveloped land containing endangered species and managed them as strict nature reserves. Land acquisition was its dominant strategy for three decades, and it is the one for which it is best known today in the United States. But that view is twenty years out of date. Two developments in conservation science during the 1980s forced TNC and others to recognize that conserving biodiversity would necessarily involve working more broadly across land- and waterscapes. First was the recognition of an early bias toward terrestrial ecosystems. Some of the most imperiled forms of life on Earth occur in freshwater, and, except for game fish, aquatic biodiversity was largely ignored by conservationists (Master 1990). The second major realization was that isolated protected areas could not conserve all endangered elements of the biosphere (Noss 1987).

These compelling scientific trends forced TNC to look beyond a simple land-purchase strategy to suites of conservation approaches across watersheds and larger landscapes that included networks of reserves embedded within considerable human enterprise. In other words, it became clear that working at the local scale would never be enough to accomplish the group's conservation mission. While strategic local action is still a hallmark of TNC, the organization also began to work across many geographic scales and sociopolitical realms. There was also a more pragmatic reason for TNC's move beyond land acquisition. The organization expanded into the international conservation arena in the early 1980s, often to places that have larger populations and land tenure systems that are different from the U.S. system. With the move from isolated nature reserves to landscapes and a geographic expansion beyond the United States, it quickly became obvious that accommodating sustainable human use in conservation strategies would be critical to effectively conserving biodiversity.

THE NATURE CONSERVANCY COMES TO CHINA

In 1995, after fifteen years of international experience in Latin America and the Pacific, TNC was presented with its first opportunity to conserve biodiversity in mainland Asia. It was invited to work with the Chinese government on new conservation initiatives in the mountains of northwest Yunnan. While the global biodiversity importance of the area was well documented (Myers et al. 2000), unfamiliar political terrain triggered a cautious analysis by TNC's governing board, which eventually authorized a project. Formal partnership with the Yunnan provincial government began in June 1998 and became known as the Yunnan Great Rivers Project (see map 2). Right from the beginning, TNC recognized and embraced the extraordinarily complex cultural and sustainable-livelihood context of its conservation work in northwest Yunnan: three million rural inhabitants governed by a strong centralized authority and belonging to more than ten official ethnic groups, although represented by considerably greater cultural diversity than these administrative ethnic categories indicate.

This invitation was not the only move China made toward increasing conservation activity during this period. Not least was a nearly logarithmic increase in the government's designation of nature reserves across the country following the Cultural Revolution (Coggins 2003, 14). Soon after TNC's entry into Yunnan, the central government also launched several broad-scale development and conservation initiatives. Foremost among them was the Great Western Development strategy in 2000 (Tian 2004), a long-term central government program aimed at raising economic standards in western

China to levels created in the east during the previous quarter century. In Yunnan, the initial manifestations were rapid infrastructure expansion and industrial tourism development. At the same time, the central government launched two large conservation programs, a ban on state-run commercial logging in 1998 (Zhang Peichang et al. 2000) and reforestation of steep-slope cropland through the Sloping Land Conversion Program, initiated in 1999 (Xu Zhigang et al. 2004). At the provincial level, most of northwest Yunnan was listed as a natural World Heritage site in 2003 (Ives 2004). Rapid shifts in the economy, with exposure to regional and global economic pressures caused by these and other programs, were predicted to have a sizable impact on both people and landscapes in Yunnan.

ESTABLISHING REGIONAL CONSERVATION PRIORITIES

Given the context of extraordinary biological and human diversity combined with mounting development pressure and new, often overlapping government programs, both the Yunnan government and TNC agreed that there was an urgent need to establish regional conservation priorities for the Yunnan Great Rivers Project (Groves 2003, 389). In fact, TNC, or any NGO, faces this situation wherever it works and whatever its mission: how to prioritize investment in the face of urgent need and limited funds. During this period, the organization used a combination of biodiversity value, urgency, and feasibility (often having to do with sociopolitical conditions) to prioritize places identified for specific local action and the broad-scale strategies required to support those actions (Groves 2003).[3]

While biodiversity was the primary focus of TNC's work in Yunnan, partnership with the provincial government brought the people of northwest Yunnan to the fore. Biodiversity and the development of social goals related to cultural diversity and sustainable livelihoods were given equal consideration in setting priorities for regional conservation. Well-connected Yunnan social scientists advising the project drove the cultural focus of provincial sponsors, which TNC embraced from the start. The resulting "Conservation and Development Action Plan for Northwest Yunnan" (JPO 2001), developed between late 1999 and early 2001, outlined cultural, economic development, and biodiversity priorities for the region (see ch. 4 in this volume for a review of the "Action Plan"). The overall objective of the "Action Plan" was to assess broad-scale patterns of biological and cultural diversity in the region in order to identify areas of cultural and biodiversity significance, regionwide or multisite threats to biocultural diversity, and the appropriate conservation and sustainable economic development activities for maintaining and enhancing this diversity (Ou 2002).

For TNC's China program, the regional planning process had two equal objectives: (1) produce a credible first iteration of biodiversity and cultural conservation priorities, as described above, and (2) introduce to China a transparent, systematic approach to setting priorities that includes interdisciplinary collaboration. These dual objectives of outcome and process, along with cultural conservation, were unique in the organization at the time. Most of TNC's regional priority setting focused only on the biodiversity part of the first objective (Groves 2003). In fact, an internal review of the biodiversity component of this plan was rather negative. The peer reviewers assessed the Yunnan project against standards developed in the United States, where social welfare and capacity-building objectives were generally not considered (although they are now). TNC's Yunnan team defended its approach and the extra effort needed to establish a transparent, interdisciplinary process with cultural and sustainable livelihood objectives, even if it distracted somewhat from a more rigorous biodiversity assessment. In the context of China at the time, a systematic approach to designing conservation actions was new, as was interdisciplinary collaboration. In the end, more than eighty Chinese experts from thirty-five institutions contributed to the "Action Plan," including biological and cultural scientists, economists, and development planners, with TNC playing a facilitating role.

Unfortunately, at the end of the priority-setting process for the Yunnan Great Rivers Project, the cultural module and the biodiversity module stood as independent tracks, with no integration of analysis and recommendations. Several factors appear to have contributed to this lack of integration. One was the very short time frame the provincial government established for production of the plan. Communication barriers also inhibited full integration of the two modules, including persistent communication obstacles between social and biological scientists and between Chinese experts and TNC expatriate facilitators. As Ou Xiaokun, a Yunnan University ecologist and one of the government leaders, put it, "[T]he larger and perhaps more difficult challenge to efficient idea exchange and cooperation are the different methods the Chinese and American partners have in conceptualizing and solving problems" (2002, 75). For example, in finding solutions to institutional barriers that slowed progress, Chinese participants most often tried to solve these problems within existing administrative channels. If the barriers persisted, TNC expatriates would readily attempt to create new pathways for resolving them. Proposals for circumventing established norms regularly created friction. As a result, recommended cultural actions were related largely to tangible culture (e.g., architecture and dance), with only general recommendations regarding cultural interactions with species and ecosystems (e.g., traditional knowledge applied to sustainable resource use). Specialist groups from the cultural team produced ethnographic and ethnobiological assessments from short field sessions; these narrow case studies of a few select villages were not broadly applicable or useful in assessing natural resource use patterns of ethnic groups at a regional scale.[4]

Another unfortunate outcome was that the cultural conservation recommendations languished after the "Action Plan" was complete. The cultural portion of the plan was developed largely by academics from research institutes and universities who did not have the institutional mandate or capacity to advocate for turning the recommendations into actions, as TNC did for biodiversity. On the positive side, the planning process did introduce biologists to social scientists, which led to later collaborations. The ethnographic case studies were important to implementing programs in specific conservation areas, such as in the Khawa Karpo (Ch. Meili) Snow Mountains (Guo 2000a). Also, the Yunnan NGO Center for Biodiversity and Indigenous Knowledge built on this earlier work to implement biocultural and livelihood programs with Tibetans at Bahang, Gongshan County (Wilkes 2006), and Jisha, Shangrila County (Xu Jianchu, Li, and Waltner-Toews 2004).

LOCAL ENGAGEMENT WITH TIBETAN COMMUNITIES

The "Action Plan" was completed during the first half of 2001 and received final approval from the provincial government in May. Many of the biodiversity priorities, however, were known by mid-2000, when the second phase of the Yunnan Great Rivers Project began: implementing conservation actions in areas of high biodiversity significance. Assessing its internal capacity and invitations received from county governments, TNC chose to assist conservation at five of the nineteen priority sites identified by the biodiversity module of the "Action Plan" (Ou 2002). The Khawa Karpo massif, in an ethnically Tibetan area along Yunnan's border with the Tibet Autonomous Region (see map 2), was one of those sites (Salick and Moseley 2012). TNC's work at this site exemplifies interactions with villagers and local officials in designing and implementing conservation strategies that go beyond a singular focus on biodiversity and incorporate cultural sensitivity, traditional knowledge, and sustainable human use.

Following broad-scale priority setting, the primary analytical tool that TNC uses to achieve place-based conservation is the Conservation Action Plan (Poiani et al. 1998). In brief, the plan identifies focal biodiversity targets at a site, prioritizes current and future stressors to target viability, and identifies strategies that maintain species viability and ecological health. Concurrently, the organization conducts an analysis of sociopolitical conditions that assesses the linkages between proximate stressors (e.g., overharvesting of snow lotus by villagers) and the more distal drivers of those stressors (e.g., global commercial demand for natural medicines), which aids in designing strategies. A Conservation Action Plan is collaborative and dynamic and can be adjusted to accommodate new information and changing situations. The methodology has been tested and refined at many sites around the world.[5]

The Deqin County government initiated the process at Khawa Karpo by hosting a conference in October 2000. Among the eighty participants were villagers, local and provincial officials, ethnographic researchers, local religious leaders, domestic and international NGOs, and international tourism and park experts. The primary outcome of the conference was a set of recommendations from three breakout sessions: Policy and Public Participation, Cultural Preservation, and Biodiversity Conservation (Deqin County and The Nature Conservancy 2000). These recommendations provided clear direction for beginning development of a comprehensive conservation program. (Another prominent issue at the conference, a ban on mountaineering on Khawa Karpo Peak, is described in Litzinger 2004 and in the introduction to this volume.)

The conference set in motion a hectic schedule of information gathering. First, Yunnan scientists conducted biodiversity field inventories that cataloged and mapped the vegetation, flora, and fauna of the site (e.g., Ou et al. 2006). This basic biological information is fundamental to making competent decisions about conservation programs. Second, the planning team gathered expert opinion on priorities from a wide range of groups with knowledge or interest in Khawa Karpo conservation. TNC insisted that broad public input be integral to conservation decision making, reflected in the importance given this topic at the Deqin conference. Much of the early public input was gathered in a series of workshops, which followed the basic Conservation Action Plan process outlined by Moseley (2000). Several workshops were held with local officials, a local conservation NGO, and Kunming-based

FIGURE 5.1   Zhila Village lies on the eastern slope of the Khawa Karpo massif in Deqin County, Yunnan. Village-level Conservation Action Planning workshops took place here and in five neighboring villages. Photo by Robert K. Moseley.

biological scientists. In addition, workshops, in the form of modified Participatory Rural Appraisals, were held in villages to gather their views on conservation priorities (fig. 5.1). With Photovoice, another participatory tool, villagers used cameras to independently document their priorities and interactions with the environment (China MAB 2005). This photo-novella technique was first developed for a rural reproductive health project in southern Yunnan, and its goals were to "empower rural women to record and reflect their lives, especially health needs, from their own point of view . . . and to inform policymakers and the broader society about health and community issues that are of greatest concern to rural women" (Wang, Burris, and Xiang

1996, 1391). TNC's use of the Photovoice technique in northwest Yunnan had similar general goals, with environment replacing reproductive health as the subject of interest and an expansion to other segments of the village population that included a balance of age, gender, and economic status. At Khawa Karpo, forty-three photographers from seven villages took part in the project, producing fourteen thousand photos and accompanying stories (Salick and Moseley 2012, 29).

Although the Conservation Action Plan process is logical to follow, and TNC used it successfully to gather local information and implement conservation at the five Yunnan Great River Project sites, it still represented a top-down process driven by outside technicians, both Chinese and expatriate. It is now clear that TNC did not fully comprehend villagers' perceptions and values related to nature, conservation, the organization itself, and its affiliation with the Chinese government. Later synthesis of opinions from all the workshops, in combination with employment of biodiversity data and sophisticated information technologies, further created a power differential between villagers (and county resource managers) and outsiders. Even Photovoice, whose aim was to enable villagers to be heard and to equalize power relations by having them drive the documentation and dissemination of knowledge, was not well integrated into the standardized Conservation Action Plan process. Photovoice was somewhat experimental then, this being the first time the technique had been used for conservation planning, and there was a significant lag between the availability of information and the Conservation Action Plan timeline. The sheer volume of information collected by Photovoice also presented analysis and synthesis challenges. TNC later developed a cultural Conservation Action Plan process in Central America after Yunnan planning was complete. All of these efforts to incorporate local perspectives in conservation, however, will probably never fully equalize the conservation discourse in China between villagers and powerful outsiders, be they government agencies or NGOs.

Another disadvantage of the standard Conservation Action Plan process is its near-exclusive focus on threats to biodiversity as the basis for developing conservation strategies. While it became clear over time that culturally driven attributes at Khawa Karpo could overlap with conservation objectives, they did not fit well into the existing process. In fact, a summary of the early Conservation Action Plan at Khawa Karpo (Moseley et al. 2004) did not mention any cultural opportunities. Only strategies directly related to stressors on biodiversity were taken seriously. Despite this, TNC staff

FIGURE 5.2   Khawa Karpo Peak looms above Mingyong Village and is the abode of an eponymous god important to Buddhists throughout the Tibetan world. The sacred status of this peak has created a sizable sacred geography across the massif that has positive implications for conservation. Photo by Robert K. Moseley.

decided to step outside of the formalized process and engage ethnographers and ethnoecologists in an effort to explore new ways of integrating cultural knowledge into the design and implementation of conservation strategies (Salick and Moseley 2012). This propensity of local staff to buck top-down organizational standards that overlook cultural knowledge has been observed elsewhere (Alcorn 2005).

Here we describe two examples of local staff using cultural knowledge in designing conservation programs at Khawa Karpo. The first example involves the sacred geography of Tibetan Buddhism. The status of Khawa Karpo Peak (fig. 5.2) as a holy mountain to Tibetans is well known and is reviewed in the introduction to this volume. Still more widely known is the contribution that sacred landscapes, such as holy mountains, make to conservation worldwide (Verschuuren et al. 2011), in eastern Tibet (Studley 2011), and in Yunnan (Pei 2011; Xu Jianchu et al. 2005). At the regional level, supporting practices that maintain sacred landscapes was one of the conservation strategies recommended by the cultural module of the "Action Plan" (JPO 2001). Cultural geographies were initially outside the experience of most TNC staff, who found them difficult to understand. Luckily, an ethnographer from the Yunnan Academy of Social Sciences, Guo Jing, a passionate advocate for local knowledge and rights, helped the organization explore the spatial relationships of sacred mountain worship around Khawa Karpo (Guo 2000b). Guo later handed off the ethnographic work to two colleagues from the academy and Yunnan University, both local Tibetans. Fully recognizing from the beginning that it is spiritually based and does not depend on the principles of ecological science, they documented a spiritually driven zoning system on Khawa Karpo that nevertheless makes significant contributions to biodiversity conservation (Anderson et al. 2005; Salick et al. 2007). This work later evolved under the direction of Tibetan TNC staff members and was integrated into the strategies that the organization was implementing at Khawa Karpo (Salick and Moseley 2012), although it still did not flow from the threat-based Conservation Action Plan process.

A second example involves the traditional ecological knowledge of local Tibetans. One of the more absurd aspects of the standard process at the time was that local conservation staff were compelled to tell villagers that they were a threat to biodiversity (e.g., in relying on fuelwood as a primary energy source), and this was often treated as a type of transaction cost on the way to effective conservation (e.g., reduce their fuelwood use in order to save primary forest). At best, this was an awkward way to begin collaboration, and, at worst, it was morally and sometimes factually wrong (Moseley 2006, 2011). Another way to approach this, again outside the formal process, is to recognize that Tibetans have been stewards of biological diversity at Khawa Karpo for centuries and that they possess knowledge about sustainable management that is outside the usual threat-based information gathering (Ou 2002). Essentially, TNC staff took a humble approach, recognizing that Tibetans need not simply wait for top-down "enlightened intervention by the ecological scientific community" (Litzinger 2006, 75). Beginning in 2001,

TNC teamed up with ethnoecologists from the Missouri Botanical Garden to explore the relevance of traditional Tibetan land management to conservation at Khawa Karpo. Botanical Garden researchers were highly successful in identifying Tibetan practices that contribute to conservation at many scales, from the agrodiversity of village crops to climate change adaptation across landscapes (Byg and Salick 2009; Gunn et al. 2010). Their prolific findings do not, however, valorize all Tibetan land uses. For example, the commercial harvest of some high-elevation medicinal plants for national and international markets was clearly unsustainable (Law and Salick 2005).

Missouri Botanical Garden research provided new models that allowed us as TNC staff members to learn from and reinforce these traditional practices and help equalize power relations in the biopolitics of sustainable development and conservation. For example, the models incorporate the perspectives of diverse groups of experts in setting research and conservation priorities for Tibetan medicinal plants; locally trained and Lhasa-trained Tibetan doctors were consulted, along with professional botanists (Law and Salick 2007). At another level, the research team quantified the conservation contribution of intangible elements of Tibetan culture, such as sacred forest groves in villages (Salick et al. 2007). This collaboration between ethnoecology researchers and conservation practitioners from the beginning of the project created a Tibetan-community-centered approach to conservation at Khawa Karpo, especially compared to the central-government-driven initiatives and regulations that largely ignored local knowledge and traditions (Salick and Moseley 2012). Put another way, local Tibetan knowledge and traditions were not treated as simply transaction costs on the way to conservation outcomes (West and Brockington 2006).

POSTSCRIPT ON THE NATURE CONSERVANCY IN YUNNAN

The events described above occurred during 2000–2005 (see ch. 4 in this volume for a discussion of TNC in Yunnan after 2005). Expatriate staff started and directed the Khawa Karpo program for TNC during 2000–2002, and Tibetan staff led the project until 2009. Two dramatic events occurred in late 2008 and early 2009 that decreased TNC's presence at Khawa Karpo. The first was the global economic recession that began in late 2008 and dramatically reduced the private philanthropy that supports the organization's programs throughout the world. TNC reduced its staff 10 percent worldwide in 2009, and this included major program cutbacks in China. At the same time, a leadership change in TNC China led to a different vision for the program, especially in light of dramatically tightened budgets. The difficulty foreign NGOs encounter while operating in Tibetan areas of China after 2008 was an additional factor in decisions about the Khawa Karpo project. Consequently, TNC's presence in Yunnan and at Khawa Karpo was reduced. The center of gravity for the organization in China shifted from Yunnan to Beijing and was reoriented toward place-based work in other provinces and engagement with national and regional initiatives.

TNC's Deqin office closed in 2010, although it continued to be engaged in the Meili Snow Mountains National Park project. Nearly from the beginning of its work in China, TNC recognized that the Chinese "nature reserve" designation was not appropriate for all situations and that another type of conservation area was needed that allowed a greater level of human use and occupation. This idea originated in the IUCN classification scheme of global conservation areas but also stemmed from the intense need for local officials to generate income as part of the Great Western Development strategy. Starting with Yunnan, TNC worked to expand the suite of conservation designations to include what became known as "national parks," a conservation area that accommodates greater human use compared to nature reserves (Grumbine 2010, 60). First applied at Pudacuo, Shangrila County (Zinda 2012a) (also see ch. 4 in this volume), the model is now being implemented at Laojun Mountain in Yulong County (Zhou and Grumbine 2011) and in the Meili/Khawa Karpo mountains of Deqin County (Zinda 2012b) (see also ch. 4 in this volume). Tensions between conservation and economic development were apparent at Pudacuo and Meili, as well as between TNC as a conservation advocate, local governments as the primary "owners" of parks, and their tourism development companies, whose mission is to maximize income (Zinda 2012a, 2012b). In late 2011, TNC ended its involvement in the Meili park project because these differences could not be reconciled to its satisfaction. TNC remains involved in the Laojun Mountain National Park project, where local community participation and benefit goals are stronger.

WESTERN SOCIAL SCIENTISTS CRITIQUE
THE NATURE CONSERVANCY

Almost from the inception of the Yunnan Great Rivers Project, a corps of Western social scientists has studied, written, and presented on how TNC engaged and interacted with different elements of Chinese and Tibetan society. The organization provided an attractive research objective: one of the biggest transnational conservation NGOs in partnership with the largest Communist government working with an ethnically diverse and economically impoverished population inhabiting a beautiful mountain region. We left China in 2005, and up to that time, seven Western social scientists had studied various parts of TNC's work.[6] A new wave of Western researchers has taken up where these scholars left off.[7]

Their critiques span the range of geographic and social scales and involve different facets of social science research. They touch on global conservation financing, partnership with the Chinese government, national conservation programs, regional conservation planning, site-level conservation approaches, tourism sustainability, and interactions with domestic experts and local communities, among others. Three thematic areas emerged from our examination of these critiques that yield insights on how to improve conservation practice, such as the weaknesses discussed above, and, more generally, suggest ways that social scientists can better engage conservationists in helping them negotiate the transition from a legacy of seeing people only as threats to nature to an approach that is culturally just and sustainable.[8]

Scales of Engagement

Effective modern conservation requires action at all scales. Addressing environmental stressors at the local scale (e.g., climate warming impacts on medicinal plant populations and yak butter production) will solve only part of the problem and must be addressed simultaneously at the national (e.g., governmental policies that hinder local climate adaptation) or even global scale (e.g., reducing greenhouse gas emissions). While much of the critique of TNC and other international NGOs focuses on their size, extent of geographic and political reach, and embeddedness in global capitalism, conservation investments made at the local scale can be wasted if larger scales are not addressed. For instance, an investment made in fuel-efficient stoves that reduce reliance on fuelwood can be wiped out (literally) by ignorance of river-damming hydropower development plans at the broader policy level. All social scientists who studied TNC in the early years (1999–2002) seemed from our perspective to misunderstand its motivations in setting regional conservation priorities with the provincial government at one scale and place-based conservation in villages at the other. This may be due to poor communication. To be clear, TNC's approach holds that conservation strategies are most effective when integrated across scales and, while priority setting is best done across biophysical units such as river basins, that conservation will always be implemented by political entities, be they villages, counties, provinces, or nations.

Related to this is the criticism that describes TNC as naive or even having ulterior motives in engaging higher levels of the Chinese government. This plays out in most critiques with regard to TNC's interactions with local cultures. While the organization gets some credit for trying to empower villagers, most critiques point out (with some validity) that TNC failed to understand the nuanced complexity of local culture and misrepresented this at higher political levels. The organization's cooperation with the Chinese government is represented as bad, either explicitly or implicitly, and is generally thought to have been motivated by the desire for more power and the ability to raise more money. The reality is that engaging higher political levels is a conscious choice made with the stakes for local places in mind. In fact, Brosius and Russell (2003, 52) recommend this focusing-up approach, in which "effective conservation must be grounded in the effort to change wider structures." As they put it, persistent structural problems favor ruling elites and their allies by maintaining perverse incentives that local communities alone cannot resist. But the cards are stacked against this struggle to change perverse structural inertia. In our view, TNC and all conservation NGOs combined are but a speck compared to the truly hegemonic economic and development forces that are homogenizing global diversity, both biological and cultural (Redford and Brosius 2006).

Whose Knowledge Counts?

Social scientists vigorously debate the meanings of apparently simple adjectives, such as "traditional," "indigenous," "native," "local," and "community-based," arguing that they are in fact enormously complex and demonstrating the political implications of their use. In critiques of TNC in Yunnan, this debate seems to us to be over who is the authentic voice for culture and conservation. While some argue that all voices, in all their complexity, should count, most critiques explicitly or implicitly suggest that one group or another represents the true interests and identities of a particular polity in a specific time and place. This crisscrossing discourse, inconsistent across the various critiques, is confusing and difficult for conservation practitioners, and practical guidance from social theorists on how to negotiate this tricky realm would be welcome.

Much has been written about TNC's attempt to use Tibetan spiritual beliefs, specifically, sacred landscapes, as a foundation for conservation. This effort has been subjected to a wide range of critique, from simple naïveté about the effectiveness of these landscapes for protecting nature to appropriation of Tibetan sacred geography for sinister marketing motives. The common thread that links these criticisms appears to be the question of who can legitimately speak for and about local sacred landscapes. In retrospect, the project did not adequately take into account the fact that the concept of nature originates in Western knowledge traditions and has little meaning in Tibetan societies (Huber and Pedersen 1997). It became more evident over time that maintenance of culture was the primary motivation for Tibetans who engaged with the project and that this concern for culture means that a biodiversity component cannot be easily compartmentalized (Yeh 2007).

Nevertheless, TNC's decision to promote the use of Tibetan sacred landscapes as a foundation for conservation was informed by a broader global discourse. The relationship between conservation and spiritual beliefs, generally, and sacred natural lands, specifically, has been widely acknowledged in the literature (e.g., Berkes 2008; Verschuuren et al. 2011). Scientists and activists have documented Tibetan case studies of sacred landscapes and environmental protection (e.g., Guo 2000b; Huber 2004; Studley 2011). The Central Tibetan Administration also expresses this view, though social scientists have pointed out both the rationales for and the problems with these representations (Huber 1997; Lopez 1998, 199; Yeh 2009a).

Similarly, Chinese ethnographers have pleaded for recognition of local cultural landscapes in an otherwise centralized, top-down conservation hierarchy. Their entreaties came through loud and clear from Chinese social scientists with whom TNC worked to create the regional "Action Plan." In order to assure that this momentum continued at Khawa Karpo, the project relied on Chinese as well as local Tibetan ethnographers to design the program. Tibetan staff members collaborated with a local NGO, the Khawa Karpo Culture Society (see ch. 1 in this volume), to continue this work. Throughout these collaborations, local religious leaders and guides interpreted the sacred landscape around villages. The documentation of sacred geographies convinced some TNC staff that a Chinese nature reserve was not appropriate for Khawa Karpo due to the possibility that onerous, centralized regulations would supplant conservation traditions that, in some cases, are centuries old. In fact, if Tibetan spiritual beliefs are maintained, no modern protected area designation may be needed at all. It remains to be seen whether the new national park concept being rolled out at Khawa Karpo will do that. The current prognosis for success is mixed (see ch. 4 in this volume).

It is instructive to note the contrast between Western and Chinese social scientists in terms of the threats on which they focus. On the one hand, Chinese ethnographers (both TNC collaborators and those outside the project) have recently begun advocating for ways to legitimize local traditions, beliefs, and knowledge in a strongly centralized governance system that has suppressed them in the past (Hathaway 2010a). On the other hand, Western social scientists expressed concerns about authenticity and authority that did not appear to recognize or acknowledge the known threats to Tibetan culture emanating from the state and the broader political context that were the concern of the Chinese specialists. Other commentators questioned TNC's attempts to legitimize local traditions within the larger Chinese government system, suggesting that this arrangement was fraught with the threat of appropriation.[9]

These differences in approach between Western and Chinese social scientists may stem from historical baggage in both Western (Brosius 2006) and Chinese (Litzinger 2000) social science. Just as early natural scientists witnessed the loss of biological richness in places where they lived and became conservationists, Yunnan social scientists are witnessing the loss of a rich cultural diversity and are desperate to find ways of stemming that loss. At Khawa Karpo, for example, it was these scholars who persistently pointed out the unseen sacred geographies of Tibetan Buddhism that were outside the biophysical geographies TNC ordinarily maps for conservation. Rightly or wrongly, these Chinese social scientists seem less hung up on theoretical deconstruction than their Western counterparts and take a much more practical approach to culture and conservation. And because conservationists are nothing if not applied scientists, they tend to listen to practical solutions.

Several Western social scientists raised another issue about authority and representation, this one involving TNC staff in China. During the organization's early years in Yunnan (ca. 1999–2002), expatriate American staff were the most visible and possibly the most approachable for Western researchers. As a result, some of the critiques allude to an international NGO staffed by foreigners, apparently implying questionable legitimacy. While this was never the case (even in its early years, TNC had an even mix of expatriates and Chinese), it definitely was not the case by 2005, when the China Program staff of more than fifty included very few expatriates. Further, ethnic minorities from northwest Yunnan have always been part of TNC's staff, including its first employee in China. Until the Yunnan office was downsized in 2009, they filled positions at all levels of the organization, including leadership (see the introduction to this volume). These staff members, as ethnic "elite," are often considered contaminated, inauthentic, and corrupted and are ignored, as was found in a study of the Yao in Guangxi (Litzinger 2000). While some Western anthropologists seem to dismiss anyone who is not a villager as incapable of authentically representing minority ethnic interests and identities, these ethnic elite also represent legitimate voices in the biopolitics of northwest Yunnan and are uniquely and productively working across the necessary scales of conservation.

Application

TNC uses an adaptive management framework whereby it adjusts strategies based on new knowledge and changed situations. With peer review as an integral part of the process, the organization is constantly learning from multiple disciplines and adjusting strategies in response to new knowledge. Although easily stated, learning across disciplines is much more difficult in practice, especially between the social sciences and biological sciences (Fox et al. 2006). One of the major factors inhibiting meaningful collaboration between these disciplinary realms is that conservation biology is, at its core, an applied science, and it appears that much of Western social science tends not to be, at least in our Yunnan experience. While examining theoretical dimensions is fundamental to any discipline, we believe that in conservation, particularly, it is important to translate theory and rhetoric into practice.

In the case of Yunnan critiques, this would mean reaching beyond the social science academy and offering more than the simple deconstruction of environmental discourse. Anthropologists and social theorists could take up the challenge by communicating their critiques "in and through a process of meaningful engagement with those whose practices they are examining. Rather than standing on the outside, we need to work with conservation practitioners and offer our analyses in ways that subject our own critiques to examination" (Brosius 2006, 685).

This sort of engagement may help social scientists eliminate the high number of factual errors observed in the Yunnan critiques, some passed along from one journal article to another. The conservationists studied by social scientists may be less dismissive of critiques of their practices if such errors were reduced. It would also help to place research in a temporal context. Although the studies sometimes state the dates of research, the narratives often come across as confidently timeless. To us, the events covered by these narratives seemed like ancient history by the time the research results became publicly available. Economic and development trends in China are changing at blinding speed. Conservation is no different, and TNC programs in Yunnan had to rapidly evolve and adjust to changing situations and new knowledge that were not reflected in the critiques. Related to this, research excursions on which the Western critiques were based were of short duration, ranging from one meeting to two years. Although usually not acknowledged as such, these were just snapshots in time, especially compared to the longer residency of subjects and programs being studied. These and other factors created walls between social scientists and conservation practitioners and unnecessarily inhibited acceptance of valid criticisms.

One outcome of an engagement between academic social science and practicing conservationists would be translation of the critical perspective of modern social theory into understandable language and applications that challenge conservationists to think differently about their interactions with society. The natural sciences teach us that turning theory and data into application takes time and is not easy. At the least, it means altering vocabulary and communication style. Much more difficult to redress is the lack of rewards given to application in current academic social science. In the past, these and other factors have been barriers to cross-discipline collaboration (Mascia et al. 2003), but conservation now appears ready to collaborate with social scientists as never before.

CONCLUSION

Like most NGOs and many government agencies involved in conservation these days, TNC is trying to integrate appropriate human use and social goals into actions that maintain and restore the Earth's biosphere. But there are social costs and social benefits to conservation programs. Conservation organizations have tended to emphasize the benefits (e.g., clean air and water, sustainable water supply, maintenance of nature-based ways of life) and downplayed or been silent about the costs (e.g., disruption of social systems, economic limitations on resource use) (Springer 2009). So it was with conservation in the Yunnan Great Rivers Project: TNC and its government partners were focused on social benefits, and Western social scientists pointed out the social costs incurred in implementing biodiversity conservation strategies that routinely involve decisions about land use and access to natural resources. As reviewed above, TNC was ill prepared in many ways to deal with the cultural setting into which it stepped in northwest Yunnan in 1998. Reliance on Chinese social scientists helped incorporate social benefits at the local level, but, possibly because the scientists were aligned with government institutions, the project did not place enough stress on the social costs. In the end, TNC made mistakes, learned lessons, and adjusted conservation strategies based on contributions from all disciplines, including the social sciences.

Encouragingly, the integration of social science into applied conservation problem solving is becoming more common among both academics and practitioners. TNC now has several social science disciplines represented among its program leaders, from human ecology to indigenous rights to resource economics. This is part of a larger trend among conservation organizations, most notably the International Union for Conservation of Nature, which has the longest history in this endeavor. It has integrated social science and culture into several of its commissions; for example, the Commission on Environmental, Economic and Social Policy is organized into a number of thematic discussion groups that include social scientists, biologists, and conservation practitioners, and the World Commission on Protected Areas has a Cultural and Spiritual Values Specialists Group. Cross-discipline collaboration is taking place in professional societies, including the Society for Conservation Biology, which formed a Social Science Working Group in 2003 with the mission, among other things, of building social science capacity among conservation practitioners. Academic social scientists are also bringing their intellects to bear on this, with case studies by anthropologists and geographers that explicitly acknowledge the stakes of ecological degradation on both natural and social systems (Stevens 1997). Recent case studies reconciling conservation action with its social costs include unsustainable timber harvest in Finland (Berglund 2006) and wildlife conservation in southeastern China (Coggins 2003).

These hopeful trends toward integration and cross-discipline collaboration bode well for the future of conservation in Shangrila. These theoretical underpinnings and social science applications, which were not readily available at the time TNC launched its Yunnan project, will allow future conservation practitioners to better discover and explain the social context in which they work, similar to what conservationists have done biophysically for decades. Integrating social sciences into conservation will not be a panacea. Many issues will still be extraordinarily challenging, for example, addressing multi-scale stressors on cultural integrity and the environment and the chronically unequal power relations in conservation. But the consistent and persistent focus of early conservationists on preserving remnants of primeval nature is now untenable. While it succeeded in elevating biodiversity conservation in the global consciousness, that single-mindedness is no longer beneficial. It is now time to blend social science seamlessly into the many disciplines of conservation to create the best outcomes for a sustainable planet that allows all life to flourish.

5. THE NATURE CONSERVANCY IN SHANGRILA

1   See Stephenson and Chaves 2006 for a critical analysis of the *Washington Post* coverage and TNC's response in the aftermath.

2   Moseley was among the handful of Chinese and expatriates who established TNC in northwest Yunnan beginning in 2000. Mullen came to China in 2003 as part of a central science team, to test and refine conservation planning methods in new places around the world. We both worked for TNC operating units before coming to China and after we left in 2005.

3   TNC now uses sociocultural outcomes, including human well-being, along with biodiversity in prioritizing conservation action and measure success.

4   Xu and Wilkes (2004) later put the ethnobiology case studies in a regional context.

5   For a review of the initial process for Khawa Karpo, which took place from 2000 to 2003, see Moseley et al. 2004.

6   Pre-2005 social scientists who studied TNC in Yunnan are Erlet Cater, professor at University of Reading (Cater 2000); Ralph Litzinger, professor at Duke University (Litzinger, 2004, 2006, 2007); Giovanni da Col, then a PhD candidate at the University of Cambridge (da Col 2006a, 2006b); Kenneth Bauer, then a PhD candidate at the University of Oxford (Bauer 2006); Justin Zackey, then a PhD candidate at the University of California, Los Angeles (Blaikie and Muldavin 2004; Zackey 2005); Michael Hathaway, then a PhD candidate at the University of Michigan (Hathaway 2004, 2006, 2007, 2009, 2010a); and Setsuko Matsuzawa, then a PhD candidate at the University of California, San Diego (Matsuzawa 2007). We would like to thank Giovanni da Col and Ralph Litzinger for many long discussions about this body of research.

7   Post-2005 social scientists who studied TNC in Yunnan are not included in our analysis because we were not personally involved in some of the programs they critique: Jennifer Dinaburg, master's candidate at Prescott College (Dinaburg 2008); Katherine Fritz, undergraduate student at New York University (Fritz 2009); Edward Grumbine, professor at Prescott College (Grumbine 2010; Zhou and Grumbine 2011); Juhyung (Jenny) Cho, master's candidate at the University of Oslo (Cho 2011); John Zinda, a PhD candidate at the University of Wisconsin (Zinda 2012a, 2012b).

8   Our analysis includes the fifteen references cited in note 6. Our objective is not a point-by-point rebuttal of individual critiques but a synthesis of what they collectively tell us about conservation practice and the interaction of Western social scientists with conservationists.

9   There are numerous examples of Western society conflating indigenous peoples with nature, maybe most famously the Western romance with Tibetans (Lopez 1998).

CHAPTER 6

Transnational
Matsutake Governance

• • •

ENDANGERED SPECIES, CONTAMINATION, AND THE
REEMERGENCE OF GLOBAL COMMODITY CHAINS

Michael J. Hathaway

A T dawn during the late summer and early fall, one can stand on a hill-side in the Sino-Tibetan borderlands and look down as hundreds of lights flick on in valley villages, like the stars emerging, but in reverse, for the night is ending rather than beginning. Unlike stars in the sky, these points of light are moving. They are flashlights, carried by villagers walking up into the mountains to hunt for a mushroom the Japanese call *matsutake* and the Chinese call *song rong*. People collect all morning and return home when the dealers arrive at a village market or drive along the roads, buying from mushroom hunters as they go, for the matsutake is highly valued in Japan. The mushrooms are carried in a shoulder satchel, often hand-fashioned from fertilizer or pig food bags, the durable everyday sack of rural China. The mushrooms are carefully cushioned in these satchels, as they can be easily damaged during a long hike over steep terrain. When hunters find a prize specimen, they wrap it in a layer of thin plastic film, or they may snap off the tip of a rhododendron branch, place the mushroom against it, and wrap grass around the mushroom, cinching it snugly, like a baby in a cradle. Over the season, millions of the mushrooms travel from these borderland villages to local buying centers and bulking stations, and then to Japan, all within forty-eight hours, for they are very delicate and insects are already starting to eat them.

How did matsutake, barely known in Yunnan's markets thirty years ago, become the province's largest agricultural export crop, now providing employment for well over half a million people (Yang et al. 2008, 270)? What does the rapid rise of Yunnan as the most important production site for the matsutake trade, globally worth billions of dollars a year (Amend et al. 2010), tell us about the changing dynamics of nature and society in the Sino-Tibetan borderlands? The Chinese state's position toward the environment has undergone a remarkable transformation over the past half century (Hathaway 2013), from the Mao-era "war against nature" (Shapiro 2001) to the goal of building an "environmental state" or "ecological state," one that actively pursues a number of environmental priorities (Goldman 2001; Lang 2002; Mol and Buttel 2002).

The matsutake economy reveals important aspects of environmental governance and the workings of an environmental state. Forms of governance are often regarded as a set of rules created and enforced by states. Many scholars of governance incorporate perspectives from Michel Foucault, who argued that power is not wielded by leaders but is diffused widely through capillary networks, yet many still often imply that the state is the source of new forms of discipline and management (Brown 2006). However, it is clear in the matsutake economy, and in many other cases, that governance is shaped by a range of actors, both domestic and transnational.

Studies of the ecological state can be generally divided into two groups, normative and critical. On the one hand, motivated by the need to achieve environmental sustainability, normative scholars focus on how states become more environmentally friendly (Dryzek et al. 2003). Critical scholars, on the other hand, are concerned about the negative outcomes of state-based conservation programs, particularly for rural subaltern communities in the Global South. They ask how conservation may dispossess such groups of land and resources needed for a decent living, such as firewood, water, or agricultural land (Goldman 2001; Peet and Watts 1996; Peluso 1993). Although both groups take distinctly different positions, each tends to view the state as the main social actor and citizens either as relatively powerless to enjoin the state to assume greater ecological responsibility or as resistant subjects working to lessen the blow of state-led conservation efforts.

In order to understand the dynamics of environmental management in contemporary China, we need a broader view that goes beyond the "state as container" model and explores how management policies and activities are affected by other states and a range of private and private-public engagements, including international conservation organizations, networks of traders, and scientists. For example, Chinese scientists' concerns that matsutake is threatened by overharvest led to its inclusion in international legislation for endangered species, and Japanese consumers' fears about matsutake being contaminated by pesticides have led Chinese nongovernmental organizations to initiate campaigns to reduce the use of chemicals in rural Yunnan. In other words, a transnational perspective provides greater insights into how and why environmental management is changing in contemporary China, particularly in the Sino-Tibetan borderlands, where these connections are deeply shaped by particular historical and social conditions. Rather than seeing resource governance as engineered by the state, we can deploy a perspective that shows how demarcations of nature-as-commodity are dispersed, multiple, and overlapping. The network of state and non-state actors in the matsutake trade links an international commodity chain with local resource management practices in a region that was embedded within expansive overland trade networks before 1949. In this context, contemporary international laws regulating traffic in endangered species, efforts to enhance matsutake growth in Japan by decreasing air pollution levels in China, and techniques for reducing pesticide contamination in mushrooms are among a panoply of environmental governance practices that affect people and nature in a region that is often thought of as "remote" but is experiencing the reemergence of global trade.

A BRIEF HISTORY OF TRADE AND RULE
IN THE SINO-TIBETAN BORDERLANDS

A transnational approach is not only helpful for understanding the contemporary period but also useful in looking at the past, even before the rise of the nation-state itself. The very fact of calling these areas "borderlands" hints at problems with the "container model" of the state. The term suggests that rather than projecting the boundaries of contemporary nation-states such as China, India, Myanmar, Thailand, and so forth back into time, we might look instead at how these areas have been historically influenced by several sources of imperial power that radiated outward in uneven ways (Winichakul 1997). Rule was less singular and absolute than plural and frequently challenged, in part because identities and loyalties were multiple and in flux (Giersch 2006).

Before officials in the People's Republic of China severed many informal connections with neighboring lands, the Sino-Tibetan borderlands were a thriving zone for the movement of people, goods, and ideas. For centuries, caravans of mules, horses, and yaks have plied these routes, stretching from lowland tropical rain forests to some of the highest places on earth.[1] Located near the Southern Silk Road that brought goods east and west, the area was also transected by a route running north and south called the "Ancient Tea-Horse Road" which connected southern Yunnan and Southeast Asia with the Sino-Tibetan borderlands and India (Hill 1998; Mu 2001; B. Yang 2004). In addition to the traffic in horses and fermented tea, there was a vigorous trade in silver and other metals, wool, musk, and medicinal plants (Lu 1997). It was also the site of much military activity, with many battles fought among diverse groups such as imperial armies, local warlords, and religious factions.

Some scholars argue that these borderlands can be thought of as belonging to Zomia, a zone created by people who fled centralized imperial power and strove for local autonomy (Scott 2009). There is evidence that some groups arrived in this region while fleeing coercive rule, but for many, their actions were less motivated by the desire for isolation and are better understood as active efforts to forge selective connections (Jonsson 2010). Groups were part of multiple and shifting trade, governmental, religious, and military relations, with overlapping alliances and lingering disputes.[2] These groups were often dispersed, working with and against various incursions of imperial armies and officials, which ebbed and flowed with cycles of power, and were often devastated by disease and the high cost of ruling at a distance.

The story of matsutake reveals that the Sino-Tibetan borderlands are currently undergoing forms of re-internationalization. Since the 1980s, one of the many remarkable transformations in this region has been the important role of long-distance social and economic relations, which are not new but reemerging. In particular, transnational connections in the realms of trade, tourism, and nature conservation are increasingly shaping people's everyday lives. Japanese consumers and businesspeople play a significant role in these changes, as they import large amounts of matsutake and other foods (such as trout, wasabi, and konjak) and actively participate in tourism and tourism development.

THE RISE AND FALL OF JAPAN'S DOMESTIC MATSUTAKE PRODUCTION AND THE GLOBAL SEARCH FOR IMPORTS

Yunnan's participation in the worldwide matsutake economy was fostered by Japan's passion for the mushroom. Over the centuries, matsutake in

Japan transitioned from an elite domestic food to an increasingly cheap product that is mainly imported. Historically, matsutake was a sumptuary good in Japan, and there were laws against it being eaten by commoners— it was considered a food fit only for the imperial court (MacMurray 2003). Japan's production peaked in 1940, at a time when wartime victory in the Pacific seemed likely and a year before its forces attacked Pearl Harbor. By this point, matsutake had become an increasingly common luxury food for many people, but then Japan's production began to plummet. Between the 1940s and the 1970s, domestic production dropped approximately fivefold every fifteen to twenty years.[3]

Matsutake's precipitous decline in Japan was considered a national trag- edy, and many tried to explain why the mushrooms were disappearing. Biol- ogists discovered that forests were in decline, and it took scientists another decade to find that acid rain was damaging trees. Although they had long known about domestic air pollution, in the 1990s they showed for the first time that pollution was coming from abroad, mainly from Chinese coal- burning factories (Wilkening 2004).[4] Subsequently Japan, already China's most important trade partner and source of international development aid (Muldavin 2000), poured massive funds into retrofitting Chinese factories (Wilkening 2004).

Thus transnational connections shaped trade and environmental man- agement in China and Japan and influenced their governmental and non- governmental relations. In part, the expansion of the matsutake economy from a domestic to a global network was precipitated by the spread of pollu- tion from China to Japan, which undercut Japan's ability to provide for itself. Second, Japan's knowledge of pollution and pollution abatement, as well as its financial and technological support, stimulated a greater attempt by the Chinese state to document and ameliorate pollution.

As late as the 1970s, almost every matsutake eaten in Japan was produced domestically, but then imports began to explode. In 1980, Japan imported 362 metric tons; domestic production and imports were roughly equivalent, and soon after, imports increased. Within nine years, imports had increased almost sevenfold to 2,210 metric tons (Bracey 1990, cited in Redhead 1997). It was not that existing markets in other countries were redirected to Japan but instead that Japanese scientists and businessmen traveled abroad to search out new matsutake populations. Starting in 1978, Canada began shipping matsutake from British Columbia to Japan. Some pickers reportedly earned $1,000 in a week, even with the relatively low value of about C$10 per kilogram (Redhead 1997). In the same year, two Japanese researchers published a paper showing matsutake's distribution in the United States and Canada, revealing new places that pickers in Canada did not know about (Kinugawa and Goto 1978) and encouraging the development of a U.S. market.[5]

We do not have equally detailed accounts of the origins of the Chinese matsutake trade, but the Japanese colonial legacy stimulated China's first trade in the northeast in the late 1970s. Japan had known about matsutake there since its invasion of this region in the early twentieth century, when researchers surveyed exploitable natural resources, including minerals, timber, and mushrooms. After Japan's defeat in World War II, it pulled out of China, and until the 1970s, the rest of China, including the southwest region of the Sino-Tibetan borderlands, was terra incognita for Japanese scientists.

A number of stories tell of the origins of Yunnan's matsutake trade. I heard several times in Lijiang that Yunnan's matsutake were first brought to international attention in 1987 by a team of visiting Japanese scientists, who, posing as butterfly collectors, were actually searching for matsutake. They discovered it growing on the side of Jade Dragon Snow Mountain (Yulongxue Shan) and filled their sacks. Coming off the mountain, they were stopped and questioned by police and forced to reveal their true purpose.

In Japan, however, I learned that as early as 1981, three Japanese scientists—Yasuto Tominaga, Ryoko Arai, and Toshio Ito—traveled in search of Yunnan matsutake. They found it growing in the autonomous prefectures of Chuxiong, Dali, Lijiang, and Diqing and published their findings in the *Bulletin of the Hiroshima Agricultural College* (Tominaga, Ami, and Ito 1981). Their article does not reveal how they established contacts with Chinese, and it is nearly certain that they relied heavily on Chinese hosts as guides. In fact, much of the region north of Lijiang remained off-limits to foreigners until much later, so travel may have been quite difficult. They found that trade with Japan already existed but at a low level.[6] The mushrooms were driven to Kunming, flown to Beijing, and then proceeded onward to Japan. Word about China's matsutake quickly spread in Japan, as there are strong links between dealers and scientists, and Tominaga was one of Japan's prominent researchers.

By the mid-1980s, trade between the Sino-Tibetan borderlands and Japan became well established, mainly through a Chinese state-run system. The system used one of the enduring features of the Mao era, thousands of collection sites called "foreign trade stations" (*waimao zhan*), which had been built during the 1950s. Rural products were collected there and then sold by the national government, which controlled foreign trade.[7] Discussions with older matsutake pickers in the borderlands suggest that these stations exercised a virtual monopoly on matsutake purchases through the 1980s. Some of the stations tried to ship fresh mushrooms, but the mushrooms often suffered during their travels. The stations had few trucks, and these were mechanically unreliable on the rough roads to Kunming. Consequently, the stations dealt almost entirely in dried goods, such as herbal medicines and animal hides, which were sturdy and could be stored for long periods of time, unlike fresh mushrooms, which are quite perishable and delicate. Thus, mushrooms were pickled and shipped without refrigeration. They were washed and packed in salt water in plastic vats and fitted with tight-sealing lids so that they could last for weeks, if not months, but their value was low. By the 1990s, more independent buyers entered the fray, often first as petty traders. They would crowd into the back of a truck with other traders and sell a large basket of matsutake at a regional trade center, such as Zhongxin Town in Shangrila (see map 1, C) or Nanhua County in Chuxiong Prefecture.

During the 1990s, as the government slowly relaxed its monopoly on foreign trade, some private exporting companies started to specialize in matsutake, trading in other goods during the ten-month off-season. In some cases, the head managers for the Kunming-based private companies were former staff of the foreign trade stations and were able to use their contacts in China and Japan to cultivate relationships for their new company. This was part of a wider phenomenon, in which Chinese companies hired former government employees for their bureaucratic knowledge and social connections.

It took sustained effort and time, along with massive infrastructure change, before fresh Yunnan matsutake could predictably arrive in Japan in good condition.[8] This infrastructure included both hard and soft aspects, an organized system of people, markets, refrigeration, good roads, and coordinated airplane transportation. Even into the early years of the first decade of the 2000s, sections of the main arterial road connecting northwest Yunnan and Kunming were still unpaved and fitted with hand-laid cobblestones. As the matsutake season overlaps with the end of the monsoons, dealers face landslides that block high-mountain roads. These were some of the same roads used for centuries by mule caravans transporting goods within and beyond the Sino-Tibetan borderlands.

As matsutake has become increasingly important in the lives of people in northwest Yunnan, resource governance has intersected with changing social relations. The matsutake economy has fostered forms of intervillage conflict, but it has also stimulated a resurgence in the construction of Tibetan houses with vernacular art and architectural features that express new forms of cultural identity and wealth. Conflict was motivated by the high value of the mushroom as well as the history of shifting and ambiguous property rights and village boundaries, which has led to clashes over rights to especially productive areas (Yeh 2000). Such conflicts create a number of challenges; even when villagers devise management systems on village lands (see ch. 7 in this volume) or make agreements with their neighbors, more guards are sometimes required when matsutake's price skyrockets.

At the same time, however, the matsutake economy has allowed some families to earn salaries many times higher than those of city-based workers (Arora 2008).[9] The influx of cash into matsutake-wealthy areas has sponsored a building boom of "matsutake mansions" that has continued through 2011: large Tibetan homes made of massive structural posts, with intricate window carvings and colorful interior paintings.[10] Older women state that new homes and vehicles are the most important purchases they make with matsutake money and worry that their husbands squander money by gambling, which has increased with these new flows of cash. As people usually do not sell their homes,[11] houses represent a relatively safe and permanent investment, yet homes are rarely able to create wealth, unlike investments in vehicles. Some use their new vehicles to engage in matsutake trade or the tourism economy, but the latter often requires personal relations beyond the village and competition with more tourist-savvy operations in places like Shangrila and Deqin.

In 2007, the highest price for Japanese matsutake rose above $4,000 per kilogram (Murata et al. 2008), but prices fluctuate quickly, even within a single day. Such fantastically high values, now almost mythical, breed stories of fortunes won overnight. These stories help fuel the continued interest in picking and trading matsutake, even though prices in North America were closer to $60 per kilogram in recent years, while the price tends to be much lower in China.

Northwest Yunnan has been recently envisioned as both a new center for tourism and an ecological hotspot. In many ways, the expansion of trading networks has piggybacked on the infrastructure designed to facilitate tourism (such as improved roads, cell phone coverage, airports, and so forth), and so, too, has the growth of the conservation economy. Especially since the logging ban in 1998, regional officials and conservationists have been increasingly interested in fostering alternative sources of income; compared to long-established livelihoods such as pastoralism, matsutake has received disproportionate interest as an ecologically friendly possibility (see also Fedor 2006). International conservation organizations such as the World Wide Fund for Nature (WWF), the Nature Conservancy (TNC), and Conservation International (CI) took different approaches but often devoted their energies to creating official protected areas, such as Pudacuo National Park (see ch. 4 in this volume). These organizations often regarded human activities as environmentally detrimental and tried to restrict activities such as collecting fuelwood and medicinal plants in protected areas (Hathaway 2010a; Law and Salick 2007; Litzinger 2004).

TNC, which had often focused on promoting nature tourism as a way of providing local incentives for environmental conservation in areas south of Shangrila, fostered the idea of "sacred lands" in areas to the north. Especially given the stimulus of Bob Moseley's efforts (see ch. 5 in this volume), the organization documented, mapped, and supported official recognition of such lands. It argued for parallels between its own interest in official protected areas and long-existent practices of protecting certain sites, especially around temples or sacred places, from hunting and plant gathering. TNC staff spoke with disapproval of the ways cultural tourism operated as "song and dance shows" in Yunnan, such as Kunming's Ethnic Minority Village, and were concerned that such formats would be duplicated in Shangrila. TNC's efforts at ecological and cultural tourism included Yubeng, a relatively remote village located near a sacred waterfall on the Khawa Karpo pilgrimage circuit, which subsequently received international press, including a *New York Times* article and a show on National Public Radio (see the introduction to this volume).

In 1995, a few years before TNC's official opening in Yunnan, WWF left its initial project site in Yunnan's southern tropical rain forests (Hathaway 2010b) and established studies and projects in the northwest centered on the

White Horse Snow Mountain (Baimaxueshan) Nature Reserve (see map 2). WWF staff worked with reserve staff to advocate the formation of village-based management committees that would create a list of village-based rules around environmental sustainability and social equity, such as where and when to graze animals, collect firewood, and gather medicinal plants or matsutake. The rules tended to be relatively similar among villages, which were working off a fairly standard template.[12] By 2005, such rules had spread to more than fifty villages near White Horse Snow Mountain alone (Fedor 2006), yet a number of these rules proved difficult to enforce or were not always followed. Some rules, such as creating a "slack day" when no one was allowed to gather, have been largely abandoned (see ch. 7 in this volume). This was especially true for villages that are well endowed with matsutake and can have regular village-based markets. Dealers prefer to travel in a circuit to buy and sell, finding a route that is relatively efficient and profitable, and some said that village slack days make coordinating their stops more challenging. Furthermore, villagers, who have competing demands on their time, tend to gain and lose interest in matsutake in relation to its fluctuating value, another challenge to local management (Robinson 2012) (but see ch. 7 in this volume on different considerations for caterpillar fungus).

Key state programs that indirectly stimulated interest in matsutake through a reduction in other economic alternatives were the Sloping Land Conversion Program, which reduced grazing and set aside agricultural lands for reforestation, and the Natural Forest Protection Program, which imposed a logging ban. Logging revenues reached a peak in the early 1990s in Deqin, where it constituted as much as 80 percent of local government funding, earning more than ¥50 million annually (Xu and Wilkes 2004).[13] Permanent employees at government-run logging centers were promised new jobs, such as in tree-planting, whereas the temporary workers, often villagers, were not compensated for their loss of employment. In northwest Yunnan, temporary work with logging companies was one of the few wage labor opportunities before the development of the tourism economy. Soon after the logging ban, WWF conducted surveys near the White Horse Snow Mountain Nature Reserve in Diqing Prefecture and found that almost 95 percent of village income came from the sale of non-timber forest products; 80 percent was from matsutake alone (Chen 2001; Menzies and Li 2010).

The reduction in grazing and agricultural lands also changed social and natural landscapes. Officials enjoined villagers to plant seedlings in grasslands and cracked down on their use of fire to stop the spread of trees into grazing areas. Villagers were paid with grain and money to replace their farm plots with trees.[14] These actions worked against farming and grazing and unintentionally promoted the mushroom economy, but a new set of laws that made the matsutake an officially protected species had other effects.

ENDANGERED SPECIES AS A NEW FORM
OF ENVIRONMENTAL GOVERNANCE

One of the ways post-Mao China engaged the world was through participation in global environmental governance. In 1973, eighty countries signed the Convention on International Trade in Endangered Species of Wild Fauna and Flora (CITES), the first international agreement to manage the trade in endangered species. In 1981, China signed CITES, one of its earlier commitments to international legislation. For some time, China was largely passive, affected by CITES regulations that banned or reduced the flows of animals and animal parts (used as medicine, for food, or in making other products) from other countries. It established a CITES office in Kunming that specialized in policing the importation of endangered animals from Southeast Asia into China.[15] Eventually, plants began to be listed and policed as well.

Yet fungus was generally ignored by protected species rules, so it was quite surprising to many observers when in 1999, some Chinese scientists petitioned to have matsutake included on China's "Second-Class Protected Species" list.[16] After the inclusion was approved, matsutake were brought within the ambit of new forms of governance. The effects of this designation in terms of trade are not entirely clear—contrary to popular belief, the listing of a species as endangered or protected does not stop all trade. Instead, the key to CITES is the regulation of transnational trade: legally, traders must obtain official permits from the host country and may also need to negotiate permits with the recipient country. Thus, in Yunnan, matsutake-exporting companies must now obtain permits from the Chinese CITES office. One of the main effects of CITES status has been to ban international trade in small matsutake (less than five centimeters across), but Kunming-based dealers are now trying to create a domestic market in these smaller mushrooms.[17] Although a number of villages have rules against collecting small mushrooms, many still end up in Kunming, where they are often washed, frozen, and shipped domestically.

The threat of pollution and contamination influences regimes of environmental governance, especially those connected to trade goods. As mentioned earlier, Chinese air pollution damaged Japanese forests, prompting Japan to offer aid in remediating China's factories. One of the most challenging issues for Yunnan's matsutake trade concerns the possibility of contamination; this threatens to stop the entire industry, which has more than half a million participants. In 2002, Japan found pesticide on a shipment of Chinese matsutake and banned that importer for the rest of the year.[18] Since that time, pesticide detection machines have been installed at major export companies so that shipments of contaminated mushrooms can be identified before they leave China. These screenings now also include metal detectors, as villagers and dealers would add slivers of iron to the matsutake in order to increase their weight and, hence, their value.[19] Japan's suspicion that China is more generally an unreliable and unsafe source of food was reinforced in 2008, when Japan experienced what some called "global food terror" after a number of people were sickened by Chinese pork dumplings (Rosenberger 2009). The incident stimulated some public acknowledgment that Japan relies heavily on cheap imported foods, and many consumers were shocked to hear that China, as a single country, provided more than half of their total vegetable imports from around the world (Dyck and Ito 2004). Media reports emphasized that Japanese food is relatively safe but also acknowledged that it was too expensive for most ordinary citizens to rely on; likewise, as toxics-laden goods from China are discovered in other places, such as North America and Europe, there is a growing wariness of Chinese goods and at the same time a sense of resignation (Chinoy 2009).

While people in other countries may feel powerless to combat this threat, a number of people in China are proactive in dealing with potential problems stemming from both intentional pesticide use and unintentional contamination of mushrooms. Pesticides are widespread in China; for decades, the country has prided itself on the manufacture of agricultural chemicals and made significant efforts to encourage their use. The vast majority of rural households farm using agricultural chemicals, including on crops for their own consumption; there are few organic farmers. Pickers or dealers may apply chemicals to protect the matsutake from insects.

Most cases of contamination, however, likely occur unintentionally. In Yunnan, most agricultural plots are small and widely dispersed. The forests where matsutake are found are often relatively close to fields—unlike the vast matsutake forests in places like North America, which generally are found far from farms. As many farmers in China use pesticide sprayers, the chemicals can drift on the wind and enter the forests. Pesticides may also enter the commodity chain through the cloth sacks that pickers use for both matsutake and farm products.

Although many animal species, such as deer, pigs, and birds, seek out and enjoy matsutake, insects are the most common and serious threat. Indeed, it is quite rare to find mature matsutake without any insect damage. Although relatively large pests such as slugs chew slowly on the fungus and are easily removed, other pests search out the mushroom by crawling though soil and/or flying through the air. In many cases, insects lay eggs in the mushroom, and the larvae hatch and create small tunnels in the soft flesh. They are impossible to physically remove without destroying the mushroom itself. Thus, pickers and dealers have a strong incentive to reduce insect damage. Not only do insects harm individual mushrooms, but when dealers are bulking their goods, sometimes for more than twenty-four hours, thousands of mushrooms can be packed in close quarters, and the whole shipment is at risk of damage. Some told me that they use a "secret formula" to keep the mushrooms looking fresh but insisted that it was perfectly safe.

Thus, the dynamics of environmental governance include harvesting rules based on concerns for the mushroom's sustainability, as well as standards on pesticide contamination originally devised in Japan to increase food safety. Such standards now motivate the work of domestic NGOs promoting organic agriculture, which hope to leverage this threat to the province's most important export crop (Yang Xuefei et al. 2008) and shape agricultural practices throughout Yunnan. Chinese citizens, from scientists, to NGO activists, to villagers, are responding creatively to these regulations by developing methods that will foster chemical-free farming or reduce the risk of mushroom contamination.

For example, villagers use a variety of techniques to deal with insects. One innovation, said to have started in the region around Lijiang and Dali, has been to sprinkle a bucket of sand over the mushroom. This covering poses a challenge to flying insects, which have little ability to dig. Another option, more widely practiced by 2009, is to place a clear plastic tent over the mushroom, weighting it down around the sides to prevent flying insects from crawling under the edge. Some pickers say that the tent increases the internal humidity and warmth, making the mushroom grow faster. The use of either sand or plastic, however, increases the mushroom's visibility to other pickers. In most places, matsutake-picking grounds located close to villages are extremely well traveled and searched, with many people covering the same ground every day during the growing season. Although pickers often disguise their prize by sprinkling duff over sand- or plastic-covered mushrooms, they are more reluctant to risk discovery by other pickers in highly traveled areas.

The nonchemical techniques villagers use to protect their mushrooms from insects are also influenced by the kind of tenure regime that exists. In some villages, gathering rights for productive matsutake mountains are auctioned off to the highest bidder, and guards patrol the land. During the 1990s, there was a campaign to divide village forest lands into family plots, but in many cases, even where this happened, villages with more widely distributed matsutake decided to recollectivize the land, at least for the purpose of matsutake gathering. Where this has happened, it is acceptable to harvest any mushroom on village lands, and only rarely can one claim a growing (but not yet picked) mushroom as one's own.

Another major force advocating change in the Sino-Tibetan borderlands is the Yunnan Matsutake Association, which comprises the province's major exporting companies. The provincial government now limits the number of exporting companies, and they in turn have created a matsutake consortium. By 2006, only twenty companies had export licenses, and a number of these companies were led by people with extensive governmental networks, sometimes with a history of working at foreign trade stations in the 1980s. In 2011, the association's leaders expressed increasing interest in creating a "Yunnan Brand" for matsutake that is associated with purity but admitted that there are several weak points in the commodity chain. The sheer proliferation of sites and people who pick matsutake, as well as the frequency with which the mushrooms change hands,[20] means that tracing a particular mushroom "from field to table" has been nearly impossible. In contrast, vegetables grown for export on large commercial farms are often easy to trace.

Without a method for tracing mushrooms, it has been quite difficult to assign responsibility for pesticide contamination in the mushroom commodity chain. Some dealers blame villagers, many of whom are aware of this accusation. During my fieldwork in Tibetan villages in 2002, 2009, and 2010, many villagers declared that they never used pesticides, arguing that it was not part of their custom. Some even pointed to a widespread fungal blight on barley fields and claimed its presence as evidence that when problems arise, they do not turn to agricultural chemicals but instead just accept fate. Others suggested that the problem lay in the proliferation of petty matsutake dealers who briefly jump into the business, unconcerned about their reputation over the long term or the morality of their everyday actions over the short term. Indeed, numerous matsutake dealers at different scales have turned to new careers such as driving taxis, operating vegetable stands, or cutting hair.[21]

When the matsutake arrive in Kunming, most are sold wholesale in city markets, especially in those specializing in mushrooms, or brought directly to one of approximately a dozen major exporting firms that constitute the Yunnan Matsutake Association, all funded mainly by domestic support but with strong ties to Japan. The association supports the work of some scientists and helps fund international workshops, such as the one I helped organize in 2011, with researchers from North Korea, Japan, China, the United States, and Canada. Members of the association are quite interested in increasing Yunnan's matsutake yields, in part as they are under pressure from scientists and officials who worry that the mushroom may be overharvested. One of the association's major projects involves teaching villagers and local government officials how to borrow techniques from Japan that will increase matsutake production. To this end, the association paid for the translation of a key book from Japan that offers theory and methods for creating "matsutake mountains"; it instructs people on how to modify trees, forest duff, and soil to increase levels of production. After the book was translated into Chinese, the association printed and distributed it to officials and villagers in some of the main matsutake areas in northwest Yunnan. The association brought the author, Dr. Yoshimura, to the 2011 international workshop in Yunnan, where he gave a talk and offered suggestions during a field trip to some major matsutake sites.

The Yunnan Mushroom Association is also addressing the main concern of its member companies, the threat of pesticide-contaminated matsutake arriving in Japan. They are trying to build chains of responsibility, in which individual dealers are accountable for the mushrooms they deliver to the export companies. However, many of these higher-level dealers also buy from lower-level dealers, who buy from potentially hundreds of pickers. One effort, begun in 2009, was to make and distribute mushroom-picking bags with a set of rules printed on them and convince villagers to use these bags only for mushrooms, thus reducing the chances of accidental contamination at this level in the commodity chain.

In addition to reducing the risk of contamination within Yunnan, the

Yunnan Mushroom Association is hoping to improve business in several ways. First, its members are trying to better understand Yunnan's position in the world market. They are keen to grasp Yunnan's place among its international competitors, and a number of Chinese scholars have begun to investigate Japan's trade with Korea, the United States, and Canada in order to create new trade strategies. They have been asking such questions as, when are these other mushrooms produced, what kinds of prices are they receiving in Japan and why, and how does the price change over the season? They are also trying to better understand diversity within Japan: Do various markets demand different kinds of matsutake? Within the global ripening cycle, Yunnan's mushroom season is neither the earliest nor the latest; mushrooms that ripen earliest often fetch higher prices, as do those at the end of the season, when supplies are more limited. The association has also been trying to foster domestic interest in matsutake. For example, some dealers now sell frozen packs of matsutake that are too small for CITES approval to Chinese urban markets.[22] Some of these small frozen mushrooms travel on the same flights to Shanghai as the larger mushrooms bound for Japan that are shipped fresh, never frozen. Thus, while it is not clear that CITES has necessarily led to a reduction in the matsutake trade, it has unintentionally created a bifurcated market and fostered interest in stimulating domestic sales. CITES regulations have also given the state more control over exports, created a source of revenue, and ended up reducing the number of exporting companies.

CONCLUSION

The Chinese state remains powerful and has not been "hollowed out"—that is, weakened—by transnational corporations and nongovernmental agencies. In its emphasis on efforts to address desertification, flooding, air and water pollution, biodiversity loss, and so forth, the Chinese state has become increasingly "ecologized." The Sloping Land Conversion Program inspired many local government leaders to encourage the matsutake trade and has increasingly pushed villagers to turn away from logging and toward collecting non-timber forest products. Yet, forms of environmental governance are not simply monopolized by the Chinese state. These days, almost everyone involved in the harvest is aware that pesticides constitute a major problem, a far cry from China's celebratory posters of the 1960s, which showed young women proudly using insecticide foggers in large fields. A wide range of actors, Chinese and Japanese, including scientists, dealers, pickers, and customs inspectors, contributes to the working out of environmental governance.

This panoply of actors coming together in the governance of matsutake as a market resource in turn contributes to significant socio-ecological change in the Sino-Tibetan borderlands. At the same time, however, matsutake markets do not represent the first arrival of long-range trade in the area. They often utilize ancient trade routes formed over centuries of movements of a wide variety of goods and a wide range of people—not only traders but also pilgrims, soldiers, and officials. The shape of this economy, in turn, has been affected by recent developments in tourism and conservation—that is, by the processes of shangrilazation and the ecological state—which are bringing new constraints and opportunities to the region, but in ways that do not always unfold as predicted.

Even though matsutake prices have fallen since early in the first decade of the 2000s, hundreds of thousands of people still regularly participate in the matsutake market and invest their profits widely, such as by buying new homes or motorcycles or, in a few cases, sending their children to college in the United States. During the matsutake boom, a number of families started to sell off their herds of cattle, cattle-yak hybrids, and yaks, whereas now, herding may be on the rise, as people are warier of the vicissitudes of the market and as tourist demand increases the value of yak meat and butter. The region's rising wealth has also contributed to a growing connection with the larger Tibetan diaspora, and it appears that more Tibetan young men, especially, are coming back from their sojourns in India, where they studied Buddhism and learned different languages, including English. They are joining a diverse set of actors in this rapidly transforming social terrain, creating new ecological and economic landscapes and working to foster stronger connections to Japan and beyond. These borderlands are not created through their separation from other zones of political and economic power but are constantly being remade through their ongoing connections.

6. TRANSNATIONAL MATSUTAKE GOVERNANCE

This chapter stems from my participation in the collaborative Matsutake Worlds Research Group, with Tim Choy, Lieba Faier, Miyako Inoue, Shiho Satsuka, and Anna Tsing.

1   Scholarship on the "Tea and Horse Caravan" trade, often across present-day bor-

ders, includes Atwill 2005; Giersch 2006, 2010; Gros 2011; Lu 1997; Mu 2001; and B. Yang 2004.

2 Chinese accounts of border areas have often portrayed these places as isolated and "opened up" by China for the first time, as though they were too far from major imperial centers (Berman 1998; Lü Yiran, Ma, and Xin 1991; Ma Ruheng and Ma 1990; Wade 2000). James Scott (2009), in contrast, reads such distance as the result of conscious intent, viewing Zomia as a zone of escape from governmental domination, a place where people practiced the "art of not being governed." Influenced by work such as Thongchai Winichakul's *Siam Mapped* (1997) and C. Patterson Giersch's *Asian Borderlands* (2006), I am less inclined to view this as a place of unintentional or intentional isolation and more inclined to read these borderlands as places of overlapping and complex engagements (see also Sturgeon 2005). For a critical discussion of James Scott's use of the term "Zomia," see Jean Michaud's edited collection in the *Journal of Global History* (2010).

3 In 1940, Japan produced and marketed more than 12,000 metric tons of matsutake, but within a decade, the amount had decreased by almost half, to 6,448 metric tons. Japan's consumption has never recovered to its 1950 levels, even with massive imports from a number of countries. By 1965, domestic production fell to 1,291 metric tons, and in 1984 it was less than 200 metric tons, a number that remained relatively stable over the next few decades. These figures are approximate. Unlike manufactured goods such as cars that are produced in large factories and are easily quantified, quantities of wild products such as matsutake are known only by those goods that appear at major markets and are subject to regular and reliable surveys. China's export figures and Japan's import figures rarely match. Only in 2000 did the Yunnan government begin to actively aggregate data on matsutake production; previously, such data were generated by different government sectors and offices, and mushroom species were often combined or mixed with other non-timber forest products such as bamboo shoots.

4 Another explanation for the forest decline points to Japan's rural exodus: rural people had regularly cut hardwood trees for fuelwood and raked away forest duff for animal bedding, activities that created excellent matsutake habitat. Pine trees, already aging and weakened by acid rain, also suffered from an introduced insect pest, a nematode, which further diminished production (Amend et al. 2010; Faier 2011; Saito and Mitsumata 2008).

5 As in the Sino-Tibetan borderlands, there was earlier interest in North American matsutake before active trade began in the 1970s. In the United States, Japanese Americans hunted matsutake in places like Oregon's Mount Hood by the 1930s, and Japanese Canadians discovered matsutake at World War II internment camps (Togashi and Zeller 1934; Shiho Satsuka, pers. comm., 2011). Although some mushrooms were shipped back to Japan, they decomposed long before reaching their destination.

6 Most scholars concur that before the 1980s, matsutake generated little interest or worth in the Sino-Tibetan borderlands, either for domestic use or for export. Daniel Winkler found mention of one exception in the *Forestry History of Ganzi*

Tibetan Autonomous Prefecture, which claims that "between 1909 and 1912 ten tons of matsutake at a total value of four hundred kilograms of silver were exported from Kangding [in present-day Sichuan]" (Winkler 2008a, 9). To my knowledge, this is the only citation on China's matsutake trade before the 1970s. I am not completely convinced, however, that this *song rong* is indeed *Tricholoma matsutake*. We have no further details, such as where these mushrooms were sent, but the shipments would have likely been dried, as fresh ones deteriorate quickly.

7   There has been little written about the foreign trade stations, in part because of the widely repeated perception that Mao-era China was an autarky with almost no foreign trade. However, rural stations were actually vital in providing the state with foreign exchange. For exceptions, see studies on the role of *waimao zhan* in wildlife harvests by Chris Coggins (2003) and Peter J. Li (2007). Li reports that by 1978, China legally exported US$150 million worth of wildlife products annually, a substantial part of foreign trade. This was equivalent to the combined value of all of China's exports in mutton, beef, sheep hides, and products from ten other farm animals. Some of these goods were quite lucrative. For example, the glands of musk deer (used in making perfumes and industrial scents) were highly desired in Japan. It is estimated that between 1978 and 1986, smugglers brought more than forty-five thousand ounces of Chinese musk to Japan (P. J. Li 2007).

8   Compare the commodity chain for matsutake with that for caterpillar fungus discussed by Michelle Olsgard Stewart, in chapter 7 in this volume. The latter can be dried and stored for a long time, while the matsutake retains its high value only if fresh. Caterpillar fungus is sold mainly to Chinese, whereas almost all of the marketable matsutake is shipped to Japan.

9   Åshild Kolås, who carried out fieldwork in 2002 and 2003, provides some information that puts these earnings in perspective. During the August–September peak season in some areas, a household could make at least ¥100 a day, or ¥4,000 a year, from matsutake. With an exchange rate of ¥8 per U.S. dollar, this would be less than US$500 for a family of perhaps six a year, not a substantial sum, but when compared with selling a cow for ¥300, it is lucrative indeed (Kolås 2004,123).

10   The resurgence of traditional Tibetan architecture is also occurring outside key matsutake areas, often spurred by attempts to stimulate tourism. Few matsutake villages, however, have become part of tourist circuits, so these transformations are not necessarily motivated by interest in tourism.

11   My fieldwork outside Lijiang early in the first decade of the 2000s indicates an emerging market for selling homes, not as property, but for materials (mostly wooden posts and beams). The buyers were mainly based in Lijiang's "Old Town," where the demand was exacerbated both by UNESCO World Heritage regulations stipulating that building restoration should use "traditional materials" and by a logging ban, which made fresh timber more difficult to acquire.

12   These matsutake collection rules are elaborated from village rules and popular contracts (*xianggui minyue*), which were aimed mainly at protecting village forests and water sources and centered around harvesting forest goods such as fuelwood and animal bedding materials. Other rules include not digging up

patches of mushrooms and not harvesting them when they are too small or when the caps are fully open (with the notion that maintaining mature mushrooms will provide spores and enable future production). More village rules are described in Menzies and Li 2010.

13 While estimates of losses from logging revenue are widely quoted, and likely generated by county leaders eager to gain compensation for their financial losses, Stedman-Edwards (2000) notes that these counties were already receiving support from Beijing (as poor and frontier places), and so logging revenue may be actually have been closer to 20 to 40 percent (9).

14 The program's "carrots and sticks"—the offer of grain as compensation and the threat of punishment—were not carried out vigilantly and uniformly but operated quite unevenly in Yunnan and elsewhere (Fedor 2006; Lang 2002; Y. Yang 2001).

15 The illegal wildlife trade occurs on a large scale. One journalist found that in Yunnan, forestry police and customs agents seized twenty-five tons of wildlife products in 2003 alone. *China Daily*, "Confiscated Contraband Poses Dilemma" March 4, 2004, http://www.china.org.cn/english/2004/Mar/89234.htm (accessed May 29, 2012).

16 Three years later, in 2002, when Chinese delegates attended the international CITES conference, they joined with Japanese delegates in opposing the inclusion of fungus under CITES, arguing that it was too difficult to determine if fungus was threatened by trade (Thomas 2005). Subsequently, China agreed that CITES should continue to consider adding fungus, but Japan registered an official reservation against the plan. Based on these actions, it seems as if Japan and China wish to manage the mushroom themselves, but not necessarily through international oversight.

17 This ban on smaller mushrooms is inspired more by economic than ecological considerations, as there is no net ecological difference between removing small and medium-size mushrooms that are not yet producing spores. Spores should not be confused with seeds. Mushrooms are more like apples than apple trees; mushrooms are fruiting bodies that come from vast underground networks of mycelia. They spread through the release of spores, although it remains largely unknown what allows spores to change into mycelia and what triggers mycelia to produce matsutake fruiting bodies.

18 Japanese reports did not specify where the matsutake were from. Chinese officials are also unclear, and those in the southwest often point to northeast China. Japanese quarantine officials found 2.8 parts per million of dichlorvos, an organophosphoric agent used in fumigation and pesticides; the limit is 0.1 parts per million ("Chemical Residue Found on 'Matsutake' Imports," *Japan Times*, August 30, 2002). This discovery led to decreased Japanese demand for Chinese mushrooms and increased interest in matsutake from places deemed "safe," such as Canada and Sweden.

19 The addition of other ingredients that cut the purity of valuable goods or increase the heft of objects sold by weight—for example, of bundles of wool or medicinal roots—is a common technique elsewhere in China and around the world (Laveaga

2009; Williams 2002). Many of these common adulterants (sand, water, dirt) create no real threat to consumer health, but contamination with pesticides raises serious issues.

20   David Arora once watched a basket of matsutake change hands six times at a market in the course of several hours (pers. comm., 2008).

21   In twenty-first-century China, entrepreneurialism is common and trading in matsutake is just one of the many possibilities for "business," made necessary by soaring unemployment.

22   Although a number of village rules stipulate that no mushrooms with caps smaller than five or six centimeters across are allowed to be sold, a number are sold anyway. As Nicholas Menzies and Li Chun (2010) report, regional officials in northwest Yunnan are trying to clamp down on these sales by rewarding prefectures that obey these regulations and denying permits to dealers that truck in these small matsutake. Nonetheless, in 2009 and 2011, I saw dealers in Kunming offering many small matsutake for sale.

CHAPTER 7

Constructing and Deconstructing the Commons

• • •

CATERPILLAR FUNGUS GOVERNANCE

IN DEVELOPING YUNNAN

Michelle Olsgard Stewart

ACH year, thousands of Tibetans climb to the high alpine grasslands of
the Tibetan Plateau in search of the rare parasitic fungus *Ophiocordyceps sinensis*, commonly known as "caterpillar fungus" (Ch. *dongchong xiacao*). Caterpillar fungus is one of the most expensive and valued traditional Chinese medicines, which has made it a choice gift for Chinese government officials from wealthy businessmen in China's unique *guanxi* economy. The gift economy is not inconsequential: commonly exchanged fifty-gram gift box sets sell in traditional Chinese medicine stores for US$800–1,000, equivalent to the rural per capita income of Chinese citizens in 2010 according to the Chinese Bureau of Statistics.[1] Though caterpillar fungus harvesters see but a fraction of the profits from the fungus, most earn 50–80 percent of their annual household cash income by collecting it during its fruiting season from May to July. Caterpillar fungus collecting areas grow increasingly crowded each year. In response, harvesters (re)produce rules and practices governing access to and control over these resources.

Drawing together field-based observations from two caterpillar fungus collecting areas in northwest Yunnan from 2007 to 2011, this chapter

175

examines local caterpillar fungus governance. Juxtaposing the governance arrangements between these case studies highlights not only the existence of strong village-level caterpillar fungus governance arrangements in some areas, which have not been described to date, but also the ways in which both local and nonlocal power relations and structures significantly shape governance realities in different areas.

The political ecology approach to natural resource governance and tenure employed here is concerned with how property rights at various scales (e.g., the state, community, household) influence access to resources and land, and what kinds of human-environmental outcomes are produced through these claims on resources (Neumann 2005, 102). Property rights are not only rules or institutions that structure human interaction and use of resources (Ostrom 1990) but also *political processes* and the "expression of the social relations of production, forged in specific places in specific political-economic contexts and embedded in locally generated meanings of land and resources" (Neumann 2005, 104). Political ecology is useful here for its analytical insistence on exploring the ways in which situated histories, political economy, human-environmental interactions, subjectivities, and scale simultaneously produce environmental governance realities in contemporary caterpillar fungus collection areas. An open reading of governance that is grounded in political ecology and science and technology studies suggests a shift away from "biologizing" frameworks of resource governance, toward more explicit attention to how and why context and social relations matter in governance.

CATERPILLAR FUNGUS PRODUCTION
AND GOVERNANCE CHARACTERISTICS

Caterpillar fungus is a flask fungus that parasitizes the root-boring larvae of several ghost moth species endemic to the Tibetan Plateau (Wang and Yao 2011). The literal translation of its name in Tibetan (Tib. *yartsa gunbu*; Wyl. *dbyar rtswa dgun 'bu*), "summer-grass winter-worm," reflects the indigenous knowledge of its annual life cycle and varied morphological stages. As soon as fungal spores attach to and intrude into their subterranean larva host— likely in late summer—the fungal mycelia grow within the larva and ingest its vital organs and tissues throughout the winter ("winter worm").[2] In the early spring, the fungal fruiting body, or stroma, grows from the head of the larva as a hornlike structure that is anchored vertically in the top five

FIGURE 7.1　A harvester carefully removes a caterpillar fungus individual from the ground. Only the dark, uppermost portion of the fruiting body was visible above the soil when the harvester spotted it, and the remainder of the larval body is still encased in a layer of soil. When removing the caterpillar fungus from the soil, harvesters are cautious not to separate the fruiting body from the larval body because doing so dramatically decreases its economic value. Photo by Michelle Stewart.

FIGURE 7.2　Caterpillar fungus as it appears when it is traded and purchased by consumers. When caterpillar fungus is collected by harvesters, the larval body is coated in a layer of silk and then soil. These are cleaned off with a toothbrush by harvesters or buyers in order to display the golden body of the larva as it is traded. Photo by Michelle Stewart.

centimeters of the soil (figs. 7.1, 7.2). The stroma is visible to harvesters as a blade of grass in the high alpine grasslands during its fruiting season from May to July each year ("summer grass"). The timing and duration of the fungal fruiting season vary based on moisture and temperature conditions that range, depending on geography (e.g., elevation, slope, and aspect), climate, and weather events. The Tibetan Plateau, which has characteristics of a non-equilibrium rangeland ecosystem, exhibits high interannual variability in its climate; caterpillar fungus growth and reproduction is subject to this variability.

Much biological and ecological knowledge of caterpillar fungus reproduction and growth patterns is lacking. As a parasite, caterpillar fungus likely exhibits predator-prey population fluctuations, which makes interannual variability difficult to interpret due to lack of baseline understanding of fungus and larvae populations and how the two populations vary in relation to each other. Tibetans have been harvesting caterpillar fungus for hundreds of years, a factor that adds another long-term relationship into caterpillar fungus's population fluctuation. The majority of caterpillar fungus harvesting pressure occurs before sexual reproduction (see Stewart 2009); however, it remains unclear whether this pattern of harvesting affects future resource viability.[3]

These gaps in scientific understanding have to date precluded the development of sustainable resource management guidelines characteristic of most Western conservation approaches, which also form the basis of most conservation and resource management efforts in the Sino-Tibetan borderlands today: prescriptions for securing "sustainable yields." In the U.S. Pacific Northwest, matsutake research and management have focused on resource *yield* assessments and implicit comparisons between resource conditions under harvesting and hypothetical "pristine" natures where humans do not disturb the resource at all (Tsing and Satsuka 2008, 248). Basing conservation ideals and interventions on unrealistic or inaccurate ecological baselines can produce unintended social and environmental consequences (Fairhead and Leach 1996; Schroeder 1997; Neumann 1997). Sustainable yield assessments that fail to adequately account for matsutake's long history of harvesting and high interannual variability in growth can interpret resource abundance fluctuations inaccurately as indicators only of harvest-induced impacts. Instead, a more appropriate approach for matsutake science is to take anthropogenic forests, rather than an idyllic norm, as a starting point (Tsing and Satsuka 2008). This suggests attention to the positioned or "partial" (Haraway 1988) nature of all knowledges, and how "Western scientific" knowledge is but one of many kinds of expertise that could be mobilized in efforts to understand human-resource relationships. While "Western scientific" knowledge is often privileged in many international development and conservation schemes, including in contemporary China, there is a critical need for researchers and practitioners to examine the assumptions underpinning their research design, conduct, and goals, in order to most accurately interpret and examine the contextual specificities of different resource polities.[4] To date, most conservation-focused caterpillar fungus studies have employed a "sustainable yields" approach to frame and examine harvester-fungus interactions (Shrestha and Bawa 2013; Cannon et al. 2009); this has in some cases produced misleading truth claims about fungal population trends. For example, a recent claim that a "drastic decline" in Nepal's caterpillar fungus populations in 2012 was due to trade-induced overexploitation was based on quantitative data showing a per capita decrease in the amount of collected and traded caterpillar fungus (Shrestha and Bawa 2013). These findings were not analyzed in conjunction with the social and political relations of production—the increased number of harvesters, varied harvesting skills, and patchy fungal distribution—which would influence the amount of caterpillar fungus a harvester finds in a day or a harvesting season and render per capita declines in and of themselves an inaccurate indicator of fungal population trends.

Situated within a sustainable yield framework, most caterpillar fungus conservation research to date suggests that the lack of ecological baseline data on the abundance and distribution of caterpillar fungus in unharvested "pristine" grasslands is the primary impediment to the production of sustainable management guidelines.[5] Despite the problems this knowledge gap poses for conservation science, Tibetan caterpillar fungus harvesting communities in Yunnan have begun developing caterpillar fungus governance arrangements even in the presence of biological and ecological uncertainties. How is it that two approaches to governance are at such different stages in their development if they are addressing the same set of relationships between harvesters and caterpillar fungus resources? How might their discrepancies illustrate different ideas of what "environmental governance" is and what it should be?

Research examining resource governance in the Yukon sheds light on these questions. Contrary to the agricultural metaphors that permeate wildlife management research and science, which assume that wildlife are an annual "crop" of animals that can be managed and controlled, Kluane First Nations hunters do not subscribe to the idea that they *control* the animals they hunt. Instead, for them, wildlife management—hunting—is about the maintenance and management of social relations both among humans and between humans and animals (Nadasdy 2011, 142). For Kluane people, hunting is associated with many culturally significant rituals and norms, which makes the practice more meaningful than just an act of "management." In the words of a hunter who was reacting against the agricultural metaphor of "managing" wildlife in a wildlife management meeting, "Animals manage themselves; they make their own decisions about when to reproduce and where to go, decisions that are quite independent of any human desires. Wildlife management . . . is not about managing animals; it is about managing people" (ibid.).

These two approaches to wildlife management differ in their ideas of governance as management of nature versus management of people. For the Kluane, governance in hunting is inherently about relationships with both people and nonhuman nature because it is about the managing of social relations. Like hunting, harvesting caterpillar fungus is an "organizing principle governing social relations" (Nadasdy 2011, 142), and managing the resource is inherently about managing people. The social relations of governance are produced not only between harvesters and villages, and through the practice of harvesting, but also in relation to situated histories and political economic contexts.

GOVERNANCE AND DEVELOPMENT:
COMPARISONS BETWEEN DONGWA AND SHUSONG

Dongwa Township and Shusong Village are located in Yunnan's Diqing Tibetan Autonomous Prefecture (see map 1, D), a region recently described as a model among China's "many Tibets" for its successful achievement of economic growth and social stability over the past decade (Hillman 2010). Diqing is a region experiencing rapid development transitions related to China's Great Western Development strategy, which seeks to equilibrate economic conditions in China's lagging west and those in its booming eastern seaboard (Goodman 2004a), in part by taking advantage of the west's unique opportunities for tourism-based industry.

Diqing's geographic and cultural diversity have made tourism a viable option for generating prefectural revenue since the mid-1990s, and even before the logging ban of 1998, the Diqing prefectural government was exploring alternatives to its timber-focused revenue.[6] Nature- and culture-based tourism was an especially feasible option for Diqing's growth model given the established, successful tourism traffic that was already flocking to the nearby towns of Lijiang and Dali (Hillman 2010). Through a combination of state-based investments, subsidies, grants, and soft loans from provincial authorities, as well as the remarkable place branding in the renaming of Zhongdian as Shangrila, Diqing gradually made tourism a primary source of regional gross domestic product (GDP). By 2007, approximately ¥3.2 billion of Diqing's regional GDP of ¥4.4 billion was tourism-based (ibid., 274).

State investments in most Tibetan areas have concentrated on infrastructure projects and state administration, which generally benefit minority elites with access to state jobs and the droves of migrant laborers seeking construction, tailoring, food production, or other service jobs (Fischer 2005; Hillman 2008). These kinds of technological and industry-focused investments produce highly heterogeneous landscapes, where some communities and places are subject to rapid transformations while others are not. Though Diqing's tourism-led development strategy is said to deliver more inclusive growth than most other models in which there are only fiscal transfers from above,[7] it still fails to directly provide new labor opportunities to the majority of rural Tibetans,[8] who are either too remote to access new job markets or simply lack the skills to be considered for them (Hillman 2008). In addition to labor opportunities, processes of market liberalization and tourism produce variegated landscapes, human-environmental relationships, and patterns of local ownership and access to resources.

Dongwa and Shusong are positioned differently in their relationships to the rapid tourism-based development transformations taking place in the region. In particular, they differ in their proximity and involvement in the expansion of the "hardware" of shangrilazation, its road networks, air travel, hydropower generation, and telecommunications systems. On the one hand, Shusong Village and its caterpillar fungus collecting areas are located immediately alongside National Highway 214 (Guodao 214), the major road connecting Shangrila to Deqin, and thus the village is subject to many influences and processes associated with a major project for its expansion. Shusong's shangrilazation process draws attention to both the concessions local communities and their environments have to make in order to enable the road network to take form and the opportunities that arise. Dongwa, on the other hand, is not located next to a major "hardware" development project like Highway 214 and is physically removed from the major Shangrila-Deqin tourism-based development corridor. However, this does not mean that villages like Dongwa remain insulated from the transformations that are constitutive of Yunnan as it undergoes shangrilazation. The rising caterpillar fungus market and local efforts to govern the resource in reaction to it are but some of the many shifts associated with the rise of tourism-based development in the region. The case studies of caterpillar fungus governance arrangements in Dongwa, and the disbanding of such arrangements in Shusong, demonstrate how uneven power relations between villages and the state play a major role in the construction and deconstruction of the caterpillar fungus commons in northwest Yunnan.

Dongwa: "Villagers Own the Mountains"

> Villagers own the mountains; they decide how much they will benefit from them, and they come up with their own rules.
> —Dongwa Township government official, June 2011

> The rules were created [by the administrative village] to show people that the mountains belong to them, and all resources on the mountains are theirs. And if others are going to use their resources, they need to benefit from them. The villages, not the township government, made the rules,. The mountains are village-owned, so village-managed.
> —Elderly male caterpillar fungus harvester from Dongwa, June 2011

The two quotes above describe Dongwa's caterpillar fungus collecting areas as village-owned, a tenure arrangement with its roots in China's pastoral reforms of the 1980s. During that time, the government disbanded the commune system and replaced it with the household responsibility system. Households were granted greater autonomy in managing their farms, livestock was privatized and distributed to households, and livestock-production marketing channels were liberalized, which enabled households to profit from their decreased-quota surpluses. Grassland parcels—some of which are now valued primarily as caterpillar fungus collecting areas—were generally allocated to the administrative or natural village and occasionally to small groups of kin-related households. The size of pastures allocated to different groups and villages was determined based on the number of livestock distributed per household (infants, children, seniors, and adults counted equally as household members) (Banks et al. 2003; Bauer 2005).

This initial partitioning of grasslands and livestock continues to evolve through changing legal and regulatory frameworks but generally still features the following: all grasslands continue to be owned by the state or the collective, where the term "collective" is generally interpreted as the administrative or natural village; long-term use rights (generally fifty-year terms) are assigned to individual households via grassland-use certificates and contracts; and stocking rates are supposed to be assigned based on the area and seasonal type of the pasture (Banks et al. 2003). In many parts of the Tibetan Plateau, household use rights to pasture have been formalized, and winter (only rarely summer) pasture is sometimes leased to other households for livestock grazing (Yeh and Gaerrang 2011) and caterpillar fungus collecting (Yeh and Lama 2013). In Yunnan, caterpillar fungus collecting areas are in summer pastures, which entire administrative villages use in common for grazing (Banks et al. 2003).

Dongwa Township (see map 2) consists of five administrative villages, each of which has approximately twelve natural villages within its territory. While this chapter draws from research conducted across several natural villages in Dongwa Township, these villages are collectively referred to here as Dongwa. At the time of the reforms, commune work teams and production brigades were dissolved and reorganized into smaller units that better matched the scale at which livelihood actions had been organized before the 1950s. The administrative levels of the collective era—the commune, production brigade, and production team—generally became the township, administrative village, and villager small group, which in this area is also a natural village, respectively (Bauer 2005, 56; Ho 2001). When pastures were distributed in Dongwa Township during the reforms, the five administrative villages were apportioned pastures and thus collective claims to caterpillar fungus harvesting areas.

After the caterpillar fungus economy began to grow rapidly during the late 1990s, the natural villages requested an intervillage meeting for creating rules of equal access to the township's collecting areas. One administrative village, for example, did not have caterpillar fungus in its pastures and thus had to make arrangements so that its residents would have the same income opportunities as other township residents. Over time, a system of fees was developed to allow all Dongwa harvesters the opportunity to collect caterpillar fungus, but fees varied according to the harvesters' village of origin—whether someone was from the administrative village that owned the harvesting area, outside the administrative village but from Dongwa Township, or outside the township. In 2009, residents from the administrative village that owned the harvesting area did not pay a fee to collect caterpillar fungus, and fees were in the range of ¥100–300 for Dongwa Township residents and ¥700–1,000 for nonresidents. People who marry out of their village can return to their home-village collecting areas to harvest (without a fee if they are from the village that owns a given harvesting area), but their spouses and children have to pay the fee associated with their own village of origin.

The amount of the fee is continuously negotiated. One natural village leader said in 2009 that there were discussions to set the Dongwa resident fee at ¥400 but that the villagers decided on ¥300 because they didn't want the fee to be too high for township residents. In 2011, the Dongwa residents' fee had gone up to ¥400–500 and was ¥1,000 for nonresidents. The fees are determined by the village that owns a particular harvesting area at meetings that are usually held in the harvesting camps at the onset of the season. One female harvester said that the 2011 meeting for her village was quite lively when they were determining fees for nonresidents; some argued that the price should be higher, while others thought it should be lower. Some of the contention around the nonresidents' fee is attributed to the perspective that non-Dongwa harvesters don't have the same sense of respect and care for their shared resources. During a group interview in one of Dongwa's harvesting areas in 2011, one elderly male harvester said that non-Dongwa harvesters (Ch. *waidiren*) destroy the land and discard garbage when they collect caterpillar fungus, so it is fitting that they have to pay a high fee. His explanation not only illustrates the strength of Dongwa village-ownership claims over its caterpillar fungus harvesting areas—they can exclude or include other users on their own terms—but also reflects the collision of values and practices that accompanies the rise of the caterpillar fungus economy. Village leaders claim that the collected harvesting fees are distributed across the households of the village that owns a given harvesting areas.[9]

The harvesting fee is generally collected one-third of the way through the harvesting season in Dongwa, which allows harvesters the opportunity to earn income so that they can pay the fee. Harvesters must pay even if they do not find caterpillar fungus.. When fees are due, the administrative village leader and other village-level officials gather at a designated area— the convergence of trails heading up to the high collecting pastures in Dongwa—where they collect fees and record names in a ledger. Harvesters and village leaders monitor and enforce payments collectively (for a similar practice with livestock resources, see Banks et al. 2003); however, there are no rigid sanctions and methods for punishing those who do not pay. One village leader explained in 2009 that some people occasionally run away on the designated payday but that it is very hard to run away without consequences because it will be "hard to come back the next year." When asked how he knew who ran and who didn't, he explained that they all know one another, that the rule is not that strict, and that those who leave without paying are not followed in order to obtain their fees. The choice to not enforce the collection of fees suggests that in Dongwa, the caterpillar fungus market has not become disembedded from its social relations (Polanyi 2001 [1944]). This contrasts with recent studies of livestock- and pasture-contracting in Qinghai, where high prices and exploitation of price differences suggest a deepening of calculative logics and the disembedding of the market from social relations (Yeh and Gaerrang 2011, 169). While Dongwa's harvesting fee is relatively high, the fluidity of the approach to its enforcement suggests the central place of social relations in exchange.

Shusong: Transitions in Home, Land, and Caterpillar Fungus Governance

Contrary to Dongwa and its strong village control over caterpillar fungus resources, Shusong currently exhibits weakened and fuzzy control over its collecting areas. Shusong (see map 2) is an administrative village in Benzilan Township, which includes within its administrative territory approximately thirteen natural villages, referred to collectively here as Shusong. When I first visited Shusong in 2007 and 2009, its caterpillar fungus governance arrangements were some of the clearest and most detailed in my case studies. When I returned in 2011, however, most of the earlier rules of membership and exclusion had eroded. While governance arrangements and rules are not rigid and fixed (Peluso 1992; Fortmann 1995), the political economic context, histories, and multi-scalar interactions—between Shusong villagers, White Horse Snow Mountain (Baimaxueshan) Nature Reserve, and the Chinese state—coproduce local claims of authority over place and resources. Shusong harvesters must negotiate not only intervillage interests through their governance arrangements, as is the case as well in Dongwa, but also the interests and highly uneven power structures associated with the nature reserve and Chinese development infrastructure.

Shusong's caterpillar fungus harvesting areas lie entirely within White

Horse Snow Mountain Nature Reserve, which comanages all resources within the reserve boundaries according to different zones of use (Weckerle et al. 2010). The reserve was established in 1983 to protect the Yunnan snub-nosed monkey, and it has had conflictual relationships with local residents since its formation because of its authority to regulate social activities within reserve boundaries. The major conservation organizations World Wide Fund for Nature and the Nature Conservancy, as well as conservation scientists, have had long-standing relationships with the reserve, which has introduced an additional set of power relations and control over the resources. In 2009, reserve managers granted conservation scientists research permission to collect caterpillar fungus samples from within Shusong Village harvesting areas, but rather than negotiating access to caterpillar fungus with residents of Shusong, the scientists hired a non-Shusong harvester to collect the samples and did not offer any compensation. This encounter not only excluded Shusong residents from caterpillar fungus conservation negotiations and decisions but placed the burden of conservation science on the village by drawing from its shared fungal resources without compensation.

Before 2007, Shusong administrative village developed clear rules of exclusion for all non-Shusong harvesters. In contrast to Dongwa, Shusong villagers considered even township residents to be "outsiders," and there was no system of fees in place to allow other villagers access to the collecting grounds. To make sure outsiders were excluded, Shusong created a formal monitoring system in 2006, a year in which fifty to sixty non-Shusong harvesters came to the area to collect. In 2007, the village paid twenty-four monitors to watch for outsiders, and they were not allowed to collect caterpillar fungus while they were monitoring. The village leader said in 2007 that a few harvesters from the township had come to Shusong's collecting area that year but the monitoring system had greatly limited the number of outsiders. Shusong harvesters themselves pay approximately ¥20 each for the season's monitors (also noted in Weckerle et al. 2010), which contrasts with the village's monitoring system for matsutake, which pays monitors with fees collected from buyers at Shusong's matsutake market.[10] According to Shusong's assistant village leader when interviewed in 2007, Shusong villagers initiated the rules excluding outsiders because they thought that outsiders, unlike locals, did not care for the environment, digging and leaving large holes while collecting caterpillar fungus, whereas Shusong harvesters always fill in the holes afterward.

In contrast to Dongwa, Shusong implemented a set of rules related to its harvesting camps, which included the following stipulations: harvesters' tents had to be alongside Highway 214, harvesters were not allowed to cut down trees around their camps for use in constructing their tents or for fuel, rubbish was not to be left lying around the camps, and there were not to be any fires in the forests. Since Shusong's camps are located within White Horse Snow Mountain Nature Reserve and along Highway 214—camps are visible from tour buses, for example—it is no surprise that these rules can be traced back to the reserve. According to reserve staff in Deqin, the harvesting camp rules were created to make sure that harvesters are not harming the environment around their camps, and reserve staff travel to the camps several times each year to monitor compliance.

The rules governing access to caterpillar fungus and Shusong's harvesting camps had persisted from their implementation through 2009, but by 2011, the rules excluding non-Shusong harvesters and the use of monitors were no longer in effect. Making sense of these erasures requires a fuller explanation of the environmental and social transformations that were taking place and their effects on the daily lives of harvesters during that time as a result of tourism-based state development interventions. In 2010, the expansion project for Highway 214 was set in motion, and by 2011, the material effects of construction in Shusong Village and its harvesting areas were indisputable. There were piles of construction rubble and debris along and on the road stretching from Shangrila to Deqin, dirt slides of up to one kilometer running downslope from the freshly scored mountains, and dust and noise filling the air as excavators, levelers, and grinders worked around the clock. Dynamite explosions could often be heard in the background during my 2011 interviews in the harvesting camps.

The material transformations associated with the Highway 214 project were immediately evident in Shusong, but the effects of its construction on the social lives of villagers and harvesters were only gradually unveiled through conversations. In previous years, Dongwa and Shusong harvesters generally described a slight increase over time in the number of harvesters as more households sent more members up to harvest. Thus, when I asked a female harvester in the camp about her perspective on the number of harvesters in 2011, I expected her to reply that there were about three hundred to four hundred people harvesting that year, given my figures for 2007 and 2009. To my surprise, her response was quite different:

Last year there were 400 people in this area, but this year there are 100 to 150 people. This is because the road is being built and affects the houses and fields it has to pass through. If the road passes through a particular family's house or farming plot, the government compensates the family so that they can rebuild. Those families whose houses were along the road are busy rebuilding this year, so they didn't come up to harvest.

She then launched into an unprompted narrative about Highway 214 that explained some of the many ways the expansion project and state development visions for the area have significantly transformed Shusong villagers' relationships with and sense of ownership of their lands and resources:

When the road started being built in Shusong, there were many arguments. The government did not pay Shusong villagers for the trees and saplings that the road was cutting through. Saplings are important for villagers because they can give good wood; [villagers] can sell it or make furniture. They are very good resources, but the government does not care about them or compensate villagers for them. We are much smaller than them [the state (*guojia*)] and can't do anything to them. They are just destroying the trees and rocks but not doing anything for the villagers. Take, for instance, the big trees on Shusong villagers' land—the government compensates villagers with ¥2,000–3,000 if the road passes through them, but this compensation is given only once, when in fact these trees are good money over time.[11]

Her narrative illustrates a politics of scale at work in these landscapes, where the state's vision and imaginary for the region conflicts with local claims on and meanings of a landscape. In this case, different values for the land and resources collide, and Shusong villagers are forced to settle the incongruities in monetary terms, which begs the question of whether both parties agree to their commensurability as "goods." In general, villagers are compensated ¥100,000 if the road passes through their houses and ¥30,000 per *mu* if the road passes through their land. While the compensation for houses is supposed to enable villagers to rebuild their homes, the land compensation is not intended to allow villagers to clear forests and rebuild their fields; instead, they are given ¥600 per year to buy vegetables and grain. According to one villager, these stipends are problematic because if they are given to household elders,[12] the stipends do not transfer to the household or its new members and are discontinued when the elders pass away. This arrangement thus removes not only the land and the capacity to produce vegetables and grains for subsistence needs but also the option of procuring these foodstuffs monetarily. Displaced villagers are then subjected to further social and economic marginalization in the rapidly expanding cash-based economy of the region. Socioeconomic marginalization is most pronounced among those whose erstwhile land enables development in the region to proceed.

Villagers have not in the past assessed the value of their homes and land for the purpose of agreeing on a settled amount for exchange. An older woman from Shusong Village claimed that when it comes to road compensation fees, there are two different kinds of people: those who have the road cross their homes and ask, "Why me? I have money. I would rather be working in the field," and those who ask, "Why not me? Why don't I get money from the road crossing?" Whether or not they are compensated — and whether or not the road passes through their houses and land—all residents who are affected are dissatisfied with the compensation settlements because they did not solicit the transactions and most of them are forced to make a permanent transition away from the life they have known. In some cases, the compensation is simply inadequate: one Shusong villager who had an injured leg was compensated ¥100,000 for the road's passage through his traditional three-story home. For him, the money was not adequate for building a new house because he would have had to hire people to help with the construction.[13] The man is vocal about his situation, saying that he is homeless and has nowhere to go.

Lack of uniformity in the fees and negotiation processes further complicates local frictions resulting from the compensation process. Some families have been able to negotiate higher payments, whereas others have not. According to one Shusong resident:

> Other families were getting lots of money from the government through compensation because they know how to bargain. Some had received almost ¥1 million for their house, while others don't know how to bargain and didn't get enough. When the government developers were taking notes and bargaining with villagers for their houses, they would say to some, "Your house is worth ¥100,000," and the villagers would trust the government officials and accept this amount. Later, however, these people would ask their neighbors about their compensation and learn that they had earned ¥900,000.

The villagers' skill at bargaining is not what is truly problematic about these transactions, however. Bargaining for goods and services is a common practice in this region, and settling on exchange values is a deeply socialized process. In bargaining with a state official for compensation fees for one's home or land, however, the terms of engagement are not as well defined, and it is uncertain whether local villagers have the power to bargain with the state at all. For some, state interests and power preclude local negotiations in the first place: some villagers reportedly tried to refuse to let the road go through their houses and were told that they could either take the money or not but the road would go through their houses anyway. Reflecting on this, one woman explained that if the road belonged to the village, villagers could reject its expansion if the effects or costs weren't agreeable, but there is nothing the villagers can do about Highway 214 because it is for the state. In other words, local and state bargaining power are hardly symmetrical. These kinds of asymmetries illustrate the role of power in the relationships between local political struggles and state development initiatives in determining control over resources (Agrawal 1999).

Just as Highway 214 has transformed Shusong villagers' valuation of and ownership claims to their homes and land, the development of the road has reconfigured their caterpillar fungus governance arrangements in diverse ways. Prior rules of exclusion have been discontinued for several overlapping reasons. For one, the "outsiders" the Shusong villagers were monitoring have changed in both composition and number. One elderly Shusong villager, whose children were collecting caterpillar fungus for the household, said that harvesters could not chase the outsiders out anymore, and that in 2010, the village had a meeting about stopping the outsiders, but in 2011, outsiders were no longer banned. Other harvesters mentioned that the village leaders had not met with Shusong villagers at all in 2011 to talk about caterpillar fungus rules, which suggests a shift in attention toward other matters. When asked who the outsiders were, the elderly woman explained that the outsiders were the people who were building the road—they worked on the road during the day and collected caterpillar fungus at night. While harvesting caterpillar fungus at night would be nearly impossible given how difficult it is to find even during the day, her narrative illustrates the many ways in which highway expansion has invaded the social lives of Shusong residents.

As previously described, most state-led development projects across Tibetan regions benefit migrant laborers who are brought in to perform services that require certain skills (Fischer 2005; Hillman 2008; Yeh 2013).

While some Shusong villagers have joined construction teams as unskilled laborers (earning ¥50–120 per day), migrant laborers work on the road in contracted sections and currently perform the majority of Highway 214 construction labor. Migrant laborers put a strain on local systems of customary rights because they utilize local resources (e.g., water and fuelwood) without necessarily knowing or abiding by the rules of use for these resources. Resource use for basic needs is perhaps locally acceptable if there is a general shared idea of equal access for subsistence needs, but collection of high-value caterpillar fungus draws attention to the ways asymmetrical power relations likely factor into the current acceptance of migrant laborers' fungus collecting.

According to Shusong's previous definition of "outsider," Highway 214 migrant laborers should be characterized as "outsiders" and excluded like all other "outsiders," such as villagers from neighboring Benzilan Township. In practice, however, this is not the case, and road laborers are not excluded because they have very different social relations with Shusong harvesters. As Highway 214 laborers, road workers are in effect appendages of the state, and the same uneven power relations that characterize Highway 214 resource and land negotiations with Shusong villagers also characterize access and control over caterpillar fungus resources. Local contestations with road workers over access to caterpillar fungus go beyond interpersonal and intervillage politics and become contestations with the state, because road workers' claims to the area are legitimized through their connection to state interventions taking place in these landscapes. While all non–Shusong villagers might be regarded as interlopers in Shusong's harvesting areas, some "outsiders" are more legitimized and less excludable than others. This observation expands our thinking on environmental governance by illustrating one of several ways local control over resources is not determined solely by the design or implementation of governance institutions but is rather enabled and constrained through social relations and the political economic context.

In addition to the ways power asymmetries contribute to the loosening of the rules of exclusion, the rapid influx of migrant laborers to the area overwhelms Shusong's earlier governance arrangements in practical ways. Previously, monitors patrolled the area for unfamiliar faces and might have discovered a handful of nonresident caterpillar fungus collectors who would then be asked to leave. The same monitoring system would now find hundreds or thousands of unfamiliar faces, and collecting caterpillar fungus is no longer the only reason people come to the area.

The discontinuation of exclusion rules is also likely attributable to a less defined and multifaceted transformation in the ways Shusong residents value caterpillar fungus and the labor associated with its collection. Though not all villagers participate in the construction of Highway 214, the unskilled labor opportunities are desirable to some, because it increases their income earning potential beyond harvesting caterpillar fungus for eight to ten hours per day. One male harvester explained that some villagers who were not finding much caterpillar fungus had decided to leave the camp early and go back to their construction jobs. The more stable income from construction is appealing for some. Not all harvesters feel the same way; in earlier interviews in Shusong in 2009, when some villagers were pursuing Deqin construction opportunities, many harvesters said that they preferred caterpillar fungus collecting to road or building construction because of the "freedom" associated with it. Some said that caterpillar fungus collecting allows one to rest when one wants to rest and eat when one wants to eat—unlike the conditions of construction work, with a foreman determining the day's schedule and supervising the workers.

Though Shusong villagers' reception of compensation fees is uneven, the injection of state funds into the region recalibrates ideas of value in palpable ways. In one harvester's words: "People are saying that if the road crosses your house, you get good money: ¥100,000. In your whole life, you will never find ¥100,000 in one day, so it is very good money." While caterpillar fungus collection has to date provided households with relatively high sums of money, the profits and labor associated with collecting are now being compared to exorbitant onetime state compensation, which, as suggested above, reconstitutes ideas of labor value and personal assessments of what one's labor, time, and effort should be worth. Most harvesters today claim to find less caterpillar fungus than they did in previous years. Combined with the overall amount of fungus available, the ability of a harvester to find caterpillar fungus is contingent on practice, patience, focus, and a personal sense that the time and effort spent searching is worth it. Narratives of decline may be interpreted in a number of ways: a decline in the overall amount of fungus, a decline in per capita collection because the number of harvesters is increasing each year, or a decline in the personal value harvesters assign to collecting as a practice. The extent to which harvesters think that the time and effort they invest in collecting caterpillar fungus is worthwhile is intimately related to its market price and how much they can earn collecting it. Harvesting caterpillar fungus requires hours if not days of searching, and if harvesters feel that these hours could otherwise be spent in more meaningful (or profitable) ways, they are more likely to perceive caterpillar fungus quantities as acutely limited.

For example, during a conversation with a group of harvesters in Shusong's camp in 2011, the most vocal of the harvesters, who had been digging caterpillar fungus for twenty years, commented that quantities are decreasing each year. Before, he said, he could find two hundred pairs of caterpillar fungus per day because there were not many harvesters, but now he could find only one pair per day.[14] "In the past, you could earn lots of yuan in one day collecting caterpillar fungus—in 2008, you could earn ¥1,000 per day but only ¥300–400 per day this year." In 2008, caterpillar fungus collection was the major source of income for Shusong households, and household interviews in 2009 revealed that 50–80 percent of annual cash income was derived from collecting. These incomes are now assessed in comparison to lump-sum state compensation and wages from other labor opportunities.

Paradoxically, the sense and experience of finding fewer caterpillar fungus—with the sense of "more" being related to both historical narratives and the overall sense that the energy and time invested in searching meet with sufficient rewards—can diminish the desire to invest in governance arrangements. In the same group interview, several harvesters mentioned that in 2008–9, they had a village meeting about stopping the outsiders, but now they no longer really care about the outsiders. When asked why, they explained that "there's so little caterpillar fungus, and the outsiders can't find much because they are from Deqin." In a separate interview, a harvester similarly explained that in 2008–9, they had stopped outsiders but were not doing so in 2011. Because harvesters in 2011 found so few compared to the past, it seemed "a little strange" to stop the outsiders. According to economic logics, a decrease in supply causes an increase in value (price) when demand is constant. Thus, it would make sense for Shusong harvesters to want to tighten control over their resources if the supply is noticeably declining. Here, harvesters are paradoxically loosening control over their resources while perceiving a decline in supply and then claiming that it is "a little strange" to stop outsiders even though this was a goal of governance two years ago. Not only is the value of caterpillar fungus contextually defined and continuously shifting in relation to political economic changes in the area, but caterpillar fungus governance is also an intimate function of its social value.

The transformations in Shusong's caterpillar fungus governance arrangements from 2007 to 2011 reflect the complex ways in which local claims of ownership and access to resources are coproduced by their histories, broader political economic contexts, and geographies. While Shusong residents once exercised strong village-level ownership of their caterpillar fungus resources, these claims have recently been weakened and revised as new sets of interests, values, and power relations have been mapped onto the region. These transitions, resulting from the shangrilazation of the region, influence and rework the daily lives of residents and landscapes in uneven and materially important ways.

CONCLUSION

> When the government came in, when they first started building the road, there was only a meeting with the very high leaders and they did not ask the locals if they wanted it. If they destroy the mountain, they say, "You will get a good life in the future." If they wanted them to really get a good life in the future, they would pay them every year. They say, "If the country develops, you can also develop. It's good for you—in the future you can get a good life."
> —Shusong caterpillar fungus harvester, June 2011

Despite the intense flows of state capital into developing Yunnan, caterpillar fungus harvesting continues to be the most important source of income for the majority of rural, pastoral Tibetans. The critical role of caterpillar fungus in contemporary Tibetan economies and lives makes the rules of access to and exclusion from fungal resources important matters for social relations, in which the governance of resources is intimately about the governance of people.

In Dongwa, historical pasture tenure arrangements provided an important foundation for today's strong village-based rules of access and control over shared caterpillar fungus resources. This village-level resource control has continued to shift over time while remaining strong because villagers and village leaders actively maintain them through practices (e.g., village meetings) that connect governance arrangements with local social and cultural norms. Strong social relations among villagers strengthen governance arrangements because they are able to monitor harvesting areas themselves and collectors are committed to abiding by the rules of access. Though caterpillar fungus has rapidly become commoditized and is thus highly important to local household incomes, the market and governance have not become disembedded from their social relations of production but rather operate through them.

The loosening of Shusong's control over its caterpillar fungus resources illustrates the significant ways political economic context conditions the formation and persistence of environmental governance arrangements. While Shusong villagers, like those in Dongwa, previously had strong control over their shared fungal resources, local control has significantly weakened as the Highway 214 expansion project, which enables and represents the imagined future of the region as Yunnan's version of "China's Tibet," has run through Shusong Village and its collection areas. The highway has materially reconstructed the landscapes and destroyed the mountains and has also reconfigured local claims to villagers' homes and land, perceptions of the value of work and caterpillar fungus income, and the collective benefits of previous investments in governance arrangements such as monitors. These transformations in Shusong's governance arrangements illustrate how access and control over resources are not fixed and static but instead are continuously produced and negotiated through multi-scalar and highly uneven relations of power. They are political processes.

As conservation interests in caterpillar fungus governance continue to grow internationally and among Chinese conservation scientists (Cannon 2011; Shrestha 2012; Zhang Yongjie et al. 2012), the development of "environmental governance" of caterpillar fungus production areas in Diqing and elsewhere is in need of scrutiny. Scholars have recently suggested that the vagueness and malleability of environmental governance that have enabled its widespread acceptance and deployment across a range of circumstances "may be proportional to its capacity to elide or conceal critical distinctions" (Bridge and Perreault 2009, 475). Like concepts of "sustainability" and "development," environmental governance is defined by certain frameworks and sets of assumptions and truths and is mobilized in order to produce particular outcomes. When environmental governance is deployed as an intentional process or organizing concept, it is inherently about "*both* the social organization of decision making with respect to the environment, *and* the production of social order via the administration of nature*" (Bridge and Perreault 2009, 477; emphasis in original). The interests of a range of actors are at stake in the governance of caterpillar fungus, and decisions about the resource—especially who makes decisions, and how and why—have significant consequences for the thousands of harvesters who rely on it for income.

As China's tourism-based developments continue to map onto Diqing and other Tibetan areas, investments in infrastructure and state administration will continue to produce uneven social and environmental outcomes. In

Diqing, the expansion of one major road network closely tied to the region's shangrilazation has significantly transformed human-environment relationships, systems of value and meaning, and local access and control over resources in the areas it has traversed. Highway 214 and other expansions of development hardware throughout the region not only produce visible material transformations and destroy the mountains but also permeate and alter other important aspects of the daily lives of people, such as caterpillar fungus governance. The tensions of shangrilazation turn on collisions between Chinese state imaginaries of what the region should become and current local realities, needs, and customary arrangements. As an act of environmental governance, shangrilazation is an intentional process and organizing concept for the reciprocal production of desired social and natural orders in contemporary Yunnan.

6. CONSTRUCTING AND DECONSTRUCTING THE COMMONS

1   National Bureau of Statistics of China, http://www.stats.gov.cn/was40/gjtjj_en_
     detail.jsp?searchword=per+capita+income&channelid=9528&record=2 (accessed
     February 22, 2012).
2   Mycelia are hairlike structures of the fungus that generally grow underground;
     with caterpillar fungus, the mycelia grow within the body of the larvae.
3   Fungi have the capacity to reproduce both sexually and asexually, and it is unclear
     at present whether caterpillar fungi reproduce asexually before they reproduce
     sexually. If they do, genetic diversity might decline in high-intensity harvesting
     areas, but the overall abundance and distribution of caterpillar fungus at the
     population level would not be dramatically affected by harvesting.
4   For discussions on the ways "Western scientific" knowledge is often privileged in
     international conservation and development interventions, see Campbell 2002;
     Goldman 2003; Irwin 1995; Nadasdy 2005; Tsing and Satsuka 2008.
5   Shrestha and Bawa 2013; Cannon et al. 2009; Weckerle et al. 2010; Winkler 2008b.
6   During the mid-1990s, timber revenues had begun to decline in Diqing due to
     trade liberalization and increasing competition from Southeast Asia.
7   Diqing has seen a large expansion in its private sector, which accounts for half of
     its GDP, where tourism has created opportunities for many Tibetan small businesses and traders with options for interest-free loans (Hillman 2010, 274).
8   While some households certainly do have individuals engaging directly with
     tourism-related opportunities in the area—working at hotels and restaurants or as
     drivers—this is not very common.
9   A handful of individuals from some of these households said in 2009 and 2011
     that their households did in fact receive a sum of money related to these fees. They

did not, however, have an explicit memory of the total amount, which is curious given the proclaimed contestation of the actual fee amounts.

10   During the harvesting and selling season (July to September), Shusong has a matsutake market located in its village, which consists of a row of booths along both sides of a small alley branching off Highway 214. The market was created to enable, regulate, and locate buyer-collector interactions for the time-sensitive market demands for the fungus. Each afternoon and at the end of the harvesting day at approximately five o'clock, matsutake collectors return to the village to sell their collected fungi to buyers, who rapidly transport them to Shangrila so that the fungus will reach its prime market in Japan within forty-eight hours (Yang Xuefei et al. 2008; Yeh 2000). Buyers had to pay to enter the market, with fees ranging from ¥2 per day (for those from Shusong) to ¥5 per day (for those from outside Shusong). The 2006 village records show that Shusong collected ¥3,149 from buyers in 2006, and the funds were apportioned across matsutake management (¥300), cleaning the market (¥310), rebuilding and maintaining the market (¥200), paying for two monitors (¥200 each), record keeping (¥192), and management (¥400). The monitor and management fees were for services related to Shusong's "rest days," which were initiated in 2005. Every five days, according to a predetermined schedule, all harvesters were supposed to rest, and four to five villagers were selected to monitor the rest days to make sure no one was going out to collect. The assistant village leader said that the rest days had been difficult to enforce at first, but the situation was improving in 2007 (the interview, however, took place at the beginning of the season).

11   Based on my 2009 household interviews, households in Shusong earned approximately ¥2,300 per year, and the income range was ¥900–5,000, depending on the number of trees a family owned. Families sell the walnuts to buyers who use them to make walnut oil.

12   I did not ascertain whether these stipends are given in perpetuity (for the lifetime of the person being given the money) or just for a certain number of years, as is more often the norm for state compensation packages.

13   It remains unclear how the process of rebuilding homes fits into these compensation plans. Recipients would have to secure use rights to another plot of land in order to rebuild a home, which is made difficult by the fact that the state is presumably not allowing resettled villagers to clear forests for new land on which to build.

14   When harvesters sell caterpillar fungus individuals to buyers, they sell them in pairs. This may relate to the common idea among harvesters that there is a male and a female caterpillar fungus and that when a harvester finds one, the "mate" is generally nearby. When caterpillar fungus is bought and sold among buyers and later to consumers, it is priced by its gram weight and not by individuals or pairs.

PART III

CONTESTED LANDSCAPES

• • •

Harmonious Society
and Sovereign Territories

THIS last section probes new kinds of environmental subjects and the new natures that they speak for and from in borderland regions now under the governing regime of the Harmonious Society. The building of a "harmonious society" in China, announced by Hu Jintao as a guiding principle for government policy in 2005, was initially aimed at addressing the threat to regime stability posed by the tens of thousands of protests that erupt across China every year over issues such as rural land expropriation, illegal fees and taxes, environmental pollution, and labor disputes. Along with the construction of the New Socialist Countryside (Shehui Zhuyi Xin Nongcun), launched in 2006, the Harmonious Society signified an intention to move away from the model of economic growth at all costs that had dominated China for more than a decade and toward a more "people first" development model that would address growing rural-urban and regional disparities as well as environmental problems. Hu defined it as a society "which gives full play to modern ideas like democracy, rule of law, fairness, justice, vitality, stability, orderliness, and harmonious co-existence between humankind and nature" (CCP 2007). Concrete policy measures of the New Socialist Countryside have included the elimination of agricultural taxes, the extension of the rural cooperative medical system, and elimination of tuition fees for compulsory education. However, in the priority areas of education, labor productivity, living standards, availability of medical personnel, and access to potable drinking water, results have been modest at best, with the most progress made in China's wealthy eastern provinces (Guo Xiang-Yu et al. 2009).

Though stability has been at the core of the Harmonious Society since its inception, early formulations made relatively few references to minority areas. Setting a deadline of 2020 for the achievement of the Harmonious Society, the Sixth Plenum stressed the Party's role in leading the "Chinese people of all ethnic groups" but did not emphasize minorities beyond a call for the promotion of "the harmony of relationship between . . . ethnic groups" and the statement that the "ethnic foundation for social harmony should be consolidated" (China.org 2006). Instead of concrete measures for promoting interethnic harmony, the Harmonious Society is supposed to work on minorities through development subsidies, which are assumed to improve their livelihoods and make them grateful to both the state and the "elder brother" Han. This gratitude in turn is presumed to produce "stability"—the absence of challenges to state power—and an enhanced sense of belonging to the Chinese (*Zhonghua*) nation and thus improved interethnic relations.

These presumptions have proved difficult to maintain. In 2008, an unprecedented wave of more than one hundred protests across the expanse of the Tibetan Plateau, carried out by rural and urban Tibetans, laity and clergy, young and old, cadres and peasants, caught officials by surprise and provided stark evidence of a failure to impose stability on the state's terms. Despite the fact that the vast majority of the protests were peaceful, official media focused on violent unrest in Lhasa, whipping up Han nationalism against Tibetans, to the detriment of actual interethnic relations. These protests and other apparent manifestations of instability have been met with two kinds of state responses. First, they set off further attempts to create harmony through the "gift" of development (Yeh 2013). At the same time, those who challenge the existence of the Harmonious Society are relegated to what Giorgio Agamben has called a zone of indistinction between violence and law, the "threshold on which violence passes over into law and law passes over into violence" (1998, 32). The increasing deployment of the sovereign element of the sovereignty-discipline-government triad since the protests of 2008 has been evident in the intensified militarization and surveillance of the Tibetan Plateau, as well as increasingly frequent periods in which Tibetan areas have been completely closed off to foreigners, and mobility and daily life practices restricted for local residents. Further heightening the state of emergency, between 2009 and the time this book was going to press in the spring of 2014, at least 125 Tibetans self-immolated, mostly in the Sino-Tibetan border areas of Sichuan, Gansu, and Qinghai (ICT 2013).[1] The state has responded with further clampdowns, including fatal police shootings of unarmed demonstrators and bystanders, and the closing off of large areas of the Tibetan Plateau.

While the intentions of all those who have chosen to self-immolate cannot be fully known, the acts are, if nothing else, both intersubjective and social, and a fiery reclamation of sovereignty over individual bodies, in a time and space of greatly heightened struggle over sovereignty at all scales, from an imagined Tibetan territory writ large to the realm of the personal self. As governmentality in the Harmonious Society assumes the form of the ecological state, and indigenous culture is treated as a renewable and marketable resource, Tibetans (and other minority *minzu*) are reviving, restoring, and reinventing indigenous places, cultural practices, and identities. In this process, they are compelled as never before to reckon with a crisis of consent (in the Gramscian sense), having to choose whether to create new Tibetan subjectivities, culture(s), and landscapes or to refuse to participate in the cultural politics of a colonial system. If the terms of participation require, or are understood to require, the loss of national identity and inevitable assimilation into an undifferentiated multiethnic nation (one that ultimately co-opts dissent and obliterates difference), ritual acts of suicide may be embraced as the most potent offering to the cause of Tibetan sovereignty. In effect, those in the borderlands who are not compelled by hopes of indigenous reterritorialization are using their bodies to publicly insist on not being "made to live" under a regime in which even their own attempts to reclaim sovereignty are appropriated by the state as part of the Great Western Development strategy. The chapters in this section are, by contrast, about those who have chosen other ways of navigating the current crisis of consent.

Crackdowns and protests have happened simultaneously with the promotion of the Harmonious Society, which thus works not unlike the older term *minzu tuanjie*, or "unity of the *minzu*," aptly described as a "hegemonic management device" (Bulag 2002). It names both a goal and a condition already assumed to have been reached. Violations of the appearance of harmony are eliminated through the exercise of sovereign power. The Harmonious Society has been promoted simultaneously with the decline of opportunities for interethnic cooperation through civil society, particularly through the NGO form. This is ironic only if the Harmonious Society is interpreted as being aimed at improving ethnic relations, rather than as a tool for reinforcing state territorial sovereignty. Instead, the Harmonious Society should be understood as a move away from an emphasis on actual interethnic relations and toward a focus on governing China's minorities through sovereign power. It signals a stifling of the emergent potentials of subaltern cosmopolitanism, an ethic of living together with strangers, toward a reinforced statist multiculturalism (see Mayaram 2009; Yeh 2009c). At the same time, it deepens neoliberalism and the power of the market.

In chapter 8, Chris Coggins highlights and reflects on his collaborative work with Gesang Zeren, a descendant of aristocratic chieftains who was heavily persecuted by the local state for most of his formative and young adult years but who later became the founder of the Hamugu Village Indigenous Conservation Area (Hamugu Minjian Baohuqu) and the Hamugu Village Center for the Protection of Indigenous Ecology and Culture (Hamugu Minjian Shengtai Wenhua Baohu Zhongxin) in Shangrila County, Yunnan. The author's field research on supernatural landscapes in ten villages of Shangrila County shows how fully geopiety is woven into the routines of everyday life, and why it is seminal in the politics of nature, territory, personhood, and economic development in Hamugu Village and beyond. From 2004 to 2011, Gesang's purposeful fusion of native and nonnative environmental discourses has given rise to an alternative conception of modernity that foregrounds Tibetan territorial identity as a function of reciprocal relations with nonhuman beings animating the local landscape, while placing Tibetan nationalism within the contingent conditions of the Great Western Development strategy and its call to "develop a locally specific economy" (*fazhan jingji tese*) through "sustainable development." After 2008, his efforts to develop Hamugu as a model for sustainable development subsided significantly, but his conceptions of alternative ecological modernity continued to be no less trenchant. While there are important points of incommensurability between Tibetan supernature, with its animate landscapes, and contemporary nature conservation of a formal scientific kind, there is much to be learned from Gesang's narratives about the ways in which the two can be brought into conceptual harmony.

In chapter 9, Charlene Makley explores through her research with Amdo Tibetans in Qinghai's Rebgong (Ch. Tongren) the implications of contestations over the authenticity of Tibetan deity mediums (Tib. *lhawa*) in the context of intensifying state-sponsored development pressures accompanying the Great Western Development strategy in the first decade of the 2000s. This study shows that the personhood of what might be thought of as "natural" features—in this case *zhidak* (territorial deities often abiding within mountains)—constitutes a field of resistance to state sovereignty, especially when it collides with (re)inventions of spiritual landscapes that animate local identities and offer new forms of power in borderland regions riven by conflicting narratives of moral and material value. Makley argues that it is the compatibility of shifting *zhidak* relations with the desires, power, and violence inherent to state-sponsored capitalism, and the threat of their escaping state, Buddhist monastic, and household disciplines, that have placed local officials in an adversarial relationship with a powerful genius loci and engendered new contestations over the mediums whose bodies "host" the *zhidak* on behalf of the village.

In the final chapter, Emily Yeh examines the rise of a particular kind of environmental subject, "the Green Tibetan," at the conjuncture of contingent articulations between local Tibetan communities, Chinese environmentalists, and transnational actors early in the first decade of the 2000s. In what proved to be an ephemeral social formation, Tibetan culture became the agent for the salvation of China's nature, particularly in the Sino-Tibetan borderlands. These interethnic and translocal networks exemplify a kind of harmonious society, but not one that could endure the events of 2008, when the state's Harmonious Society became hegemonic. Yeh focuses on her interactions with Rinchen Samdrup, who rose from being a spokesperson for a new regard for nature in his home village in Chamdo to a renowned exemplar of the Green Tibetan; he was later tried and imprisoned by the Chinese government for attempting to enforce anti-poaching laws meant to protect the nation's wildlife resources. Yeh argues that Rinchen Samdrup's case is emblematic of a (re)turn to governing China's minorities by way of sovereign power and its attendant "statist multiculturalism" and neoliberal governmentality.

All three chapters describe landscapes in which the Harmonious Society initiative and struggles for Tibetan sovereignty simultaneously (or successively) converge, conflict, and vie for supremacy. These landscapes inform and embody ideological and cosmological conflicts that involve the visible and the invisible, the animate and the inanimate, the inert matter of nature as marketable resource and the animate matter of supernature, where deities abide within networks of social relations. The supernatural cannot be appropriated for mercenary or utilitarian ends alone, which provides one explanation for the less-than-harmonious relations between modern conservation efforts and indigenous sacred landscape practices. This is a critical source of tension between Tibetans' efforts to promote grassroots, indigenous nature conservation and the ecological state's will to sovereignty through zonation and commodification (described in chs. 4–7 in this volume). The latter holds a powerful monopoly on the economy of scale that underwrites nearly all transnational nature conservation schemes, whereas the former holds the potential to radically reconfigure landscape ecology so that it encompasses the human and the nonhuman in dialectical embrace. All three chapters show that these potentialities may persist in the Sino-Tibetan borderlands for some time to come, but only if the Harmonious Society or the policies that succeed it promote just and serious intercultural engagement.

PART 3. CONTESTED LANDSCAPES

1   See Carole McGranahan and Ralph Litzinger, "Self-immolation as Protest in Tibet," Fieldsights—Hot Spots, *Cultural Anthropology Online*, April 9, 2012, http://www.culanth.org/fieldsights/93-self-immolation-as-protest-in-tibet. (accessed July 11, 2013)

Animate Landscapes

• • •

NATURE CONSERVATION AND THE PRODUCTION
OF AGROPASTORAL SACRED SPACE IN SHANGRILA

Chris Coggins with Gesang Zeren

The disenchantment of the world means the extirpation of animism.
—MAX HORKHEIMER AND THEODOR W. ADORNO,
DIALECTIC OF ENLIGHTENMENT

[A]bsolute space . . . is a fragment of agro-pastoral space. [It] appears as
transcendent, as sacred (i.e. inhabited by divine forces), as magical and
cosmic . [I]ts mystery and its sacred (or cursed) character are attributed
to the forces of nature, even though it is the exercise of political power.

HENRI LEFEBVRE, *THE PRODUCTION OF SPACE*

B EFORE 1949, governance in the Sino-Tibetan borderlands was subject
to negotiation, expedience, fortune, and alliance. The projection of
state power from afar was mediated by local polities that resisted domination by following cosmological orderings attuned to local livelihoods and
other interests. Local ritual practices and everyday understandings of sacred
space helped deflect territorial claims by distant states; today they continue
to challenge official distinctions between religion and politics, the human
and the nonhuman, and nature and culture. In Diqing Tibetan Autonomous
Prefecture, in northwest Yunnan, the formal governing bodies and cultural
institutions of China and Tibet have long competed for influence, and politi-

cal administration was tripartite from the sixteenth century to 1949. Tibetan monastic clergy of the ruling Gelugpa sect, who were linked to Lhasa, shared power with local nobility and representatives of China's Qing dynasty civil administration. Informal governance, the everyday, ongoing, and intimate relations between humans and their environs, necessitated still more intricate social arrangements in which space itself—inhabited by indwelling divinities—assumed power within the polities of town and village.

Many of these practices continue to produce meaningful landscapes in the basin and range country of Shangrila County today (see map 1, C). Here, snowcapped peaks loom above broad valley prairies known locally as "seas" (Ch. *hai*), the grazing grounds for yak, cattle, goats, horses, and pigs. Following the summer rains, the prairies flood, providing wetland habitat for the autumn migration of black-necked cranes and bar-headed geese. With the dry cold season, the floodwaters descend into subterranean limestone caverns to make their way down into the hot, dry gorges of the Yangzi, Mekong, Salween, and their tributaries, where cacti and drought-resistant scrublands form a sharp contrast to the humid upland forests nearby. Seasonal cycles of village land use and labor compose regular rhythms within the longer, broader patterns of regional production and trade. From at least the first century, horse husbandry was important in the local economy since horses were the key to transportation and a major trade item on the Ancient Tea-Horse Road (Ch. Chama Gudao)—a trade route with branches extending from Southeast Asia, through Yunnan, to central Tibet and India. In addition to their former role as producers and traders of horses for this long-distance network, Diqing Tibetans have long practiced agropastoralism, growing barley, buckwheat, potatoes, turnips, maize (in the dry valleys), and other crops, while also raising yaks in a transhumant pattern that rotates from high mountain pastures in summer and fall to valley pastures in the colder months. Transhumance-based agropastoral production requires large hinterlands for each village community, with a high degree of altitudinal zonation in familial and communal land use, common property resources, and frequent activity in a variety of landscapes from dry river valleys, to high valley wetlands, to alpine forests, and up to the montane tundra above the tree line. As with Tibetans of other regions, Diqing residents believe that deities reside within the land, the waters, the sky, and the subterranean realms. These beings are dangerous when disturbed but beneficent when propitiated appropriately and reverently, providing wealth in the form of livestock, crops, and other material and nonmaterial forms of good fortune. The sites of greatest power are associated with *zhidak* (Ch. *shanshen*), or territorial gods commonly abiding within mountains, and the political ecologies surrounding these deities present a significant provocation to contemporary assumptions about resource management, nature conservation, and the boundaries defining nature, personhood, and polity. (See Belleza 2005; Goldstein and Kapstein 1998; Huber 1999a, 1999b; Karmay 1994; Nebesky-Wojkowitz 1998 [1956]; Makley 2007; and ch. 9 in this volume.)

As Lefebvre (1974, 48) notes in the epigraph above, to consign agropastoral sacred space to the category of religion is to erase its political significance, for what he calls "absolute space" signifies sites that are always both "religious and political in character—a product of the bonds of consanguinity, soil and language." This description conforms closely to the territoriality of Tibetan communities; throughout the Sino-Tibetan borderlands, an enduring politics of supernature animates the shifting arrangements (alliances, conflicts, rapprochements) between humans and their no-less-idiosyncratic deities. In Lefebvre's treatment, absolute space prevailed in precapitalist societies, and did so with unconditional power, that is, without reference to other ways of dividing up and producing the lived world. Largely overtaken by the *abstract space* of capitalism, absolute space still "survived as the bedrock of historical space and the basis of representational spaces (religious, magical and political symbolisms)" (Lefebvre 1991, 48).[1] Modern secular attempts to obliterate or appropriate Tibetan sacred spaces have included first the Marxist-Leninist-Maoist productivism enforced through a command economy; second, state-capitalist commodification of nature and culture within a liberalizing market economy; and third (and inseparable from the second trend), efforts to align these spaces with contemporary nature conservation. This latest effort may seem more benign than the first two, but it is both blessed and challenged by the discontinuity between modern conceptions of nature as a thing separate from humans and culture, on the one hand, and indigenous conceptions of animate landscapes as abodes and embodiments of deities endowed with personhood, on the other. Intervening in the borderlands of this discontinuity are Diqing Tibetans who are fluent in both cosmologies; it is to their work within the context of capitalist commodification of "nature" and "culture," along with ongoing political struggle in the borderlands, that we devote this study.

FIGURE 8.1 View of Hamugu Village and Mount Chuji from Jueju Village (to the north). Houses in the foreground are part of Jueju. Chuji is the small mountain directly behind Hamugu. The trees covering Chuji's north slope are a recently restored sacred forest of larches and other conifers. Photo by Chris Coggins.

DIVINE ELOPEMENT IN THE BORDERLANDS

I learned my first lesson on the nature of marginal alliances in Diqing while standing on a vast alluvial fan that reaches down to the western edge of an even larger wet prairie called Napahai, in Shangrila County (see map 2). In late May 2004, while gazing out at Rising Sun Spirit Lake (Ch. Rizhang Shenhu) with Gesang Zeren (also known as Liu Zan)[2] and Lazong Ruiba (Tib. Lobsang Rinpa), community organizers from the nearby village of Hamugu, I recalled the story that they had told that morning about the two god-mountains, Shika and Chuji, which soared above the Duji Gorge to the west (fig. 8.1):

> Shika and Chuji came from the holy land of the Ngari (Ch. Ali) region, in
> western Tibet. Shika was a handsome, talented young nobleman, sincere

and upstanding. From a young age, he loved his homeland dearly and reveled in a free life of adventure on the high plains and snow mountains, where he grew to be strong and hardy. Influenced by his social and physical environment, he understood the hardships of pastoral life and enjoyed helping the poor. Chuji was an upright and beautiful admirer—simple, hardworking, and diligent—a very good young woman who was born into the poor class of herders. All of her family worked as laborers on Shika's family estate. From a tender age, Shika and Chuji played together happily, riding horses, herding livestock, and growing as close as kin. Reaching adulthood, they had developed a deep affection for each other but never dared to express their love—such sentiments could not be shared between people of such different classes.

When Shika was about twenty, his family selected a bride who was also a member of the nobility. Although Shika was extremely vexed, he could not confront his parents. He could only ponder his situation and cry all alone through the night. At night, Chuji appeared in his dreams—a beautiful woman of elegant bearing. Shika realized deep in his heart that it didn't matter whether Chuji was from a poor family of serfs; there was no more beautiful and virtuous woman in the world. Perhaps through the work of the gods, the young people of the village arranged to have a tea party, where Shika found Chuji. They expressed their mutual love and, determined to stay together, cut ties with their respective social classes and decided to elope.

The next day, before dawn, they traveled to Yamdrok Lake to pray for the blessings of the Buddha. After several hours, a *dakini* emerged from the surface of the lake and said, "You two are of one mind in your mutual love, and you seek the blessings of the Buddha. If you can spend fifteen days and nights together, and keep the yaks with you, you will reach a land of clear streams, splendiferous flowers—a magical pureland. That is where you will establish your treasured home." She also added that if they could not spend fifteen days and nights, the marriage bond would fail. Before departing, the *dakini* gave them a pair of yaks, some yak butter, and fried noodles.

After that, the two rode the yaks day and night without stopping. Crossing snowy mountains and fording three rivers, they traveled for exactly fifteen days, and they finally arrived at a place with level ground and dense forests—a veritable sea of green—with a cliff emerging above the trees. Just below the top of the cliff lay a cave resembling a Buddhist temple. The two lovers wondered whether this could be the holy land that the *dakini* had described. The sun was just setting behind a mountain to the west. Shika untied the yaks' halter ropes and began to tie the yaks to a tree branch. The two lovers also began to prepare a fire and haul water. Before dark, a thunderbolt rang out, the sky turned black, and a huge downpour began. The yaks, spooked by the lightning and thunder, broke the ropes and fled into the forest. Shika bolted after them, searching high and low. He searched until dawn but could not find the yaks. His efforts to manage the yaks for fifteen days and nights had failed; he lost his chance to secure the bonds of matrimony with Chuji, and he was heartbroken. Remembering what the *dakini* had said, he wondered how this could possibly be his fate. He vowed never to marry, and then he turned into a *zhidak*. When Chuji realized that Shika would never return from chasing the yaks, she wailed loudly, crying ceaselessly. Her tears formed the Rising Sun Spirit Lake. This beautiful and virtuous herding girl, having lost her lover, prayed daily for Shika's good fortune and health. Afterward, she, too, turned into a *zhidak* [near Shika], the Chuji Spirit Mountain that lies just behind Hamugu Village.

The unconsummated marriage of Shika and Chuji can be glossed, in broad terms, as a legend of animation—an account of how inert matter, in this case, a pair of mountains, was endowed with life, breath, and personhood. In Tibetan tradition, the story conforms to Tantric conceptions of magic landscapes, and, as Gesang Zeren goes on to explain, in both oral and written versions, the Duji Spirit Cave, which is imbued with the powers of the lovers, served as an abode where a series of Nyingma, Kagyu, and Gelugpa masters performed three- to seven-year Tantric meditation retreats over the course of several hundred years starting before the 1600s.[3] Tibetan and Chinese inscriptions on the cave walls explain much of this history, which is unique to Hamugu but in no way exceptional within the geographic context of the borderlands region. Many Tibetans in northwest Yunnan experience animate landscapes as agentive and volitional gods or spirits with personhood or, more aptly, super-personhood. These experiences disallow a distinct separation between "natural" and "cultural" environments and render "sacred geography" more a matter of everyday practice and ritual performance than one of absolute spatial demarcation (in a physical or cognitive sense) (Allerton 2009; Bird-David 1999; Mazard and Swancutt, forthcoming; Nadasdy 2011; Overstall 2005; Sullivan 2010; and Viveiros de Castro 1998, 2004). This perspective constitutes a cosmological subject position that stands in direct contradiction not only to the state and the

Chinese Communist Party but also to the hegemonic, modern ontological position through which the world is made sensible by way of the endless process of "purification" and separation of the nonhuman and nature from the human and culture (Latour 1991, 11). In acts of religious or other ideological conversion, the agency of spiritual landscapes becomes a matter of ultimate concern; missionaries and modernizers attempt to purge the environment of its powers by inscribing it with normative signs and practices in a process of deterritorialization and reterritorialization (Agnew 2009; Deleuze and Guattari 1987). The colonized, or those who would be converted, often resist these efforts, engendering "new forms of conversation with the landscape, including re-enchantments, religious syntheses, [and] reassertions of the landscape's potency" (Allerton 2009, 235). In Diqing (and throughout the borderlands), these processes manifest themselves in the reclamation of Tibetan territorial identity through continuing (re)inscription of sacred places through both the writing of texts and the ritual demarcation of space. This reterritorialization has been both bounded and produced by state policy on religious practice and nature conservation in a period of transnational capital investment in ecological and cultural resources.

ECOLOGICAL CAPITALISM AND ANIMATE LANDSCAPES:
RETERRITORIALIZING THE MARGINS

At the turn of the twenty-first century, northwest Yunnan was the epicenter of cultural, political, and economic changes that continue to shape the production of space, place, and identity throughout the Sino-Tibetan borderlands and beyond. First, as a project of governmentality and power projection over processes of place-making, the Great Western Development strategy unleashed a wave of capital investment and transnational mediation of landscapes designed to maximize cultural and ecological values in the name of "sustainable development" (Ch. *kechixu fazhan*) (Hakkenberg 2008; Hillman 2003, 2010; Kolås 2008; Litzinger 2004). The rapid mobilization of international and domestic environmental nongovernmental organizations and transnational investors was matched by a groundswell of local environmental and social activism and entrepreneurialism, along with intensive Chinese and foreign scholarship, media coverage, and explosive growth in tourism. Indigenous stewardship over natural resources became a guiding vision, a foundation for multiple regional and local economic development projects. Growing political and economic support for indigenous culture and ecology seemed to indicate the regional advent of both an "ecological phase of capital"—in which nature was no longer "treated and defined as an external and exploitable domain" (Escobar 1996, 47)—and "the culturalization of the economy" (Yúdice 2003, 19).[4] Working in tandem, nature conservation and eco-cultural tourism provided a redemptive vision for central state planners, local state officials, and many people who call the area home.

Nature conservation and ecotourism in Diqing are largely premised on the idea that Tibetan agropastoral traditions of sacred landscape management are highly compatible with the scientific management of biodiversity in conjunction with new forms of community development (Salick et al. 2007; Hakkenberg 2008). Although the 2001 "discovery of Shangrila" in Zhongdian County has rightly drawn criticism and a plethora of scholarly and popular commentary (see the introduction to this volume), multilateral support for village-based restoration of damaged, compromised, and otherwise fragile landscapes can be lauded as among the first of its kind in China. These projects have been activated within a complex web of international discourse on indigenous knowledge and depend on international funding and at least tacit support from the Chinese government (see chs. 4 and 5 in this volume).

In conjunction with these discursive changes, many rural communities throughout Diqing have revitalized and reinvented sacred landscapes and local religious practices in an assertion of the village as a distinctly indigenous territory—one that is "Tibetan" to the extent that it was historically (before Liberation) endowed with an ecological conscience that obviated the need for modern nature conservation and policing by Han officials.[5] As Gesang Zeren put it during our first meeting in 2004:

> On the one hand, you could have forest regulations from the forestry
> officials, but in reality, if you wantonly take resources from the mountains,
> you will be penalized. If you enter the territory of a *zhidak* and fell trees, as
> some foolhardy young men dare to do, in the end there is the same result—
> the heavens penalize them. After they've cut a few trees, they get shoulder
> injuries. This is true. So once again, they're afraid to cut. They say, "This is
> Duji Cave, where the masters lived. We can't mess with anything." Then, in
> a few more years, people go for the big trees. After the logs are on the trac
> tor, the driver's hand will be broken, or his leg will be broken. Again they'll
> be afraid; they will not dare to go in and cut, saying, "Oh, isn't that how I
> offended the *zhidak*?" After a while, though, [they] seek fuelwood to slide

down the mountain. Two or three years ago, a family with a nine- or ten-year-old boy was pulling trees down the mountain; the mother was down below collecting firewood, and a tree slid down the mountain, killing her. Later, through ritual [involving a medium], we inquired about the situation, asking, "Do you think the *zhidak* has been offended?" and the voice of the mother coming off the mountain said that it was so. . . . So now we say, the *zhidak* will always demand its debt from those who offend it.

In terms of our ecological protection and our educational system, no other *minzu* have this [particular] traditional protection system. It is built into our culture. We don't need the government to invest a bunch of money in it. That would be ineffective. We ourselves have a traditional conservation system.

Sustainable development strategies advocated by Diqing officials enable animistic beliefs and practices to figure prominently in the reinscription of village landscapes in accordance with local cultural identities and aspirations. Here, "animate landscapes" refers to mountains, lakes, springs, trees, and other nonhuman environmental features that are believed to be the abodes (Wyl. *gnas*) of gods or spirits, the most salient among Diqing Tibetans being the *zhidak*, *yullha*, or gods of the locale, and the *lu* (Wyl. *klu*), serpent-like spirits that abide in or near trees and water sources (see the introduction and ch. 9 in this volume). Material from Gesang Zeren's writings and our ongoing dialogues, in conjunction with site visits and treks in Hamugu and its vicinity, illustrate how texts, the landscape itself, and complex, collective, community conservation and development initiatives inform the inscription process. These findings on animate landscapes are supported by field data from nine additional villages in Diqing.

In this context, animate landscapes are, in ontological and cosmological terms, radically different from, and not always commensurable with, scientific conservation practices and interests. While sacred landscapes and conservation objectives often coalesce around specific natural features—which are constructed in modern scientific ontologies as organisms, ecosystems, and geomorphic features—Tibetan geopiety is not a panacea for sustainable ecological development.[6] The idiosyncratic personalities of specific gods, the significant disconformity between sacred landscape practice and modern conceptions of embodiment, and the ever-changing affective dimensions of labor and leisure complicate the notion that Diqing's animate landscapes are ideal foundations for nature conservation and sustainable development based on ecotourism. The degree to which local people are aware of this slippage is evident in the extent to which community development plans such as those in Hamugu involve a complex array of active management strategies intended to enforce community compliance and counter the demands and pressures of rapacious development projects, even those operating under the rubric of "ecotourism" (Ch. *shengtai lüyou*). Given these caveats, animate landscapes and geopiety in the prefecture appear to be durable components in the production of space; they hold important vernacular political standing in landscapes that demarcate the borders between "Tibetan" and "Han" and, in the popular imagination, between a sacred indigenous space that defines the center and a hegemonic, disenchanted world of possessive individualism that marks a vast and powerful periphery. The deeply political and territorial power of animate landscapes and the flexibility of animist cosmology may ensure that local religious beliefs and practices continue to articulate, albeit in less than predictable ways, with transnational networks of nature conservation and sustainable development.

GOVERNING ECOLOGICAL AND CULTURAL CAPITAL IN DIQING LANDSCAPES

The Sixth Plenary Session of the Seventeenth Communist Party of China Central Committee, which convened on October 15–18, 2011, marked a millennial high point in the governance of culture as a national priority. Its mandate was to "deepen reforms in the cultural system" and promote "national cultural soft power" in order to enhance China's status in international geopolitics. Noting the inseparability of cultural production from economic development and the "construction of environmental civilization" (Ch. *shengtai wenming jianshe*), the Politburo report called for greater "cultural awareness," "cultural self-confidence," and stronger guarantees of "the people's basic cultural rights and interests." While the promotion of cultural production and the culture industry were deemed critical to the future of "socialism with Chinese characteristics," the most direct reference to religious or spiritual culture was a call to more deeply establish the Chinese people's "collective spiritual home" (Ch. *gongyou de jingshen jiayuan*). Cultural mobilization was to be balanced by measures that would "safeguard harmonious social stability" and "guard against all kinds of potential hazards"; this required official vigilance and political responsibility for cultural development at all administrative levels (CCP 2011).

Constructing definitions of "culture" and "ecology" as an expedient for development requires lapidary precision; the central state's omissions and silences in policy formulation are as significant as clear and intricate theoretical calculations by the local (or regional) state. A collection of essays by Diqing's Party cognoscenti, *Collected Essays from a Research Conference on Theories for Constructing Harmonious Society in Diqing Prefecture* (Jiang Wenjuan 2006), calls for a "scientific outlook on development" (Ch. *kexue fazhan guan*) based on the protection of "ecological environments," biological diversity, "Harmonious Society," and "religious culture." The advent of ecological capital in Diqing is represented in terms of a turning away from the "traditional practices" of the production power state and the transition to the ecological state (see the introduction to this volume). The term "production power state" refers to resource management systems based on resource extraction, which were promoted by the CCP during 1949–99 (the preindustrial past is conveniently elided from this account):

> In the past, people assumed that only by harvesting natural resources could they enter commercial markets, and only this could be considered natural resource utilization with use value for the people of Diqing; anything else was considered wasteful. This is a kind of traditional and one-sided viewpoint. It ignores a very important understanding of value, specifically that humanity's largest and most important capital consists of beautiful ecological environments with biological diversity and native vegetation as their essential structural features; in an intensely competitive market, this is Diqing's late-developing advantage. Only because of its existence, Diqing's mountains are green and its waters are clear, it is a landscape adorned with color, it is a renowned [UNESCO] World Heritage site, and thus the ecotourism resources are abundant. Only because of the existence [of this nature] can Diqing's rivers flow unimpeded, providing all *minzu* in the region with water for their livelihoods and productive activities, including a secure source of hydropower. Therefore, to protect and improve the precious natural ecology and biodiversity of this land is the most important historical mission of the people of Diqing. . . . Following the accumulation of experience in development practices, and informed by advancements in global thinking and the completion of scientific research for the establishment of Three Parallel Rivers [World Heritage site], people gradually realized that Diqing's most valued natural resources should be biological diversity, the uniqueness and preciousness of its ecological features, and its fragility. (Pan 2006, 77–78)

The author, a Diqing official, describes how in the 1970s and 1980s Diqing's forests were treated as vast and inexhaustible, and how the resulting wave of timber cutting—the so-called timber wars (between competing government agencies and individuals)—left much of the mountain range deforested and barren. Whereas in the 1960s the forest area was 1,309,000 hectares, by 1990 it had been reduced to 822,000 hectares (a 37 percent decrease), water resources dried up, the environment deteriorated, and geological hazards became more severe (Pan 2006). The moral of the story is that in the context of environmental history, the long-term economic value of nature in Diqing is found in the preservation of biological diversity and in "natural landscapes [that] are famed for their lofty heights, great depths, strangeness, and grandeur, [and furthermore] their spirituality, mystery, and elegance are what people yearn for" (ibid., 79).

In regard to the role of Tibetan spirituality and indigenous knowledge in the long-term management of Diqing's natural resources, the official party line is devoid of commentary. Of foremost concern is how best to guide religion into "mutually adaptive" harmony with socialism and to suppress "heterodox (or perverse) cults" (Ch. *xiejiao*) such as Falun Gong and Mentuhui (which is based on quasi-Christian doctrine). Religious belief is recognized as "[the believer's] objective spiritual need"; thus, it is reasoned that "only by earnestly respecting and protecting their freedom of religious belief and satisfying their spiritual needs can they be united around the party and the government" (Peng and Ma 2006, 63). "Normal religion" (Ch. *zhengchang zongjiao*) is valorized insofar as it contributes to the inexorable historical movement toward a socialist "middle class (materially prosperous) society" (Ch. *xiaokang shehui*), and while Tibetan Buddhism—the majority religion in Diqing—is deemed normal, it requires vigilant surveillance to prevent the "infiltration of separatist" proponents and the activities associated with the "Dalai Clique" (Peng and Ma 2006) (also see ch. 9 in this volume). As with all "believers," Diqing's Tibetan Buddhists are not to be told to abandon religion but instead instructed "to deeply love the mother country; embrace the socialist order; embrace CCP leadership; respect national laws, regulations, and policies; and pursue religion in ways that serve the highest interests of the country and the people" (Peng and Ma 2006, 66). When believers are brought into the ambit of socialist modernization, they will "emerge from the psychological illusion of a future paradise into the reality of establishing a hopeful life in the real world" (ibid.).

While ritual practices associated with *zhidak*, *yullha*, *lu*, and other genii loci could easily be classified as heterodox, they are not explicitly addressed as subjects for regulation or concern in CCP doctrine. Heterodox cults are defined by their criminality and associated with specific beliefs and activities, including brainwashing, kidnapping, excessive tithes, illicit sex, belief in the end of the world, and the exploitation of impressionable youth (Yang Hongying 2006). Because the cults are believed to be most active in remote villages where state surveillance is weak, emphasis is placed on the efficacy of training lower-level officials who represent the local state in rural communities. As is the case with "normal religion," heterodox cults are to eventually give way to Marxist philosophy, materialism, atheism, natural science, and law (ibid.).

REINSCRIBING SACRED LANDSCAPES
THROUGH VILLAGE RITUAL PRACTICE

From 2004 to 2008, working closely with staff from the Tibetan Studies Research Center in Shangrila and with other local Tibetans, I conducted five rounds of fieldwork in nine villages of Shangrila and Deqin, focusing on the status of local beliefs and practices involving sacred landscapes and their ecological significance, especially in light of the severe suppression of religious activities between 1949 and 1979. In 2011, I returned to Shangrila for follow-up work with Gesang Zeren. I had known that Tibetan communities from Ladakh and northern Nepal to the Chinese borderlands share multiple local and regional variations of geopiety based on hierophany, the manifestation of the sacred within the mundane world (Eliade and Sullivan 1987). It quickly became clear that Tibetan geopiety is also associated with theophany, the manifestation of specific deities and spirits within mundane objects, in this case, terrestrial features such as mountains, forests, waterfalls, springs, and rocks.[7] As part of a complex of theophanic geopiety, the history of Tibetan sacred sites predates Tibetan Buddhism. Tibetan-speaking communities distinguish three realms: the sky or upper region (Tib. *nam*; Wyl. *gnam*), the atmosphere or intermediate space (Wyl. *bar*), and earth (Wyl. *sa*), including lakes, rivers, and the underworld. These realms are porous, as is the distinction between the two types of beings that are mainly involved with the sacralization of mountains, especially *neri*, or "abode mountains," *zhidak*, and *yullha* (see the introduction to this volume). One class of beings is the fierce *nyen* (Wyl. *gnyan*), who are yellow in color and usually associated with mountaintops, where they live among trees and rocks. The other, the *tsen* (Wyl. *btsan*), is a very powerful class of beings who dwell in the atmospheric realm, where the sky touches the ground, especially at the summits of mountains or inside rocks.[8] *Nyen* and *tsen* are among the most feared and respected deities in the region, having the power, as a Tibetan healer from Adong Village in Deqin County explained, to shoot holes into offending humans, causing more than 1,500 kinds of disease.[9] Whereas *nyen* and *tsen* can traverse the three realms, and *lha* (higher deities) inhabit the sky or specific terrestrial sites or objects, the *lu* abide in or near water sources and trees. While residing in specific places any spirit may be called a *sadak* (Wyl. *sa bdag*) (master of the soil).[10]

Sacred precincts associated with deity-mountains are delineated roughly by a boundary between the upper and lower elevation zones near midslope. It is marked by transition points called *rigua* (Wyl. *ri 'gag*), "door of the mountain" or "barrier." In basic terms, the *rigua* marks a boundary between the divine world of the gods at the higher elevations and the mundane world of humans below (Litzinger 2004; Moseley et al. 2003). The term derives from the idea that humans must give up all resources that lie above the line to a mountain god that forever plays the role of host and may at any time exact revenge for transgressions of any kind. The line is not always sharp, clear, or straight, however, and the presence of human settlements below the line, yet within the mountain abode, is based on a contractual relationship of reciprocity between gods and humans. Tree cutting, hunting, or fishing even in certain sacred areas *below* the *rigua* line is believed to lead to retribution in the form of disease, natural disaster, or other misfortunes (see Gesang 2005, 2011; Huber 1999a; Ma and Chen 2005; Moseley et al. 2003).

While Khawa Karpo is the only *neri* in Diqing, there are hundreds of other sacred mountains that date from Tibet's pre-Buddhist cultural foundations in the Tibetan imperial era. Mountains associated with *zhidak* or *yullha*, specifically where *nyen* and *tsen* deities reside, can be classified as male, female, nuns, or monks. These mountain deities are worshiped by, and associated with, specific groups of villages, individual villages, or even individual households (Abe 1997; Coggins and Hutchinson 2006; Huber 1999b). As with the *neri*, the gods residing within these mountains "own" all of the local lands and have retreated to their mountain strongholds to allow humans to settle as guests in arable lands at their feet. As guests of these territorial gods of the land, humans are required to behave as one would with the master of a household in which one is a visitor. This pious regard is enacted through communal and individual rituals. Unlike the *neri*, the *zhidak* are not pilgrimage destinations. They compose a less literary, more oral, and yet universal Tibetan territorial practice.[11] Their ecological significance is evident by the fact that although most of the Zhongdian basin was severely deforested by national timber-cutting operations from the 1970s to the 1990s, *zhidak* and *yullha* mountain forests are plainly visible on slopes behind villages across the basin. Some are forest patches that survived intensive logging due to their locations within *rigua*; others have been planted or have regenerated following the restoration of traditional religious practices since the 1980s.

Zhidak and *yullha* are inscribed in the landscape and in local consciousness through folklore and through a cycle of daily, monthly, seasonal, and annual ritual observances. For each mountain deity, there are also specific prayers for specific occasions, many of which have been preserved in ritual texts called *songyi* (Wyl. *bsang yig*). On the first, eighth, and fifteenth day of every lunar month, people visit shrines in the forests or at the foot of the mountain, where they offer barley, rye, wheat, buttermilk, wine, incense, and other items to the gods, who can be quite vicious when offended. The largest ritual occurs just after the new year on the Tibetan calendar, when each household is required to send at least one male representative to a predawn procession that ascends the mountain of the *zhidak* starting before dawn and often not arriving until the afternoon. Each man inserts a bamboo pole representing an arrow into a stone ritual cairn (Tib. *zangbon*; Wyl. *rtse phung*), barley wine and barley grains are thrown into the air, and prayers specific to the abiding deity are recited (see ch. 9 in this volume). These acts bind families and individuals within community and cosmos, leaving the visible symbolic mark of cairns and arrows atop numerous peaks in the region through all seasons. Due to traditional assumptions that women are ritually impure, most villages still forbid them from ascending summits of major male god-mountains; females can ascend with males during the new year renewal ceremonies only if a family has no male representative. In some communities, they can also climb mountains associated with female *zhidak* for ritual or other purposes. A forty-nine-year-old woman from Jisha Village told me that the restrictions seem fair to her; women conduct the main rituals at *lu* sites, give offerings to the *zhidak* and *yullha* at household and community shrines in the village, and, as she said, "Men have to leave the village to work, and they need more protection."[12] The forests are as closely associated with the *zhidak* and *yullha* as are the mountains themselves, and these locales serve as refugia for spruce, larch, pine, oak, rhododendron, birch, and other subtropical and temperate tree species. As mentioned, though most sacred mountains are associated with entire communities, smaller mountains are exclusive sites or foci of worship for individual families and households. For example, in Nedu Village, which lies north of the Zhongdian basin but still within Jiantang Township, there are four *zhidak* and twenty-four *yullha* mountains, one associated with and worshiped by each household in the village.[13]

In addition to the forest and wildlife conservation function of traditional sacred geography, there are also hydrological conservation functions. Mountain forests not only conserve water in catchment zones above village settlements but also help prevent flooding during periods of high rainfall or snowmelt. Maintaining a supply of clean drinking water in dense settlements with an abundance of human and livestock wastes was no doubt an important impetus in the development of microgeographic forms of geopiety targeting water sources. In this regard, every village in my survey had community and household sites for the propitiation of *lu*. In the village center and its immediate periphery, individual families or groups of families manage small groups of trees as abodes for *lu*. Snakes, frogs, and other reptiles and amphibians are associated with *lu*, either as guardians, possessions ("livestock"), or representatives. It is not difficult to imagine that the presence of healthy individuals or populations of reptiles and amphibians near wooded water sources might be associated with the "wealth" of the *lu* and, in modern ecological terms, the quality of the water source. *Lu* are also considered to be guardians of secret treasures. Ritual acts at the familial *lu* sites are often prescribed by a local reincarnated master or *tulku* (Wyl. *sprul sku*) as a means of curing illness. *Lu* are closely associated with diseases of the skin, such as leprosy, and an offense against the *lu*, which can include contaminating a waterway, will lead to retributive illness. To cure a family member afflicted by a *lu*-related disease, of which there are more than 420, a person can bury tricolored cloth, grains, and other offerings in a cooking vessel at the base of one of the trees in the grove. As a Tibetan doctor and ritual master in Deqin County explained, "When the *lu* is sick, people can get sick."[14] At such times, offerings can be made to the *lu* in order to heal it, just as herbal medicine is given to the patient.

In addition to familial groves, there are also larger communal *lukong* (Wyl. *klu khang*), "palaces" or "temples" for the *lu* in the form of small stone altars or cairns near community wells, springs, ponds, streams, or other nearby water sources, and these shrines are associated with water sources and surrounding groves and forests larger than those of household *lu* sites. Here, members of each family burn incense and make other offerings at regular intervals, and in spring and early summer, women gather to sing prayers for rain when the barley crops are young and vulnerable. Thus there is an association not only between the *lu* and terrestrial hydrology but also between these deities of the aquatic realm and atmospheric sources of precipitation.

ANIMATE LANDSCAPES INSCRIBED: COMMUNITY-BASED CONSERVATION IN HAMUGU

In 2002–3, Gesang Zeren and Lazong Ruiba established the Hamugu Village Center for the Protection of Indigenous Ecology and Culture. As Gesang Zeren explained in 2004:

> Our village is remote and poor. The average income is not even ¥300; we
> grow enough grain to fill our stomachs. So many years after Liberation,
> our production systems—raising livestock and planting crops—are about
> the same. We have thirty-plus families, about 260 people. When we started
> this project, we already had some kind of foundation. When I was a cadre,
> I already had some idea about resource conservation. I had these ideas
> about conservation, and the government even contributed ¥400,000 for
> water resource management, to move water down from the mountain into
> the fields. The problem is that our people are poorly trained and poorly
> educated. Everyone depends on the crops. And if the heavens bring rain, we
> eat; if it doesn't rain, we don't eat. In twenty to thirty years, our standard
> of living hasn't improved much—we just fill our bellies—so we hope to
> begin to bring some benefits to our village. We already had an ideologi-
> cal foundation, and local people believed in us. If we told local people to
> do something, they would willingly do what we suggested. [Later on, he
> explained that the central government had forced them to meet unrealistic
> crop production quotas before the 1980s, so in a very real sense he contrasts
> his own leadership with the poor collective and commune leadership of the
> past.]
>   The first thing we did was to develop tourism resources. First, we
> needed to protect the resources, . . . so we had a big meeting with all of
> the villagers. It wasn't just us making rules, saying you should do this and
> that. Men sat down, women sat down, old people sat down. After much

discussion and much work, we came up with a common understanding, a consensus, a path for protecting resources, a way out of our troubles. By developing common ideas, we figured out ways of protecting the resources; we had an action plan. Everyone agreed on this plan, and everyone signed the contract. Every household signed; the operating principles for ecological protection were agreed on by everyone. The contents include establishing a cultural ecology area. Why protect the culture and ecology? Because they are inseparable. Because Chinese influence has been too pervasive. The clothing I am wearing right now was made by Chinese people; the clothing I am wearing wasn't made by Tibetans. As different cultures come into contact, the local culture, the host culture, is itself diminished.

Gesang Zeren chronicled the history of Hamugu and wrote a guide to its sacred geography. He used my translation of it to apply for conservation and development grants from the state and from NGOs. Although not originally from the village, Gesang resided there with his wife, who was a villager, and before her death, he convinced each household to pool contributions and grant money from the World Wide Fund for Nature and a number of national organizations in China in order to erect a traditional rammed-earth-and-timber-frame building to house facilities for local environmental and cultural education. When the Pulitzer Prize–winning journalist and globalization pundit Thomas Friedman visited Hamugu during a tour of green development initiatives in Shangrila in 2005, he wrote, "The good, and surprising, news I found in Shangri-La was how much the poor villagers here were coming up with their own green growth solutions. For instance, the 39 families in the village of Hamugu have bundled their savings to build a lodge for ecotourists drawn by the wetlands. 'We just need a Web site,' the manager told me."[15]

In 2004, Gesang hoped that the center would include courses on literary Tibetan (few people in the region outside of Buddhist monasteries can read or write), English, and remedial standard Chinese, along with traditional artisanal skills, religious traditions, and ecological knowledge. From 2004 to 2008, villagers also maintained small-scale ecotourism services offering horse packing into the village's rugged hinterlands, a low-impact trek up the sacred Duji Gorge to spend a night in log herders' huts in a yak-grazing meadow next to Chuyun Spirit Lake, and a climb to the summit of Shika Mountain, which, according to local people, cannot be defiled by small numbers of hikers (fig. 8.2).

FIGURE 8.2 Mount Shika as seen from the slopes of another god-mountain (Mount Jiza) farther west. In the middle ground is Chuyun Spirit Lake, with nearby yak herders' huts belonging to Hamugu families who bring their stock to this and other nearby high-elevation meadows in the warm season. Hamugu Village (not visible) is in the valley next to the Napahai Prairie, to the left and far down the slope of Mount Shika. Photo by Chris Coggins.

Gesang's role as an advocate for sustainable development is tied to his literacy.[16] He is one of the few older villagers fluent in standard Chinese; he is also a former cadre and a gifted writer, and thus he became the primary interpreter of the landscape and local identity for a growing number of curious visitors. His written guide to Hamugu describes the village and its hinterlands in microgeographic detail, providing a textual "map" of the Napahai Prairie, which the village abuts in the valley, the Duji Gorge, the high-elevation yak-grazing meadows, the sacred lake, a cave where numerous spiritual masters attained enlightenment, and the myriad wonders of floral and faunal splendor associated with different elevation zones (listed with common names in standard Chinese) (Gesang 2005, 2011). As an *inter-*

pretation of Tibetan geopiety made legible to outsiders, the work emphasizes the pastoral qualities of the landscape and the harmonious relations between humans and nonhumans, a peaceable kingdom infused with Buddhist values and teeming with biological diversity.

> Autumn and winter transform the grassland into a golden-yellow sea. The distant and mysterious peaks, Shika and Meiduosila Snow Mountains, are reflected on the surface of the lake. At this time of year the spirit lake and prairie become a paradise for migratory birds. Huge flocks of rare species like the black-necked crane, bar-headed goose, ruddy shelduck, mallard, black stork, herons, and egrets congregate on the wet prairie. Now flying through the sky, now flocking together to display their aerial choreography, their resounding calls pierce the blue sky above the snow land plains. . . . According to tradition, the black-necked crane and the Tibetan people both prayed before the Buddha in ancient times, thus Tibetans across the generations have refrained from killing it or driving it off, and the crane vowed never to encroach on our croplands. The crane does not eat a single grain of barley, and on the head of the crane grow three barley grains. Although this is just a legend, Tibetan people have a profound respect for nature, and traditional beliefs concerning the natural harmony between humans and birds is amply illustrated here. . . . Hamugu residents inhabit white-walled Tibetan-style timber frame houses set among winding streams. All along the village pathways grow hawthorns. Upon entering the village one senses the simple respect and thanks that residents express toward the gods, who provide generations of villagers with blessings and protection. Daily work activities, household production and reproduction, rites and rituals, and important festivals all express deference for nature and ecological constraint. (Gesang 2005, 3)

During the same time period, the neighboring natural villages of Bulun, Cuogu, and Jinugu, which, like Hamugu, are part of Nishi Administrative Village, pursued a very different development plan. They leased their lands, which include the south side of Shika Mountain, to a Hong Kong–based corporation for fifty to one hundred years enabling construction of a cable car system from near the valley floor to the summit of the god-mountain. When the system was under construction in the summer of 2005, many Tibetans in the Zhongdian basin attributed a regionwide drought to Shika's anger, but there were no overt challenges to the project, and today the cable cars shuttle thousands of tourists to Shika's summit each year. By 2011, house-holds in the three villages were earning an estimated ¥5,000 ($785) per year over their base income, while Hamugu households continued to pursue their own strategies of economic diversification.

Despite the efforts of Gesang Zeren, Lazong Ruiba, and other villagers, the Hamugu Village Center for Cultural and Ecological Protection as well as the village's small-scale ecotourism scheme failed to thrive, but Gesang did not give up hope. As he noted in June 2011:

> In terms of marketing, a small village like this does not receive substantial support from the government. So while taking this idea into the marketplace, [one must note that] it is a "high-end" (Ch. *gaoduan*) mode of tourism; it is not facing the same kind of problems associated with mass tourism. The clientele come from relatively developed countries, and they are relatively wealthy people. They can appreciate the beauty of nature. We don't have the opportunity to connect with that kind of market, and this is a severe obstacle.

At that time, I asked him if he felt that the *zhidak* and *lu* were fairly stable cultural traditions, and he responded:

> Of course! These traditions have been handed down over several thousand years! How could one say that tomorrow *zhidak* will suddenly be be gone?! For twenty or thirty years, before the Reform and Opening period, after Liberation (1949), it was widely propounded that ghosts and spirits do not exist. "Belief in gods is forbidden! Belief in ghosts is forbidden!" Did this change anything? Nope—no changes. Minority peoples' beliefs are inevita-ble beliefs. This has gained legal standing as the laws that ensure freedom of belief. This simply cannot be changed. Over thousands of years, it has been unalterable. In each dynasty, it has been unsusceptible to change. How can we now manage to go and change it? Even where science is fairly developed, economic knowledge stands as the scientific version of development. That is merely a kind of faith or belief as well.

CONCLUSION

The functionality of Diqing's Tibetan sacred landscapes in the protection of ecosystems is well documented (Hakkenberg 2008; Ma and Chen 2005; Salick et al. 2007), but it is important to keep in mind several fundamental ontological and cosmological distinctions, first, for a clearer understanding of animate landscapes and, second, for an appreciation of why they are not necessarily the gods' gifts to nature conservation. The materialist logic of agropastoral sacred landscapes is manifest in the fact that forests, wildlife, pastures, mountain slopes, water sources, and settlement sites are sustainable only if resource offtake is restricted to certain zones, times of year, and specific users. Restrictions must be maintained through systems of collective protection of the commons based on powerful affective associations such as fear, reverence, devotion, and the like. While this may go some distance toward explaining the ubiquity and durability of animate landscapes, it does not go all the way—animism encompasses a full range of subjects and objects, many of which fall far outside the modern Western social categories associated with "resource conservation" (see ch. 9 in this volume). In terms of origins, some anthropologists have argued that the high level of complexity required for human social behavior favored the evolution of social intelligence that was then extended to objects of nature ("erroneously" or not is a matter of perspective). Such a dichotomous view incorrectly presumes a fundamental a priori division "between the inanimate and the animate, between the non-human and the human, and between the natural and the social."[17] It also assumes that "life and mind are interior properties of individuals that are given, independently and in advance of their involvement in the world." As an alternative view, Tim Ingold states:

> To "talk with a tree" . . . is a question not of (mistakenly) attributing to it an inner intelligence and then configuring how it might decide to react to what one does but of perceiving "what *it* does as one acts towards it, being aware concurrently of changes in oneself and the tree." Responsiveness, in this view, amounts to a kind of sensory participation, a coupling of the movement of one's attention to the movement of aspects of the world. . . . Human beings everywhere perceive their environments in the responsive mode not because of innate cognitive predisposition but because *to perceive at all they must already be situated in a world and committed to the relationships this entails.* (Bird-David 1999, 82; italics mine)

The last point speaks to the ontological depth of being "situated in a world" and how our very responsiveness, whatever forms it takes, depends on the complexity of the social relations entailed therein. In Diqing, the personal idiosyncrasies of *zhidak* loom large. The remarkable array of transactions between god-mountains and local people captures their socially complex, idiosyncratic, and deeply affective interrelationships. Human fortunes may rise and fall with the wrath or beneficence of these powerful deities, gods who are not strictly bound by codes of conduct or a moral order but who respond, not always predictably, to acts of devotion or violation carried out by their mortal guests. Whether we consider them forces of nature or transcendent and sacred beings, *zhidak* comprise an absolute space that is fundamentally political.

In summary, the complex sociality of humans and supernature that composes agropastoral sacred space ensures the persistence of certain forms of ecological stewardship in Tibetan communities throughout Diqing. Geopiety is a strong foundation for alliances with conservation organizations (Ma and Chen 2005), but animate landscapes and their denizens cannot be reduced to the governable subjects and governable spaces of nature conservation alone, at least not for the time being.

CHAPTER 8. ANIMATE LANDSCAPES

This research was made possible by the ASIANetwork Freeman Student-Faculty Fellows Program and the American Philosophical Society.

1   Lefebvre (1991, 48) describes the political and religious nature of absolute space as "made up of fragments of nature located at sites which were chosen for their intrinsic qualities (cave, mountaintop, spring, river), but whose very consecration ended up by stripping them of their natural characteristics and uniqueness. Thus natural space was soon populated by political forces." Lefebvre's assumption of "natural space" is problematic but conforms to his project of establishing an emancipatory "rhythm analysis" in which "the laws of nature and the laws governing our bodies . . . overlap" (1974, 206). Building on Marx, Lefebvre posits that in the process of abstracting labor from its reproductive social and communal functions (during the rise of Europe's bourgeois towns and cities), abstract space became "[t]he dominant form of space, that of the centres of wealth and power . . . [which] seeks, often by violent means, to reduce the obstacles and resistance it encounters [in peripheral spaces]" (1991, 49).

2   Gesang Zeren, a retired agricultural technologist who was persecuted during the Cultural Revolution because of his descent from a local family of nobles (Ch. *tusi*), played the lead role in organizing Hamugu community development projects. Like many Tibetans in the area, he has a Chinese and a Tibetan name.

3   I have translated the oral and written accounts, which appear here in modified form.

4   Yúdice (2003, 17) notes, "This culturalization of the economy has not occurred naturally; it has been carefully coordinated via agreements on trade and intellectual property, such as GATT and the WTO, laws controlling the movement of

mental and manual labor. . . . In other words, the new phase of economic growth, the cultural economy, is also political economy."

5 For more on the discursive formation of "indigenous space" in southwest China, see Hathaway 2010a.

6 The term "geopiety" denotes the worship of and awe and reverence felt for natural landscape features or the spiritual forces that animate or dwell within them (Cosgrove 2000; Huber 1999a, 1999b).

7 Eliade and Sullivan (1987) distinguish between theophany and kratophany (hierophany associated with supernatural power *not* associated with spirits or deities). On Tibetan theophanies, see also Belleza 2005; Huber 1999a; Makley 2007; and chapter 9 in this volume.

8 Wang Xiaosong, personal communication, Zhongdian, Diqing Tibetan Autonomous Prefecture, 2006.

9 Sinang Dorje, personal communication, Adong Village, Deqin County, Diqing Tibetan Autonomous Prefecture, 2006.

10 Wang Xiaosong, personal communication, Zhongdian, Diqing Tibetan Autonomous Prefecture, 2006; and Giovanni da Col, personal communication, Shengping Township, Diqing Tibetan Autonomous Prefecture, June 2004.

11 This is not to suggest that there are no texts associated with the mountain deities; see the description of *songyi* (Tib. *bsang yig*) in the next paragraph.

12 Yangzong, personal communication, Jisha Village, Diqing Tibetan Autonomous Prefecture, 2006.

13 Aun Paba, personal communication, Nedu Village, Diqing Tibetan Autonomous Prefecture, 2006.

14 Sinang Dorje, personal communication, Adong Village, Deqin County, Diqing Tibetan Autonomous Prefecture, 2006.

15 Friedman's (2005, 1) assessment of local efforts was laudatory, and he noted that the stakes were high for the country as a whole: "Put simply: if development doesn't come to Shangri-La and other rural areas, the divide between haves and have-nots will widen and destabilize China. But if the wrong development comes here, it will add to global warming and ravage the rural environment where many of China's indigenous cultures and species are nested."

16 See Schein 2000 for comparison to "self-appointed scribes" among the Miao who served as collectors of what was perceived to be vanishing or imperiled culture.

17 See Ingold's response to Bird-David and others in the forum discussion in Bird-David 1999.

The Amoral Other

• • •

STATE-LED DEVELOPMENT AND

MOUNTAIN DEITY CULTS AMONG

TIBETANS IN AMDO REBGONG

Charlene E. Makley

IN recent years, the Sino-Tibetan borderlands, especially in the Tibet
Autonomous Region (Central Tibet), and also in western Sichuan, Gansu,
Yunnan, and Qinghai (Amdo and Kham), have seen political and economic crises perhaps unmatched since the Maoist years. A series of dev-
astating "natural" disasters in the wake of Chinese state-led development
and resource extraction since the late 1990s (floods, grassland deterioration,
earthquakes, mudslides) exacerbated many rural Tibetans' sense of vulnerability and marginalization in their mountainous home regions. The protests that broke out across Tibetan regions during China's vaunted "Olympic
year," in 2008, led to a military crackdown and intensified state rhetoric
vilifying the Dalai Lama and his "separatist clique" as instigators and liken-
ing Tibetan protesters to "terrorists" (Barnett 2009; Makley 2009). By 2012,
those tensions culminated in an unprecedented series of self-immolations by
young Tibetan monks, nuns, and laity calling attention to the ongoing militarization of their regions and heightened state scrutiny of their activities.[1]
Just as in 2008, central state media accounts worked to individualize and
pathologize these new protesters, depicting them either as mentally unstable
individuals or as tragic dupes of cunning anti-state organizers.

Such efforts on the part of central leaders attempt to deflect attention
away from the troubled history and cultural politics of landscape and ter-

ritory in the Sino-Tibetan borderlands since the beginning of Chinese Communist Party intervention in the region in the early to mid-twentieth century. This chapter brings an anthropological perspective to bear on these most recent events by considering post-Mao state-led development agendas in the region, framed in claims to the technocratic management of objective market forces, as themselves a cultural politics with long-term consequences for Sino-Tibetan relations. An emphasis on "cultural politics" draws attention to the fact that all human experience is necessarily intersubjective, mediated by particular, historically grounded interpretive practices, as well as by unequal access to the prestige, authority, or resources necessary to render those practices authoritative or dominant. From this perspective, the meanings, causes, and consequences of all things and events are under constant, sometimes violent, negotiation (Irvine 1989; Keane 1997; Sahlins 2000a).

In this light, anthropologists of economics and development have approached capitalism as itself a cultural process or a "moral economy," emphasizing the great transnational charisma of triumphalist narratives of capitalist globalization and free markets since the 1980s especially (Comaroff and Comaroff 2000; Graeber 2001; Tsing 2002). Among national elites, we have seen a heady mix of, on the one hand, a profound faith in the salvific potential of capitalist growth and development and, on the other, the *moral* promise of economic methods for discovering objective or universal truths and primary causes of market behaviors driving social processes. Indeed, Deng Xiaoping, the much-hailed new leader of the post-Mao People's Republic of China in the early 1980s, famously promoted his pragmatic market reforms with the slogan "[economic] development is the first principle (Ch. *ying daoli*, lit. 'hard truth')." Such economistic premises have undergirded the massive restructuring of life in China over the past thirty years. Simultaneously with state officials' claims to be presiding over a "New China" and a new moral economy, or "socialism with Chinese characteristics," uneasy alliances between state and private interests have channeled resources and labor into the construction of new institutions, technologies, and infrastructure for the creation and movement of global capital,[2] even as, in the early reform years, Maoist state investments in education and social welfare were withdrawn or increasingly threatened.[3]

These processes in the Sino-Tibetan borderlands play out in ongoing contestations over the material and epistemological grounds of space, personhood, and value. Drawing on fieldwork (2002–11) among Amdo Tibetans in the rapidly urbanizing town of Longwu, the seat of both Huangnan Prefecture and Tongren County in the center of the famous Tibetan region of Rebgong in Qinghai (see map 1, F), this chapter focuses on the vigorous (re)emergence of local Tibetan cults of *zhidak* (Wyl. *gzhi bdag*) (see also ch. 8 in this volume), territorial deities commonly abiding within mountains, under post-Mao reforms. That revival occurred despite state-sponsored efforts to encourage Tibetans to abandon their "backward" ways and prioritize instead the "vision of commodity production" (Ch. *shangpin shengchan yanguang*) necessary for newly liberated markets. Under intensifying state-sponsored development pressures in the first decade of the 2000s, the particularly contested position of the Tibetan deity medium (Tib. *lhawa*; Wyl. *lha pa*), the person whose body hosts the *zhidak* on behalf of a village, points up the stakes and consequences of the inherently indeterminate nature of human meaning and agency (the capacity to act socially). This is in part because spectacular claims to close relationships with the warlike deities threatened to embody and apotheosize an amoral Other in the midst of market reforms, a selfish and desirous, yet place-based (capitalist?) subject escaping state, Buddhist monastic, or household disciplines.

Zhidak in Rebgong are powerful, mostly masculine deities lodged in surrounding mountains and linked to particular Tibetan villages or nomad encampments as divine rulers of the watersheds that sustain them. They are supposed to be "tamed" to serve Buddhist incarnate lamas in the famous monastery of Rongwo, the erstwhile human rulers of the region. Yet, as commanders of vast entourages of divine minions, mountain deities specialize in protecting and mediating access to worldly fortune and wealth for lay villagers and their households.

Scholars argue that Tibetans' relationships with such autochthonic deities are centuries old, predating even the introduction of Buddhism from India in the seventh to ninth centuries, but in such eastern Tibetan frontier regions as Rebgong, contemporary *zhidak* cults are intimately bound up with the history of Buddhist sectarian and monastic expansion eastward from Lhasa. Particularly important deities were established or tamed primarily by Buddhist lamas as a village's protector when the village entered into reciprocal patron-preceptor relations with a monastery—especially in the seventeenth to eighteenth centuries when Rongwo monastery converted to the ascendant Geluk sect, and the Shartshang lineage of incarnate lamas consolidated rule over patrilineal networks of Tibetan farmers and nomads, which were later called the "twelve patron tribes of Rongwo" (Wyl. *rong bo nang shog bcu gnyis*) ('jigs med theg mchog 1988; Stevenson 1999; T. Yangdon Dhondup 2011).

With the 1980s revival of Tibetan ritual practices that had been proscribed during the Maoist years (1950s–70s), annual festivals for *zhidak* were vigorously revived in the valley's main urbanizing villages, while monastic institutions and festivals were reorganized on a much smaller scale than before. And in 2005, elders in Jima Village (pop. approx. 2,100),[4] the central urban village in town and home to some of the wealthiest Tibetan beneficiaries of market reforms, with donations from Jima households as well as from foreign NGOs, organized the expansion of perhaps the most magnificent mountain deity shrine in the province for what they take to be the most powerful mountain deity in Rebgong—Amnye Shachong, divine ruler of the entire Rebgong region. Meanwhile, beginning early in the first decade of the 2000s, Tibetan businessmen across the valley revived the annual practice of sponsoring offerings and meals for Rongwo's monk assembly during the fifth lunar month, but they added a new practice at the culmination of the event: a communal incense offering to various protector deities, including their favored *zhidak*, on the ridge just above the monastery, a site well chosen for its visibility to the town below.

DEVELOPMENT AND INFRASTRUCTURE AS CULTURAL POLITICS

What should we make of such practices and the contestations they engender in the contemporary context? An analytic of cultural politics suggests that we need to see them as emerging in dialogue with post-Mao economic development projects that have both expanded on and challenged Tibetans' understandings of space, personhood, and value. The most consequential rubric of state-led development efforts affecting Rebgong Tibetans in recent years has been the Great Western Development (Xibu Da Kaifa) campaign, launched by central leaders in 2000. Assessments of the campaign in the middle of the first decade of the 2000s suggest that it was not meant as a fundamental redirection of central development priorities to the west. Instead observers noted that it was a relatively modest central investment in major "infrastructure" (Ch. *jichu sheshi*) projects designed to both consolidate central state control over western landscapes (figured as manageable "resources" [Ch. *ziyuan*]) and bring about a grand vision of national economic integration largely benefiting the more "open" (Ch. *kaifang*) east (Oakes 2004; Holbig 2004). The Great Western Development campaign thus encapsulated the dilemmas facing reform-era PRC state officials (including Tibetans) at all levels by the first decade of the 2000s: the campaign heightened pressures for "total economic [read: 'market'] solutions" (Goodman 2004b, 381) at the same time that officials struggled to secure central state legitimacy amid the lures of privatization and the seeming decline of socialist ideals.[5]

Importantly, campaign planners from the beginning were strongly pre-occupied with financing the construction of infrastructure, which they took to be material structures and technologies (roads, railways, dams) that would automatically enhance integration (Holbig 2004, 348–49).[6] In this, Chinese technocrats, many of whom had studied economics abroad and looked specifically at the United States as a model for westward expansion and development, were drawing on a long legacy of Western social thought that relegated the material to an inert or concrete ground for the progressive projects of rational actors. Meanwhile, in the context of statist seculariza-tion efforts and the rise of Western science in China as elsewhere, terms for "religion" or "magic" connoted the appeal benighted ideas about causes and effects had for irrational or uneducated people (cf. Sahlins 2000b).

By contrast, a focus on cultural politics would lead us to ask: What *counts* as materiality and agency, and to whom, in particular situations? What practices objectify, materialize, and thereby prioritize or devalue per-sons and things, and with what consequences? From this perspective, we could not take the technologies and networks that are widely recognized as material infrastructure for granted as just inert "channels" for global flows (pace, e.g., Larkin 2008). Instead, they are actually the contingent outcome of competing "scale-making projects" (Tsing 2002, 69) that work to build cultural-material frameworks (or assemblages) for human and nonhuman participation and value creation (Goffman 1981).[7]

Taking such a cultural politics as the starting point, then in the context of globalizing capitalisms, any assertion that something is infrastructure would have to be taken as part and parcel of larger frameworks in which particular types of agents, spaces, and times are valorized and foregrounded, while others are devalorized and obscured (Sassen 1999; Lee and Lipuma 2002; Humphrey 2003). The technocratic focus on (material) infrastructure and all the related investment rhetoric thus could be seen as justifying, even moralizing claims to a naturalized, unmarked ground against which the fig-ures of transcendent capitalist agents (i.e., entrepreneurs, securities traders, enlightened state officials, development and NGO officials, etc.) appear. In practice, notions of infrastructure as inert, material background allow for

such agents to claim socially *unmediated* actions and consequences (Mazzarella 2004; Keane 2008)— that is, such premises allow development agents to
refute corruption charges and strategically deny the ongoing embeddedness
of construction projects in conflicts over responsibilities for and access to
the flows of investments they unleash.

CONTESTED NOTIONS OF MATERIALITY:
THE INDETERMINACY OF DEITY RECOGNITION

Tibetans' recent revival of *zhidak* cults in Qinghai are grounded in alternative notions of materiality, participation, and value invoked by situated
persons and collectives, a cultural politics emerging within and against competing state, capitalist, and Buddhist frameworks under post-Mao reforms.
Further, it is a hindrance to simply characterize these practices as the conservation of Tibetan (lay) "religion" in the face of "modernizing" pressures
(e.g., Blondeau 1995; Karmay 1994),[8] or just as new responses to perceived
market vulnerabilities or unfulfilled aspirations (e.g., Comaroff and Comaroff 2000; cf. Kapferer 2002; Taussig 1980).

In fact, Tibetans across the Himalayas have long figured their landscapes,
bodies, households, and regional networks as constantly vulnerable to the
interventions and operations of outside (human and nonhuman) agents and
forces (see ch. 8 in this volume). Human agency under such conditions was
recognized and evaluated in various efforts to evidence, materialize, and
control such outside agents and forces. Historically, especially as the Geluk
sect moved east, it was the Buddhist lamas' promise, via their tantric ritual
prowess, to tame and to channel such forces on behalf of Tibetan communities that justified the incorporation of humans and deities as monastic
patrons or protectors. In the case of Rebgong's Jima Village, for example, the
famous seventeenth-century lama founder of the ruling Shartshang lineage
at Rongwo monastery is said to have given lay Buddhist vows to Jima's main
mountain deity, Amnye Shachong.

But as monastic centers in the frontier zone attracted trading towns and
rival regimes into the early twentieth century, the transcendent agency and
moralizing ethics associated with the Buddhist lama always came up against
the indeterminacy and generativity of deity recognition.[9] No one could fully
control when and how a divine agent would be manifest and recognized.
Buddhist monastic discourses from the period include much derision and
skepticism of laypersons' various claims to unmediated access to divine

FIGURE 9.1 Amnye Shachong in his human Hero aspect. Exterior mural. Shachong temple, Jima Village, Rebgong, summer 2005. Photo by Charlene E. Makley.

agency—especially when lay specialists like local mediums were claiming, in spectacular public trance states, to embody those deities whose mundane activities trafficked in what Buddhist discourses construed as the baser desires of human individuals and collectivities (Lama Tsanpo 1962 [1820]).

In this context then, the indeterminacy of *zhidak* recognition among Tibetans past and present can be seen as epitomizing the indeterminacy of human agency and meaning in general. Amid the sedentarizing and centralizing efforts of Buddhist monasteries and competing outside regimes in the frontier zone into the twentieth century, mountain deities, substantialized in offering rites and regularly embodied via lay mediums presiding over village socio-ritual propriety, were thus positioned as potentially threatening, uncontrollable Others to both monastic and state officials. Cults of *zhidak* were proscribed in Rebgong, along with all public Buddhist practices, after Chinese Communist Democratic Reforms in 1958. But with post-Mao reforms, villages throughout the valley found new, younger mediums with the blessings and confirmations of rehabilitated incarnate lamas,[10] and they organized to reestablish annual village offering rites to *zhidak* on an increasingly grand scale. This surge in village-level practices officially labeled "folk" custom (Ch. *minjian*) in the 1980s and 1990s occurred even as state officials focused their wary scrutiny and regulation on the revival of institutionalized "religious" (Ch. *zongjiao*) practices centered on Buddhist monasteries and Muslim mosques in the region (Goldstein and Kapstein 1998; Makley 2007). Importantly, with the launch of the Great Western Development campaign in 2000, these cultural politics of materiality and agency intensified in the Rebgong valley in perhaps unprecedented ways.

THE THREAT OF THE OTHER UNDER WESTERN DEVELOPMENT

As early as the mid-1980s, Qinghai development planners had sought ways to alter the province's national reputation as a site of "black (i.e, secret) infrastructure" and construct it instead as an extension of an expanding Chinese "market" (Ch. *shichang*), a repository of untouched human and natural capital that could be put to work for foreign and domestic investors.[11] In development and education circles, "human capital theory" imported from the United States and Europe replaced earlier Marxist-Leninist objectifications of people as labor units (Bass 1998). Qinghai residents could now be objectified and valorized as potential stores of measurable skills for participation in the market, and into the 1990s the trope of "quality" (Ch. *suzhi*) came to be the standard measure for evaluating the overall quantity and usability of the human capital embodied in individuals, sectors, regions, and indeed in whole *minzu* groups (Anagnost 2004; Yan 2003).[12] But frustrated provincial planners found that the region could not compete with the lucrative networks of capital and influence in the preferred eastern provinces under reforms, and Chinese and Tibetan elites alike began to look for causes in the low "quality" of Qinghai's "backward" ethnic minority populations (e.g., Wang and Bai 1987).

By 2000 then, the Great Western Development campaign was a broad *moral* rubric under which competing central and provincial economic development efforts could be brought to bear on Tibetan communities. Campaign projects and rhetoric sought to both maintain the region as a site for the exploitation of resources and to highlight ideally entrepreneurial, "high-quality" market agents whose profits there were supposed to fuel *national* economic growth.[13] In this context, the participation of local Tibetan villagers in *zhidak* cults and especially the activities of *lhawa*, or *zhidak* mediums, became particularly problematic as claims to alternative frameworks for materiality and value.

FIGURE 9.2   Tibetan *lhawa* possessed by village *zhidak* at the annual harvest festival, summer 2008. Photo by Charlene E. Makley.

Tibetan mountain deities embody the increasing unmanageability and expanding scope of newly privatized consumerist motivations under post-Mao reforms in the valley. More importantly, in this context, mountain deities threaten to apotheosize an amoral, specifically Tibetan (masculine) subjectivity that is grounded in the dangerous compulsions of both bodily desires and obligatory exchange. In the valley, this played out most crucially in intergenerational, lay-monastic, and state-local conflicts over control of ritualized social networks for creating and accessing increasingly mobile capital, a process that amounted to the rise of new "unruly coalitions" among local elites (Verdery 1996, 193). Thus under reforms and increasingly into the 1990s and the first decade of the 2000s, the figure of the *lhawa* emerged as a newly indeterminate medium for a cultural politics of materiality: he embodied the heightened stakes under the Great Western Development campaign of competing efforts to assert and maintain relatively backgrounded infrastructures for morally problematic individual and collective aspirations. In other words, under the intensifying scrutiny of both state and popular economic practices against the standard of an ideally open national-global market, the spectacular visibility and corporeality of the *lhawa* in public trance rendered discomfortingly noticeable the place-based social networks, jurisdictions, and material efficacies among Tibetans that had been relatively (and expediently) unmarked in the early reform years (Chau 2005, 239).

As many observers have pointed out, Chinese imperial courts have for centuries attempted to control or incorporate local deity cults, and the rationalism and authority of state bureaucracies were often the ground against which local mediums were portrayed as *individually intentioned* charlatans and swindlers.[14] In the twentieth century, Chinese nationalist regimes attempted to define and regulate ritual practices as folk "superstition" (Ch. *mixin*) or institutionalized "religion" (Duara 1991). Under the official materialist atheism of the ascendant Chinese Communist Party, accusations of individual trickery could be leveled at any ritual specialist in order to justify central control or eradication (Goldstein et al. 2009). Yet with post-Mao reforms and the 1982 reinstatement of "freedom of religious belief," state officials had to negotiate a delicate balance, especially in Tibetan regions, between regulating and allowing scope for the revival of both lay ethnic "traditions" (Ch. *chuantong*) and Buddhist monastic "religion" (Ch. *fojiao*), even as the practice of folk "superstitions" was still defined as illegal. As Ann Anagnost has pointed out, the 1980s saw intensifying public debates and state scrutiny in Han regions directed at a perceived boom in folk ritual practices and deity cults, including mediumship, that was seen to be channeling excessive amounts of resources to ritual specialists. Most importantly, it was the "social relational" aspect of such practices, manifest in the perduring obligations created in gift exchanges, that was most threatening to state officials at the time: "the idea that [ritual specialists] may indeed be social creations directly confronts the state's attribution to them of motivated self-interest" (Anagnost 1987, 52).

In Tibetan regions like Rebgong, however, the exigencies of ethnic politics after brutal forced assimilation efforts during the Maoist years meant that lay "folk" practices, including *zhidak* cults, were *less* subject to state scrutiny than Buddhist lamas, monks, and monastic institutions, the erstwhile rulers of the region. It was only in the late 1990s and early in the first decade of the 2000s, and especially with the reemergence in central state discourse of the old category of "heterodox (or perverse) cults" (Ch. *xiejiao*),[15] that there were increasing calls in Qinghai to extend state supervision and regulation to lay "folk" practices, including *zhidak* cults. The category of "heterodox cult" emerged most prominently in 1999, on the eve of the Great Western Development campaign.[16] It famously appeared in central legislation aimed at containing, indeed crushing, the expanding Falun Gong movement, whose practitioners included increasing numbers of government officials and Party members. Especially with post-9/11 fears of "terrorist" organizations, the discourse of *xiejiao* intensified scrutiny of lay ritual practices, and in Qinghai, the term was taken up within ongoing debates among academics and policy makers about the nature of "religious morality" and "social stability" under rationalizing economic development. As prominent Tibetologists at Qinghai's Academy of Social Sciences argued in 2001:

> in Tibetan regions, the social economy lacks development, the masses
> widely believe in Buddhism, and religious views are particularly strong.
> This is also one of the central regions in which the Dalai Lama faction and
> international powers exploit religion and *minzu* issues to interfere with us,
> pursuing splittist activities. Thus correctly recognizing and managing all
> kinds of religious problems is a crucial aspect of protecting the social stabil-
> ity of this region. (Pu and Can 2001, 1; cf. L. Wang 2002)

In Qinghai, where a large proportion of the population consists of ethnic minorities ensconced in Buddhist or Muslim communities, public security pundits and Tibetan Buddhist scholars alike thus struggled to delineate "normal religion" (Ch. *zhengjiao*) from illegal, "terrorist" heterodox cults on the model of Falun Gong. Importantly, a heterodox organization was defined as a secret, "closed network" of duped practitioners operating across provinces from Beijing down to local levels and controlled by a cunning individual leader who posed as divine in order to greedily extract capital from them

(Sun 2002; Muchi Yundeng Jiacuo 2003). In this light then, *xiejiao* discourse in Qinghai was a most recent manifestation of an older state-local dynamic: as the Great Western Development campaign intensified efforts to recruit locals to participate in the (moral/national) economic rationalities that would open the region to national and global markets, the stark terms of this discourse recognized the enemy within. Indeed, as state officials at all levels struggled to both control and morally distance themselves from lucrative "local mafias" amid market reforms (Barmé 1999; Dutton 2005), the figure of the heterodox cult could be seen as an emergent abject Other for the state's precarious vision of a moral-rational and thus nationally transcendent market economy— the guerrilla-terrorist Other at its very heart.

Importantly, as the market's Other, *xiejiao* is not an easily apprehended individual person but an alternative infrastructure, that is, alternative, unmarked spaces, practices, and networks that create types of persons and transcendent values in non-national (i.e., unpatriotic) and uniquely compelling ways. Low quality is then the measure of such participants, those who orient themselves to the national market not primarily as human capital in search of abstract, asocial capital under state auspices but as socially and locally mediated subjects with indeterminate motives and loyalties. Given the utopian nature of such visions of a state-led, abstract market, *most* Chinese citizens, from uneducated farmers to government and Party technocrats, are potentially low quality. Thus it is no surprise that Sun Baohua, a teacher at the Qinghai Police Management Vocational College, characterized *xiejiao* in the urgent and sweeping moral terms of Maoist rhetoric: "the anti-human, anti-science, anti-social [*xiejiao*] . . . is a social poison, a great threat to humankind. For the sake of the safety and peace of the people, of families and of society, we must persist in rooting it out" (2002, 88).

CONTESTED MEDIATIONS:
THE PRECARIOUS FIGURE OF THE *LHAWA*

This larger context then sheds light on the public debates and private anxieties I encountered in Jima Village about the future status of the *lhawa* in the summer of 2005. Village elder men were debating the proper roles of the village Party secretary and the *lhawa* in supervising village affairs, and especially in organizing and fund-raising for the annual festival offering to Amnye Shachong. Indeed, at the annual picnic for elder men (to which I had been graciously invited), where the men were feting the successful expansion of Amnye Shachong's temple,[17] the Jima Party secretary and de facto "village head" (Wyl. *sde dpon*) loudly announced that he was fed up with the villagers' disunity and constant complaints about his leadership in temple affairs and that he would be resigning the next day. Elders admonished him that such talk was "Communist Party affairs," not for such festive occasions. And they urged him to wait to resign until after the village's annual festival offering, in part, as I learned later, because Jima's young *lhawa*, the ritual specialist whose authority is supposed to mediate its organization, had moved to the provincial capital, Xining, after a dispute with some village elders over his legitimacy as a medium of the deity. Meanwhile, villagers nervously wondered in private whether unprecedented prefecture government plans to circumscribe the central role of the village *lhawa* would fundamentally alter village life in these particularly precarious times.

Indeed, such rumors of impending government regulation of mediums were linked for some to broader prefecture plans to recentralize town administration based on reconfigured urban "communities" (Ch. *shequ*) spanning several erstwhile farming villages. In effect, that reconfiguration would consolidate and complete the process of state-sponsored decollectivization, urbanization, and market integration in the central valley that had been ongoing since 1980. With the advent of the household responsibility system in the early 1980s, village households were once again the main units of production and consumption. In centrally located Jima, households' reallocated farmlands on the valley floor were gradually taken over by the prefecture government for urban expansion in exchange for cash and, in many cases, rights to lucrative roadside lots for commercial buildings. By the late 1990s, most of Jima's 190 households were completely market dependent, relying for cash income on wage labor, burgeoning business networks, and, especially for the wealthiest households, rents on commercial real estate in town (Makley 2013).

In this context, it is easier to grasp how the figure of the *lhawa* in Rebgong could become the material pivot (or index) of the specter of heterodox cults for all involved. His ritual authority in and outside of trance states hinged on his capacity for authentic possession by the village *zhidak* (Irvine 1982). In the valley, divine possession consists in a patterned set of gestures and performances indicating the overwhelming force of the transcendent deity "descended" (Wyl. *babs*) into the mortal body of the *lhawa*.[18] But such a practice materializes claims to divided or intersubjective selves and deferred authorities that are inimical to state, business, and Buddhist authorities'

FIGURE 9.3 "Lenghu Road Chief Financial Center / Investing is for making a PROFIT!" Billboard at construction site, Xining City, summer 2005. Photo by Charlene E. Makley.

efforts to pin down and rationalize individual motives and responsibilities. Indeed, despite constant contestation in Tibetan communities over the proper regional scope and position of mountain deities in divine hierarchies, the lay medium operates within the same general logic of materiality, embodiment, and intersubjective exchange as does the historically ascendant Buddhist incarnate lama: human bodies, just as other objects, can serve as "supports" or "containers" for aspects of divine presence with whom humans must enter into consequential, enduring exchanges (see ch. 8 in this volume).

New state-local and lay-monastic business networks and real estate transactions produced new dependencies and new profits in the valley, raising the stakes for control of access to mobile capital. Meanwhile, the influx of Han and Hui (Muslim Chinese) merchant and construction family networks had heightened the pressures for Tibetan market participation in this Tibetan Autonomous Prefecture. Indeed in Jima and other central urban villages, Tibetan households were precariously dependent on the market success of Han and Hui merchants; they often owned the very commercial buildings in which those merchants operated. With ongoing struggles over state taxation eating into their profits, and anxieties over inflation, the lack of government services, affordable health care, education, or lucrative jobs for their children, Tibetan villagers early in the first decade of the 2000s were acutely aware that the magic of the market, touted in advertising and government slogans, was *not* risk-free.

In this context, the burgeoning role of lay *zhidak* cults in Tibetan villages literally positioned the entranced *lhawa*-as-deity at center stage in intensified contests over the recognition of individually intentioned fraud versus socially produced (ethnic) transcendence and value.[19] Rather than functioning exclusively as a communal and unifying force among lay Tibetans, mountain deity practices have always played out in tensions between collective ideals and the competing interests of households and individuals.[20] Indeed, as many have pointed out, Tibetan villagers' conceive of fortune or vitality (Wyl. *g'yang*), in contradistinction to a notion of abstract capital, as a naturo-social potentiality or essential force, and that potentiality has long been conceptualized as embedded in *households* (Wyl. *khyim tshang*), ideally under the guidance of patriarchs, as the main units of production and reproduction (Da Col 2007; Makley 2013; Mills 2003). The status of such household fortune is always at risk. Household members' intentional and unintentional socio-ritual missteps can anger deities or invite demonic intervention and thus allow fortune to leak out or be captured by others. Individuals are thus supposed to interact with the *zhidak* of their birthplace (Wyl. *skyes lha*) (i.e., through individual prayers and offerings, placement of blessed "arrows" in "treasure vases" in homes and at *zhidak* altars) primarily as members of households seeking propitiation and thus the protection and expansion of household fortune.

But it is in communal rites like regular chanting sessions conducted by elder men at the temple, or especially the annual public offering festivals at village *zhidak* temples, that the authority of household patriarchs is supposed to coalesce, under the household-transcending auspices of the deity, as a villagewide *generational* authority, and a committee of elders can legitimately fund-raise and organize the festivals on behalf of village prosperity (cf. Chau 2005). The communal rites could thus be seen as attempts to constitute a moral frame for household wealth accumulation. They worked to instantiate the basic parameters of a Tibetan village moral economy: wealth and fortune gained by households under the proper guidance of patriarchs are the legitimate product of ongoing reciprocal relations with the *villagewide* protector deity. The socio-ritual propriety of household members and their patriarchs is supposed to benefit all under the deity's jurisdiction, in large part because their mutually constituted fortune is both displayed and shared at such feasts hosting the deity (da Col 2012).

The elders' legitimate mediation of household and village prosperity is then (precariously) dependent on the *lhawa*'s bodily mediation of the deity. The three-day marathon of the annual offering festival, in which the *lhawa*-as-deity is the celebrated master of ceremonies and village disciplinarian, is a delicate dialogue between the ruling presence of the transcendent deity and the minute orchestrations of village elders. The elders minister to and (passively) direct the deity as he gesticulates through his various ritual duties, checking regularly with the deity to see if their generationally organized dance and burnt food offerings are satisfactory so as to ensure village prosperity and unity in the coming year. Indeed, it is the deity via the entranced *lhawa* whose authority during the festival is supposed to supersede that of the village headman or Party secretary. He can fine households for not participating and, most dramatically in his final judgments to gathered villagers, haul up and beat young men who have reputations for socio-ritual misbehavior.[21] These are the basic frameworks and technologies of materiality and value in *zhidak* cults that remained expediently unmarked in the early reform years in the valley.

But in the ferment of recent years in Rebgong, the figure of the *lhawa* in Tibetan villages came under increasing government scrutiny just as his status *and* that of the mountain deity as mediators of socio-moral fortune for village elders became increasingly indeterminate. In the earliest reform years, elders from central villages like Jima were in an awkward position as they sought to revitalize their mountain deity cults. As Party members and government officials, many could not be seen to be endorsing such "backward" practices as deity possession. Thus the first few festivals were organized without mediums or with an elder appointed as a *lhawa* surrogate (Wyl. *lha pa tshab*) (Epstein and Peng 1998). But as rehabilitated Buddhist lamas could once again confirm a *zhidak* possession, older mediums gradually began to practice again, taking on younger apprentices, so that most villages had recognized mediums by the early years of the first decade of the 2000s.

However, the violent ruptures and painful betrayals of the Maoist years, along with the political and economic ferment of the reform years, had radically altered the grounds for deity recognition in the valley. For one thing, the moral and legal status of the incarnate lama was also increasingly precarious into the 1990s and the first decade of the 2000s (Makley 2007, 2010).[22] For another, by 2000, after the initial period of revitalization, new young mediums, educated in secular schools and lacking long apprenticeships in local deity cults, were modifying and curtailing their ritual practices and social roles, facilitating a general shift among villagers to a more skeptical relationship with them.[23] Meanwhile some young mediums, claiming a lack of traditional village support and income, were refusing to take on the role. Villagers across the valley wondered why contemporary mediums rarely spoke while possessed, unlike the mediums of the past. Instead, the new mediums mainly gesticulated or grunted their messages, leaving harried elders to interpret as best they could. In some villages downriver, elders resorted to making newly recognized mediums thumbprint a contract obligating them to take on the duties the role required, rather than neglect them in favor of pursuing cash income elsewhere (snying po rgyal and Rino 2008, 170).

In Jima, elders were scandalized when one of two chosen young mediums refused the role so that he could pursue long-distance trade and, they concluded with knowing looks, ended up dying in a horribly violent truck accident. The other young *lhawa*, after presiding over several village festivals, clashed with certain village elders, including the Party secretary, when he questioned their authority to lead the annual festival. The elders' supporters then pointed to how the young medium had demanded that the village help him buy a piece of roadside land, ostensibly so that he could maintain himself in the village. They represented this as an unprecedented and selfish demand for real estate capital, and some began to wonder whether he was actually faking his possessions or was possessed not by Amnye Shachung but by a lower malevolent demon. Angered by their lack of faith, the medium left Rebgong for Xining and refused to come back for the 2006 festival, even after a group of Jima elders traveled there to invite him.

Such conflicts over deity recognition in the valley reflect the moral quandaries of agency among Tibetans across the community under the pressures of market reforms; that is, the increasing unmanageability of privatized motives and "unruly coalitions" brought the *zhidak* cult perilously close to the immoral terms of the *xiejiao* Other. As in many urbanizing Tibetan communities, household-based market participation and dependencies under reforms increased income gaps among village households. In Jima, the wealthiest earned many times the income of the poorest, mainly from real estate investments, close relations with state officials, and canny inroads into Han-enclaved construction businesses at the same time that ethnic business networks pressured Tibetans to find allies in their own enclaved networks in the valley and beyond.[24]

Indeed, by 2005, "development" efforts in Jima village seemed largely to be carried out on behalf of particular households and their kin or neighbor networks, so that the wealthiest of urban villages, where many households were building gorgeous new compounds, had no public sanitation system or paved roads.[25] Meanwhile, new exigencies and aspirations for translocal market participation lured young people away from villages and households, their aspirations threatening to focus on the individual pursuit of amoral cash versus household-based fortune. Further, increasing competition for capricious translocal capital pressured Tibetan elites, including Buddhist lamas, to view ritual-versus-secular development investments in the valley as a zero-sum game. One particularly cosmopolitan lama in Rebgong, for example, said that he was "very angry" with his own people, explaining that "they do nothing while Han and Hui make progress." His own ultra-rationalist portrayal of Buddhism as a "scientific" body of knowledge about karma and the mind that could help subjects live better socio-moral lives echoed government development rhetoric, and he explicitly blamed lay Tibetans' lack of progress on their regionalist disunity and wasteful preoccupation with practices like mediumship or offerings to *zhidak*. Mountain deities, he opined, function best to motivate people to "preserve nature": "[The deities] have been working so hard," he exclaimed. "Now we have to protect them, and get people not to walk on them!" In effect, the lama was arguing for allowing *zhidak* to retire from their central roles in Tibetan regional politics and exchanges, relegating them to enclaved protectors of an abstract "environment" (see also ch. 10 in this volume).

Hence the increasing scrutiny from all sides of the *lhawa*'s claims to deferred authority, the performative relationship between his ordinary persona(e) and a divine Other. For village elders and for the *lhawa* himself, who is often the owner of a small business or even a government official, authority rests on his recognition in trance as a fully transparent medium of divine presence—*un*mediated that is, by the intentions of his unentranced self. In the context of post-Mao disillusionment with public speech among Tibetans, the brutal legacy of popular suspicions about the relationship between one's "mouth" or "speech" (Wyl. *kha*) and "heart" (Wyl. *khog*) (Makley 2005), one way of understanding the *lhawa*'s lack of speech in trance states under reforms would be to consider it as a turn to bodily-material

FIGURE 9.4   Possessed *lhawa* dances after cutting his head with a knife, demonstrating the deity's control over his body. Annual harvest festival, summer 2008. Photo by Charlene E. Makley.

indicators, which are claimed to be more powerful and direct signs of divine presence versus the interventions of unreliable human speech, at the same time that the greater ambiguity of those signs allows interpretive leeway to all involved under indeterminate state scrutiny (Morris 2000). Indeed, for all of my Tibetan interlocutors, the most spectacular material signs of *zhidak* presence, themselves evidence of the deity's material size, weight, and ferocity, were the ways in which the medium's face swelled and puffed, as well as the forms of physical violence the deity wrought on the medium's body, such as cutting the head with a knife.

CONCLUSION: THE AMORAL OTHER

Yet such efforts could not fully stave off the specter of the *xiejiao* Other against the lure of the market. Indeed, the village elders' very hold on the *lhawa*/deity as mediator of socio-moral wealth was based in the dangerously *amoral* compulsions of bodily desires and obligatory exchange at the heart of Tibetan ritual technologies. In fact, the liturgies of invocation, propitiation, and offering for Jima's Amnye Shachung, for example, chanted daily by the temple caretaker and monthly by a group of village elders, appropriated tantric Buddhist techniques of deity yoga to invoke and bind the mountain deity to human agendas via the impersonal and amoral workings of lavish feast offerings:

> You mountain deities and your retinues, eat! Then destroy all adversity facing our people and our wealth and provide us with all positive conditions. Do everything you can to fulfill all our wishes the way we want![26]

As many have pointed out, gift exchanges confront capitalist claims to magical returns from impersonal contracts with the persistence of reciprocal social relations over time (Graeber 2001; Klima 2002; Mauss 1990 [1925]). But in Tibetan *zhidak* ritual, this was not necessarily a claim to an alternative morality. In the invocation ritual's framework, the practitioner conjures massive amounts of desirable things and desirous beings (the deity and his entourage) pervading space and time. He relies on the sheer compulsiveness of the gorgeous and delicious offerings to overcome the deities' transcendent indifference to humans and to bind them via automatic obligation to return the favor—the moral character or intentions of either party are irrelevant. Importantly, it is only after the practitioner has requested the deities to fully consume the offerings that he uses the most agentive verbs in the imperative mood to ask them to do his (even violent) bidding in order to capture fortune and wealth:

> All you attentive protector deities, we exhort you to stand up and get to work! Amnye Shachong, go to the enemy! Shachong's soldiers, go to the enemy! Expand your troops and brandish your weapons! . . . Fill up the enemies' lands with your troops! Destroy their fortress walls from the foundations! Pulverize the enemies' life force and chop it to bits! Feast on the enemies' blood and flesh! Cut off the enemies' lineages at the roots! Loot and feast on all their possessions!

In that vision of divine agency, the *zhidak* appears as a powerfully intentioned, yet desirous and temptable being, whose efficacy, once captured in obligation, transcends space and time to violently eliminate (i.e., through military conquest of enemy deities and demons) all barriers to the practitioner's equally massive desired returns—fabulous wealth, health, and prosperity.

Here we can appreciate the emergent threat of the increasing indeterminacy of mountain deity recognition in Rebgong: the unmanageable *xiejiao* potential at the heart of *zhidak* relations. In the villages, the amoral and compulsive nature of the forces harnessed by such ritual technologies threatened to take *zhidak* agency out of the control of village elders. Indeed, elders could not legislate how individual villagers, especially young men, engaged with the *zhidak* as a personal birth deity. "So few of our young men are any good anymore," confided one old man to me at the picnic in 2005. Increasingly, I learned, and recalling the new communal incense offerings to *zhidak* from Rebgong Tibetan businessmen, young men sought the might of their *zhidak* to conquer in business ventures, gambling, and trade.

Personal invocations (or hostings) of the deity often prioritized another form of fortune over *g'yang* as a reward: *lungta* (Wyl. *rlung rta*; lit. "windhorse"), a capricious and quixotic, short-term form of luck, associated with the laborless value of sudden windfalls and gambling wins, that is, income and fortune unrelated to or outside household obligations (da Col 2007, 2012; Karmay 1998). Thus village elders joined lay intellectuals and state and Buddhist elites in expressing moral concerns about the fate of the next generation under market reforms. As we saw, the young *lhawa* was crucial for mediating the moral authority of the elders' household-based business networks in the face of new market dependencies. In this light, the powerfully place-based and Tibetan nature of *zhidak* frameworks as they were communally and publicly performed were important aspects of Tibetans' very modern attempts to create intergenerational and trans-household networks for accessing mobile capital.

But in the face of state claims to legitimating economic rationality under the Great Western Development campaign, that very solidarity threatened to appear as the illegitimate manipulations of a "heterodox" organization, especially since many village men held state positions. And yet, the efforts of prefecture officials to recentralize the town under new urban districts and appointed headmen also threatened the social parameters that had worked to keep *zhidak* practices within the moral framework of household-based wealth accumulation under village patriarchs.[27] In such a context, efforts at increasing market integration held out to young people the allure of the impersonal magic of the market, a process that perhaps presented the greatest threat to competing authorities—that shifting *zhidak* relations would apotheosize mountain deities as a powerful, specifically Tibetan masculine subjectivity that yet recognized and was exceedingly compatible with the bodily desires, social power, and violence inherent to state-sponsored capitalism. In such a context, the powerful bodily violence that the deity wrought on the *lhawa* in spectacular public trance could not but render that recognition uncomfortably visible. As against competing authorities' efforts to position themselves in various moral economies, the possession of the *lhawa* threatened to expose the indeterminacies and cultural politics on which they all rested.

By 2007–9, these tensions came to a head not only in Rebgong's Jima village but also across the valley. In 2005, CCP officials called in to investigate the conflict between Jima elders and the *lhawa* ruled that the *lhawa* had overstepped his bounds when he had, for the first time, chosen a new village head while possessed by Shachong. With support from the opposing faction of elders, the officials took the opportunity to declare that Jima no longer needed its own village head because it was now incorporated into the new urban district, a move that effectively ended Jima's status as a village with the right to administer its own land and elections and relegated the *lhawa* to the role of colorful tourist attraction in the prefecture-promoted annual harvest festival (see Makley 2013).[28]

And after unrest and protests broke out in the streets in 2008, the military crackdown in the valley was accompanied by patriotic and legal education campaigns for students, officials, and protesters. Under the explicit threat of violence, those efforts linked good citizenship to the promotion of ideal spaces, persons, and values grounded in the "scientific" materialities of a national market under the Communist Party's enlightened rule of law. As President Hu Jintao's ubiquitous slogan on Rebgong TV and streets in the spring and summer of 2008 put it: "promote the worldview of scientific development." Further, an article included in the Qinghai CCP committee's teachers' guidebook on the 2008 protests argued that "we must value even more the good forms of development and stability." By 2012, massive central investments in the region materialized state-led "development" as the preferred response to Tibetan unrest (Fischer 2012), unleashing yet another construction boom in Rebgong, as elsewhere. In this, the new national five-year plan renewed calls to "develop the west," touting, as before, the expansion of infrastructure as the key to the "success of the region."

CHAPTER 9. THE AMORAL OTHER

1   By October 2013, a total of 122 Tibetans are known to have self-immolated (103 men and 19 women) in China, 102 of whom died, and 42 of whom were from

Ngawa (Ch. Aba) Tibetan and Qiang Autonomous Prefecture, Sichuan, which has been under particularly strict military control since protests broke out among Tibetan Buddhist monks there in 2008. The self-immolations started there among young monks and then spread to other regions. Self-immolation as protest was virtually unknown among Tibetans before this time, and there is little Buddhist doctrinal or ritual precedent for it (ICT 2013).

2   Most prominent among these new institutions and networks were the tax-sheltered export-processing manufacturing zones of the east coast special economic zones.

3   In Tibetan regions, state investments in education and social welfare were reduced until early in the first decade of the 2000s. Then, in part to address priorities laid out in the Great Western Development campaign and in part to respond to increasing unrest, central state subsidies for education and social welfare increased dramatically. But that did not necessarily mean allocated funds made it to rural locales (Bass 1998; Goodman 2004a).

4   This village name is a pseudonym.

5   From the mid-1980s onward, and especially after the Tiananmen crackdown, popular and state scrutiny of and anger at "corruption" among government and Party officials and their families who are parlaying state access into lucrative business deals have been increasingly highlighted in mass media, protest demonstrations, and legislation.

6   "Accelerating infrastructure construction" was the first of five main goals of the Great Western Development campaign listed in the initial report released by the State Council in 2000.

7   Here I rely on Goffman's famous concept of "participation frameworks" (vs., for example, a Geertzian notion of "cosmology" or "cultural system") to get at the simultaneously cultural and material ways in which embodied interlocutors mutually define social realities. I prefer Goffman's notion to a Deleuzian understanding of "assemblages" or a Latourian notion of "networks" because it provides specific analytic tools for getting at meaning-making as embodied and intersubjective practice.

8   Indeed I see no analytic use for the term "religion" as anything other than an emic category.

9   Perhaps the main practice by which Buddhist monks and lamas attempted to regulate deity recognition was to materialize and (in the case of *zhidak*, violently) hierarchize them in written, visually presented, and ritually performed tantric mandalic taxonomies. European and American Tibetologists widely took on such taxonomic activities as a foundational practice for their own academic science (e.g., Nebesky-Wojkowitz 1998 [1956]; cf. Dalton 2011).

10   Little is known yet about the actual processes of finding such new mediums in Rebgong under Dengist reforms. Some were chosen out of groups of young men who went into trances at village rites; others were discovered via divination, or through lineage links to former mediums. Some apprenticed with old former mediums, while others had to learn as they went. All, however, were supposed to

seek confirmation from important incarnate lamas in the monasteries that they were indeed possessed by recognized mountain deities and not by opportunist demons (cf. mkhar rtse rgyal 2005, 2009; snying po rgyal and Solomon Rino 2008).

11   *Xibu diqu kaifa zhinan* 1988; Wang and Bai 1991; and see Rohlf 2003 and Goodman 2004a. Qinghai, with its vast tundra and remote mountainous landscape, was targeted during the Maoist years as the site for the construction of mines, prison and labor camps, military bases, nuclear-weapons testing sites, and experimental state farms and factories (Naughton 1988; Rohlf 2003).

12   Yan Hairong (2003) discusses the 1987 national conference on *suzhi*, in which such evaluations were officially formulated and then materialized in the conference report.

13   Elsewhere, I address Tibetan officials' development dilemmas in Rebgong in broader contexts, especially in light of the 2008 protests and military crackdown (Makley 2013).

14   See Hymes 2002; Kleeman 1994; Shahar and Weller 1996; and Von Glahn 2004.

15   Here the term "cult" would include its more recent pejorative sense.

16   Then president Jiang Zemin publicly endorsed anti-*xiejiao* legislation in the very months during which he was preparing to announce the launching of the Great Western Development campaign.

17   According to some Jima elders, the temple dates from the early seventeenth century, when Rongwo monastery's central incarnate lama had it built at the same level on the mountainside as his own chambers. It was destroyed in 1958 and then rebuilt in 1980. With help from U.S. NGOs and fund-raising drives among Jima households, more than ¥350,000 was collected for a major renovation of the temple in 1999, on the eve of the Great Western Development campaign and *xiejiao* legislation. The village's four wealthiest households contributed ¥10,000 each, with others contributing ¥200–5,000 each. In 2005, further funds were raised for the expansion and renovation of the temple's side buildings and courtyard space (cf. Epstein and Peng 1998; 'brug thar and sangs rgyas tshe ring 2005; Xirejiancuo 2005, 2008).

18   I have seen at least eight *lhawa* from different villages in trance in Rebgong, and all indicate their trance state with recognizable bodily signs of the force of the deity: constant puffing while vibrating the lips, salivating, rhythmic shaking and hopping, feats of strength, or infliction of pain, including cutting the head with a knife and smashing alcohol bottles against the head. The trance state during the annual offering festivals is particularly exhausting for *lhawa*, as they have to be in and out of trance for a marathon three days.

19   Up to thirty separate villages in the Rebgong valley, not all of them recognized as "Tibetan," are said to participate in or hold annual offering festivals (Tib. Lurol; Wyl. *klu rol*) for their respective mountain deities (ri gdengs 1994; mkhar rtse rgyal 2005, 2009; Nagano 2000; Epstein and Peng 1998; Xirejiancuo 2008; Buffetrille 2008; snying po rgyal and Rino 2008). The visibility of such practices with the *lhawa* at center stage was of course greatly enhanced with state and tourist

interest in them, which has burgeoned from the mid-1980s onward. The annual festivals are regularly filmed for television documentaries and tourist media.

20   Evidence suggests that Jima's festival emerged only in the nineteenth century, when farming villages were expanding and Jima villagers adopted Lurol by extending the village's annual rites at deities' mountaintop "cairns" (Wyl. *labtse*) and expanding the roles of deity mediums in order to celebrate victory, and thus the favor of Shachung and other deities, in a bloody intervillage land dispute (Makley 2013; Xirejiancuo 2008).

21   In one account of the revitalization of the annual *zhidak* offering festival in a Rebgong village in the early 1980s, informants waxed nostalgic about how the previously disunited and chaotic village, in which young men frequently drank and fought, was quickly pacified and reunited by the emergence of a powerful *lhawa* (Stuart et al 1995; cf. snying po rgyal and Rino 2008).

22   Because of this precariousness, it is not surprising that the Tibetan scholar Muchi Jiacuo, writing in a Qinghai social science journal (2003), goes out of his way to distinguish lama reincarnation (*zhuanshi*) from illegal *xiejiao* practice.

23   Though I heard a few educated young people (mostly young men) express such skeptical views about village mediums, this did *not* necessarily mean Tibetans widely doubted the existence of mountain deities and other invisible beings.

24   I was told that by the middle of the first decade of the 2000s, the richest of these Jima households, benefitting from rapidly rising land-use prices, owned several commercial buildings and brought in more than ¥100,000 a year, while most Jima building owners averaged about ¥35,000 a year in rental income. This contrasted sharply with per capita incomes of rural farmers, nomads, and poor households in Jima, who received only several hundred yuan per month in welfare subsidies.

25   This was the scene just before the launch of a suite of reform and "people first" development policies in rural Tibetan regions, in part as a central and provincial state response to the increasing rural-urban and class divides among Tibetans and the threat of ethnic unrest. Such policies have seen renewed central support and funding, especially since the 2008 protests and crackdown. By 2011, under the rubric of the New Socialist Village campaign, almost all Rebgong villages had paved roads and running water facilities paid for with central funds, but all households were required to contribute fixed sums of cash, which unleashed further conflict (Fischer 2012; Yeh 2013).

26   "dkar phyogs skyongs ba'i yul lha se ku bya khyung la dbang gi 'phrin las gtso bor bsgrub par bskul tshul gyi cho ga 'dod dgu'i char 'beb shes bya ba bzhugs so" (Procedure for entreating the virtuous regional deity Seku Shachung to use his powerful action to shower down all wishes). I thank Amdo Lekshay Gyamtso for his invaluable help in translating this and related texts. All subsequent excerpts are from this text.

27   Tibetans' long history of grappling with the moral implications of relations with this-worldly protector gods like *zhidak* is perhaps best exemplified in ongoing Buddhist and lay debates vis-à-vis specific deities as to whether they are "white"

(benevolent) or "black" (malevolent), and what kinds of offerings (vegetable or live sacrifices) are morally appropriate (cf. Dalton 2011).

28   By then, the festival was a striking anachronism in Jima, as households no longer engaged in farming.

The Rise and Fall
of the Green Tibetan

• • •

CONTINGENT COLLABORATIONS
AND THE VICISSITUDES OF HARMONY

Emily T. Yeh

I FIRST met Rinchen Samdrup at breakfast on the opening morning of the "Sharing, Cooperation, and Scaling Up" meeting of environmental civil society organizations in Dujiangyan, Sichuan, in June 2004. Jointly sponsored by the Conservation International (CI) China program (CI-China) and the Critical Ecosystem Partnership Fund (CEPF), the meeting was intended as a networking and exchange opportunity for environmental groups that had applied for, or would be eligible for, funding from CEPF within the Mountains of Southwest China biodiversity hotspot, which was declared in 2000. Significantly, more than 80 percent of the area of the designated hotspot coincides with Sino-Tibetan borderland areas in parts of Sichuan, Yunnan, Qinghai, Gansu, and the eastern Tibet Autonomous Region (TAR).

Altogether there were more than 125 participants, representing about seventy projects and organizations, including nature reserves, academic research institutes, international organizations, student associations, and grassroots groups. In the crowd of activists wearing button-down shirts, slacks, and summer dresses, several Tibetan monks in maroon robes stood out, as did Rinchen Samdrup, a ruddy-faced, tall man then in his late thirties, who was dressed in a beige *chuba*, a long-sleeved Tibetan robe, hitched up at the waist with a belt from which hung a short sheathed knife with a yak-bone handle. Curious, I sat down at his table. There was animated conversation all around him, but no one spoke to Rinchen, not even the professor who had set up his own research organization to study Tibetan sacred mountain culture, or my environmental educator friend, who had confided to me on the bus ride to the conference that the happiest time in her life had been when she lived in a Tibetan village and studied the significance of Tibetan circle dancing for her master's degree. I found this rather surprising, as Rinchen's self-presentation, from his *chuba* to his knife to his necklace of turquoise, coral, and precious *gzi* beads, did nothing if not announce his Tibetanness. Only after talking to him did I realize why: Rinchen Samdrup doesn't speak Chinese.

But the Tibetan man who was sitting next to him, and who turned out to have brought him to this meeting, did. Trador, dressed in a T-shirt and black jeans, was the vice secretary of the Sanjiangyuan Environmental Protection Association. Formally registered in Qinghai in November 2001, it was one of the earliest environmental NGOs in a Tibetan area. At the plenary session a few hours later, he told a remarkable story about Rinchen's remote village in Chamdo, a Kham area of the eastern TAR, to which his organization had recently started providing "some advice and direction." The area, he told his audience of Chinese environmentalists, is remote and still follows many traditions; every family has its own "soul-tree"[1] and "soul-spring," and during the summer Universal Prayer Festival, the villagers are so consumed with religious activities that no one can be found working in the fields. In fact, he said of the villagers, "50–60 percent of their lives are devoted to their sacred mountains." A few years earlier, Rinchen had organized the village to start rehabilitating its main sacred mountain by planting trees that had been cut down during the Cultural Revolution. In addition, the villagers had also organized sanitation efforts and drawn up a set of regulations against hunting and other actions that harm the environment, as well as a list of fines for those who fail to comply.

Trador's PowerPoint presentation explaining these grassroots environmental protection efforts included photographs of the villagers circumambulating their sacred mountain with ritual flags and scenes of deforestation, logging trucks, Tibetan village women hauling large buckets of water on their backs up to the new seedlings, and an old man leaning on a staff, crying next to a gargantuan tree stump, all that was left of his family's soul-tree. Trador's narrative was well received by the audience, and his poster about Rinchen's village won the prize for best poster presentation of the conference. It seemed to perfectly embody CI-China's goal for its new Sacred Lands program in the Mountains of Southwest China hotspot, "the revival of Tibetan cultural value towards nature and traditional land protection mechanisms." Indeed, throughout the conference, many of the Han participants repeatedly emphasized the need to revive the ecological wisdom that traditional Tibetan culture possessed and use it, not only in the service of conserving biodiversity, but also as a model to "encourage Chinese society to adopt a more sustainable lifestyle."[2]

That evening, Rinchen showed me several thick stacks of photographs from his valley, and explained that the 1,347 members of Tserangding, a cluster of eleven hamlets in Gonjo County (see map 1, G), had all agreed to form an environmental protection association. He also produced a set of documents, in Tibetan, about the environment there. The first, written in 1997, was a long essay about the history of the sacred mountain and a discussion of why villagers should care for the trees on the sacred mountain in order to avoid incurring the wrath of territorial deities who could retaliate by inflicting disease and disaster. In addition, there were guidelines, written in 2003, for the members of the association, including a list of fines for violating various rules, and the names of villagers who had volunteered to take supervisory roles in the association. Also from 2003 was another essay he had authored, which further elaborated upon both the rules and the rationales for their implementation, in terms of the need to protect the natural environment for the good of humanity. It read, in part:

> Our forefathers had since early times decoded the secret of the interdependency of various aspects of the environment, and hence they always took care of nature and found ways to create a balance in nature. We should pay attention to these rich traditions, which are miraculous and beneficial, worthy of experimentation, and acceptable. They have much in common with modern science. They are something that we can be proud of. . . . If promoted, these traditions might be helpful for researchers in their search to understand nature.

He had brought copies of these essays to the meeting to distribute to other interested environmentalists but was disappointed to realize there would be no point, given the language barrier. He gave me a set, however, stating that he would like these to be translated into English as part of his effort to network and make the villagers' efforts to protect the Tibetan environment, which he saw as being critical to the well-being of the earth at large, more widely known.

Rinchen's essays are but a few in the proliferation of Tibetan writing in China in the first decade of the 2000s that asserts the affinities of traditional Tibetan cultural-religious idioms and concepts with contemporary environmental concerns and that argues that Tibetan culture is thus valuable for conservation. Such claims can be found in an outpouring of essays and books, in both Chinese and Tibetan, by social scientists, influential Tibetan Buddhist leaders, and leaders of new grassroots organizations (e.g., Dawa Tsering 2004; klu rgyal thar 2007; Tsering Samdrup 2004; Tsultrim Lodroe 2003). The Tibetan borderland areas of Qinghai, Sichuan, Yunnan, and Gansu also witnessed a flourishing of newly formed grassroots and regional environmental protection organizations dedicated to maintaining or reviving cultural practices of conservation. The villagers of Tserangding were unique in being the only Tibetan environmental NGO formed in the TAR during this period. Much tighter political control in the region meant even stricter control of NGOs, greater fear of the state's reaction to their formation, and thus fewer connections to domestic and transnational environmental organizations in comparison to the rest of the Tibetan Plateau.

The story of Rinchen Samdrup illuminates the factors that facilitated the emergence of Tibetan environmental associations as well as Tibetan environmental identities and subjectivities in China early in the first decade of the 2000s. A set of contingent articulations between the interests of local Tibetan communities, Chinese environmentalists, and transnational actors allowed for interethnic and translocal collaboration around Tibetan environmental protection, manifested in the articulation of a "Green Tibetan" discourse —the claim that Tibetan culture and Buddhism have traditionally fostered environmental protection. Chinese and Tibetan environmentalists came together to mobilize Tibetan culture to save China's biodiversity, creating a space for Tibetan culture to be expressed and for Han and Tibetan actors to agree on both mutual cultural respect and coordinated activities. Thus, it created the potential for significant harmony, in the sense of living peaceably together with others, in a way that has not been adequately explored in the political ecology critique of conservation projects (e.g., Brockington, Duffy, and Igoe 2008; Neumann 1998, 2004; Walley 2004; West 2006; Zerner 2000).

The promise of this moment is clearest in its aftermath. The space for Tibetan cultural claims through environmental protection shrank considerably after the 2008 demonstrations across the Tibetan Plateau; that is, possibilities for Han-Tibetan cooperation decreased even as the state stepped up the discourse of the Harmonious Society after 2005 (see the introduction to this volume). Thus, the trajectory of the rise and fall of the figure of the Green Tibetan, told through the story of Rinchen Samdrup, also provides a comparison between the contingent, but fragile, collaboration that emerged between Han, Tibetans, and Westerners in the Sino-Tibetan borderlands early in the first decade of the 2000s and the statist multiculturalism of the Harmonious Society, which deploys sovereign power to enforce a state-defined harmony.

ENVIRONMENTALITY, TRANSLATION, AND COLLABORATION

The emergence of the Green Tibetan, and more specifically the shift in Rinchen's writing away from local deities and toward "environmental protection," can be understood as a process of environmental subject formation—the production of subjects for whom the environment constitutes a conceptual category that organizes thought and practice. Two recent approaches to the formation of environmental subjectivities can be productively read with and against each other in understanding these processes in Tibet.

Developing a framework of environmental governmentality, or "environmentality," in his 2005 book, Arun Agrawal opens with two visits to Hukam Singh, a villager in northern India who in 1985 does not particularly care about the cutting of trees but by 1993 has been converted to the cause of environmental conservation. From the perspective of environmentality, the shift from centralized to decentralized environmental regulation, and in particular community-based forest councils as a new form of regulatory community, has led to the production of environmental subjects like Singh. Participatory, decentralized management sets conditions through the arrangement of repeated, embodied action for the production of self-governing subjects who desire the right thing; through bodily participation in monitoring and enforcement of village forest council rules, the rhetoric offered by villagers for why they wish to protect the forests comes to echo precisely the objectives pursued by the colonial Forest Department more than a century ago (ibid.). In this view, environmental subjectivity through community-based natural resource management becomes, like the proliferation of conservation-and-development projects and NGOs more generally, a symptom of neoliberal governmentality, the effect of a technique of self-government that makes subjects responsible for internalizing government desires (Bryant 2002; T. Li 2007; McCarthy 2005; Rose 1999; Sharma 2006).

Agrawal does not provide much detail about Singh; we do not learn more about him or his narrative about the specific process through which he came to articulate his interests and desires with respect to caring for the environment, or the specificities of the political economy, contingent moments in the life of social movements at different scales, or the localized categories of personhood that may also have played a role in effecting this shift. In this framework, transformations of subject positions at the scale of the individual can only be explained as "probabilistic" (Agrawal 2005, 163), an approach that leaves "little satisfying to say about the complex and deeply biographical practices through which environmental subjects 'make themselves' and equally 'are made'" (Raffles 2005, 184).

Though it does not explicitly address the question of environmental subject formation, Anna Tsing's (2005) study of environmentalism as the product of translation and the frictions of collaboration offers a different approach to this process. She suggests that the array of critical perspectives offered by anthropologists, geographers, and others on transnational conservation, NGOs and the disciplinary effects of conservation present "a historical metanarrative of imperial modernization in which nothing can ever happen—good or bad—but more of the same. Familiar heroes and villains are again arrayed on the same battlefield. It is difficult to see how new actors and arguments might ever emerge" (161, 214). What is needed instead is attention to the processes of collaboration between forest dwellers, student activists, environmentalists, aid workers, academics, and others; the unstable and unexpected outcomes of collaborations across difference produce new interests and identities. This can lead to success because of (and not just in spite of) disagreements and divergent understandings of common words and concepts. This "productive confusion" of collaboration can result from the way in which knowledge moves through processes of translation, where translation is understood as a "necessarily faithless appropriation, a rewriting of a text in which new meanings are always forged by the interaction of languages" (Tsing 1997, 253; 2005, 246). Rather than stressing the articulation of environmental interests as an effect of governmentality, then, environmentalism can be understood as an emergent cultural form, the contingent effect of global encounters and translations across difference (Tsing 2005, 3).

This chapter develops an explicit analysis of environmental subject formation, but one that stresses articulation, the contingent and conjunctural ways in which certain kinds of discourses come to be enunciated by certain subjects in both speech and text. Details of the ways in which forms of power get translated and reworked must be attended to, in order to avoid both an uncritical celebration of the transnational, on the one hand, and the reproduction of a theory of an all-encompassing form of power in which nothing new can ever happen, on the other (Ghosh 2006, 526).

GREEN TIBETANS

Rinchen's 2003 essay seems to echo the Green Tibetan discourse that emerged in exile in the mid-1980s and is now an indispensable element of the exile and transnational Tibet Movement's representations of Tibetanness (Huber 1997, 2001). For example, according to a Tibetan writer in India more than a decade earlier, Tibetans—like other ecologically wise indigenous peoples—have always lived in harmony with nature because their Tibetan Buddhist outlook fostered an understanding of ecological interdependency and respect for all living things:

> A general taboo against exploiting the environment was a direct result of
> our Buddhist knowledge and belief about the inter-relationship between all
> plants, animals, as well as the non-living elements of natural world. . . . Fur-
> thermore, we Tibetans have always been aware of the interdependent nature
> of this world. . . . [F]or centuries Tibet's ecosystem was kept in balance and
> alive out of a common concern for all of humanity. (Atisha 1991, 9)

This apparent similarity between exile and PRC articulations of the Green Tibetan premise suggests that it is an assemblage (Ong and Collier 2004) or an allegorical or activist package (Tsing 2005, 234), a story or discourse that is unmoored or extracted from its original cultural and political context and reassembled, reformulated, or reattached in another political and cultural context. Such packages can be reassembled and reattached only in specific conjunctures in which they are capable of gaining traction, in part by finding a receptive audience. The first incarnation of the Green Tibetan was an intercultural production between exile Tibetans and their Western supporters. Struggles over sovereignty in Tibet and the explicit rejection within China of everything seen as emanating from Tibetan exiles and the "meddlesome" West made any kind of direct translation or travel to China impossible. The second, which emerged in China, is instead an intercultural production between Tibetans in Tibet and Chinese environmentalists that resembles but also explicitly disavows certain elements of the earlier (and still globally circulating) version of the Green Tibetan.

This points to three key differences between the articulation of the Green Tibetan in exile in the mid-1980s and the appearance of a similar discourse in China beginning in the late 1990s: authorship, audience, and political aim. First, the authors of these narratives are different. The earlier discourse responded to the condition of exile. It could be traced back to a "very small circle of individuals that constitute a part of the exiled Tibetan political, religious, and intellectual elite in Dharamsala . . . [who] not only generate the images in question, but also continue to manipulate and disseminate them" (Huber 1997, 106; 2001). In Tibet, by contrast, authors of Green Tibetan texts are not political elites and frequently, as in the case of Rinchen, not intellectual or religious elites either.

A second related difference is the intended audience. Many of the exile Green Tibetan texts appeared first in English before being translated and edited for publication in Tibetan, which, coupled with the high production standards of these publications in comparison to others, suggests that they were intended primarily for a Western audience (Huber 1997, 111). As a result, they were at that time arguably irrelevant not only for the vast majority of Tibetans, who live within the political boundaries of the People's Republic of China, but also for the vast majority of Tibetan exiles. In fact, in the late 1990s, other than a small circle of young, educated, and cosmopolitan Tibetans who spoke English and had frequent contact with Westerners, Tibetan refugees were neither well versed nor interested in Tibetan greenness (Huber 2001, 368). In Tibet today, by contrast, materials such as those of Rinchen are being written in Tibetan, for a local Tibetan audience, and translated only later if at all into Chinese and English.

The third major contrast is in political aims. The exile representations were quite explicitly part of a larger effort to create support for Tibet among a liberal Western audience; given the rapid growth in visibility of the transnational Tibetan struggle in the late 1980s and throughout the 1990s, this was quite a successful strategy. These narratives of eco-friendliness were intertwined with claims about the massive destruction that China has wrought on the Tibetan environment and heavy criticism of the Chinese government (Yeh 2009a). Thus, these narratives could not simply travel across the Himalayas to be asserted in Tibet. Instead, the Green Tibetan claims of the first decade of the twenty-first century originated from a new conjuncture in which environmental claims were very carefully made to indicate an adherence to—rather than a protest against—the Chinese state's laws and policies. Indeed, the very first paragraph of the bylaws of the association Rinchen Samdrup founded, the Voluntary Environmental Protection Association,[3] reads:

> Understanding the significance of the kind policies laid down by the Central Government for Tibet is very important. These policies have made our society prosper . . . by uniting people from different parts of the country. . . . One should learn how to dispel superstitious beliefs and other bad customs . . . We must promote the following measures under the guidance of the Central Government.

Only after performing the loyalty of its authors to the Chinese state does the document proceed to make claims about the benefits Tibetan culture held for nature.

TRANSNATIONAL/TRANSLOCAL COLLABORATION: SACRED LANDS AND CHINA'S ENVIRONMENTAL MOVEMENT

On the front cover of Conservation International's China Program brochure when the organization first started to work in China in the middle of the first decade of the 2000s was a photograph of a fresco in a Tibetan monastery in the Kham Tibetan area of Sichuan presenting Tibetan culture as a symbol of Chinese conservation. According to the brochure, the primary goal of the organization's Sacred Lands program was to support "the revival of Tibetan cultural value towards nature and traditional land protection mechanisms" through measures such as the following:

> Understand the traditional Tibetan cultural value and land protection system; Refurbish and promote a cultural value in Tibetan communities through local social institutions such as NGOs, governmental agencies and monasteries; Legally recognize Tibetan Sacred Land Protection as a form of protected area management.

CI-China's program resembled that of the World Wide Fund for Nature and the Nature Conservancy, which were also starting to work more intensively in Tibetan areas of China at the time. These programs were based on the dual premise that certain forms of development had choked the "ecological vitality" of biodiverse areas and that transnational conservation organizations could ameliorate the situation by helping Tibetan communities observe their already-existing Buddhist traditions, according to which they "aspire to live in harmony with the land, treating certain mountains, forests and rivers as sacred sites." The program became an umbrella for a number of different conservation efforts in the Mountains of Southwest China hotspot, including a survey of biodiversity in sacred mountains, in which scientists set out to demonstrate that traditional Tibetan sacred areas were more biodiverse than areas that were not protected in this way (D. Anderson et al. 2005; Luo, Liu, and Zhang 2009; Shen et al. 2012); declaration of several new nature reserves that overlap significantly or are defined by the boundaries of traditional sacred areas; and efforts to mobilize Tibetan religious leaders to promote biodiversity conservation.

Transnational actors clearly played a crucial role in the articulation of Green Tibetan identities and ideas within China (see also discussion of the Tibetan Doctors Association in the introduction to part 2 of this volume). Yet it would be a mistake to conclude, as some observers have, that transnational interest in sacred lands was no more than an appropriation of Tibetan indigenous worldviews, that they were incommensurable with Tibetan geopiety, and that the effect was simply to limit and circumscribe Tibetan identities. Instead, attention to the specificities of the emergence and effects of the Green Tibetan discourse shows it to be part of a process of global and translocal encounters across difference that contingently produced new interests, identities, and projects. These socio-natural projects of mobilizing Tibetan culture to conserve biodiversity were emergent within a historically specific conjuncture that went far beyond local people merely reacting to or parroting dominant conservationist discourses.

Indeed, CI-China's Sacred Lands Program brochure bore a striking resemblance to the Sanjiangyuan Environmental Protection Association's description of its own Sacred Mountains and Lakes Programs:

> One of our goals is to restore and promote traditional respect for natural resources. The values reflected from traditional Tibetan culture will be carried forward. Sacred mountains and lakes will be legally established as locally-managed conservation areas.

In fact, CI-China's Sacred Lands program was sparked by a trip by the Chinese director of both CI-China and the Critical Ecosystem Partnership Fund in China took with Trador through Sichuan's Ganzi Tibetan Autonomous Prefecture. The notion of sacred lands for conservation originated much more with him than from the suggestions of international conservation actors. Furthermore, when CI-China and the Sanjiangyuan association began working together on environmental education, they found many *khenpos* and lamas (Tibetan Buddhist teachers) eager to take up the message and spread it to villagers as part of their religious teachings.[4] Many of these teachers came from the Sertar Buddhist Institute in Larung Gar, which, since the late 1980s, had become not only a key training institute for monasteries throughout the Kham region but also a center for Buddhist modernist-inspired movements of radical vegetarianism and compassion toward animals (Gaerrang 2012). The Green Tibetan was thus not merely a top-down imposition by transnational conservation organizations; rather, it was forged out of the production of local and translocal Tibetan interests and identities arising out of radically different frameworks and communities (see also Yeh 2012).

At the same time, the Green Tibetan could find a receptive audience and gain traction within China only if the notion of ecologically friendly Tibetan culture was accepted and promoted by Chinese environmentalists. From the 1950s until well into the 1980s and beyond, most Han imagined Tibetans as barbaric, dirty, superstitious, and violent, based on the few representations of Tibetans available to them, such as the 1960s film *The Serf* (Nongnu). Exoticized images of Tibetans, particularly the "erotic 'minority' Tibetan girl," began to appear in the early 1980s as part of a broader shift in the Han imagination about ethnic minorities. By the late 1990s, multiple and somewhat contradictory Chinese understandings of Tibetans existed together: Tibetans as grateful to the "older brother Han" *minzu* for liberation, science, and development; Tibetans as barbaric and backward; and Tibetans as primitive and erotic. Amid this heteroglossia, another Chinese conception emerged, of Tibet as a mysterious land with a special connection with nature. It entailed a sense of nostalgic longing and a view of Tibetans as repositories of ancient spiritual and ecological wisdom, symbols of a simpler, purer time. This new development resulted from a convergence of forces: state promotion of leisure culture (J. Wang 2001), tourism as a development strategy in Tibet, the rise of Chinese backpacker culture, and the search for and resurgence of religion, particularly among residents of wealthy coastal cities (Yü 2012).

This new Chinese relationship with Tibetans, problematic as it was, partially enabled the emergence of the Green Tibetan. It included expressions such as the formation of a "Love Tibet Association" in 2001 by the China Tibet Information Center. Boasting more than fifteen thousand members, its stated goal was to "construct a spiritual home for people who love Tibet."[5] More specifically, it helped its members network, organized trips to Tibet, and provided information about tourism. In addition to making "a spiritual home" for lovers of Tibet, the association also promised to "serve Tibet" through activities such as organizing talks on college campuses "to spread the word about Tibet" and "Tibetan culture appreciation month." Members also engaged in travel for various purposes, including to donate money to Tibetan orphanages and "to protect the environment" by driving their own cars to Tibet; there was even a trip for "photographers going to Tibet to rescue cultural heritage."

Among the travelers who began visiting Tibetan areas were urban, college-educated youth who became leading environmental activists. Indeed, China's environmental movement developed in the 1990s in relation to issues of species protection in culturally Tibetan areas. This was due in large part to the fact that wildlife conservation has been seen as a relatively nonpolitical and thus safe issue, and culturally Tibetan areas, which cover about one-quarter of China's total land area, have far more charismatic megafauna left than most other parts of China. Two of the earliest campaigns by China's first prominent environmental NGO, Friends of Nature, that galvanized Chinese college environmental activists, were located in Tibetan areas: the campaign to save the snub-nosed monkey in Diqing, Yunnan, and the campaign against the poaching of the Tibetan antelope for the making of *shahtoosh* shawls in the Kekexeili region of Qinghai. These campaigns also motivated the formation of Green Camps, expeditions of elite Beijing-based college students to China's former frontier areas with severe environmental problems, including a number of Tibetan areas, from 1996 to 2006. These trips brought China's new environmentalists face-to-face with Tibetans, inspiring many to both form their own environmental organizations and respect Tibetan culture.

A convergence of many factors thus created a receptive audience for the idea that Tibetan culture is beneficial for the environment. Among these were the travel of transnational discourses of ethnobotany, religion and the environment, and traditional ecological knowledge, which contrasted sustainable livelihoods supported by indigenous ways of knowing against the environmental ravages of development. The rise of independent tourism (see chs. 2 and 3 in this volume) and changing representations of ethnic minorities in China were also important. The idea that Tibetans might have something to offer mainstream Han society represented a dramatic departure from the long-standing belief that Tibetans are backward and inferior and could only be improved by becoming more like the Han (Heberer 2001). The geographic contingencies of species distribution also resulted in an emergent environmental movement developed in relation to Tibetan areas. Chinese environmentalists became increasingly interested in the potential of Tibetan culture to save China's biodiversity (Guo Jing 2000b; Xie Hongyan, Xiaosong, and Xu 2000; Xu Jianchu 2000; Xu Jianchu et al. 2005; Zhang Shi 2000). A spate of ecological studies, by both Chinese and international scientists, sought to rigorously demonstrate the contributions that Tibetan sacred lands have made to vegetation condition and biodiversity (D. Anderson et al. 2005; Luo et al. 2009; Nan 2001; Salick et al. 2007; Shen et al. 2012).

Because of the Chinese state's concerns about sovereignty in relation to transnational organizations (Litzinger 2006; Turner and Lü 2006), many transnational environmental and development organizations work in China with minimal expatriate staff. Thus, both transnational and translocal interest in Tibetan culture's potential for biodiversity conservation has worked through Chinese conservation organization staff, activists, and scholars.[6] This resulted not only in scientific investigations of biodiversity but also in funding for various projects and conferences that further validated the ideas underpinning the Green Tibetan. It also created opportunities for networking among grassroots Tibetans and between Tibetans taking up environmental subject positions and Han and foreign conservationists.

This wave of interest in the potential of Tibetan culture for biodiversity conservation opened up a space for the formation of a number of Tibetan community environmental protection organizations through most of the first decade of the twenty-first century, some with very direct outside support and direction, such as the Tibetan Doctors Association in Diqing and Green Kham, in Ganzi. Others, such as the grassroots association in Chamdo established by Rinchen Samdrup, formed without direct financial or logistical support from outsiders. Along with the proliferation of Tibetan writings about the environment, the formation of these organizations meant that the years from the early to middle of the first decade of the 2000s were a time of great ferment in terms of this new articulation of a Tibetan environmental subjectivity, as well as great optimism for the potential of nongovernmental organizations. Grassroots associations focused on development and the environment sprung up across the Tibetan borderland regions of Kham and Amdo. Educated Tibetans, often those with English-language training and exposure to foreigners, aspired in large numbers to form their own NGOs. The future of Tibetan environmental associations, supported by Chinese environmentalists, looked promising.

THE VOLUNTARY ENVIRONMENTAL PROTECTION ASSOCIATION AND THE MAKING OF AN ENVIRONMENTAL SUBJECT

An organic intellectual, Rinchen Samdrup never attended school. He learned to read and write first from his mother and then, toward the end of the Cultural Revolution, from a monk who taught children in the hamlet, hiding when state authorities arrived. Later he studied with a lama, focusing on texts from which he learned to make Tibetan medicines. He began to lead other villagers up to the nearby hills twice a year to collect medicinal plants and made medicines, which he distributed for free. He also began intensive study of the texts of Nyala Changchub Dorje, an early twentieth-century Nyingma master revered throughout the region, many of whose original texts had been buried in the village during the Cultural Revolution.

According to Rinchen, his concern for the environment was originally sparked by the local sacred mountain. As with many important religious sites in Tibet, special significance is attached to ritual circumambulation of this mountain once every twelve years. Rinchen first became concerned during the 1997 propitiation event when he saw that the mountain had not only been deforested but was also littered with garbage. This prompted him to write an essay about the history and importance of this sacred site, as well as reasons to protect it. The twenty-two-page essay quotes long passages from religious texts and is devoted to what these texts say about the negative consequences of harming the place: "Destroying mountains, blowing up boulders, defiling springs, disturbing the *gnyan*, logging the forests, killing animals . . . will cause fortune and power to be lost and suffering of strange diseases. . . . There will be diseases associated with disturbing the *klu* and the *sa-bdags*. . . . All of these will lead to death of livestock, destruction of crop by hailstorms, infestation of pests on the crops." The essay is couched in Tibetan religious terms and uses the grammatical form of religious texts. It does not self-consciously present "nature," "religion," or "culture" as abstract concepts. Its rationales for environmental protection are specific to the territorial deities and other beings that inhabit the local place, rather than based on general principles of ecology or interconnectedness.

After he wrote this essay, Rinchen Samdrup began to talk to other villagers about the need to protect the environment, but at first, nobody was particularly interested. In fact, he said, in the beginning, "they laughed at me because they said that I am a person from a small village, thinking about matters related to the world." Two things eventually changed the villagers' minds. First, he was persistent. Whenever he visited his neighbors, Rinchen talked about the need to protect the environment, and "since we all have good relationships, they were willing to listen at least. Gradually, they started to agree." The other catalyst was a visit by his younger brother Karma Samdrup. Karma had left home at an early age to become a *gzi* (precious agate bead) trader and eventually became a very wealthy businessman. He also founded the Sanjiangyuan Environmental Protection Association, though Trador did most of the day-to-day work. When he visited home and spoke with his older brother, he learned of Rinchen's essay about the sacred mountain and sent it to Trador. In 2003, Karma and Trador returned to the village together. By that time, most of the villagers were on board and had begun some small-scale tree planting and were trying to stop outsiders from fishing (fishing is taboo for religious reasons, but the high-altitude fish had become a delicacy for local officials). However, they were concerned about attracting too much attention, fearing possible punishment from the government for doing anything out of the ordinary. Trador discussed his environmental organization with Rinchen and the villagers and assured them that environmental protection work was in fact supported, not punished, by the government.

The visit solidified the villagers' determination, and soon all of the adult residents of Tserangding agreed to organize themselves into the Voluntary Environmental Protection Association. They drew up a detailed list of regulations and developed a plan for major afforestation efforts on previously deforested land. The first two years alone, they planted a total of four hundred thousand sea buckthorn saplings, forty thousand spruce trees, and sixty thousand poplars, all with village labor, with a goal of planting twenty thousand trees per year for the next ten years. After the second year, they began to receive sea buckthorn and spruce saplings free of charge from the County Forestry Bureau, which had saplings available as part of the Sloping Land Conversion Program but few takers among other townships and villages.

Other activities taken up by the association included community garbage cleanup activities, monthly wildlife patrols against poaching, and monitoring wildlife with binoculars, supported indirectly by CI-China. Monitoring fit especially well with CI-China's goals, given that the area's extraordinary biodiversity included endangered and threatened species such as black-necked crane, blue sheep, musk deer, gazelle, lynx, and brown bear. Beginning in 2005, the community association organized environmental education activities during the annual summer festival, when the entire community gathers together for about ten days. They asked the abbot of the local monastery to give teachings about the relationship between Tibetan Buddhism and environmental protection and also to voice his support for the association's activities. The villagers organized a quiz program, essay contests, and role-playing skits about the environment.

An important principle of the association since its formation has been to inextricably intertwine their environmental protection work with the broader goal of promoting Tibetan culture. As a sixty-year-old association member told me, "Our main purpose is to promote Tibetan religion and the customs of the place, and on the side, we stop hunting and plant trees." Similarly, Rinchen stated, "Cleaning garbage and other activities are branches of our work. The most important goal is to protect our culture." Thus, along with the group's tree-planting work, Rinchen from the very beginning also organized the compilation of a Tibetan-language environmental journal. Key association members selected excerpts from historical Buddhist and Bön texts with implications for environmental protection, quotes from Chinese laws and leaders from Mao to the present day, and essays about environmental protection by well-known *khenpos* and local villagers. They also established a Tibetan-language website on environmental protection and tried to set up a rural Tibetan-language library.

Rinchen continued to write, though after the formation of the association, much of his effort was directed toward the journal and various brochures and booklets for association members. There are a number of noticeable differences between the language he chose after 2003, compared to his earlier essays. While the 1997 essay mentioned the term "environmental protection" only once, the terms "environmental protection," "natural environment," "balance," and "interdependence" appear frequently later. His earlier work is fundamentally concerned with specific types of illnesses and harms that can result from the disturbance of local territorial deities. His more recent work (quoted above), by contrast, emphasizes the conviction that traditional Tibetan practices are both similar to, and will eventually be evaluated very highly by, scientific research. The former also is concerned primarily with a detailed history of a local place, while the latter emphasizes that protecting these local places "also benefits the world." Even the term "culture" appears only in the latter documents, which build on the ideas expressed in a localized and specific vocabulary in the early writings but rearticulate them in a way that is self-consciously *environmental*.

Rinchen's contact with Trador in 2003 catalyzed both the formation of the association and the process of his becoming an environmental subject. Trador served as a cultural and linguistic translator of Rinchen's concerns to a broader Chinese public, bringing him to training workshops and meetings, where he met Chinese environmentalists and journalists. A few Beijing-based environmentalists traveled to Chamdo to learn more about the group's work and successfully nominated the association for several national-level environmental awards; it won third place in the national Alax SEE environmental award in 2005 and, in 2006, first place in the Ford Motor Company's China Environment and Conservation Grant competition. This national-level recognition brought the group the funds to continue its work, as well as further recognition among Chinese environmentalists who were enthusiastic about its work and about the broader potential for similar groups to mobilize traditional Tibetan culture to preserve biodiversity.

Although Rinchen and others like him insisted that Tibetan culture had always had the concept and practice of environmental protection, even if the term itself was new, they also maintained that there were clear differences between the ways they understood the environment and its protection and the way it was understood by the Chinese and foreign conservationists they encountered. However, by aligning themselves with conservationists and their discourses and institutions of science, Tibetans simultaneously distanced themselves from the possibility of their cultural practices being labeled as "superstition," and thus dangerous, illegitimate, or anti-state (see ch. 9 in this volume). What their collaboration in conservation efforts produced, then, was not only better conditions for the survival of other species but also a space in which Tibetans could make a bid for the legitimacy of cultural practices in a way that had been unthinkable (and would soon be so again).

FRAGILITY AND LIMITATIONS

Translocal and transnational collaborations can work not just in spite of but also because of differences and the inevitable slippages and faithless appropriation that characterizes all translation (Tsing 1997, 2005). In some circumstances, however, these slippages can also make the resulting collaborations fragile. Even in 2004, at the workshop that first brought Rinchen Samdrup into contact with broader environmentalist networks, the limits to the depth of intercultural collaboration were apparent. Rinchen and others like him were, like foreign and Chinese environmentalists, genuinely interested in the protection of "nature." At the same time, however, their environmental subjectivities were constituted in part by the fact that the environment provided a way to talk safely about other aspects of Tibetan life and culture that were too politicized to discuss on their own terms. Han proponents of the Green Tibetan discourse saw Tibetan culture largely as a way of protecting the environment, whereas Tibetans saw the environment not only as something to be protected but also as a way of making space for Tibetan culture.

The depth of their collaboration in the middle of the first decade of the 2000s was limited in part by the fact that some of the political constraints faced by Tibetans were virtually invisible to non-Tibetans. For example, on the second day of the 2004 conference, about fifteen people, half of them Tibetan and half Han, participated in a working group on "remaining problems in traditional culture and environmental protection." One participant was a Beijing University student, a serious-looking young Han man, who was very adamant that "the *real* root of all environmental problems is the loss of traditional culture." He raised numerous examples to support his point, such as the fact that the traditional Tibetan reluctance to eat fish, once seen as superstition, is now recognized as environmentally friendly. Other Han participants proposed that the Critical Ecosystem Partnership Fund should "spread information about the ways in which Tibetan culture is good for the environment" and "support monasteries." Their basic message was summarized in the statement of one Han environmental activist: "Our goal is to change the minds of policy-makers by spreading the word about the *good* aspects of traditional culture. We should protect cultural diversity, and we should use Tibetan religion for environmental protection." They enthusiastically agreed on the use of traditional religious practices for environmental protection and that they should promote the legal recognition of Tibetan sacred mountains as a form of protected area management.

After almost an hour of discussion, one of the quiet Tibetans finally spoke up, trying to explain that this would be more difficult than some of the activists seemed to believe. He didn't mention that many traditional practices, such as rituals to prevent hail, are regularly labeled superstitious and thus are seen as a threat to the state. He did explain, however, that there are still restrictions on monasteries. In the past, he stated, monks set aside certain areas as sacred mountains and forbade logging in those areas. Now, however, monks and lamas are authorized by the state to be involved only in those activities that the state deems to be "religion." This means, he explained, that they certainly do not have the right to tell citizens whether or not they can cut down trees; lamas no longer have the right to declare sacred mountains. None of the participants followed up with a comment. Indeed, it was as if no one had heard his remarks. The conversation continued with more declarations about the importance of traditional culture.

After a while, another Tibetan spoke up in flawless standard Chinese. "Look—the problem is politics . . . Before I came to this conference, I was warned that I should be very, very careful about what I said here." The Tibetan who had spoken up earlier looked relieved, as this was the point he had tried to convey. He added, "Probably, it's we Tibetans that understand this best. There are still some things that are very hard for us to do." Their comments were again met with silence—not a hostile silence, but one that suggested a lack of comprehension, as if these Tibetans, in talking about the constraints that they might face in trying to implement the Han activists' optimistic goals of "reviving local religious culture in service of the environment," were speaking a language that the Chinese environmentalists could not or would not engage with at the time.

THE CONJUNCTURE BREAKS APART

The political terrain shifted dramatically for Tibetans after the unprecedented wave of more than one hundred protests that swept the Tibetan Plateau in 2008 and unleashed a torrent of Chinese nationalist backlash (see Barnett 2009; Yeh 2009d). During the Olympic Games, hotels in Beijing were not open to Tibetans (or Uyghurs). Even afterward, Tibetans often found that as soon as they showed their identification cards, previously vacant hotels mysteriously became full. Taxi drivers and restaurants refused to serve them. The Tibetan Plateau entered a state of lockdown, with People's Armed Police soldiers stationed on every street corner of Lhasa, new surveillance technologies, and helicopter patrols of the city. In Lhasa, residents reported a noticeable worsening of interethnic relations. The extensive policing, surveillance, and always-tight political control in the TAR was extended across cultural Tibet, permeating the Sino-Tibetan borderlands, which witnessed a horrifying series of self-immolations beginning in 2011.

Contact with foreigners became a liability, making transnational collaborations dangerous. Foreign NGOs that had long done development work in Tibetan areas were declared to be enemies, and local residents were banned from receiving any kind of foreign money. NGOs in general became suspect, first in Tibetan areas and later, in 2011, with democratic protests breaking out across North Africa and the Middle East, throughout all of China. No longer able to function without funds, local civil society organizations fell apart. Tibetan aspirations to found or work for NGOs fizzled in the face of this severe political pressure. Many young English-speaking Tibetans, once motivated to improve the environment and local livelihoods and revive local culture went to work as civil servants, including, in some cases, Public Security Bureau officers. Others, citing the impossibility of doing anything through civil society, turned toward a business model and the language of social entrepreneurship. International NGOs that found a way to continue working in Tibet also did so by switching their model away from development, environmental protection, and culture and toward business development and ecotourism. The emphasis shifted to turning Tibetans into successful entrepreneurs. The language of sustainability and the new exalted figure of the entrepreneur fit well within China's larger turn toward an increasingly neoliberal form of governance, in which all citizens must cultivate themselves to become more rational actors and better entrepreneurs of themselves, so that China may gain its rightful place of domination in economic globalization (Yan 2008; Zhang and Ong 2008).

SOVEREIGN POWER AND HARMONY IDEOLOGY

However, a far worse fate than the withdrawal of funding was in store for Rinchen Samdrup and the Voluntary Environmental Protection Association in Tserangding. Rinchen and his younger brother Chime Namgyal were detained in August 2009. Chime was sentenced without trial to twenty-one months in a labor camp on charges of endangering state security by having "illegally compiled three discs of audio-visual materials on the ecology, environment, natural resources and religion of Chamdo Prefecture," illegally possessing materials from "the Dalai clique abroad," and "supplying photographs and material for the illegal publication 'Forbidden Mountain, Prohibited Hunting,'" a reference to their Tibetan-language environmental protection journal. Furthermore, he was accused of having broken the law by assisting Rinchen in applying for registration for their environmental NGO. Chime had been partially handicapped before his detention and was reportedly tortured and beaten to the point of being unable to walk or eat without assistance (ICT 2010).

Rinchen was held without trial and without being officially charged for almost one year, when he was sentenced to five years in prison on charges of "incitement to split the country." His lawyer stated to the *Times* of London that the main charge centered around the posting of an article on the environmental association's website that indirectly mentioned that the fourteenth Dalai Lama had been awarded the Nobel Peace Prize. Rinchen denied in court that he had posted it. None of the activities that Rinchen and Chime were accused of are in fact against the law. The association applied repeatedly for official registration but was consistently denied. When Chime was sentenced, however, these attempts at legal recognition were simply declared illegal. Similarly, there is no law in China against possessing or posting photos of the Dalai Lama or making references to him, certainly not references as obscure as the one Rinchen Samdrup was accused of having posted. Yet this, too, was simply declared illegal.

In the aftermath of 2008, even as state authorities stepped up calls for a "harmonious society," sovereign power marked Tibetans as always already guilty subjects. In their position, guilt is not about transgression of the law. It does not refer "to the determination of the licit and the illicit, but to the pure force of the law, to the law's simple reference to something" (Agamben 1998, 27), which makes an actual violation of an actual law irrelevant. Giorgio Agamben further writes that the "almost constitutive exchange between violence and right that characterizes the figure of the sovereign is shown more nakedly and more clearly in the figure of the police than anywhere else" (ibid., 104). Thus, it is not surprising that Rinchen, Chime, and a number of other villagers were subject to police violence and that their troubles actually began with the police. Though the environmental protection association had long had good relations with Forestry Bureau officials, it also had a long-standing enmity with the (Tibetan) head of the County Public Security Bureau. An essay published in the association's journal indicated that things started to go poorly for them in 2005, the year the Harmonious Society was declared. Villagers accused the official of sending people to hunt wildlife that they were trying to protect and of beating them when they tried to prevent poaching. There were other disputes related to grassland boundaries, sacred mountains, a village deity, and compensation for the trees the villagers had planted for the Sloping Land Conversion Program, along with further poaching and beating of villagers. The members of the association eventually attempted to bring their local police chief to court and to petition regional and national levels of government. Retribution from officials who had been petitioned against or embarrassed by the process, or from their political patrons, led ultimately to the arrest and sentencing of the environmentalists on state security charges. Karma Samdrup, Rinchen's other younger brother and a very well-known environmentalist, philanthropist, and businessperson, was also arrested and sentenced to fifteen years in 2010 as he sought to mobilize support to help get his brothers out of detention.

These arrests and the state violence mobilized against the members of the association ended their ability to do environmental work, let alone continue to realize their goals of cultural revival. While Chime and Rinchen were detained, Chinese environmentalists worked behind the scenes to demonstrate the brothers' innocence, highlight their environmental protection contributions, and secure their release. In doing so, they were forced to navigate the new precariousness of their own positions, as Tibetan environmental protection became a dangerous rather than celebrated cause. These efforts were unsuccessful. In the meantime, both transnational environmental organizations working in China, and domestic NGOs, have largely moved on from their focus on sacred lands and indigenous knowledge. The combination of shifting donor priorities within transnational conservation finance, increased Chinese state regulation and pressure on NGOs, and the shift toward a greater emphasis on sovereign power in the sovereignty-discipline-government triad after 2008 led away from sacred lands and toward issues of adaptation to climate change, payments for ecosystem services, and more generally "selling nature to save it." Though the Chinese environmentalists who had been involved in championing a space for Tibetan cultural assertion did not themselves change their minds or start seeing Tibetan culture differently, the Chinese public at large became less willing to trust Tibetans or believe in the positive potential of Tibetan culture. Thus the space that once existed in which the Green Tibetan could gain traction and produce material results in the world closed down even as the Harmonious Society was being heavily promoted.

A number of scholars have read the interest of transnational conservation agencies in sacred lands as an appropriation and closure of indigenous territoriality, an extension of the territorialization and enframing of space that comes with the declaration of new ecoregions. Still others have interpreted the emergence of local environmental NGOs and the production of environmental subjects as the carriers of new forms of imperial sovereignty and neoliberal governmentality. While this perspective is a useful corrective to the triumphalist mainstream literature that reads Chinese NGOs only in terms of their potential for Western-style democratization, the possibility of recognizing change is foreclosed by too insistent a reading of the emergence of subjects who care for and guide their own behavior in particular ways in relation to "the environment" as merely a new form of government "acting at a distance."

While the emergence of the Green Tibetan in China may be these things, it is also much more. Rinchen Samdrup's essays before and after his engagement, through a cultural and linguistic translator, with translocal and transnational understandings of environmentalism and Tibetanness reveal how concern for a local place and its territorial deities were reworked and re-presented as concern for the world's environment. At the same time, the program activities of a transnational conservation organization meant to protect sacred mountains and lakes were formed very much in relation to the concerns of people like Rinchen. These encounters were thus cultural productions, resulting in new identities and interests for all of their participants. For a brief period of time, the productive slippages of translated interactions with distant others created a space in which Tibetans could not only actively argue for nature protection but also articulate claims about the inherent value of their culture. However, this conjuncture proved fragile and fleeting in the face of the state's reassertion of sovereign power as a favored mode of governing Tibetans after 2008. Ultimately, contingent collaborations of Chinese and Tibetan environmentalists in mobilizing Tibetan culture to conserve biodiversity were far more beneficial for interethnic harmony than the state-led project of a forced harmony ideology.

CHAPTER 10. THE RISE AND FALL OF THE GREEN TIBETAN

This research was made possible with a grant from the National Science Foundation (BCS 0847722). I am grateful to the many colleagues who have commented on versions of this paper over several years, as well as to Rinchen Samdrup, Trador, and numerous other environmentalists in China. All mistakes are my own.

1   A "soul tree" (Wyl. *bla shing*) is one that stands in sympathetic relationship with a particular person's or clan's life force.

2   *Sacred Land: Refuge for Nature*, CI-China brochure (undated).

3   The full name of the organization is (in Wylie transliteration) mdo smad ahn
     chung seng ge gnam rdzong rang mos skye khams khor yug srung skyong mthun
     tshogs, or Voluntary Association for the Protection of the Natural Environment
     of Domed Anchung Sengge Namzong (a local place-name).

4   A *khenpo* is an advanced degree given in the Nyingma school in the study of
     Tibetan Buddhism.

5   Love Tibet Association, http://www.tibetinfor.org/friend-tibet/index/11newyear.
     htm (site discontinued).

6   By "translocal," I refer to connections as well as unevenness and inequalities link-
     ing localities within China. See Oakes and Schein 2005.

Afterword

• • •

THE AFTERLIVES OF SHANGRILA

Ralph Litzinger

For some time now, the idea of Shangrila has been picked apart, deciphered, and thoroughly deconstructed. For me, the great unraveling began in the early 1990s, when, browsing a bookstore in Seattle, I happened upon a used copy of Peter Bishop's *The Myth of Shangri-La*. It might not be too much to say that this book launched a kind of academic cottage industry charting the multiple lives of Shangrila. None of us can think of Shangrila today without also referencing Donald Lopez's 1998 *Prisoners of Shangri-La*, Tsering Shakya's "Tibet and the Occident," Orville Schell's 2000 *Virtual Tibet*, Dibyesh Anand's *Geopolitical Exotica*, and a host of other books, articles, and websites. These interventions create a must-read list for anyone serious about understanding the history of Shangrila's multiple significations and uses, its many afterlives. We can no longer think of Shangrila without addressing histories of British colonialism in Asia (and elsewhere); the ugly and racist geopolitics of the Great Game, of Chinese and Russians and Americans and European powers vying for trade and other advantages; the Nazis turning to Tibet to test their detestable theories of Aryan superiority; Hollywood mythmaking; celebrity activism; and even Chinese nationals trying to save the country's reputation when free-Tibet protesters confronted the Olympic torch as it made its way across the world to Beijing. Shangrila belongs to a troubled history of mostly Western desire and mythmaking, to histories of violence and the desire for domination and control, and to the Western craze for collecting all things exotic and other. Through Hollywood, the popularization of the *Tibetan Book of the Dead*, and the New Age movement, the idea of Shangrila is also linked to the desire for alternative forms of spiritualism and to the ongoing struggle to free Tibetans from what many—mostly outside China—see as the genocidal madness of the Chinese Communist state.

Mapping Shangrila, acutely aware of these complex histories, adds yet another twist to the story of Shangrila by giving us the first collection of close ethnographic readings and analyses of China's many Shangrilas. In the hands of hucksters and entrepreneurs and government officials looking for a quick buck, Shangrila has been reborn in China. It lives again through the production of new circuits of commodity production and consumption, middle-class Chinese tourist encounters with Tibet, new film and documentary productions (both Chinese and, more recently, by Tibetan intellectuals in China), the relentless "opening up" of the Tibetan plateau for resource extraction, new ecological discourses about planetary and Third Pole crises, the forced migration of nomads to lifeless new towns, and the seemingly never-ending Chinese state project to, once and for all, liberate the Tibetan masses from their eternal backwardness. The chapters collected here thus show us that Shangrila is no longer singularly a Western fantasy, even though it continues to be recycled in the West, is still used to create resorts and name botanical gardens, motor raceways, tourist agencies, albums, museum collections, and private residences. As we learn from this wide-ranging collection of case studies, China is now in the Shangrila game in a big way, and the stakes are high for a range of different actors. Conservation scientists, the people at the United Nations Educational, Scientific and Cultural Organization (UNESCO) who manage the World Heritage sites, mushroom and medicinal herb collectors, Tibetan villagers and nomads who have been promised a say in their futures through new "participatory" modes of development, national park and nature reserve planners, mining and construction companies, hydropower investors, and even the lowly paid tour operator haltingly explaining to the tourist why Tibetans are self-immolating—all are part of the story of the making of a new Shangrila imaginary, this time with Chinese characteristics.

The rebirth of Shangrila in China—as a specific place called Xianggelila—can be approached through differing theoretical perspectives: neoliberalism, governmentality, resource competition, and ethnic revitalization. For almost all commentators in this volume, whether working in Xianggelila or other places, the reform-era state has created complex forms of state capitalism, which, in turn, have unleashed new forms of desire at the local level—for prestige, visibility, identity, and capital. In the far reaches of northwest Yunnan, the making of Xianggelila is a story of how local entrepreneurs, some Tibetan, many not, imaginatively linked themselves to this grandest of European colonial fantasies, to a British novel and popular U.S. film (translated into Chinese and widely distributed). This recuperated colonial past was then grafted onto a developmental model for the ethnic borderlands that would take mass tourism as the key link. The aim was nothing less than to transform a little-known town in the northwest corner of Yunnan into a major tourist destination.

The story often overlooked in this narrative is how the reinvention of Shangrila got entangled in a global ecological imaginary of biodiversity conservation. In the mid- to late 1990s, after nongovernmental organizations (NGOs) had experimented for a decade, intent on figuring out the cause of poverty and advising the government on the best courses for poverty alleviation, northwest Yunnan and other parts of the Tibetan Plateau came to be viewed as a working laboratory for a new kind of collaborative global environmentalism. As some of the chapters in this book illustrate, the making of Shangrila as global ecological laboratory necessitated working with government, at all levels of the Chinese bureaucracy. At the same time, the global biodiversity project sought to transcend the fixed administrative and ideological boundaries of the prefecture, the province, and, yes, even the nation-state. This new environmentalism, this transregional, transnational, and planetary ecological imaginary, was meant, in part, to assist China in getting over the political hangover of the Maoist past, which many environmentalists viewed as an ecological disaster. Science would now serve development. The ecological would finally find a secure place in China's developmental planning. This would happen not just in the northwest corner of Yunnan, where the mythological Shangrila was being reassembled into Xianggelila, but in multiple locations across the Tibetan borderlands.

• • •

My first encounter with China's Shangrila came in the summer of 2000. I was invited to be a self-funded participant at an event in Kunming called the Cultures and Biodiversity Congress (CUBIC). This gathering of the global biodiversity tribe aimed to create a policy document, which would eventually come to be known as the Yunnan Initiative. This visionary document was to be presented to the Yunnan provincial government in a bold attempt to convince the leadership that ethnic minority cultures and biodiversity were intricately linked; that Yunnan's unique cultures and biodiversity were under extreme threat from shortsighted government policies and the expansion of local, regional, and international markets and, in some instances, by locals themselves; and that the future of "local livelihoods" depended on new planning regimes, new resource management models, and new forms of cooperation between governments, nongovernmental actors, and commercial interests.

CUBIC was not just a huge meeting spanning many days of lectures, breakout sessions, and PowerPoint presentations (in those days, incidentally, all prepared on IBMs). It was also meant to be a traveling practicum for those who wished to get into the "field." We thus became a mobile research unit, traveling from Kunming to Xishuangbanna in the far south of Yunnan, and then back north, high on the Tibetan Plateau. Looking back at my field notes and recalling my many conversations with other participants, I realize that it was the trip to the Tibetan Plateau that most energized my traveling companions. It was essential, we were told, to see the biodiversity and cultural plentitude of northwest Yunnan firsthand. To get close to the land. To feel it and smell it. To meet local people.

Though we traveled with government officials from various bureaus and were hosted at multiple sites by officials, there was a paradoxical sense that it was necessary to sidestep the official state-speak of the government if we were to really experience the new Shangrila in the making. Only then could we get close to the truth of what was happening on the ground. The state created a new version of Shangrila. But it might also obscure its most essential truths. How were people using forest and non-forest resources? Who was to blame for the years of deforestation? Did local Tibetans really participate in and benefit from the ghastly scourging of the forests? Were there ethnic practices that could be studied and mobilized for alternative visions of development? I remember thinking: This is an anthropological dreamworld! The possibilities for fieldwork seemed endless. I was crazed with excitement. The Chinese ethnologist and the American or British or Italian anthropologist would now stand beside the conservation biologist. Events like the CUBIC field junket allowed one to meet scholars and environmental experts from all over China. My pockets were bulging with name cards, the essential *mingpian*. I was creating a network, a web of connections that might help me in the future. I was getting to know, for example, Liang Congjie, who would become a friend and respected colleague until, sadly, he passed in October of 2010, and also younger Chinese NGO staffers, relatively new to this world of biodiversity management and environmental stewardship. Over the next decade, a handful of these people would become some of China's most visible environmental activists. All around me there was a heady mix of deep knowledge about northwest Yunnan and other regions across the Tibetan Plateau. It is as if we were inhaling biodiversity with every breath. After the ravages of Maoism and the extractive practices of the logging industry, northwest Yunnan now had a chance to be rightfully returned to a state of equilibrium, in which ethnic culture would be harmonized with nature. In this very moment, the underlying logic of the Euro-American dream machine—the idea that Tibet *must* deliver something, a personal journey, spiritual quest, an alternative civilization, a future without war, or a market or trade route—was giving way to something seemingly entirely new.

But what was this something new? And could it be sustained? Within a little less than two years, after almost a decade of quite assiduous study, backdoor maneuvering, gifting, historical re-creation and fanciful reconstruction, the Diqing provincial government would win State Council approval to change the name of Zhongdian County to Xianggelila. Pages of text have been produced since then demonstrating how this process took place, the forms of exclusion upon which it was predicated, and the differential economic outcomes for those entrepreneurially savvy enough to cash in on the new Shangrila. There has been a perpetual tension between the big government infrastructure project, entrepreneurial craft, local self-fashioning, tourist excess, and the grassroots desire of "locals" who so badly wanted to get into the game of turning their religious practices, villages, homes, song and dance, and bodies into objects of desire. Perhaps, as some scholars have asserted, there has been an ethnic upside, that what we have witnessed over the past decade is the creation of a new kind of pan-Tibetan ethnic identity (Hillman 2003; Kolås 2008), one celebrated by the harmonizing state and yet never fully controlled or represented by it. Perhaps.

At CUBIC in the summer of 2000, and in the decade to follow, the idea of Shangrila as a global ecological laboratory was slowly taking shape. I don't think we find the hunger of the ecological scientist in the deep archive of the West's many Shangrila imaginaries, nor among the great plant hunters and explorers Erik Mueggler has documented in *The Paper Road*. What was born in the late 1990s in northwest Yunnan was an ecological Shangrila, one that would be at once both national and transnational. This ecological

Shangrila would be a testing ground for new mapping strategies, in which, for example, a local villager's hand-drawn map of a forest and its multiple uses would be commensurate with the large satellite images of the Yunnan Great Rivers Project's conservation zones that hung on the corporate office walls. It would be a laboratory for testing new modes of local participation in national park planning or nature reserve management strategies, where, everyone seemed to believe, local voices, histories, and "traditional" practices would surely matter in the making of an ecological future. It would be a place in which Kodak and Fuji would team up with the Nature Conservancy (TNC) to bring cameras to villagers (TNC was not alone in this kind of endeavor). With disposable camera in hand, villagers would shoot their local environs, documenting their everyday relationship to the plentitude of nature that surrounded them. These images were then collected. Interviews conducted. Local views recorded. All of this material was then worked into masterfully organized portfolios of images and texts (usually only captions) that evidently captured both the voices and visions of the natives, as they saw the world around them. In principle, this portfolio of images was to be presented to a government official in a poverty-alleviation or tourism or construction bureau. This official might, just might, take these villagers' voices and visions, as mediated through the Photovoice project, into consideration in the next round of state planning. In too many cases, I was to learn some time later, the image-making project never successfully informed policy. Rather, the images became the means for the extraction of surplus value, enlarged into massive and beautifully crafted images and hauled off to a fund-raiser event in Shanghai, or Beijing, or San Francisco. The participatory ecological imaginary had gone global, via the traveling photo exhibit.

• • •

After CUBIC, the Nature Conservancy was gracious enough to invite me back to Yunnan the following year to track its projects, work beside its staff, attend meetings, and reflect on its many projects. Other social scientists would follow. As Robert Moseley and Renée Mullen rightly put it in chapter 5 in this volume, we didn't always speak the same theoretical language or share the same goals. Remarkably, and to TNC's immense credit, the organization let us loose at its project sites, where we learned things we didn't always like. At one point, for example, a TNC staffer on his way out shared an entire file drawer of contracts, financial agreements, reports from hired Chinese field biologists and ethnologists. I was astonished to see what people were paid, the wild divergence between different levels of staff, the money that was going to some nature reserve officials and how some were getting paid almost nothing for their labor. I thus became interested in the forms of work and labor that went into the new ecological tasks of documenting, mapping, and mobilizing local participation in the Yunnan Great Rivers Project, but this turn inward to the internal logics of the organization's operations in China was not always embraced. Suspicions arose if the gaze was not turned outward to the larger task of documenting biodiversity and convincing local villagers that they would be better off in the long run if they participated in various programs—the making of eco-villages, a large-scale biogas project, Photovoice, and new management training sessions. Could the anthropologist be trusted? What would he or she do with the data that were being collected? When ethnic tensions emerged between Naxi and Tibetan staffers, as they did, and accusations of scheming and corruption surfaced, what would the anthropologist do with these company secrets? Would the anthropologist undermine the larger project of convincing the Yunnan and, much later, central government that biodiversity was a form of national capital that should be studied and preserved? How could the dream of collaboration be maintained when differing views surfaced, not only between the leadership of the project in Yunnan and the anthropologists but also between the many Han and the ethnic minorities who staffed the projects on the ground?

Anna Tsing once wrote about how cultures are continually being coproduced in the interactions she called "friction." In my view, Tsing's vision of collaboration and the tensions and instabilities that inform it has always been at the heart of the Shangrila imaginary, whether we are referring to the utopia of *Lost Horizon*, which became a big chunk of the material for the imagining of Xianggelila, or the new ecological imaginary in which biological scientists and ecologists would work side by side with social scientists and figure out how nature and culture could be properly managed and synced. Tsing reminds us that all collaborations are about the awkward, unequal, unstable, and creative qualities of interconnection *across difference*. Collaboration is not a simple sharing of information, she tells us, and there is no reason to assume that collaborators share common goals.

In this respect I differ somewhat from a certain reading that seems to me to inform the introduction to part 2 of *Mapping Shangrila*. Here, Chris Coggins and Emily Yeh would have us believe that everything begins to change with the Tibetan uprisings of March 2008 and the subsequent global financial crisis. They see multiple signs of hope between the late 1990s and 2008—innovative projects, international staffers working with Chinese environmentalists, social scientists working with biologists, Yi and Naxi working with Tibetans, prefectural and provincial governments accepting the gift of an international ecological mapping and planning process. They see a new kind of collaborative possibility in the making, what I have called an ecological Shangrila. After 2008, a period of retrenchment sets in, and the Chinese state reasserts itself. International environmental organizations are subjected to new forms of scrutiny and even surveillance, money dries up, projects fizzle out.

But long before 2008, there are many examples of projects, funded and supported by various international conservation organizations, that go nowhere. One could point to the enormous resources wasted in terms of labor, time, and money on biogas conversion projects. One could look at long-standing and still unresolved village conflicts over matsutake and other non-timber forest products. One could look at beautifully constructed ecotourism centers in places such as Qianhushan or the Thousand Lakes District in Diqing Prefecture that today sit empty because villagers could not decide on workable management strategies and ways of sharing profits from ecotourism. One could go on forever about the eventual failure of the campaign to stop damming on the upper reaches of the Nu, Mekong, and Yangzi Rivers. One need only point to the disaster that is the Three Parallel Rivers World Heritage site, where river water resources were magically written out of the original mapping. One could point to the White Horse Snow Mountain Nature Reserve and the deal that had to be struck with provincial authorities to keep out mining interests. Today, one can walk a half hour from a village just outside the nature reserve and photograph snub-nosed monkeys "in the wild." An endangered species has been turned into a zoological specimen in order to save the mountains from mining.

Mapping Shangrila shows us that the colonial fantasy of Shangrila lives on, refusing to die. Or, rather, it continues to return to the world of the living in a bizarrely reincarnated form, disfigured yet somehow strangely familiar.

References

Abe, Ken-ichi. 1997. "Forest History in Yunnan, China (I): Tibetan God Mountain and Its Protected Forest in Jungden [Zhongdian]." Japanese. *Southeast Asian Studies* (SEAS) 35(3): 422–44.

Agamben, Giorgio. 1998. *Homo Sacer: Sovereign Power and Bare Life.* Stanford: Stanford University Press.

Agnew, John. 2009. *Globalization and Sovereignty.* Lanham, MD: Rowman & Littlefield.

Agrawal, Arun. 1999. *Greener Pastures: Politics, Markets, and Community among a Migrant Pastoral People.* Durham, NC: Duke University Press.

———. 2005. *Environmentality: Technologies of Government and the Making of Subjects.* Durham, NC: Duke University Press.

Alai. 2000. *Dadi de jieti* [The earth's staircase]. Kunming: Yunnan Renmin Chubanshe.

———. 2002. *Red Poppies: A Novel of Tibet.* New York: Houghton Mifflin.

Alcorn, Janis B. 2005. "Dances around the Fire: Conservation Organizations and Community-Based Natural Resource Management." In *Communities and Conservation: Histories and Politics of Community-Based Natural Resource Management,* edited by J. Peter Brosius, Anna L. Tsing, and Charles Zerner, 37–68. Walnut Creek, CA: Altamira.

Allerton, Catherine. 2009. "Introduction: Spiritual Landscapes of Southeast Asia." *Anthropological Forum* 19(3): 235–51.

Amend, Anthony, Zhendong Fang, Cui Yi, and Will C. McClatchey. 2010. "Local Perceptions of Matsutake Mushroom Management, in NW Yunnan China." *Biological Conservation* 143(1): 165–72.

Anagnost, Ann. 1987. "Politics and Magic in Contemporary China." *Modern China* 13(1): 40–61.

———. 2004. "The Corporeal Politics of Quality (Suzhi)." *Public Culture* 16(2): 189–208.

Anderson, Benedict. 2005. "Imagined Communities." In *Nations and Nationalism: A Reader,* edited by Philip Spencer and Howard Wollman, 48–60. New Brunswick, NJ: Rutgers University Press.

Anderson, Danica, Jan Salick, Robert Moseley, and Xiaokun Ou. 2005. "Conserving the Sacred Medicine Mountains: A Vegetation Analysis of Tibetan Sacred Sites in Northwest Yunnan." *Biodiversity and Conservation* 14: 3065–91.

Arora, David. 2008. "The Houses That Matsutake Built." *Economic Botany* 62(3): 278–90.

Atisha, Tenzin P. 1991. "The Tibetan Approach to Ecology." *Tibetan Review* 25(2): 9–14.

Atwill, David G. 2005. *The Chinese Sultanate: Islam, Ethnicity, and the Panthay Rebellion in Southwest China, 1856–1873.* Stanford: Stanford University Press.

Bai Hua. 1994. *The Remote Country of Women* [Yuanfang you ge nü'er guo]. Honolulu: University of Hawai'i Press.

Balm, Roger, and Briavel Holcomb. 2003. "Unlosing Lost Places: Image Making, Tourism, and the Return to Terra Cognita." In *Visual Culture and Tourism*, edited by David Crouch and Nina Lübbren, 157–74. New York: Berg.

Banks, Tony, Camille Richard, Li Ping, and Yan Zhaoli. 2003. "Community-Based Grassland Management in Western China Rationale, Pilot Project Experience, and Policy Implications." *Mountain Research and Development* 23(2): 132–40.

Barmé, Geremie. 1999. *In the Red: On Contemporary Chinese Culture.* New York: Columbia University Press.

Barnett, Robert. 2009. "The Tibet Protests of Spring 2008." *China Perspectives* 3: 6–24.

Bass, Catriona. 1998. *Education in Tibet: Policy and Practice since 1950.* New York: St. Martin's Press.

Bauer, Ken. 2005. "Development and the Enclosure Movement in Pastoral Tibet since the 1980s." *Nomadic Peoples* 9(1–2): 53–81.

———. 2006. "Sacred Forests and Holy Mountains: Tibetan Notions of the Environment and the Discourse of Biodiversity Conservation." Abstract. American Anthropological Association 2006 Annual Meeting, San Jose, CA.

BCSD Program Team (Biodiversity Conservation and Sustainable Development in Shangri-la Gorge Program Team). 2003. "Feasibility Study for the Establishment of Shangri-la Gorge Special Ecological Zone in NW Yunnan." The Nature Conservancy China Program.

Belleza, John Vincent. 2005. *Spirit-Mediums, Sacred Mountains and Related Bon Textual Traditions in Upper Tibet: Calling Down the Gods.* Boston: Brill Academic Publishers.

Bennett, Tony. 2006. *Critical Trajectories: Culture, Society, Intellectuals.* Oxford: Blackwell.

Berglund, Eva. 2006. "Ecopolitics through Ethnography: The Cultures of Finland's Forest-Nature." In *Reimagining Political Ecology*, edited by Aletta Biersack and James. B. Greenberg, 99–120. Durham, NC: Duke University Press.

Berkes, Fikret. 2008. *Sacred Ecology: Traditional Ecological Knowledge and Resource Management.* New York: Routledge.

Berman, Merrick Lex. 1998. "Opening the Lancang (Mekong) River in Yunnan: Problems and Prospects for Xishuangbanna." Master's thesis, Department of Asian Languages and Literatures, University of Massachusetts Amherst.

Bhabha, Homi K. 1994. *The Location of Culture.* London and New York: Routledge.

Bird-David, Nurit. 1999. "'Animism' Revisited: Personhood, Environment, and Relational Epistemology." Special issue, "Culture: A Second Chance?" *Current Anthropology* 40: 67–91.

Blaikie, Piers M., and Joshua S. S. Muldavin. 2004. "Upstream, Downstream, China, India: The Politics of Environment in the Himalayan Region." *Annals of the Association of American Geographers* 94: 520–48.

Blondeau, Anne-Marie, ed. 1995. *Tibetan Mountain Deities, Their Cults and Representations: Papers Presented at a Panel of the 7th Seminar of the International Association for Tibetan Studies, Graz 1995.* Vienna: Verlag der Österreichischen Akademie der Wissenschaften.

Booz, Patrick. 2011. *Tea, Trade and Transport in the Sino-Tibetan Borderlands.* DPhil thesis, Faculty of Oriental Studies, Oxford University.

Bourdieu, Pierre. 1990. *The Logic of Practice.* Stanford: Stanford University Press.

Bracey, R. 1990. "The Japanese Mushroom Market." Report. Tokyo. 27 pp.

Bridge, Gavin, and Tom Perreault. 2009. "Environmental Governance." In *A Companion to Environmental Geography,* edited by Noel Castree, David Demeritt, Diana Liverman, and Bruce Rhoads, 475–97. New York: Wiley-Blackwell.

Brockington, Dan, Rosaleen Duffy, and Jim Igoe. 2008. *Nature Unbound: Conservation, Capitalism and the Future of Protected Areas.* London: Earthscan.

Brosius, J. Peter. 2006. "Common Ground between Anthropology and Conservation Biology." *Conservation Biology* 20: 683–85.

Brosius, J. Peter, and Diane Russell. 2003. "Conservation from Above: An Anthropological Perspective on Transboundary Protected Areas and Ecoregional Planning." *Journal of Sustainable Forestry* 17: 39–65.

Brown, Phil, Darrin Magee, and Yilin Xu. 2008. "Socioeconomic Vulnerability in China's Hydropower Development." *China Economic Review* 19(4): 614–27.

Brown, Wendy. 2006. "Power after Foucault." In *The Oxford Handbook of Political Theory,* edited by John S. Dryzek, Bonnie Honig, and Anne Phillips, 65–84. Oxford: Oxford University Press.

'brug thar and sangs rgyas tshe ring. 2005. *mdo smad rma khug tsha 'gram yul gru'i lo rgyus deb ther chen mo* [Historical annals of the region of the Amdo Yellow River banks]. Beijing: Minzu Chubanshe.

Bryant, Raymond. 2002. "Non-governmental Organizations and Governmentality: 'Consuming' Biodiversity and Indigenous Peoples in the Philippines." *Political Studies* 50: 268–92.

Buffetrille, Katia. 2008. "Some Remarks on Mediums: The Case of the lha pa of the Musical Festival (glu rol) of Sog ru (A mdo)." *Mongolo-Tibetica Pragensia '08* 1(2): 13–66.

Bulag, Uradyn. 2002. *The Mongols at China's Edge: History and the Politics of National Unity.* Boulder: Rowman & Littlefield.

Byg, Anja, and Jan Salick. 2009. "Local Perspectives on a Global Phenomenon—Climate Change in Eastern Tibetan Villages." *Global Environmental Change* 19: 156–66.

Callon, Michel. 1986. "Some Elements of a Sociology of Translation: Domestication of the Scallops and the Fishermen of St. Brieux Bay." In *Power, Action, Belief: A New Sociology of Knowledge?* edited by John Law, 196–229. Andover, Hants, England: Routledge, Chapman and Hall.

Campbell, Lisa M. 2002. "Science and Sustainable Use: Views of Marine Turtle Conservation Experts." *Ecological Applications* 12(4): 1229–46.

Cannon, Paul. 2011. "The Caterpillar Fungus, a Flagship Species for Conservation of Fungi." *Fungal Conservation* 1: 35–39.

Cannon, Paul F., Nigel Hywel-Jones, Norbert Maczey, Lungten Norbu, Lungten Tshitila, Tashi Samdup, and Phurba Lhendup. 2009. "Steps towards Sustainable Harvest of Ophiocordyceps Sinensis in Bhutan." *Biodiversity Conservation* 18(9): 2263–81.

Carrithers, Michael, Matei Candea, Karen Sykes, Martin Holbraad, and Soumhya Venkatesan. 2010. "Ontology Is Just Another Word for Culture." *Critique of Anthropology* 30(2): 152–200.

Carter, Neil T., and Arthur P. J. Mol. 2007. *Environmental Governance in China.* New York: Routledge.

CAS 2007. *China Modernization Report 2007: Study on Ecological Modernization.* Beijing: Chinese Academy of Sciences.

Casey, Edward S. 1996. "How to Get from Space to Place in a Fairly Short Stretch of Time: Phenomenological Prolegomena." In *Getting Back into Place: Toward a Renewed Understanding of the Place-World,* 317–48. Bloomington: Indiana University Press.

———. 2000. *Remembering: A Phenomenological Study.* Bloomington: Indiana University Press.

Cater, Erlet. 2000. "Tourism in the Yunnan Great Rivers National Parks System Project: Prospects for Sustainability." *Tourism Geographies* 2: 472–89.

CCP (Chinese Communist Party). 2007. "Harmonious Society, Seventeenth National Congress of the Communist Party of China." *People's Daily,* Beijing. http://english.peopledaily.com.cn/90002/92169/92211/6274973.html.

———. 2011. "Zhongguo Gongchandang Dishiqijie Zhongyang Weiyuanhui Diliuci Quanti Huiyi gongbao" [Report from the Sixth Plenum of the Seventeenth Central Committee of the Chinese Communist Party]. http://cpc.people.com.cn/GB/64093/64387/15939604.html.

Certeau, Michel de. 1984. *The Practice of Everyday Life.* Berkeley: University of California Press.

———. 1988. *The Writing of History.* New York: Columbia University Press.

Chan, Yu Nam. 2002. "Livestock and Rangeland Management in Shangri-La Gorge, Shangri-La County, Northwest Yunnan, China." Master's thesis, Department of Environmental Science, Lund University.

Chapin, Mac. 2004. "A Challenge to Conservationists." *World Watch,* November–December, 17–31.

Chatterjee, Partha. 2006. *The Politics of the Governed: Reflections on Popular Politics in Most of the World.* New York: Columbia University Press.

Chau, Adam. 2005. "Politics of Legitimation and the Revival of Popular Religion in Shaanbei, North-Central China." *Modern China* 31(2): 236–78.

Chen, Y. 2001. "The WWF Integrated Conservation and Development Project with Communities Adjacent to the National-Level Biamaxueshan Nature Reserve (Sustainable Utilization of Matsutake Sub-project)." Project report for WWF-China. Kunming.

Chen Zhihong. 2008. *Stretching the Skin of the Nation: Chinese Intellectuals, the State, and the Frontiers in the Nanjing Decade (1927–1937).* PhD diss., University of Oregon.

China Daily. 2004. "Cooperation Declaration Inked for Tourism Development of 'Shangri-la.'" *China Daily*, October 15. http://www.chinadaily.com.cn/chinagate/2004-10/15/content_382721.htm. (accessed October 31, 2013).

China MAB (Chinese National Committee for Man and the Biosphere). 2005. "Photovoice." Special issue, *Man and the Biosphere*, 1–88.

China.org. 2006. "Communiqué of the Sixth Plenum of the 16th CPC Central Committee." http://english.gov.cn/2006-10/11/content_410436.htm (accessed October 31, 2013).

China State Forestry Administration. 2008. *Guanyu tongyi Yunnansheng lieru guojiagongyuan jianshedian sheng de tongzhi* [Notice on agreeing to designate Yunnan as a pilot province for constructing national parks]. http://www.forestry.gov.cn/sub/FstArticle.aspx?id=zwgk.5193.

China Statistical Bureau. 2013. http://www.tjcn.org.

Chinoy, Daniel. 2009. "Black-Hearted Products: The Causes of China's Product Safety Problems." *Columbia East Asia Review* 2(Spring): 20–36.

Cho, Juhyung (Jenny). 2011. *Poverty Alleviation through Ecotourism in the Three Parallel Rivers World Heritage Site, Yunnan, China*. Master's thesis, University of Oslo.

Choy, Howard Y.F. 2008. "In Quest(ion) of an 'I': Identity and Idiocy in Alai's *Red Poppies*." In *Modern Tibetan Literature and Social Change*, edited by Lauren R. Hartley and Patricia Sciaffini-Vedani, 225–35. Durham, NC: Duke University Press.

Coggins, Chris. 2003. *The Tiger and the Pangolin: Nature, Culture, and Conservation in China*. Honolulu: University of Hawai'i Press.

Coggins, Chris, and Tessa Hutchinson. 2006. "The Political Ecology of Geopiety: Nature Conservation in Tibetan Communities of Northwest Yunnan." *Asian Geographer* 25(1–2): 85–107.

Cohen, Erik. 1972. "Toward a Sociology of International Tourism." *Social Research* 39(1): 164–89.

Coleman, William M. 2002. "The Uprising at Batang: Khams and Its Significance in Chinese and Tibetan History." In *Khams pa Histories: Visions of People, Place and Authority*, edited by Lawrence Epstein, 31–56. Boston: Brill.

Comaroff, Jean, and John Comaroff. 2000. "Millennial Capitalism: First Thoughts on a Second Coming." *Public Culture* 12(2): 291–342.

Connerton, Paul. 1989. *How Societies Remember*. Cambridge: Cambridge University Press.

Cosgrove, Denis. 2000. "Geopiety." In *The Dictionary of Human Geography*, 4th ed., edited by R. J. Johnston, Derek Gregory, Geraldine Pratt, and Michael Watts, 308–9. Oxford and Malden, MA: Blackwell.

———. 2008. *Geography and Vision: Seeing, Imagining and Representing the World*. London: I. B. Tauris.

Crang, Mike. 1997. "Picturing Practices: Research through the Tourist Gaze." *Progress in Human Geography* 21(3): 359–73.

Cresswell, Tim. 2012. "Review Essay: Nonrepresentational Theory and Me: Notes of an Interested Sceptic." *Environment and Planning D: Society and Space* 30(1): 96–105.

Cronon, William. 1995. "The Trouble with Wilderness; or, Getting Back to the Wrong

Nature." In *Uncommon Ground: Rethinking the Human Place in Nature*, edited by William Cronon, 69–90. New York: Norton.

Crouch, David, Lars Aronsson, and Lage Wahlstrom. 2001. "Tourist Encounters." *Tourist Studies* 1(3): 253–70.

Crouch, David, and Luke Desforges. 2003. "The Sensuous in the Tourist Encounter." *Tourist Studies* 3(1): 5–22.

da Col, Giovanni. 2006a. "Grib and Bcud: Genealogies of Biopolitics among Tibetan Communities in Southwest China." Abstract. Ninth European Association of Social Anthropologists Biennial Conference, Bristol, UK.

———. 2006b. "Tibetan Parrhesiastes: Truthtellers, Charismatic Authorities, Mountain Keepers, and Bogus 'Living Buddhas' in the Cult of Kha ba dkar po, a Holy Peak in Northwest Yunnan (China)." Abstract. American Anthropological Association Annual Meeting, San Jose, CA.

———. 2007. "The View from *Somewhen*: Events, Bodies and the Perspective of Fortune around Khawa Karpo, a Tibetan Sacred Mountain in Yunnan Province." *Inner Asia* 9: 215–35.

———. 2012. "The Poisoner and the Parasite: Cosmoeconomics, Fear, and Hospitality among Dechen Tibetans." *Journal of the Royal Anthropological Institute*, n.s., S175–S195.

Dalton, Jacob. 2011. *The Taming of the Demons: Violence and Liberation in Tibetan Buddhism*. New Haven: Yale University Press.

D'Arcus, Bruce. 2000. "The 'Eager Gaze of the Tourist' Meets 'Our Grandfather's Guns': Producing and Contesting the Land of Enchantment in Gallup, New Mexico." *Environment and Planning D: Society and Space* 18: 693–714.

Das, Veena, and Deborah Poole. 2004. "State and Its Margins: Comparative Ethnographies." In *Anthropology in the Margins of the State*, edited by Veena Das and Deborah Poole, 3–34. Santa Fe, NM: School of American Research Press.

Dawa Tsering. 2004. *Bod kyi srol rgyun rig gnas dang deng dus kyi khor yug srung skyob* [Traditional Tibetan culture and contemporary environmental protection]. Beijing: Nationalities Publishing House.

Deleuze, Gilles, and Felix Guattari. 1987. *A Thousand Plateaus: Capitalism and Schizophrenia*. Minneapolis: University of Minnesota Press.

Deng Zhangying and Xiaoli Bai, eds. 2012. *"Weixi jianwen ji" yanjiu* [A study of *Weixi jianwen ji*]. Chengdu: Sichuan University Press.

Deqin County and The Nature Conservancy. 2000. *Proceedings: Meilixueshan Conservation and Development International Workshop, Deqin, Yunnan, China, October 11–13, 2000*. Deqin and Kunming, Yunnan: Deqin County and The Nature Conservancy.

Diemberger, Hildegard. 2005. "Female Oracles in Modern Tibet." In *Women in Tibet*, edited by Janet Gyatso and Hanna Havenvik, 113–68. New York: Columbia University Press.

Dinaburg, Jennifer S. 2008. *Making the Medicine Mountains: The Politics of Tibetan Doctors and Medicinal Plant Management in the Meilixueshan Conservation Area, Yunnan Province, PRC*. Master's thesis, Prescott College, Prescott, AZ.

———. 2011. "The Politics of Market-Based Approaches to Tibetan Medicinal Plant Management." Unpublished manuscript.

Dowie, Mark. 2005. "Conservation Refugees: When Protecting Nature Means Kicking People Out." *Orion*, November–December, 16–27.

Diqing Prefecture Development and Reform Commission. 2008. "Peiyu zhuangda si da zhizhu chanye tuijin jingji jiegou tiaozheng" [Foster and strengthen the four pillar industries, advance structural adjustment of the economy]. http://dq.xxgk.yn.gov.cn/canton_model37/newsview.aspx?id=1521951.

Dryzek, John S., David Downes, Christian Hunold, David Schlosberg, and Hans-Kristian Hernes, eds. 2003. *Green States and Social Movements: Environmentalism in the United States, United Kingdom, Germany, and Norway.* Oxford: Oxford University Press.

Duara, Prasenjit. 1991. "Knowledge and Power in the Discourse of Modernity: The Campaigns against Popular Religion in Early Twentieth-Century China." *Journal of Asian Studies* 50(1): 67–83.

Dudley, Nigel, ed. 2008. *Guidelines for Applying Protected Area Management Categories.* Gland, Switzerland: IUCN.

Durkheim, Emile. 1995[1912]. *The Elementary Forms of Religious Life.* Translated by Karen Fields. New York: The Free Press.

Dutton, Michael. 2005. *Policing Chinese Politics: A History.* Durham, NC: Duke University Press.

DXDZ (Daocheng xianwei, Daocheng xian renmin zhengfu, and Daocheng Yading fengjing mingsheng guanli weiyuanhui). 2004. *Shengdi: Daocheng Yading* [Holy land: Daocheng Yading]. Promotional video.

Dyck, John, and Kenzo Ito. 2004. "Japan's Fruit and Vegetable Market." In *Global Trade Patterns in Fruits and Vegetables*, edited by Sophia Huang and Linda Calvin, 64–76. Washington, DC: United States Department of Agriculture.

DZSL (Daocheng xian renmin zhengfu and Sichuan sheng lüyou guihua sheji suo). 2001. Daocheng xian lüyou fazhen zongti guihua (2001–2015) [Daocheng County tourism development integrated plan (2001–2015)].

Ekvall, Robert B. 1939. *Cultural Relations on the Kansu-Tibetan Border.* Chicago: University of Chicago Press.

Elden, Stuart. 2010. "Land, Terrain, Territory." *Progress in Human Geography* 34(6): 799–817.

Eliade, Mircea, and Laurence E. Sullivan. 1987. "Hierophany." In *The Encyclopedia of Religion*, vol. 6, 313–17. New York: Macmillan.

Epstein, Lawrence, ed. 2002. *Khams Pa Histories: Visions of People, Place and Authority.* Boston: Brill.

Epstein, Lawrence, and Peng Wenbin. 1998. "Ritual, Ethnicity and Generational Identity." In *Buddhism in Contemporary Tibet: Religious Revival and Cultural Identity*, edited by Melvyn Goldstein and Matthew Kapstein, 120–38. Berkeley: University of California Press.

Escobar, Arturo. 1996. "Constructing Nature: Elements for a Poststructuralist Political Ecology." In *Liberation Ecologies: Environment, Development, Social Movement*, edited by Richard Peet and Michael Watts, 46–68. London: Routledge.

Fairhead, James, and Melissa Leach. 1996. *Misreading the African Landscape: Society and Ecology in a Forest-Savanna Mosaic*. Cambridge: Cambridge University Press.

Fan Wen. 2000. *Cangmang gudao: Hui bu qu de lishi* [Endless ancient roads: The history to which there is no return]. Kunming: Yunnan Renmin Chubanshe.

Faier, Lieba, 2011. "Fungi, Trees, People, Nematodes, Beetles, and Weather: Ecologies of Vulnerability and Ecologies of Negotiation in Matsutake Commodity Exchange." *Environment and Planning A* 43(5): 1079–97.

Fedor, David. 2006. "Home on the Range: Conservation Policy, Traditional Land Use, and Yak Butter Tea on the Tibetan Plateau." Unpublished report, Goldman Honors Program, Stanford University.

Ferguson, James. 1994. *The Anti-politics Machine: "Development," Depoliticization, and Bureaucratic Power in Lesotho*. Minneapolis: University of Minnesota Press.

———. 2006. *Global Shadows: Africa in the Neoliberal World Order*. Durham, NC: Duke University Press.

Fischer, Andrew. 2005. *State Growth and Social Exclusion in Tibet: Challenges of Recent Economic Growth*. Copenhagen: NIAS Press.

———. 2012. "The Revenge of Fiscal Maoism in China's Tibet." ISS Working Paper, no. 547.

Foggin, Marc. 2008. "Depopulating the Tibetan Grasslands: National Policies and Perspectives for the Future of Tibetan Herders in Qinghai Province, China." *Mountain Research and Development* 28(1): 26–31.

Fortmann, Louise. 1995. "Talking Claims: Discursive Strategies in Contesting Property." *World Development* 23(6): 1053–63.

Foucault, Michel. 1991. "Governmentality." In *The Foucault Effect: Studies in Governmentality,* edited by Graham Burchell, Colin Gordon, and Peter Miller, 87–104. Chicago: University of Chicago Press.

———. 2003 [1976]. *Society Must Be Defended: Lectures at the College de France, 1975–76*. New York: Picador.

Fox, Helen E., Caroline Christian, J. Cully Nordby, Oliver R. W. Pergams, Garry D. Peterson, and Christopher R. Pyke. 2006. "Perceived Barriers to Integrating Social Science and Conservation." *Conservation Biology* 20: 1817–20.

Freyfogle, Eric T. 2010. "Owning Nature Responsibly." In *Imagination and Place: Ownership,* edited by K. Barth, 158–77. Lawrence, KS: Imagination and Place Press.

Friedman, Thomas. 2005. "Green Dreams in Shangri-La." *New York Times*, October 28.

Fritz, Katherine. 2009. *National Parks in China: A New Model for Nature Conservation*. ISP Collection Paper 706. Brattleboro, VT: School of International Training (SIT).

Gaerrang. 2012. *Alternative Development on the Tibetan Plateau: The Case of the Slaughter Renunciation Movement*. PhD diss., University of Colorado Boulder.

Gesang Zeren. 2005. *Hamagu yuanshengtai wenhuayou* [Hamagu cultural ecological tourism]. Unpublished guide to Hamugu Village.

———. 2011. "Shenshan wenhua de zuji" [Traces of the mountain god culture].

Ghosh, Kaushik. 2006. "Between Global Flows and Local Dams: Indigenousness, Locality and the Transnational Sphere in Jharkhand, India." *Cultural Anthropology* 21(4): 501–34.

Gidwani, Vinay. 2008. *Capital, Interrupted: Agrarian Development and the Politics of Work in India*. Minneapolis: University of Minnesota Press.

Giersch, C. Patterson. 2006. *Asian Borderlands: The Transformation of Qing China's Yunnan Frontier*. Cambridge, MA: Harvard University Press.

———. 2010. "Across Zomia with Merchants, Monks, and Musk: Process Geographies, Trade Networks, and the Inner-East-Southeast Asian Borderlands." *Journal of Global History* 5(2): 215–39.

Gladney, Dru C. 1994. "Representing Nationality in China: Refiguring Majority/Minority Identities." *Journal of Asian Studies* 53(1): 92–153.

Glover, Denise M. 2011. "At Home of Two Worlds: Ernest Henry Wilson as Natural Historian." In *Explorers and Scientists in China's Borderlands, 1880–1950*, edited by Denise Glover, 57–90. Seattle: University of Washington Press.

Goffman, Erving. 1981. *Forms of Talk*. Philadelphia: University of Pennsylvania Press.

Goldman, Mara. 2003. "Partitioned Nature, Privileged Knowledge: Community-Based Conservation in Tanzania." *Development and Change* 34(5): 833–62.

Goldman, Michael. 2001. "Constructing an Environmental State: Eco-Governmentality and Other Transnational Practices of a 'Green' World Bank." *Social Problems* 48(4): 499–523.

Goldstein, Melvyn C., Ben Jiao, and Tanzen Lhundrup. 2009. *On the Cultural Revolution in Tibet: The Nyemo Incident of 1969*. Berkeley: University of California Press.

Goldstein, Melvyn, and Matthew T. Kapstein, eds. 1998. *Buddhism in Contemporary Tibet: Religious Revival and Cultural Identity*. Berkeley: University of California Press.

Gonbo Namjyal, ed. 2005. *Journey through Labrang Culture: Labrang English Handbook*. Lanzhou, China: Lanzhou University Press.

Gongbao Nanjie [Gonbo Namjyal]. 2006. *A Dream World—Shambala, Gannan*. Lanzhou, China: Lanzhou University Press.

Goodman, David S. G. 2002. "The Politics of the West: Equality, Nation-Building and Colonisation." *Provincial China* 7(2): 127–50.

———. 2004a. "The Campaign to 'Open Up the West': National, Provincial-Level and Local Perspectives." *China Quarterly* 178: 317–34.

———. 2004b. "Qinghai and the Emergence of the West: Nationalities, Communal Interaction and National Integration." *China Quarterly* 178: 379–99.

Graeber, David. 2001. *Toward an Anthropological Theory of Value: The False Coin of Our Own Dreams*. London: Palgrave.

Great Rivers Planning Team. 2001. "Northwestern Yunnan Ecoregional Conservation Assessment." Kunming: Yunnan Provincial Planning Commission and The Nature Conservancy.

Greenberg, James B. 2006. "The Political Ecology of Fisheries in the Upper Gulf of California." In *Reimagining Political Ecology*, edited by Aletta Biersack and James Greenberg, 121–48. Durham, NC: Duke University Press.

Grenier, Katherine Haldane. 2005. *Tourism and Identity in Scotland, 1770–1914*. London: Ashgate.

Gros, Stéphane. 2011. "Economic Marginalization and Social Identity among the Drung

People of Northwest Yunnan." In *Moving Mountains: Ethnicity and Livelihoods in Highland China, Vietnam, and Laos,* edited by J. Michaud and Tim Forsyth, 28–49. Vancouver: University of British Columbia Press.

Groves, Craig R. 2003. *Drafting a Conservation Blueprint: A Practitioner's Guide to Planning for Biodiversity.* Washington, DC: Island Press.

Grumbine, R. Edward. 2010. *Where the Dragon Meets the Angry River: Nature and Power in the People's Republic of China.* Washington, DC: Island Press.

Gunn, Bee F., Mallikarjuna Aradhya, Jan M. Salick, Allison J. Miller, Yongping Yang, Lin Liu, and Xian Hai. 2010. "Genetic Variation in Walnuts (*Juglans regia* and *J. signillata*; Juglandaceae): Species Distinctions, Human Impacts, and the Conservation of Agrobiodiversity in Yunnan, China." *American Journal of Botany* 97: 660–71.

Guo Jing, ed. 2000a. *Impacts of the Proposed Kawagebo Nature Reserve on Local Communities.* Kunming: Yunnan Provincial Planning Commission and The Nature Conservancy.

———. 2000b. "A Mountain of Nature, Also a Mountain of Divinity: Indigenous Knowledge about the Space of Mt. Khabadkarpo." In *Links between Cultures and Biodiversity: Proceedings of the Cultures and Biodiversity Congress 2000,* edited by Xu Jianchu, 230–39. Kunming: Yunnan Science and Technology Press.

——— 2009. "Xueshan zhi shu jiuzhang (2): Shanming gaibian de youlai" [The book of the mountain, chapter 9, part 2: Origins of the change of the mountain's name]. In *Youfang seng de xingnang: Yong muren de yanjing kan zhe shijie* [The journal of a traveling monk: Seeing the world through the eyes of a herder]. http://azara55. blog.163.com/blog/static/1221183532009102382199926/.

Guo Xiang-Yu, Zhi-Gang Yu, Todd Schmit, Brian Henehan, and Dan Li. 2009. "Evaluation of New Socialist Countryside Development in China." *China Agricultural Economic Review* 1(3): 314–26.

Hakkenberg, Christopher. 2008. "Biodiversity and Sacred Sites: Vernacular Conservation Practices in Northwest Yunnan, China." *Worldviews* 12: 74–90.

Han Nianyong and Zhuge Ren. 2001. "Ecotourism in China's Nature Reserves: Opportunities and Challenges." *Journal of Sustainable Tourism* 9(3): 228.

Hansen, Mette. 2005. *Frontier People: Han Settlers in Minority Areas of China.* Vancouver: UBC Press.

Haraway, Donna. 1988. "Situated Knowledges: The Science Question in Feminism and the Privilege of Partial Perspective." *Feminist Studies* 14(3): 575–99.

Harkness, Jim. 1998. "Recent Trends in Forestry and Conservation of Biodiversity in China." *China Quarterly* 156: 911–34.

Harrell, Stevan. 1995. "Jeeping against Maoism." *positions: east asia cultures critique* 3(3): 728–58.

———, ed. 2000. *Cultural Encounters on China's Ethnic Frontiers.* Seattle: University of Washington Press.

Harris, Richard B. 2008. *Wildlife Conservation in China: Preserving the Habitat of China's Wild West.* Armonk, NY: M. E. Sharpe.

Hathaway, Michael. 2004. "Indigeneity and Nature Conservation in China's Yunnan Province." *Anthropology News* 45: 57–58.

———. 2006. "'Filling In': The Local, National and Transnational Politics of Indigenous Identities in Southwest China." Abstract. American Anthropological Association 2006 Annual Meeting, San Jose, CA.

———. 2007. *Making Nature in Southwest China: Transnational Notions of Landscape and Ethnicity*. PhD diss., University of Michigan, Ann Arbor.

———. 2009. "Postcolonial Science Studies and the Making of Matsutake Science in China." *American Ethnologist* 36: 393–97.

———. 2010a. "The Emergence of Indigeneity: Public Intellectuals and an Indigenous Space in Southwest China." *Cultural Anthropology* 25: 301–33.

———. 2010b. "Global Environmental Encounters in Southwest China: Fleeting Intersections and 'Transnational Work.'" *Journal of Asian Studies* 69(2): 427–51.

———. 2013. *Environmental Winds: Making the Global in Southwest China*. Berkeley: University of California Press.

HBB (Huanjing Baohu Bu Ziran Shengtai Baohu Si). 2009. *Quanguo ziran baohuqu minglu* [List of nature reserves of the entire country]. Beijing: Zhongguo Huanjing Kexue Chubanshe.

Heberer, Thomas. 2001. "Old Tibet as Hell on Earth? The Myth of Tibet and Tibetans in Chinese Art and Propaganda." In *Imagining Tibet: Perceptions, Projections and Fantasies*, edited by Thierry Dödin and Heinz Rather, 103–19. Boston: Wisdom Publications.

Hevia, James L. 2001. "World Heritage, National Culture, and the Restoration of Chengde." *positions: east asia cultures critique* 9(1): 219–43.

Hill, Ann Maxwell. 1998. *Merchants and Migrants*. New Haven: Yale University Press.

Hillman, Ben. 2003. "Paradise under Construction: Minorities, Myths and Modernity in Northwest Yunnan." *Asian Ethnicity* 4(2): 177–90.

———. 2008. "Money Can't Buy Tibetans' Love." *Far Eastern Economic Review*, April, 8–12.

———. 2010. "China's Many Tibets: Diqing as a Model for 'Development with Tibetan Characteristics'?" *Asian Ethnicity* 11(2): 269–77.

Ho, Peter. 2000. "The Clash over State and Collective Property: The Making of the Rangeland Law." *China Quarterly* 161: 240–63.

———. 2001. "Who Owns China's Land? Policies, Property Rights and Deliberate Institutional Ambiguity." *China Quarterly* 166: 394–421.

Holbig, Heike. 2004. "The Emergence of the Campaign to Open Up the West: Ideological Formation, Central Decision-Making and the Role of the Provinces." *China Quarterly* 178: 335–57.

Horkheimer, Max, and Theodor W. Adorno. 2002. *Dialectic of Enlightenment: Philosophical Fragments*. Stanford: Stanford University Press.

Hu Yan. 1995. "Wu zu gonghe kouhao de tichu jiqi yiyi" [The creation of the slogan 'unity among five ethnicities' and its implications]. *Xizang yanjiu* [Tibet studies] 1: 42–50.

Huber, Toni. 1997. "Green Tibetans: A Brief Social History." In *Tibetan Culture in the Diaspora*, edited by Frank Korom, 103–19. Vienna: Verlag der Österreichischen Akademie der Wissenschaften.

———. 1999a. *The Cult of Pure Crystal Mountain: Popular Pilgrimage and Visionary Landscape in Southeast Tibet*. Oxford: Oxford University Press.

———, ed. 1999b. *Sacred Spaces and Powerful Places in Tibetan Culture: A Collection of Essays*. Dharamsala, India: Library of Tibetan Works and Archives.

———. 2001. "Shangri-la in Exile: Representations of Tibetan Identity and Transnational Culture." In *Imagining Tibet: Perceptions, Projections and Fantasies*, edited by Thierry Dödin and Heinz Rather, 357–72. Boston: Wisdom Publications.

———, ed. 2002. *Amdo Tibetans in Transition: Society and Culture in the Post-Mao Era*. Boston: Brill.

———. 2004. "Territorial Control by 'Sealing' (rgya sdom-pa): A Religio-Political Practice in Tibet." *Zentralasiatische Studien* (ZAS) 33: 127–52.

Huber, Toni, and Poul Pedersen. 1997. "Meteorological Knowledge and Environmental Ideas in Traditional and Modern Societies: The Case of Tibet." *Journal of the Royal Anthropological Institute* 3: 577–98.

Humphrey, Caroline. 2003. "Rethinking Infrastructure: Siberian Cities and the Great Freeze of January 2001." In *Wounded Cities: Destruction and Reconstruction in a Globalized World*, edited by Jane Schneider and Ida Susser, 91–107. Oxford: Berg Publishers.

Hymes, Robert. 2002. *Way and Byway: Taoism, Local Religion, and Models of Divinity in Sung and Modern China*. Berkeley: University of California Press.

ICT 2010. "'A Sharp Knife above His Head': The Trials and Sentencing of Three Environmentalist Brothers in Tibet." International Campaign for Tibet, Washington, DC. http://www.savetibet.org/media-center/ict-news-reports/%E2%80%98-sharp-knife-above-his-head%E2%80%99-trials-and-sentencing-three-environmentalist-brothers-tibet.

———. 2013. "Self-immolations by Tibetans." International Campaign for Tibet, Washington, DC. http://www.savetibet.org/resource-center/maps-data-fact-sheets/self-immolation-fact-sheet.

Irvine, Judith. 1982. "The Creation of Identification in Spirit Mediumship and Possession." In *Semantic Anthropology*, edited by David Parkin, 241–60. Orlando, FL: Academic Press.

———. 1989. "When Talk Isn't Cheap: Language and Political Economy." *American Ethnologist* 16(2): 248–67.

Irwin, Alan. 1995. *Citizen Science: A Study of People, Expertise and Sustainable Development*. London: Routledge.

Ives, Jack D. 2004. *Himalayan Perceptions: Environmental Change and the Well-Being of Mountain Peoples*. New York: Routledge.

Ivy, Marilyn. 1995. *Discourses of the Vanishing: Modernity, Phantasm, Japan*. Chicago: University of Chicago Press.

Jacobs, Andrew. 2013. "Plans to Harness Chinese River's Power Threaten a Region." *New York Times*, May 4.

Jenkins, Mark. 2009. "Searching for Shangri-la: Two Visions of the Future Compete for the Soul of China's Western Frontier." *National Geographic*, May.

Jiang Rong. 2008. *Wolf Totem: A Novel*. New York: Penguin Press.

Jiang Wenjuan, ed. 2006. *Diqing Zhou guojia Hexie Shehui lilun yanjiuhui lunwenji* [Collected essays from a research conference on theories for constructing Harmonious Society in Diqing Prefecture]. Kunming: Yunnan Minzu Publishing Company.

'jigs med theg mchog. 1988. *rong bo dgon chen gyi gdan rabs* [Buddhist history of Rongwo Monastery]. Xining: Qinghai Minzu Chubanshe.

Jonsson, Hjorleifur. 2010. "Above and Beyond: Zomia and the Ethnographic Challenge of/for Regional History." *History and Anthropology* 21(2): 191–212.

JPO (Joint Project Office). 2001. "Conservation and Development Action Plan for Northwest Yunnan." Kunming: Yunnan Provincial Planning Commission and The Nature Conservancy.

Kang Xiuying. 2005. "Dui Ganzi Zhou wenhua lüyou chanye fazhan de sikao" [Thoughts on the development of the cultural tourism industry in Ganzi Prefecture]. Zhongguo xizang xinxi zhongxin [China Tibet information network], April 11. http://www.tibetinfor.com/t/040513zggz/200402005411162211.htm (accessed June 15, 2012).

Kapferer, Bruce. 2002. "Sorcery and the Shapes of Globalization, Disjunctions and Continuities: The Case of Sri Lanka." In *Globalization, the State, and Violence*, edited by Jonathan Friedman, 249–78. Walnut Creek, CA: Altamira.

Karan, Pradyumna P. 1976. *The Changing Face of Tibet: The Impact of Chinese Communist Ideology on the Landscape.* Lexington: The University Press of Kentucky.

Karmay, Samten. 1994. "Mountain Cults and National Identity in Tibet." In *Resistance and Reform in Tibet*, edited by Robert Barnett, 112–120. Bloomington: Indiana University Press.

———. 1996. "The Tibetan Cult of Mountain Deities and Its Political Significance." In *Reflections of the Mountain*, edited by Anne-Marie Blondeau and Ernst Steinkellner, 59–75. Vienna: Verlag der Österreichischen Akademie der Wissenschaften.

———. 1998. *The Arrow and the Spindle: Studies in History, Myths, Rituals and Beliefs in Tibet.* Kathmandu: Mandala Book Point.

Keane, Webb. 1997. *Signs of Recognition: Powers and Hazards of Representation in an Indonesian Society.* Berkeley: University of California Press.

———. 2008. "Market, Materiality and Moral Metalanguage." *Anthropological Theory* 8(1): 27–42.

Kinugawa, Kenjiro, and Toranobu Goto. 1978. "Preliminary Survey on the 'Matsutake' (*Armillaria ponderosa*) of North America." *Transactions of the Mycological Society of Japan* 19: 91–101.

Kleeman, Terry. 1994. "Mountain Deities in China: The Domestication of the Mountain God and the Subjugation of the Margins." *Journal of the American Oriental Society* 114(2): 226–38.

Klima, Alan. 2002. *The Funeral Casino: Meditation, Massacre, and Exchange with the Dead in Thailand.* Princeton: Princeton University Press.

Klingberg, Travis, and Tim Oakes. 2012. "Producing Exemplary Consumers: Tourism and Leisure Culture in China's Nation-Building Project." In *China in and beyond the Headlines*, edited by Timothy Weston and Lionel Jensen, 195–213. Lanham, MD: Rowman & Littlefield.

klu rgyal thar. 2007. "Goms srol du chags p'i bla'i rig gnas dang skye khams srung skyob skor rob tsam gleng ba" [A brief discussion of the customary culture of bla and environmental protection]. *Journal of Minorities Teachers College of Qinghai Teachers University* 1: 19–22.

Kolås, Åshild. 2004. *Ethnic Tourism in Shangrila: Representations of Place and Tibetan Identity*. PhD diss., University of Oslo.

———. 2008. *Tourism and Tibetan Culture in Transition: A Place Called Shangrila*. London and New York: Routledge.

Lafitte, Gabriel. 2013. *Spoiling Tibet: China and Resource Nationalism on the Roof of the World*. London: Zed Books.

Lai, Hongyi. 2002. "China's Western Development Program: Its Rationale, Implementation and Prospects." *Modern China* 28(4): 432–66.

———. 2003. "National Security and Unity, and China's Western Development Program." *Provincial China* 8(2): 118–43.

Lama Tsanpo. 1962 [1820]. *The Geography of Tibet ('dzam gling rgyas bshad)*. Translated by Turrell Wylie. Rome: ISIAO.

Lang, Graeme. 2002. "Forests, Floods, and the Environmental State in China." *Organization and Environment* 15(2): 109–30.

Larkin, Brian. 2008. *Signal and Noise: Media, Infrastructure, and Urban Culture in Nigeria*. Durham, NC: Duke University Press.

Larsen, Jonas. 2001. "Tourism Mobilities and the Travel Glance: Experiences of Being on the Move." *Scandinavian Journal of Hospitality & Tourism* 1(2): 80–98.

———. 2006. "Geographies of Tourist Photography: Choreographies and Performances." In *Geographies of Communication: The Spatial Turn in Media Studies*, edited by Jesper Falkheimer and André Jansson, 241–57. Gøteborg: Nordicom.

———. 2008. "Practices and Flows of Digital Photography: An Ethnographic Framework." *Mobilities* 3(1): 141–60.

Latour, Bruno. 1987. *Science in Action: How to Follow Scientists and Engineers through Society*. Cambridge, MA: MIT Press.

———. 1991. *We Have Never Been Modern*. Cambridge, MA: Harvard University Press.

———. 2005. *Reassembling the Social: An Introduction to Actor-Network-Theory*. New York: Oxford University Press.

Laveaga, Gabriela Soto. 2009. *Jungle Laboratories: Mexican Peasants, National Projects, and the Making of the Pill*. Durham, N.C.: Duke University Press.

Law, Wayne, and Jan Salick. 2005. "Human Induced Dwarfing of Himalayan Snow Lotus, *Saussurea laniceps* (Asteraceae)." *Proceedings of the National Academy of Sciences* 102: 10218–220.

———. 2007. "Comparing Conservation Priorities for Useful Plants among Botanists and Tibetan Doctors." *Biodiversity and Conservation* 16: 1747–59.

Lee, Benjamin, and Edward LiPuma. 2002. "Cultures of Circulation: The Imaginations of Modernity." *Public Culture* 14(1): 191–213.

Lefebvre, Henri. 1974. *The Production of Space*. Oxford: Blackwell.

Lévi-Strauss, Claude. 1966. *The Savage Mind*. Chicago: University of Chicago Press.

Li Guiming. 2007a. "Guanyu huigui shige de taolun" [Debates on return poetry]. *Huigui* [Return] 1: 1–14.

———. 2007b. "Yunnan wenhua huigui de shige jingshen" [The poetic spirit in Yunnan's cultural renaissance]. *Huigui* [Return] 1: 15–19.

———. 2010. *Wo de Dianxi* [My western Yunnan]. Kunming: Yunnan Keji Chubanshe.

———. 2011. "Chuancheng Dianxi shige de ziyou xuetong" [Continuing the lineage of freedom in the poetry of western Yunnan]. *Li Guiming Blog*, November 14. http://blog.sina.com.cn/s/blog_49fecb500100vy9x.html (accessed June 15, 2012).

Li, Peter J. 2007. "Enforcing Wildlife Protection in China." *China Information* 21(1): 71–107.

Li, Tania. 2007. *The Will to Improve: Development, Governmentality and the Practice of Politics.* Durham, NC: Duke University Press.

Li Yiming. 2000. "Diqing nuli peiyu si da zhizhu chanye" [Diqing assiduously fosters four pillar industries]. *Yunnan Daily*, September 12. http://www.people.com.cn/GB/channel4/989/20000912/229984.html.

Lim, Francis K. G. 2009. "'Donkey Friends' in China: The Internet, Civil Society and the Emergence of Chinese Backpacking Community." In *Asia on Tour: Exploring the Rise of Asian Tourism*, edited by Tim Winter, Peggy Teo, and T. C. Chang, 291–301. New York: Routledge.

Litzinger, Ralph. 2000. *Other Chinas: The Yao and the Politics of National Belonging.* Durham, NC: Duke University Press.

———. 2004. "The Mobilization of 'Nature': Perspectives from North-west Yunnan." *China Quarterly* 178: 488–504.

———. 2006. "Contested Sovereignties and the Critical Ecosystem Partnership Fund." *PoLAR: Political and Legal Anthropology Review* 29(1): 66–87.

———. 2007. "In Search of the Grassroots: Hydroelectric Politics in Northwest Yunnan." In *Grassroots Political Reform in Contemporary China*, edited by Elizabeth J. Perry and Merle Goldman, 282–99. Cambridge, MA: Harvard University Press.

Liu, Bo, Eryuan Liang, and Liping Zhu. 2011. "Microclimatic Conditions for Juniperus saltuaria Treeline in the Sygera Mountains, Southeastern Tibetan Plateau." *Mountain Research and Development* 31(1): 45–53.

Liu Juan. 2009. "Zhongguo zangzu zizhiqu shoupi guojiagongyuan jiang zai Xianggelila jiancheng" [The first cohort of national parks in China's Tibetan areas is being built in Shangrila]. Diqing Prefecture Tourism Bureau Administrative website. http://www.shangrila-travel.cn/Article_2_239.html (accessed July 28, 2010).

Llamas, Rosa, and Russell Belk. 2011. "Shangri-la: Messing with a Myth." *Journal of Macromarketing* 31(3): 257–75.

Lopez, Donald S. 1998. *Prisoners of Shangri-La: Tibetan Buddhism and the West.* Chicago: University of Chicago Press.

Lü Linglong and Fudi Wang. 1996. *Daocheng: Zai na yaoyuan de difang* [Daocheng: In that faraway place]. Chengdu: Sichuan Meishu Chubanshe.

Lü, Yiran, Dazheng Ma, and Yulin Xin, eds. 1991. *Zhongguo bianjiang shidi lunji* [Collected papers on China's borderlands]. Harbin: Heilongjiang Jiaoyu Chubanshe.

Lu Ren. 1997. *Yunnan dui wai jiaotong shi* [A history of Yunnan's foreign communications]. Kunming: Yunnan Minzu Chubanshe.

Ludden, David. 1992. "India's Development Regime." In *Colonialism and Culture*, edited by Nicholas B. Dirks, 247–88. Ann Arbor: University of Michigan Press.

Luo Yangfeng, Jinlong Liu, and Dahong Zhang. 2009. "Role of Traditional Beliefs of Baima Tibetans in Biodiversity Conservation in China." *Forest Ecology and Management* 257: 1995–2001.

Lutz, Catherine, and Jane Lou Collins. 1993. *Reading National Geographic*. Chicago: University of Chicago Press.

Ma Jianzhong and Jie Chen, eds. 2005. *Zangzu wenhua yu shengwu duoyangxing baohu* [Tibetan culture and biodiversity conservation]. Kunming: Yunnan Science and Technology Press.

Ma Ruheng and Dazheng Ma, eds. 1990. *Qingdai bianjiang kaifa yanjiu* [Research on the opening up of the Qing dynasty borderlands]. Beijing: Xinhua Shudian Chubanshe.

MacCannell, Dean. 2001. "Tourist Agency." *Tourist Studies* 1(1): 23–37.

Machlis, Gary E., and Donald R. Field, eds. 2000. *National Parks and Rural Development: Practice and Policy in the United States*. Washington, DC, and Covelo, CA: Island Press.

MacMurray, Jessica. 2003. "Matsutake Gari." *Gastronomica* 3(4): 86–89.

Makley, Charlene. 1999. "Gendered Practices and the Inner Sanctum: The Reconstruction of Tibetan Sacred Space in 'China's Tibet.'" In *Sacred Spaces and Powerful Places in Tibetan Culture*, edited by Toni Huber, 343–66. Dharamsala, India: Library of Tibetan Works and Archives.

———. 2005. "Speaking Bitterness: Autobiography, History and Mnemonic Politics on the Sino-Tibetan Frontier." *Comparative Studies in Society and History* 47(1): 40–78.

———. 2007. *The Violence of Liberation: Gender and Tibetan Buddhist Revival in Post-Mao China*. Berkeley: University of California Press.

———. 2009. "Ballooning Unrest: Tibet, State Violence and the Incredible Lightness of Knowledge." In *China in 2008: A Year of Great Significance*, edited by Kate Merkel Hess, Kenneth L. Pommeranz, and Jeffrey Wasserstrom, 44–56. Lanham, MD: Rowman & Littlefield.

———. 2010. "Minzu, Market, and the Mandala: National Exhibitionism and Tibetan Buddhist Revival in Post-Mao China." In *Faiths on Display: Religion, Tourism and the Chinese State*, edited by Timothy Oakes and Donald S. Sutton, 127–56. Lanham, MD: Rowman & Littlefield.

———. 2013. "The Politics of Presence: Voice, Deity Possession, and Dilemmas of Development Among Tibetans in the PRC." *Comparative Studies in Society and History* 55(3): 665–700.

Mascia, Michael B., J. Peter Brosius, Tracy A. Dobson, Bruce C. Forbes, Leah Horowitz, Margaret A. McKean, and Nancy J. Turner. 2003. "Conservation and Social Sciences." *Conservation Biology* 17: 649–50.

Master, Larry L. 1990. "The Imperiled Status of North American Aquatic Animals." *Biodiversity Network News* 3(1–2): 7–8.

Matless, David. 2003. "The Properties of Landscape." In *Handbook of Cultural Geography*, edited by Kay Anderson, Mona Domosh, Steve Pile, and Nigel Thrift, 227–32. London: Sage.

Matsuzawa, Setsuko. 2007. *The Transnational Diffusion of Global Environmental*

Concerns via INGOs in China: A New Framework for Understanding Diffusion in Authoritarian Contexts. PhD diss., University of California, San Diego.

Mauss, Marcel. 1990 [1925]. *The Gift: The Form and Reason for Exchange in Archaic Societies*. Translated by W. D. Halls. New York: Norton.

Mayaram, Shail, ed. 2009. *The Other Global City*. New York: Routledge.

Mazard, Mireille, and Katherine Swancutt, eds. Forthcoming. "The Animist Turn: Ethnographic Renewal in a Post-reflexive World." Special issue, *Social Analysis*.

Mazzarella, William. 2004. "Culture, Globalization, Mediation." *Annual Review of Anthropology* 33: 345–67.

McCarthy, James. 2005. "Devolution in the Woods: Community-Based Forestry as Hybrid Neoliberalism." *Environment and Planning A* 37(6): 994–1014.

Mei Biqiu, Jixiang Zhang, Jianming Dai, Chaohua Xie, Zhanxin Xia, and Pingbo Peng. 2010. "Xi Dongtinghu shidi baohu yu kaifa liyong diaoyan baogao" [West Dongting Lake wetland protection and development research report]. *Yueyang Zhiye Jishu Xueyuan xuebao* [Journal of Yueyang Technical Vocational College] 25(6): 42–47.

Menzies, Nicholas K., and Chun Li. 2010. "One Eye on the Forest, One Eye on the Market: Multi-tiered Regulation of Matsutake Harvesting, Conservation and Trade in North-western Yunnan Province." In *Wild Product Governance: Finding Policies the Work for Non-timber Forest Products*, edited by Sarah A. Laird, Rebecca McLain, and Rachel Wynberg, 243–64. London: Earthscan.

Michaud, Jean. 2010. "Zomia and Beyond." *Journal of Global History* 5: 187–214.

Mills, Martin. 2003. *Identity, Ritual and State in Tibetan Buddhism*. London: Routledge.

Minca, Claudio. 2007. "The Tourist Landscape Paradox." *Social & Cultural Geography* 8(3): 433–53.

Ministry of Environmental Protection. 2010. "National List of Protected Areas." Ministry of Environmental Protection Statistics Center. http://datacenter.mep.gov.cn/main/dbCenterDataList.do?tableName=ZHB_T_NEW_RESERVES_MAIN (accessed March 4, 2010).

Mitchell, Don. 1996. *The Lie of the Land: Migrant Workers and the California Landscape*. Minneapolis: University of Minnesota Press.

mkhar rtse rgyal. 2005. Interview on Qinghai Tibetan radio station.

———. 2009. '*Jig-rten mchod-bstod: mDo-smad Reb-gong-gyi drug-pa'i lha-zla chen-mo'i mchod-pa dang 'brel-ba'i dmangs-srol rig-gnas lo-rgyus skor-gyi zhib-'jug* [A worldly offering: Research on Amdo Rebgong's sixth lunar month festival and related folk culture]. Beijing: Zhongguo Zangxue Chubanshe.

Mol, Arthur P. 2006. "Environment and Modernity in Transitional China: Frontiers of Ecological Modernization." *Development and Change* 37(1): 29–56.

Mol, Arthur P., and F. H. Buttel. 2002. *The Environmental State under Pressure*. Bingley, UK: JAI Press.

Moore, Donald S. 2005. *Suffering for Territory: Race, Place and Power in Zimbabwe*. Durham, NC: Duke University Press.

Morell, Virginia, and Katherine Wolkoff. 2005. "The Mother of Gardens." *Discover Magazine*. Available at http://discovermagazine.com/2005/aug/mother-of-gardens/ (accessed July 19, 2012).

Morris, Rosalind C. 2000. "Modernity's Media and the End of Mediumship? On the Aesthetic Economy of Transparency in Thailand." *Public Culture* 12(2): 457–75.

Moseley, Robert K. 2000. "The Nature Conservancy's Framework for Site Conservation Planning in Mountain Regions." In *Links between Cultures and Biodiversity: Proceedings of the Cultures and Biodiversity Congress 2000*, edited by Xu Jianchu, 111–17. Kunming: Yunnan Science and Technology Press.

———. 2006. "Historical Landscape Change in Northwestern Yunnan, China: Using Repeat Photography to Assess the Perceptions and Realities of Biodiversity Loss." *Mountain Research and Development* 26: 214–19.

———. 2011. *Revisiting Shangri-La: Photographing a Century of Environmental and Cultural Change in the Mountains of Southwest China*. Beijing: China Intercontinental Press.

Moseley, Robert K., Sina Norbu, Ma Jianzhong, and Guo Jing. 2003. "Kawagebo Snow Mountains Sacred Natural Sites Case Study." Presented at the Fifth World Parks Congress, Durban, South Africa, September 9–17.

Moseley, Robert K., Christine Tam, Renée Mullen, Long Yongcheng, and Ma Jianzhong. 2004. "A Conservation Project Management Process Applied to Mountain Protected Area Design and Management in Yunnan, China." In *Managing Mountain Protected Areas: Challenges and Responses for the 21st Century*, edited by D. Harmon and G. L. Worboys, 252–32. Colledara, Italy: Andromeda Editrice.

Mowforth, Martin, and Ian Munt. 1998. *Tourism and Sustainability: New Tourism in the Third World*. London and New York: Routledge.

Mu, Xiang. 2001. *Lijiang mabang* [Lijiang horse caravans]. Kunming: Yunnan Renmin Chubanshe.

Muchi Yundeng Jiacuo. 2003. "Xiejiao tezheng lun" [On the special characteristics of heterodox cults]. *Qinghai Minzu Xueyuan Xuebao* 1: 9–12.

Mueggler, Erik. 2011. *The Paper Road: Archive and Experience in the Botanical Exploration of West China and Tibet*. Berkeley: University of California Press.

Muldavin, Joshua. 2000. "The Geography of Japanese Development Aid to China, 1978–98." *Environment and Planning A* 32(5): 925–46.

Mullaney, Thomas. 2010. "Seeing for the State: The Role of Social Scientists in China's Ethnic Classification Project." *Asian Ethnicity* 11(3): 325–42.

———. 2011. *Coming to Terms with the Nation: Ethnic Classification in Modern China*. Berkeley: University of California Press.

Murata, Hitoshi, Katsuhiko Babasaki, Tomoki Saegusa, Kenji Takemoto, Akiyoshi Yamada, and Akira Ohta. 2008. "Traceability of Asian Matsutake, Specialty Mushrooms Produced by the Ectomycorrhizal Basidiomycete Tricholoma Matsutake, on the Basis of Retroelement-Based DNA Markers." *Applied and Environmental Microbiology* 74(7): 2023–31.

Myers, Norman, Russell A. Mittermeier, Christina G. Mittermeier, Gustavo A. B. da Fonseca, and Jennifer Kent. 2000. "Biodiversity Hotspots for Conservation Priorities." *Nature* 403: 853–58.

Nadasdy, Paul. 2005. *Hunters and Bureaucrats: Power, Knowledge, and Aboriginal-State Relations in the Southwest Yukon*. Seattle: University of Washington Press.

——. 2011. "We Don't Harvest Animals; We Kill Them: Agricultural Metaphors and the Politics of Wildlife Management in the Yukon." In *Knowing Nature: Conversations at the Intersection of Political Ecology and Science Studies*, edited by Mara J. Goldman, Paul Nadasdy, and Matthew D. Turner, 131–51. Chicago: University of Chicago Press.

Nagano, Sadako. 2000. "Sacrifice and lha pa in the glu rol Festival of Reb-skong." In *New Horizons in Bon Studies*, edited by Samten Karmay and Yasuhiko Nagono, 567–649. Delhi: Saujanya Publications.

Nan, Wenyuan. 2001. "The Taboos in Tibetan Areas and the Role They Have Played in Environmental Protection." *Northwest Minorities Research* 3: 21–29.

Naughton, Barry. 1988. "The Third Front: Defence Industrialization in the Chinese Interior." *China Quarterly* 115: 351–86.

Naughton-Treves, Lisa, Nora Alvarez-Berr, Katrina Brandon, Aaaron Bruner, Margaret Holland, Carlos Ponce, Malki Saenz, Luis Suarez, and Adrian Treves. 2006. "Expanding Protected Areas and Incorporating Human Resource Use: A Study of 15 Forest Parks in Ecuador and Peru." *Sustainability: Science, Practice, & Policy* 2(2): 32–44.

Nebesky-Wojkowitz, Rene de. 1998 [1956]. *Oracles and Demons of Tibet: The Cult and Iconography of the Tibetan Protective Deities*. New Delhi: Paljor Publications.

Neumann, Roderick. 1997. "Primitive Ideas: Protected Area Buffer Zones and the Politics of Land in Africa." *Development and Change* 28(3): 559–82.

——. 1998. *Imposing Wilderness: Struggles over Livelihood and Nature Preservation in Africa*. Berkeley: University of California Press.

——. 2004. "Nature-State-Territory: Toward a Critical Theorization of Conservation Enclosure." In *Liberation Ecologies: Environment, Development and Social Movements*, edited by Richard Peet and Michael Watts, 179–99. New York: Routledge.

——. 2005. *Making Political Ecology*. New York: Routledge.

Norbu, Namkhai. 1997. *Journey among the Tibetan Nomads*. Dharamsala, India: Library of Tibetan Works and Archives.

Noss, Reed F. 1987. "From Plant Communities to Landscapes in Conservation Inventories: A Look at The Nature Conservancy (USA)." *Biological Conservation* 41: 11–37.

Nyíri, Pál. 2006. *Scenic Spots: Chinese Tourism, the State, and Cultural Authority*. Seattle: University of Washington Press.

Ó Tuathail, Gearóid. 1996. *Critical Geopolitics: The Politics of Writing Global Space*. Minneapolis: University of Minnesota Press.

Oakes, Tim. 1998. *Tourism and Modernity in China*. New York: Routledge.

——. 1999. "Eating the Food of Ancestors: Place, Tourism, and Tradition in a Chinese River Town." *Cultural Geographies* 6(2): 123–45.

——. 2000. "China's Provincial Identities: Reinventing Regionalism and Reinventing 'Chineseness.'" *Journal of Asian Studies* 59(3): 667–92.

——. 2004. "Building a Southern Dynamo: Guizhou and State Power." *China Quarterly* 178: 167–87.

——. 2005. "Tourism and the Modern Subject: Placing the Encounter between Tourist and Other." In *Seductions of Place: Geographical Perspectives on Globalization and*

Touristed Landscapes, edited by Carolyn L. Cartier and Alan A. Lew, 36–55. New York: Routledge.

———. 2006. "The Village as Theme Park: Mimesis and Authenticity in Chinese Tourism." In *Translocal China: Linkages, Identities and the Reimagining of Space*, edited by Tim Oakes and Louisa Schein, 166–92. New York: Routledge.

———. 2007. "Welcome to Paradise! A Sino-American Joint Venture Project." In *China's Transformations: The Stories beyond the Headlines*, edited by Timothy Weston and Lionel Jenson, 240–64. Lanham, MD: Rowman & Littlefield.

Oakes, Tim, and Louisa Schein, eds. 2005. *Translocal China: Linkages, Identities, and the Reimagining of Space*. New York: Routledge.

Ong, Aihwa, and Stephen Collier, eds. 2004. *Global Assemblages: Technology, Politics and Ethics as Anthropological Problems*. New York: Wiley-Blackwell.

Ostrom, Elinor. 1990. *Governing the Commons: The Evolution of Institutions for Collective Action*. Cambridge: Cambridge University Press.

Ou Xiaokun. 2002. "The Yunnan Great Rivers Project." Woodrow Wilson Center *China Environment Series* 5: 74–76.

Ou Xiaokun, Zhiming Zhang, Chongyun Wang, and Yucheng Wu. 2006. *Vegetation Research in the Meili Snow Mountains*. Beijing: Science Press.

Overstall, Richard. 2005. "Encountering the Spirit in the Land: 'Property' in a Kinship-Based Legal Order." In *Despotic Dominion: Property Right in British Settler Societies*, edited by John McLaren, A. R. Buck, and Nancy E. Wright, 22–49. Vancouver: University of British Columbia Press.

Pan Yousheng. 2006. "Luoshi kexue fazhan guan, zhengque chuli 'Shengtai Lizhou' yu 'Chanye Qiangzhou' de guanxi—dui Diqing ziyuan kaifa chuantong linian de fansi" [Implementing scientific conceptions of development—correct handling of relations between 'Ecological Statehood' and 'Production Power Statehood': Reflections on traditional conceptions of natural resource utilization in Diqing]. In *Diqing Zhou guojian Hexie Shehui lilun yanjiu taohui* [Collected essays from a research conference on theories for constructing Harmonious Society in Diqing Prefecture], edited by Jiang Wenjuan, 77–78. Kunming: Yunnan Minzu Publishing Company.

Peet, Richard, and Michael Watts, eds. 1996. *Liberation Ecologies: Environment, Development, Social Movements*. London and New York: Routledge.

Pei Shengji. 2011. "The Road to the Future? The Biocultural Values of the Holy Hill Forests of Yunnan Province, China." In *Sacred Natural Sites: Conserving Nature and Culture*, edited by Bas Verschuuren, Robert Wild, Jeffrey A. McNeely, and Gonzalo Oviedo, 98–106. London: Earthscan.

Peluso, Nancy Lee. 1992. "The Political Ecology of Extraction and Extractive Reserves in East Kalimantan, Indonesia." *Development and Change* 23(4): 49–74.

———. 1993. "Coercing Conservation: The Politics of State Resource Control." *Global Environmental Change* 3(2): 199–217.

Peng Wenbin. 2002. "Frontier Process, Provincial Politics and Movements for Khampa Autonomy during the Republican Period." In *Khams pa Histories: Visions of People, Place and Authority*, edited by Lawrence Epstein, 57–84. Boston: Brill.

Peng Zhenxiang and Shiming Ma. 2006. "Yindao zongjiao yu shehuizhuyi shehui xiangshiying—wei goujian Diqing Hexie Shehui er nuli" [Guiding the mutual adaptation of religious and socialist society—on efforts to build Harmonious Society in Diqing]. In *Diqing Zhou guojian Hexie Shehui lilun yanjiu taohui* [Collected essays from a research conference on theories for constructing Harmonious Society in Diqing Prefecture], edited by Jiang Wenjuan, 62–67. Kunming: Yunnan Minzu Publishing Company.

Poiani, Karen A., Jeffery V. Baumgartner, Steven C. Buttrick, Shelly L. Green, Edward Hopkins, George D. Ivey, Katherine P. Seaton, and Robert D. Sutter. 1998. "A Scale-Independent, Site Conservation Planning Framework in The Nature Conservancy." *Landscape and Urban Planning* 43: 143–56.

Polanyi, Karl. 2001 [1944]. *The Great Transformation: The Political and Economic Origins of Our Time.* Boston: Beacon Press.

Pu Wencheng and Kanjia Can. 2001. "Zangchuan Fojia yu Qinghai Zangqu Shehui Wending Wenti Yanjiu" [Research on the problem of Tibetan Buddhism and social stability among Qinghai Tibetans]. *Qinghai Minzu Xueyuan Xuebao* 2: 1–11.

Qin Heping. 2007. "Xiangcheng, Daocheng tutou tongzhi de youlai jiqi shanbian" [The origin and transformation of local tribal chiefs of Xiangcheng and Daocheng]. *Xizang Yanjiu* 2: 1–9.

Raffles, Hugh. 2005. "Response to 'Environmentality: Community, Intimate Government, and the Making of Environmental Subjects in Kumaon, India.'" *Current Anthropology* 46(2): 183–84.

Redford, Kent H., and J. Peter Brosius. 2006. "Diversity and Homogenization in the Endgame." *Global Environmental Change* 16: 317–19.

Redhead, Scott. A. 1997. "The Pine Mushroom Industry in Canada and the United States: Why It Exists and Where It Is Going." In *Mycology in Sustainable Development: Expanding Concepts, Vanishing Borders,* edited by Mary E. Palm and Ignacio H. Chapela, 15–54. Boone, NC: Parkway Publishers.

Ren, Hai. 2007. "The Landscape of Power: Imagineering Consumer Behavior at China's Theme Parks." In *The Themed Space: Locating Culture, Nation, and Self,* edited by Scott Lukas, 97–112. Lanham, MD: Lexington Books.

Research Office of the People's Government of Yunnan Province. 2006. *Guanyu Dianxibei guojiagongyuan yu chanye fazhan xianghu guanxi yanjiu de huibao* [Report on research on relationships between national parks and industrial development in northwest Yunnan]. Kunming: Research Office of the People's Government of Yunnan Province.

———. 2010a. *Laojunshan guojiagongyuan guanli tizhi yanjiu baogao* [Report on research on the Laojun Mountain National Park management model]. Kunming: Research Office of the People's Government of Yunnan Province.

———. 2010b. *Meilixueshan guojiagongyuan guanli tizhi yanjiu baogao* [Report on research on the Meili Snow Mountains National Park management model]. Kunming: Research Office of the People's Government of Yunnan Province.

Research Office and The Nature Conservancy (Research Office of the People's Government of Yunnan Province and The Nature Conservancy China Program). 2005a. *Dianxibei diqu jianshe guojiagongyuan zonghe baogao* [Comprehensive report on establishing national parks in northwest Yunnan]. Kunming: Research Office of the People's Government of Yunnan Province.

———. 2005b. *Xianggelila Bitahai Shuduhu guojiagongyuan jianshe fang'an* [Proposal for establishing the Shangrila Bita Lake–Shudu Lake National Park]. Kunming: Research Office of the People's Government of Yunnan Province.

———. 2005c. *Xianggelila da xiagu guojiagongyuan jianshe fang'an* [Proposal for establishing the Shangrila Gorge National Park]. Kunming: Research Office of the People's Government of Yunnan Province.

ri gdengs. 1994. mdo smad du dar ba'i drug pa'i glu rol [The sixth-month Lurol Festival of Amdo]. In *rma lho'i rtsom bsdus padma dkar po'i tshom bu* [The white lotus: Collected essays from Huangnan]. Lanzhou: Gansu Minzu Chubanshe.

Robinson, Brian E. 2012. *Getting More from Forests: The Effects of Management, Competition and Spatial Characteristics on Forest Livelihoods*. PhD diss., Nelson Institute of Environmental Studies, University of Wisconsin, Madison.

Rock, Joseph. 1931. "Konka Risumgongba, Holy Mountain of the Outlaws." *National Geographic Magazine* 60(1): 1–65.

———. 1956. *The Amnye Ma-Chhen Range and Adjacent Regions: A Monographic Study*. Rome: IsMEO.

Rohlf, Greg. 2003. "Dreams of Oil and Fertile Fields: The Rush to Qinghai in the 1950s." *Modern China* 29(4): 455–89.

Rosaldo, Renato. 1989. "Imperialist Nostalgia." *Representations* 26: 107–22.

Rose, Nikolas. 1999. *Powers of Freedom: Reframing Political Thought*. Cambridge: Cambridge University Press.

Rosenberger, Nancy. 2009. "Global Food Terror in Japan: Media Shaping Risk Perception, the Nation, and Women." *Ecology of Food and Nutrition* 48(4): 237–62.

Sahlins, Marshall. 2000a. *Culture in Practice: Selected Essays*. New York: Zone Books.

———. 2000b. "The Sadness of Sweetness, or, The Native Anthropology of Western Cosmology." In *Culture in Practice: Selected Essays*, 527–84. New York: Zone Books.

Saito, Haruo, and Gaku Mitsumata. 2008. "Bidding Customs and Habitat Improvement for Matsutake (Tricholoma Matsutake) in Japan." *Economic Botany* 62(3): 257–68.

Salick, Jan, Anthony Amend, Danica Anderson, Kurt Hoffmeister, Bee Gunn, and Zhendong Fang. 2007. "Tibetan Sacred Sites Conserve Old Growth Trees and Cover in the Eastern Himalayas." *Biodiversity and Conservation* 16: 693–706.

Salick, Jan, and Robert K. Moseley. 2012. *Khawa Karpo: Tibetan Traditional Knowledge and Biodiversity Conservation*. Saint Louis: Missouri Botanical Garden Press.

Salick, Jan, Yongping Yang, and Anthony Amend. 2005. "Tibetan Land Use and Change near Khawa Karpo, Eastern Himalayas." *Economic Botany* 50(4): 312–25.

Sassen, Saskia. 1999. *Globalization and Its Discontents: Essays on the New Mobility of People and Money*. New York: New Press.

Schein, Louisa. 2000. *Minority Rules: The Miao and the Feminine in China's Cultural Politics*. Durham, NC: Duke University Press.

Schroeder, Richard A. 1997. "'Re-claiming' Land in the Gambia: Gendered Property Rights and Environmental Intervention." *Annals of the Association of American Geographers* 87(3): 487–508.

Schwartz, Joan M. 1996. "The Geography Lesson: Photographs and the Construction of Imaginative Geographies." *Journal of Historical Geography* 22(1): 16–45.

Schwartz, Jonathan. 2008. "Shifting Power Relations: State-ENGO Relations in China." In *The Chinese Party-State in the 21st Century: Adaptation and the Reinvention of Legitimacy,* edited by André Laliberté and Marc Lanteigne, 58–77. New York: Routledge.

Scifo, Barbara. 2005. "The Domestication of Camera-Phone and MMS Communication: The Early Experiences of Young Italians." In *A Sense of Place: The Global and the Local in Mobile Communication,* edited by Kristóf Nyíri, 363–74. Vienna: Passagen Verlag.

Scott, James C. 1998. *Seeing Like a State: How Certain Schemes to Improve the Human Condition Have Failed.* New Haven: Yale University Press.

———. 2009. *The Art of Not Being Governed: An Anarchist History of Upland Southeast Asia.* New Haven: Yale University Press.

SDXBW (Sichuan sheng daocheng xianzhi bianzuan weiyuanhui). Daocheng xianzhi [Daocheng County annals]. 1997. Chengdu: Sichuan Renmin Chubanshe.

———. 2009. Daocheng xianzhi 1991–2005. [Daocheng County annals, 1991–2005]. Chengdu: Sichuan Kexue Jishu Chubanshe.

Sellars, Richard West. 2009. *Preserving Nature in the National Parks: A History.* 2nd ed. New Haven: Yale University Press.

Shahar, Meir, and Robert P. Weller, eds. 1996. *Unruly Gods: Divinity and Society in China.* Honolulu: University of Hawai'i Press.

Shakya, Tsering. 1999. *The Dragon in the Land of Snows: A History of Modern Tibet since 1947.* New York: Penguin Compass.

Shapiro, Judith. 2001. *Mao's War against Nature: Politics and the Environment in Revolutionary China.* Cambridge: Cambridge University Press.

Sharma, Aradhanya. 2006. "Crossbreeding Institutions, Breeding Struggle: Women's Empowerment, Neoliberal Governmentality and State (Re)formation in India." *Cultural Anthropology* 21(1): 60–95.

Shen Xiaoli, Sheng Li, Nyima Chen, Shengzhi Li, William J. McShea, and Zhi Lü. 2012. "Does Science Replace Traditions? Correlates between Traditional Culture and Local Bird Diversity in Southwest China." *Biological Conservation* 145(1): 160–70.

Shih, Victor. 2004. "Development, the Second Time Around: The Political Logic of Developing Western China." *Journal of East Asian Studies* 4: 427–51.

Shneiderman, Sara. 2010. "Are the Central Himalayas in Zomia? Some Scholarly and Political Considerations across Time and Space." *Journal of Global History* 5: 289–312.

Shrestha, Uttam Babu. 2012. "Asian Medicine: A Fungus in Decline." *Nature* 482(7383): 35.

Shrestha, Uttam Babu, and Kamaljit S. Bawa. 2013. "Trade, Harvest, and Conservation of Caterpillar Fungus (Ophiocordyceps Sinensis) in the Himalayas" *Biological Conservation* 159: 514–20.

Smith, Stephanie, and Steve Mark. 2009. "The Historical Roots of The Nature Conservancy in the Northwest Indiana/Chicagoland Region: From Science to Preservation." *South Shore Journal* 3: 1–10.

snying po rgyal and Solomon Rino. 2008. "Deity Men: Rebgong Tibetan Trance Mediums in Transition." *Asian Highlands Perspectives* 3: 1–277.

Sonam Norbu. 2009. "Kawagarbo shenshan xia de shenghuo" [Life at the foot of the sacred mountain Kawagarbo]. *Huigui* [Return] 3: 24–33.

————, ed. 2011. *Feixiang de xueshan: Deqin minjian xianzi geci huibian* [Flying Snow Mountains: Fiddle folksongs of Deqin]. Kunming: Yunnan Minzu Chubanshe.

Spengen, Wim van. 2002. "Frontier History of Southern Kham: Banditry and War in Multi-ethnic Fringe Lands of Chatring, Mili, and Gyethang, 1890–1940." In *Khams pa Histories: Visions of People, Place and Authority*, edited by Lawrence Epstein, 7–29. Leiden: Brill.

Sperling, Elliot. 1976. "The Chinese Venture in K'am, 1904–1911, and the Role of Chao Erh-feng." *Tibet Journal* 1(2): 10–36.

Springer, Jenny. 2009. "Addressing the Social Impacts of Conservation: Lessons from Experience and Future Directions." *Conservation and Society* 7: 26–29.

Stanley, Nick. 2002. "Chinese Theme Parks and National Identity." In *Theme Park Landscapes: Antecedents and Variations*, edited by Terence Young and Robert Riley, 269–90. Washington, DC: Dumbarton Oaks Research Library and Collection.

State Council of the People's Republic of China. 2009. *Guowuyuan guanyu fabu di qi pi guojiaji fengjingmingshengqu mingdan de tongzhi* [Notice of the State Council announcing the Seventh Cohort of National Scenic Areas]. Beijing: State Council of the People's Republic of China.

Stedman-Edwards, Pamela. 2000. "China: Southwestern Forests." In *The Root Causes of Biodiversity Loss*, edited by Alexander Wood, Pamela Stedman-Edwards, and Johanna Mang, 153–82. London: Earthscan.

Stephens, Joe, and David B. Ottoway. 2003. "Big Green." *Washington Post*, May 4–6.

Stephenson, Max, and Elisabeth Chaves. 2006. "The Nature Conservancy, the Press, and Accountability." *Nonprofit and Voluntary Sector Quarterly* 35: 345–66.

Stevens, Stan, ed. 1997. *Conservation through Cultural Survival: Indigenous Peoples and Protected Areas*. Washington, DC: Island Press.

Stevenson, Mark. 1999. *Wheel of Time, Wheel of History: Cultural Change and Cultural Production in an Amdo Tibetan Community*. PhD diss., University of Melbourne.

Stewart, Michelle O. 2009. "The 'Himalayan Gold' Rush: Prospectors' Practices and Implications for Management." In *Contemporary Visions in Tibetan Studies: Proceedings of the First International Seminar of Young Tibetologists*, edited by Brandon Dotson, Kalsang Norbu Gurung, Georgios Halkias, and Tim Myatt, 69–91. Chicago: Serindia Publications.

Stewart, Susan. 1984. *On Longing: Narratives of the Miniature, the Gigantic, the Souvenir, the Collection*. Durham, NC: Duke University Press.

Stuart, Kevin, Banmadorji, and Huangchojia. 1995. "Mountain Gods and Trance Mediums: A Qinghai Tibetan Summer Festival." *Asian Folklore Studies* 54(2): 219–37.

Studley, John. 2011. "Uncovering the Intangible Values of Earth Care: Using Cognition to Reveal the Eco-spiritual Domains and Sacred Values of the Peoples of Eastern

Kham." In *Sacred Natural Sites: Conserving Nature and Culture*, edited by Bas Ver-schuuren, Robert Wild, Jeffrey A. McNeely, and Gonzalo Oviedo, 107–18. London: Earthscan.

Sturgeon, Janet C. 2005. *Border Landscapes: The Politics of Akha Land Use in China and Thailand.* Seattle: University of Washington Press.

Sullivan, Sian. 2010. "'Ecosystem Service Commodities'—a New Imperial Ecology? Implications for Animist Immanent Ecologies, with Deleuze and Guattari." *New Formations: A Journal of Culture/Theory/Politics* 69: 111–28.

Sun Baohua. 2002. "Zongjiao yu xiejiao de falü jieding" [The legal definition of religion and heterodox cult]. *Qinghai minzu yanjiu* [Nationalities research in Qinghai] 4: 2–19.

T. Yangdon Dhondup. 2011. "Reb kong: Religion, History and Identity of a Sino-Tibetan Borderland Town." *Revue d'Études Tibétaines* 20: 33–59.

Tashi Nyima. 2007. "Santou niu" [Three cows]. *Huigui* [Return] 1: 27.

Tashi Nyima and Ma Jianzhong. 2010. *Xueshan zhi yan: Kawagarbo shenshan wenhua ditu* [The eye of the Snow Mountain: A map of the culture of the sacred mountain Kawagarbo]. Kunming: Yunnan Minzu Chubanshe.

Taussig, Michael. 1980. *The Devil and Commodity Fetishism in South America.* Chapel Hill: University of North Carolina Press.

Thargyal, Rinzin. 2007. *Nomads of Eastern Tibet: Social Organization and Economy of a Pastoral Estate in the Kingdom of Dege.* Leiden: Brill.

Tian Qunjian. 2004. "China Develops Its West: Motivation, Strategy, and Prospect." *Journal of Contemporary China* 13: 611–36.

Tian Shizheng and Yang Guihua. 2009. "Guojiagongyuan lüyou guanli zhidu bian-qian shizheng yanjiu—yi Yunnan Xianggelila Pudacuo guojiagongyuan wei li" [An empirical study of the changes in management systems of national parks—a case study of Pudacuo National Park in Shangrila of Yunnan]. *Guangxi Minzu Daxue xuebao, zhexue shehui kexue ban* [Journal of Guangxi University for Nationalities, philosophy and social science edition] 31(4): 52–57.

Tilt, Bryan. 2010. *The Struggle for Sustainability in China: Environmental Values and Civil Society.* New York: Columbia University Press.

TNC China Program. 2007. *The Nature Conservancy China Program Annual Report 2006.* Kunming: The Nature Conservancy China Program.

TNC China Program and International Ecotourism Research Center. 2009. *Luorong shengtai wenhua yanjiu xiangmu baogao* [Luorong eco-culture research project report]. Kunming: Ecotourism Faculty, Southwest Forestry College.

Togashi, K., and Sanford M. Zeller. 1934. "The American and Japanese Matsutakes." *Botany and Zoology* 2: 507–19.

Tominaga, Yasuto, Ryoko Ami, and Toshio Ito. 1981. "Matsutake of the People's Republic of China. 1, Matsutake of Yunnan Province." *Hiroshima Agricultural College Bul-letin* 6(4): 449–58.

Trouillot, Michel-Rolph. 2003. *Global Transformations: Anthropology and the Modern World.* New York: Palgrave Macmillan.

Tsering Samdrup. 2004. *Bod kyi skye khams rig pa spyi bshad 'dzam gling skye dgu'i spyi nor* [The ecological viewpoint of Tibetan Buddhism]. Kunming: Yunnan Minzu Publishing House.

Tsering, Topgyal. 2011. *The Insecurity Dilemma and the Sino-Tibetan Conflict*. PhD thesis, The London School of Economics and Political Science. London: LSE Thesis Online. http://etheses.lse.ac.uk/id/eprint/237.

Tsing, Anna. 1997. "Transitions as Translations." In *Transitions, Environments, Translations*, edited by Joan Scott, Cora Kaplan, and Debra Keates, 253–72. New York: Routledge.

———. 2002. "The Global Situation." In *The Anthropology of Globalization: A Reader*, edited by Jonathan Inda and Renato Rosaldo, 453–86. Malden, MA: Blackwell.

———. 2005. *Friction: An Ethnography of Global Connection*. Princeton: Princeton University Press.

Tsing, Anna, and Shiho Satsuka. 2008. "Diverging Understandings of Forest Management in Matsutake Science." *Economic Botany* 62(3): 244–53.

Tsultrim Lodroe. 2003. *Dus su bab p'i gtam lugs gnyis gsal b'i me long zhes bya ba bzhugs so* [Timely advice: The mirror that clarifies the two systems]. Hong Kong: Center for Service to the Bright Kindness of Tibetan Buddhism.

Turner, Jennifer, and Zhi Lü. 2006. "Building a Green Civil Society in China." In *State of the World 2006*, edited by Worldwatch, 152–70. Washington, DC: W. W. Norton & Co.

Urry, John. 2002. *The Tourist Gaze*. London: SAGE.

van Schendel, Willem. 2002. "Geographies of Knowing, Geographies of Ignorance: Jumping Scale in Southeast Asia." *Environment and Planning D: Society and Space* 20: 647–68.

van Spengen, Wim. 2002. "Frontier History of Southern Kham: Banditry and War in the Multi-ethnic Fringe Lands of Chatring, Mili and Gyethang, 1890–1940." In *Khams pa Histories: Visions of People, Place and Authority*, edited by Lawrence Epstein, 7–30. Boston: Brill.

Vandergeest, Peter, and Nancy Lee Peluso. 1995. "Territorialization and State Power in Thailand." *Theory and Society* 24(3): 385–426.

Varutti, Marizia. 2011. "Miniatures of the Nation: Ethnic Minority Figurines, Mannequins and Dioramas in Chinese Museums." *Museum and Society* 9(1): 1–16.

Vasantkumar, Chris. 2009. "'Domestic' Tourism and Its Discontents: Han Tourism in China's 'Little Tibet.'" In *Domestic Tourism in Asia*, edited by Shalini Singh, 129–50. London: Earthscan.

———. 2012. "Han at Minzu's Edges: What Critical Han Studies Can Learn from China's 'Little Tibet.'" In *Critical Han Studies: The History, Representation, and Identity of China's Majority*, edited by Thomas S. Mullaney, James Leibold, Stéphane Gros, and Eric vanden Bussche, 234–56. Berkeley: University of California Press.

———. 2013. "Unmade in China: Reassembling the Ethnic on the Gansu-Tibetan Border." *Ethnos: Journal of Anthropology* 78(5), 261–86.

Verdery, Katherine. 1996. *What Was Socialism? And What Comes Next?* Princeton: Princeton University Press.

Verschuuren, Bas, Robert Wild, Jeffery A. McNeely, and Gonzalo Oviedo, eds. 2011.

Sacred Natural Sites: Conserving Nature and Culture. London: Earthscan.

Viveiros de Castro, Eduardo. 1998. "Cosmological Deixis and Amerindian." *Journal of the Royal Anthropological Institute* 4(3): 469–88.

———. 2004. "Exchanging Perspectives: The Transformation of Objects into Subjects in Amerindian Ontologies." *Common Knowledge* 10(3): 463–84.

von Glahn, Richard. 2004. *The Sinister Way: The Divine and the Demonic in Chinese Religious Culture*. Berkeley: University of California Press.

Wade, Geoffrey. 2000. "The Southern Chinese Borders in History." In *Where China Meets Southeast Asia: Social and Cultural Change in the Border Region*, edited by Grant Evans, Chri. Hutton, and Kuah Khun Eng, 28–50. Bangkok: White Lotus.

Wainwright, Joel. 2008. *Decolonizing Development: Colonial Power and the Maya*. Oxford: Blackwell.

Waitz, Theodor. 2012. *Die Anthropologie der Naturvölker*. London: Ulan Press.

Walley, Christine. 2004. *Rough Waters: Nature and Development in an East African Marine Park*. Princeton: Princeton University Press.

Wang, Caroline, Mary Ann Burris, and Yueping Xiang. 1996. "Chinese Village Women as Visual Anthropologists: A Participatory Approach to Reaching Policymakers." *Social Science and Medicine* 42: 1391–1400.

Wang, Jing. 2001. "Culture as Leisure, Culture as Capital." *positions: east asia cultures critique* 9(1): 69–104.

Wang Lunguang. 2002. "Lun Xibu Da Kaifa yu jiazhi guannian gengxin" [On the Great Western Development strategy and the renewal of values]. *Qinghai Minzu Xueyuan Xuebao* 2: 15–19.

Wang Xiao-Liang and Yi-Jian Yao. 2011. "Host Insect Species of Ophiocordyceps Sinensis: A Review." *ZooKeys* 127: 43–59.

Wang Xiaoqiang and Bai Nanfeng. 1991 [1987]. *The Poverty of Plenty (*Furao de pinkun*)*. Translated by Angela Knox. New York: St. Martin's Press.

Weckerle, Caroline S., Yongping Yang, Franz K. Huber, and Qiaohong Li. 2010. "People, Money, and Protected Areas: The Collection of the Caterpillar Mushroom *Ophiocordyceps Sinensis* in the *Baima Xueshan* Nature Reserve, Southwest China." *Biodiversity and Conservation* 19(9): 2685–98.

Wen Pulin. 2003a. *Mangmang zhuanjing lu* [The endless prayer road]. Lhasa: Xizang Renmin Chubanshe.

———. 2003b. *Jieyuan Bajia Huofo* [Making friends with Bajia Rinpoche]. Lhasa: Xizang Renmin Chubanshe.

West, Paige. 2006. *Conservation Is Our Government Now: The Politics of Ecology in Papua New Guinea*. Durham, NC: Duke University Press.

West, Paige, and Dan Brockington. 2006. "An Anthropological Perspective on Some Unexpected Consequences of Protected Areas." *Conservation Biology* 20: 609–16.

West, Paige, James Igoe, and Dan Brockington. 2006. "Parks and Peoples: The Social Impact of Protected Areas." *Annual Review of Anthropology* 35: 251–77.

West, Patrick C., and Steven R. Brechin. 1991. *Resident Peoples and National Parks: Social Dilemmas and Strategies in International Conservation*. Tucson: University of Arizona Press.

Wilcox, Emily. 2012. *The Dialectics of Virtuosity: Dance in the People's Republic of China, 1949–2009*. PhD diss., University of California, Berkeley.

Wilkening, Kenneth E. 2004. *Acid Rain Science and Politics in Japan: A History of Knowledge and Action toward Sustainability*. Cambridge, MA: MIT Press.

Wilkes, Andreas. 2006. "Innovation to Support Agropastoralist Livelihoods in Northwest Yunnan, China." *Mountain Research and Development* 26: 209–13.

Williams, Dee Mack. 2002. *Beyond Great Walls: Environment, Identity, and Development on the Chinese Grasslands of Inner Mongolia*. Stanford: Stanford University Press.

Williams, Raymond. 2008. *Tourism, Landscape, and the Irish Character: British Travel Writers in Pre-Famine Ireland*. Madison: University of Wisconsin Press.

Winichakul, Thongchai. 1997. *Siam Mapped: A History of the Geo-Body of a Nation*. Honolulu: University of Hawai'i Press.

Winkler, Daniel. 2008a. "The Mushrooming Fungi Market in Tibet Exemplified by Cordyceps sinensis and Tricholoma Matsutake." *Journal of the International Association for Tibetan Studies* 4 THL#T5571, 46 pp.

———. 2008b. "Yartsa Gunbu (Cordyceps Sinensis) and the Fungal Commodification of Tibet's Rural Economy." *Economic Botany* 62(3): 291–305.

Working Group on Drafting the Development Plan for the Northwest Yunnan Tourism Region. 2004. *Dianxibei Xianggelila shengtailüyouqu fazhan guihua (gangyao)* [Development plan for the northwest Yunnan Shangrila ecotourism region (summary)]. Kunming: Working Group on Drafting Development Plans for the Six Great Tourism Regions of Yunnan.

Wylie, John. 2007. *Landscape*. New York: Routledge.

Xiao Tanglong. 2006. *Faxian Yading* [Discovering Yading]. Daocheng: Daocheng Xian Renmin Zhengfu.

Xibu diqu kaifa zhinan [Guide to the development of western China] 1988. Beijing: China Science and Technology Press.

Xie Hongyan, Wang Xiaosong, and Xu Jianchu. 2000. "The Impacts of Tibetan Culture on Biodiversity and Natural Landscapes in Zhongdian, Southwest China." In *Links between Cultures and Biodiversity: Proceedings of the Cultures and Biodiversity Congress 2000*, edited by Xu Jianchu, 527–37. Kunming: Yunnan Sciences and Technology Press.

Xie, Jisheng. 2001. "The Mythology of Tibetan Mountain Gods: An Overview." *Oral Tradition* 16(2): 343–63.

Xie Yan, Sung Wang, and Peter Schei, eds. 2004. *China's Protected Areas*. Beijing: Tsinghua University Press.

Xinhua. 2007. "Hu Jintao Proposes Scientific Outlook on Development for Tackling China's Immediate Woes, Challenges." October 15. http://news.xinhuanet.com/english/2007–10/15/content_6883135.htm.

Xirejiancuo. 2005. Unpublished report to The Bridge Fund.

———. 2008. Klu-rol (lu-rol) *Ritual: A Symbolic Communication between Mountain Deities and Human Agency*. BA thesis, Reed College, Portland, OR

Xu Jianchu, ed. 2000. *Links between Cultures and Biodiversity: Proceedings of the Cultures and Biodiversity Congress 2000*. Kunming: Yunnan Science and Technology Press.

Xu Jianchu, Li Bo, and David Waltner-Toews. 2004. "Habitat of Tibetan Nature and Culture." *EcoHealth* 1: 327–29.

Xu Jianchu, Erzi T. Ma, Tashi Dorje, Yongshou Fu, Zhi Lü, and David Melick. 2005. "Integrating Sacred Knowledge for Conservation: Cultures and Landscapes in Southwest China." *Ecology and Society* 10(2). http://www.ecologyandsociety.org/vol10/iss2/art7/.

Xu Jianchu and David R. Melick. 2007. "Rethinking the Effectiveness of Public Protected Areas in Southwestern China." *Conservation Biology* 21(2): 318–28.

Xu Jianchu and Andreas Wilkes. 2004. "Biodiversity Impact Analysis in Northwest Yunnan, Southwest China." *Biodiversity and Conservation* 13: 959–83.

Xu Xiake. 2004. *Xiake youji* [Travel notes of Xu Xiake]. Changchun: Shidai Wenyi Chubanshe.

Xu Zhigang, M. T. Bennett, Tao Ran, and Xu Jintao. 2004. "China's Sloping Land Conversion Programme Four Years On: Current Situation, Pending Issues." *International Forestry Review* 6: 317–26.

Yan, Hairong. 2003. "Neoliberal Governmentality and Neohumanism: Organizing Suzhi/Value Flow through Labor Recruitment Networks." *Cultural Anthropology* 18(4): 493–523.

———. 2008. *New Masters, New Servants: Migration, Development, and Women Workers in China*. Durham, NC: Duke University Press.

Yang, Bin. 2004. "Horses, Silver, and Cowries: Yunnan in Global Perspective." *Journal of World History* 15(3): 281–322.

Yang Hongying. 2006. "Tuoshan chuli goujian hexie shehuizhong de yajiao wenti" [On the problem of proper management of heterodox religions in a harmonious society]. In *Diqing Zhou goujian Hexie Shehui lilun yanjiu yaohui* [Collected essays from a research conference on theories for constructing Harmonious Society in Diqing Prefecture], edited by Jiang Wenjuan, 187–91. Kunming: Yunnan Minzu Publishing Company.

Yang Xuefei, Jun He, Chun Li, Jianzhong Ma, Yongping Yang, and Jianchu Xu. 2008. "Matsutake Trade in Yunnan Province, China: An Overview." *Economic Botany* 62(3): 269–77.

Yang, Yuexian. 2001. "Impacts and Effectiveness of Logging Bans in Natural Forests: People's Republic of China." In *Forests Out of Bounds: Impacts and Effectiveness of Logging Bans in Natural Forests in Asia Pacific*, edited by Patrick Durst, Thomas Waggener, Thomas Enters, and Tan Lay Cheng, 81–102. Bangkok: Food and Agricultural Organization of the United Nations.

Yasue, Eriko, and Kazuo Murakami. 2011. "Practicing Tourist Landscapes: Photographic Performances and Consumption of Nature in Japanese Domestic Tourism." In *Real Tourism: Practice, Care and Politics in Contemporary Travel Culture*, edited by Claudio Minca and Tim Oakes, 123–42. Abingdon, UK: Routledge.

Yeh, Emily T. 2000. "Forest Claims, Conflicts and Commodification: The Political Ecology of Tibetan Mushroom-Harvesting Villages in Yunnan Province, China." *China Quarterly* 161: 264–78.

———. 2005. "Green Governmentality and Pastoralism in Western China: 'Converting Pastures to Grasslands.'" *Nomadic Peoples* 9(1–2): 9–30.

———. 2007. "Translocal/Transnational Collaboration and Environmental Subject Formation: Sacred Lands and the Green Tibetan." Paper presented at the annual meeting of the American Anthropological Association, Washington, DC, November.

———. 2009a. "From Wasteland to Wetland? Nature and Nation in China's Tibet." *Environmental History* 14: 103–37.

———. 2009b. "Greening Western China: A Critical View." *Geoforum* 40: 884–94.

———. 2009c. "Living Together in Lhasa: Ethnic Relations, Coercive Amity and Subaltern Cosmopolitanism." In *The Other Global City*, edited by Shail Mayaram, 54–85. New York: Routledge.

———. 2009d. "Tibet and the Problem of Radical Reductionism." *Antipode* 41(5): 983–1010.

———. 2012. "Transnational Environmentalism and Entanglements of Sovereignty: The Tiger Campaign across the Himalayas." *Political Geography* 31: 418–28.

———. 2013. *Taming Tibet: Landscape Transformation and the Gift of Chinese Development*. Ithaca, NY: Cornell University Press.

Yeh, Emily T., and Gaerrang. 2011. "Tibetan Pastoralism in Neoliberalising China: Continuity and Change in Gouli." *Area* 43(2): 165–72.

Yeh, Emily T., and Kunga T. Lama. 2013. "Following the Caterpillar Fungus: Nature, Commodity Chains and the Place of Tibet in China's Uneven Geographies." *Social & Cultural Geography* 14 (3): 318–40.

Yin Kaipu. 2003. "Chuan-zang xian shang de kexue kaocha wangshi." http://www.cib.cas.cn/wh/whfk/wxcz/khfz/200908/t20090814_2401769.html (accessed July 19, 2012).

———. 2010. "Koukai 'zui hou xianggelila' da men." www.cib.cas.cn/wh/whfk/wxcz/khfz/200908/t20090803_2310004.html (accessed July 19, 2012).

Yü, Dan Smyer. 2012. *The Spread of Tibetan Buddhism in China: Charisma, Money, Enlightenment*. New York: Routledge.

Yúdice, George. 2003. *The Expediency of Culture: Uses of Culture in the Global Era*. Durham, NC: Duke University Press.

Yunnan Province Environmental Protection Department. 2009. *Dianxibei shengwu duoyangxing baohu xingdong jihua (2008–2012 nian)* [Action Plan for biodiversity conservation in northwest Yunnan 2008–2012]. Kunming: Yunnan Province Environmental Protection Department.

Yunnan Province Forestry Department and Research Office of the People's Government of Yunnan. 2009. *Yunnansheng guojiagongyuan fazhan zhanlüe yanjiu* [Research on development strategies for national parks in Yunnan]. Kunming: Research Office of the People's Government of Yunnan Province.

Yunnan Province Government. 2009. *Yunnansheng guojiagongyuan fazhan guihua gangyao (2009–2020)* [Summary of the 2009–2020 plan for national park development in Yunnan]. Kunming: Yunnan Province Government.

Yunnan Province Tourism Bureau and Yunnan Province Development and Reform Commission. 2008. *Yunnansheng lüyou chanye fazhan he gaige guihua gangyao* [Key points from the 2008–2015 tourism sector development and reform plan for Yunnan]. Kunming: Yunnan Province Tourism Bureau and Yunnan Province Development and Reform Commission.

Zackey, Justin. 2005. *Deforestation Discourses: Nature, Narratives and Policy in Northwest Yunnan Province, P.R.C.* PhD diss., University of California, Los Angeles.

Zerner, Charles, ed. 2000. *Peoples, Plants and Justice: The Politics of Nature Conservation.* New York: Columbia University Press.

Zhang, Li, and Aihwa Ong, eds. 2008. *Privatizing China: Socialism from Afar.* Ithaca, NY: Cornell University Press.

Zhang Peichang, Shao Guofang, Zhao Guang, Dennis C. Le Master, George R. Parker, John B. Dunning, and Li Qinglin. 2000. "China's Forest Policy for the 21st Century." *Science* 228: 2135–36.

Zhang Shi. 2000. "Traditional Culture and Ecological Construction in Shindao Tibetan Village, Zhongdian County, Yunnan Province." In *Links between Cultures and Biodiversity: Proceedings of the Cultures and Biodiversity Congress 2000*, edited by Xu Jianchu, 309–12. Kunming: Yunnan Sciences and Technology Press.

Zhang Yongjie, Erwei Li, Chengshu Wang, Yuling Li, and Xingzhong Liu. 2012. "Ophiocordyceps Sinensis, the Flagship Fungus of China: Terminology, Life Strategy and Ecology." *Mycology: An International Journal on Fungal Biology* 3(1): 2–10.

Zhou D.Q. and R. Edward Grumbine. 2011. "National Parks in China: Experiments with Protecting Nature and Human Livelihoods in Yunnan Province, People's Republic of China (PRC)." *Biological Conservation* 144(5): 1314–21.

Zimmerman, Andrew. 2001. *Anthropology and Antihumanism in Imperial Germany.* Chicago: University of Chicago Press.

Zinda, John A. 2012a. "Hazards of Collaboration: Local State Cooptation of a New Protected-Area Model in Southwest China." *Society and Natural Resources* 25: 384–99.

———. 2012b. "Tourism Development and Biodiversity Conservation in Southwest China: Extending Growth Coalition Theory." Unpublished manuscript.

Contributors

CHRIS COGGINS is a professor of geography and Asian studies at Bard College at Simon's Rock. His book *The Tiger and the Pangolin: Nature, Culture, and Conservation in China* (2003) is based on research on environmental history, political ecology, and nature conservation in southeast China. He has also conducted research on geopiety, nature conservation, and national identity among Tibetans in northwest Yunnan and is currently engaged in a field research project on village *fengshui* forests in southern and central China.

MICHAEL J. HATHAWAY is an associate professor of anthropology at Simon Fraser University in Vancouver, British Columbia. He is the author of *Environmental Winds: Making the Global in Southwest China* (2013) and a number of articles on environmentalism, indigeneity, and commodity chains in rural China.

TRAVIS KLINGBERG is a cultural geographer and PhD candidate in geography at the University of Colorado Boulder. His research, based primarily in Sichuan, focuses on the remaking of geography through tourism. He is the coauthor, with Tim Oakes, of "Producing Exemplary Consumers: Tourism and Leisure Culture in China's Nation-Building Project," in *China in and beyond the Headlines* (2012).

RALPH LITZINGER is an associate professor of cultural anthropology at Duke University as well as director of Duke Engage, Beijing. He is the author of *Other Chinas: The Yao and the Politics of National Belonging* and has also done research and published on global conservation movements and environmentalism in China and Tibetan politics. His new project is a study of migrant labor politics in China.

CHARLENE E. MAKLEY is an associate professor of anthropology at Reed College in Portland, Oregon, and author of *The Violence of Liberation: Gender and Tibetan Buddhist Revival in Post-Mao China* (2007). Her current book project, *The Politics of Presence: Development and State Violence among Tibetans in China*, based on long-term fieldwork in a rural Tibetan region in China's northwest (2002–11), is an ethnography of state-local relations among Tibetans grappling with their marginalization under China's Great Western Development campaign and in the wake of the 2008 military crackdown on Tibetan unrest.

ROBERT K. MOSELEY has worked for the Nature Conservancy in China, Illinois, and Idaho, where he has written widely on mountain ecology and conservation. His most recent book is *Khawa Karpo: Tibetan Traditional Knowledge and Biodiversity Conservation* (2012), coauthored with Jan Salick.

RENÉE B. MULLEN is an assistant professor of environmental studies at Eureka College. Before joining Eureka College, she worked as a scientist for the Nature Conservancy for ten years. Her research on microbial ecology and biodiversity conservation has been published in *Oecologia*, *Environmental Science and Policy*, *New Phytologist*, and *Environment, Development, and Sustainability*, among others.

MICHELLE OLSGARD STEWART is a PhD candidate in the Department of Geography at the University of Colorado Boulder. She conducted her dissertation research in northwest Yunnan from 2007 to 2010, examining the politics and ecology of the *Ophiocordyceps sinensis* resource economy. Her research interests include the politics of development and environmental governance and expanded roles for local knowledge in international development and conservation schemes.

CHRIS VASANTKUMAR is an associate professor of anthropology at Hamilton College in New York. He has conducted research on the cultural politics of difference and national belonging among Tibetans and members of other Chinese nationalities in Gansu, China, and in India since 2002. His essays have been published in the *Journal of Asian Studies*, *Ethnos: Journal of Anthropology*, and *Environment and Planning D: Society and Space*. His current research interests include outbound Chinese international tourism and the anthropology of money.

EMILY T. YEH is an associate professor of geography at the University of Colorado Boulder. She is the author of *Taming Tibet: Landscape Transformation and the Gift of Chinese Development* (2013) and numerous articles on the political ecology of pastoralism, commodity chains, and property rights, as well as relationships between transnationalism, sovereignty, and cultural politics in environmental movements and identities in Tibet.

LI-HUA YING is an associate professor of Chinese language and literature at Bard College in Annandale-on-Hudson, New York. Along with articles and translations of contemporary Chinese poetry, she has published *Cihai wenhui* (Magic of the word: New trends in Chinese expressions) and *Historical Dictionary of Modern Chinese Literature*. She is currently studying travel accounts on southwest China written by Westerners at the end of the nineteenth and the beginning of the twentieth century.

GESANG ZEREN is an independent scholar in Shangrila County and the founder of the Hamugu Village Center for the Protection of Indigenous Ecology and Culture.

JOHN ALOYSIUS ZINDA is a postdoctoral research associate at the Environmental Change Initiative at Brown University in Providence, Rhode Island. His research concerns the relationship between political, social, and ecological aspects of conservation efforts in China.

Index

Page numbers in italics refer to illustrations.

A

actor-network-theory (ANT), 26n4, 251n7

Adong Village, 43–44

Adorno, Theodor, 205

aesthetics, Chinese, 73n19

Agamben, Giorgio, 201, 275

agency: divine, 234–35, 248; human, 231, 234–35; landownership and, 100; landscapes and, 22–23, 26n2, 211; materiality and, 233, 236; Tibetan, 26n2, 245; *zhidak*, 249

Agrawal, Arun, 259–60

agropastoral sacred space, 205–7, 227

Alai, 23–24, 40, 49, 50n8; Gyarong writings, 29, 46–48; on the Tibetan Plateau, 45

Amdo, 63–64; Golog people, 8. *See also* Rebgong

Amnye Shachong, 232, 234, *235*, 240–41, 248

Anagnost, Ann, 238

animate landscapes: concept, 207, 213; legends, 210; resource conservation and, 226–27; sustainable development of, 213–14

architecture, 20, 47, 72n11, 160, 171n10

articulations: of environmental subjectivity, 260, 267; of the Green Tibetan, 258, 261–62, 264; of local Tibetan communities, 203, 258

assemblages, 26n4, 251n7, 261

Axu, 31–33

B

backwardness: of ethnic minority populations, 23, 40, 236; of Tibetan culture, 45, 231, 267, 280

Bai Hua, 30, 32

Belk, Russell, 26n3

Bhabha, Homi, 29

biodiversity conservation: aquatic, 131; culture and, 109, 133–35, 138, 145, 267, 277; in Diqing Prefecture, 215–16; at Khawa Karpo, 135–38; programs, 97–98, 130; of sacred areas, 264; of Shangrila Gorge, 111, 117; threats to, 140; in Yunnan, 133–35, 281–83, 285

biopower, 12, 99, 103

bodhisattvas, 78

bodily practices, 77, 87, 89, 93

botanical exploration, 81–83

Brosius, J. Peter, 144

Buddhism, 50n3, 216, 239; culture, 69; discourses, 233–34; education, 265, 278n4; environmental protection and, 258, 270; knowledge, 246, 261; practices, 235–36; sacred geographies of, 140, 146. *See also* lamas

C

Cairang Danzhi, 61–63

capital: ecological, 96, 212, 215; human, 236, 240; movement of, 230; state investment in, 12, 16, 211

capitalism: global, viii, 143, 159, 233; moral economy of, 230; space of, 207; state, 203, 249–50, 280–81 caterpillar fungus (*Ophiocordyceps sinensis*): biology and life cycle, 176, 178, 196nn2–3; collection in Dongwa Township, 182–87; collection in Shusong, 185–87, 192–93; earnings from, 175, 192–93; governance, 176, 179, 190–91, 193–96; harvesting/harvesters, 103, 175, *177*, 178, 197n14; sustainable yields approach to, 179

Catholicism, 34–35

Center for Biodiversity and Indigenous Knowledge, 97–98, 135

Chamdo, 256, 267, 271, 274; location, *10*

Chanadordje Mountain, 78–79, *79, 87*

Chime Namgyal, 274–76

China. *See* People's Republic of China (PRC)

China Protected Area Leadership Alliance Project, 122

Chinese Communist Party (CCP), 6, 13, 215, 238, 250; ecological management, 96; improvement projects, 82; "interethnic unity" policy, 36; in Konkaling, 81; promotion of Tibetan culture, 265–66; Sixth Plenum of the Seventeenth Central Committee, 200, 214

Chinese medicine, 175

Choy, Howard Y. F., 50n8

Chuji Mountain: legend of, 208–10; photo, *208*

Chuyun Spirit Lake, 222, *223*

civilizing projects, 8–9, 11, 25

Cizhong Village, 34–35, 38

Coggins, Chris, vii, 202, 285

collaboration: instability of, 285; interdisciplinary, 134, 147–49; process, 260; translocal and transnational, 271–72, 274, 277

Collected Essays from a Research Conference on Theories for Constructing Harmonious Society in Diqing Prefecture (Jiang Wenjuan), 215

colonization, 48

commodification: of landscapes, 14; of nature, 99, 155, 207; neoliberal forms of, 99; of place, 77

commodity chains, 101; caterpillar fungus, 171n8; matsutake mushroom,

102–3, 155, 165–67

conservation: biology, 147; community involvement in, 105–6, 127, 135–38; cultural knowledge and, 138–41; designations, 142; economy, 161–63; management, 102, 105–7, 124–27; organizations, 129–30, 148, 286; programs, 130, 132–33, 148, 154; of sacred landscapes, 97, 140, 145, 204, 213, 226; social costs and benefits of, 148–49; social science/scientists and, 147–50; state power and, 16, 107; tourism development and, 85, 92; water, 220. *See also* biodiversity conservation; nature reserves; protected areas; transnational conservation

Conservation International–China (CI-China), 255, 270; Sacred Lands Program, 97, 257, 263–65

Convention on International Trade in Endangered Species of Wild Fauna and Flora (CITES), 163, 168, 172n16

cosmology, 205, 207, 213–14, 226, 251n7

cosmopolitanism, 50n3, 202

crane, black-necked, 224, 270

Critical Ecosystem Partnership Fund (CEPF), 255, 265, 272

cults: heterodox (*xiejiao*), 216–17, 239–40, 245, 252nn16–17; mountain, 17n2; *zhidak*, 231, 234–36, 239, 243–44

cultural politics: of landscape, 229; of materiality, 233, 236, 238; of state-led development, 230, 232

cultural production, 214, 277; inter-, 261–62

culture. *See* Tibetan culture

Cultures and Biodiversity Congress (CUBIC), 281–84

D

Dalai Lama, 229, 274–75

Daocheng County, 81–82, 93; competition for Shangrila name, 90–91; establishment of Yading Nature Reserve, 83–84; tourism, 85, *86*, 89

Daocheng: The Remote Land (Lü Linglong), *84,* 84–85

deforestation, 216, 219, 256, 282; highway

expansion and, 188, 197n13; in Japan, 157, 170n4

deities: Diqing belief in, 206, 225; for household and village protection, 243–44; and moral implications, 247–49, 253n27; mountain, vii, 3–4, 17nn2–3, 207, 217–19, 231–32; recognition of, 234–35, 244–45, 249, 251n9; state control of, 238; water, 220–21. *See also lhawa; yullha; zhidak*

Deng Xiaoping, 230

Deqin County, 5, *10*, 136; logging, 162

Diqing Tibetan Autonomous Prefecture: agropastoral traditions, 206, 212; GDP, 181, 196n7; national parks, 105–6, 116–17, 120–21; natural resources, 215–16; politics, 98; population, 8; religious/cultural diversity, 33–36; tourism, 20–22, 25n1, 110–11, 180–81, 195–96; tourism planners, 114–15, 116, 120

Dokar Dzong, *21*, 21–22, 72n10

Dongwa Township: administrative villages, 183; caterpillar fungus collection, 182–85; governance, 182, 194; location, *15*, 180, 181

Dream World—Shambala, Gannan, A (Gonbo Namjyal), 60–61, 67–70

Duji Spirit Cave, 210, 212

E

Earth's Staircase, The (Alai), 46, 48

ecological modernization, 99; China's, 12, 14, 96, 100

ecological state: China's transformation to, 96, 154; conflicts, 107; disunity, 124; Harmonious Society as, 201; land classification systems, 100; normative and critical studies of, 154; power and, 16, 103; projects, 14–15; shangrilazation and, 106, 169; sovereignty and, 204; TNC's role in, 130; transnational conservation and, 102, 126

economic crisis (2008), 141–42

economic development: conservation and, 130, 134, 142; cultural production and, 214; of Great Western Development campaign, 71, 232–33, 236; post-Mao, 230, 232; tourism for, 85; use of local

resources for, 69, 211

economy: conservation, 161–63; cultural, 16, 23, 85, 227n4; matsutake mushroom, 154, 160, 162–63; moral, 230, 243, 250; tourism, 81, 91, 93, 113, 162

ecotourism, 212, 274, 286; in Hamugu Village, 214, 222, 225. *See also* Greater Shangrila Ecotourism Zone

Ekvall, Robert, 66

Eliade, Mircea, 228n7

elites, 230, 236, 246, 249, 262

endangered species, 270, 286; matsutake as, 103, 155, 163; protected areas for, 131

energy development, 14, 18n11

entrepreneurialism, 173n21, 274, 281, 283

environmental governance: of caterpillar fungus, 176, 179, 190–91, 193–96; endangered species as a form of, 163; of matsutake mushroom, 154–55, 164–65, 168–69; in Sino-Tibetan borderlands, 155; village-level, 103

environmental protection: of mountains, 6, 19, 256–57, 268, 272–73, 277; of national parks, 111; organizations, 267; in religion, 270, 272–73; resident involvement in, 113–14; of Sino-Tibetan landscapes, 13; Tibetan culture and, 99, 257–58, 263, 266, 270–73, 276

ethnic minorities: biodiversity and, 282; classification of, 11, 18n9; differences, 33–34, 61, 71; folk songs of, 41–43; freedom and, 41–42; Han fetishization of, 40–41; harmony among, 200–202; identity, 12, 23, 28–29, 42–44, 49, 283; in Lhasa, 50; as "living fossils," 40–41, 50n7; markers/indicators of, 53; miniaturization of, 57–59, 61; pastoral simplicity of, 30–31; religious diversity, 33–35; as "sites," 39; sovereign power and, 204; as TNC staff, 147. *See also minzu*

ethnobotany, 97–98, 266

ethnographers: Beijing, 18n9; Chinese, 145–46; Tibetan, 140, 145

Everest, Mount, 3–4

exiles, 261–62

exploitation: market, 185; of nature, 82; resource, viii, 14, 106, 116, 236; of youth, 217

F

Falun Gong, 216, 239
Fan Wen, 23, 28, 33–39, 48
folk practices, 235, 238–39
folk songs: ethnic identity and, 42–43;
    Khawa Karpo Culture Society and, 29,
    41; revitalization of, 29, 40
food safety, 164–65
foreign trade stations, 158–59, 166, 171n7
Foucault, Michel, 12, 99, 154
freedom, concept of, 41–42
Friedman, Thomas, 222, 228n15
frontier poetics, 25, 29, 43–44

G

Gannan Tibetan Autonomous Prefec-
    ture: altitude living conditions, 70; as
    China's "little Tibet," 24, 54, 59–60;
    clothing, 70; Langmusi, 51–54, 71n1;
    population, 69; Shambala, 67–68;
    shangrilazation of, 55; tourism, 69, 71
geopiety, 202, 213–14, 220, 227; definition,
    228n6; theophanic, 217
Gesang Zeren (Liu Zan), 202–3, 210,
    227n2; on belief in mountain deities,
    225; Hamugu Village guide, 222–24;
    role in Hamugu ecological/cultural
    action plan, 221–22, 225; on traditional
    conservation, 212–13
gift exchange, 175, 238, 248
globalization: capitalist, 230; economic,
    274; tourism and, 28, 30, 41
global warming, 5–6, 228n15
gnas ri, vii–viii, 4, 217–18. *See also* Khawa
    Karpo Mountain
Goffman, Erving, 251n7
Golog, 8
Gonbo Namjyal (Gongbao Nanjie), 60,
    63–65, 68, 73n17
Gonjo County, *10,* 257
governmentality: development and,
    13; environmental, 99, 104, 259; in
    Harmonious Society, 201; neoliberal,
    204, 259, 274, 277; population and, 12.
    See also environmental governance;
    resource governance
grasslands, partitioning of, 182–83

grassroots associations, 98, 256, 258,
    267–68
grazing, 183, 206; reduction, 162–63
Greater Shangrila Ecotourism Zone, 14,
    20, 90; map of, *10;* Yunnan's location
    within, 113. *See also* Yading Nature
    Reserve
Great Western Development strategy:
    in Daocheng County, 89; in Diq-
    ing Prefecture, 180–81; ecological
    management, 103–4; infrastructure
    and economic development, 232–33,
    236, 240, 251n6; purpose of, 13, 18n10,
    132–33; shangrilazation process and,
    25; in Sino-Tibetan borderlands, 8,
    25; sovereignty and, 202; sustainable
    development and, 203, 211; Tibetan
    culture and, 69, 236
Green Tibetan, 203; decline of, 276;
    discourse, 258, 261, 264; exiles,
    261–62; Rinchen Samdrup as, 204, 259;
    Tibetan-Han relations and, 265–66,
    272
Guo Jing, 140
Gyalthang. *See* Zhongdian County
Gyarong, 29, 46–48

H

Hamugu Village: cultural/ecologi-
    cal action plan, 221–22; ecotourism
    development in, 214, 222, 225; guide
    to, 222–24; photo, *208;* sustainable
    development, 203
Hamugu Village Center for the Protection
    of Indigenous Ecology and Culture,
    202, 221–22, 225
Han: environmental activists, 272–73;
    fetishization of minorities, 40–41; and
    Hui tensions, 53–54; merchants, 242;
    nationalism, 201; population, 11; tour-
    ists, 55, 76; view of Tibetans, 265–67;
    writers, 25, 27–28, 39; in Xiahe, 66–67
Harmonious Society: Han-Tibetan
    cooperation and, 259; as hegemonic,
    204; inception and principles, 12, 200;
    promotion of, 202, 276; Tibetan sover-
    eignty struggles and, 204, 275
harmony: ethnic, 33–36, 39, 200, 258–59,

L

Labrang: culture, 61–65, 73n17; embodiment of Tibetanness, 61, 64–65, 69–70; fame, 73n14
lamas, 4, 35; incarnate, 231, 234–35, 244, 252n10
land compensation, 188–92, 197n11, 197n13
landscapes: cultural, 7, 14, 17n6, 33, 145; exotic, 30; gendering of, 38; Gyarong, 46–48; identity and, 28–29, 47, 49–50; preservation of, 37–38; representations of, 22–23, 30, 48–49; resources and, 13–14, 188; as sites of cultural memory, 33, 35, 38; spiritual transformation and, 33; supernatural, 202, 204; Tibetan Plateau, 29, 45; tourist, 24, 71, 72n5; transformation of, 14–15; Western concepts of, 55–57, 72n8. *See also* animate landscapes; sacred landscapes
land tenure, 100, 131–32
Langmusi, 51–54, 71n1
Laojun Mountain, 121, 142
Latin American writers, 40, 50n6
Latour, Bruno, 26n4, 251n7
law, 201, 275
Lazong Ruiba (Lobsang Rinpa), 19–20, 22, 208, 221, 225
Lefebvre, Henri, 205, 207, 227n1
legislation: for endangered species, 155, 163; for national parks, 120–21, 123–24; *xiejiao*, 239, 252n16
Leisha's (restaurant), 51–54
Lévi-Strauss, Claude, 57
Lhasa, 50n3, 63–64, 201, 273
lhawa: materiality and, 236–38; photo of, *237*; recognition of, 244–45; role in Tibetan villages, 231, 240–45, 250; skepticism of, 245, 253n23; in trance state, 246–47, *247*, 252n18
Li, Chun, 173n22
Li, Peter J., 171n7
Li Guiming, 23, 29, 40–44, 50n6
Lijiang, 27, 158, 171n11
Lisu people: folk traditions, 41–42; identity, 44
"Little Tibets," 24, 59–60, 64; Xiahe as, 54, 65, 67

Llamas, Rosa, 26n3
local governments: community engagement, 125–26; development strategies, 108; national park management, 102, 105–7, 111–12, 117–20, 123–27, 142; tourism promotion, 83–84
logging, 14, 82, 133, 162, 172n13
Longwu, 231
Lost Horizon (Hilton), vii–viii, 20, 90–91, 285
lu, 213, 216, 219–20
Lü Linglong, 24, 83–86, 93

M

Ma Jianzhong, 3
Makley, Charlene, 67, 203
marginalization, 39–40, 189, 229
markets: exploitation, 185; Japanese, 103, 157; matsutake, 157–160, 168–69, 170n3, 197n10; for medicinal plants, 98–99; neoliberalism and, 202; reforms, 230–31, 245, 249; tourism, 38, 55
marriage, 34
materialism, metropolitan, 30–33, 38–39
materiality: cultural politics of, 233, 236, 238; in *zhidak* cults, 236, 244
matsutake mushroom *(Tricholoma matsutake)*: commodification of, 102–3; earnings from, 157, 160, 171n9; economy, 154, 160, 162–63; inclusion on endangered species list, 103, 155, 163, 172n16; monitoring system, 186, 197n10; pesticide contamination, 155, 164–67, 172n18; pickers, 153, 165–66; in Sino-Tibetan borderlands, 170n6; smaller-sized, 163, 168, 172n17, 173n22; spores, 172n17; sustainable yield assessments, 178; trade, 155–59, 163, 168–69, 170n3, 170n5
medicinal plants, 98, 141, 161–62, 268
mediums. See *lhawa*
Meili Snow Mountains National Park, 6, 117, 119, 125, 142; name, 128n2
memory, cultural, 33, 35, 38
Menzies, Nicholas, 173n22
Miao people, 50n7
migrant labor, 181, 190–91
militarization, 78, 201, 229

Mingyong glacier, 3–6
miniaturization, 72n9, 72n11; ethnic difference and, 57–60; landscapes and, 25, 71
minzu, 23; classification, 11–12, 18n9, 53; parks, 58–59; unity, 36, 202. *See also* ethnic minorities
Missouri Botanical Garden, 141
monasteries: Konkaling, 78, 81; Labrang, 9, 62– 64; Rongwo, 231–32, 234, 252n17; Tsengu Gomba, 79–80, 87, 91, 94n6; Xiahe, 67
monks, 36–37, 229, 273; Rongwo's, 232
Moseley, Robert, 102, 150n2, 161, 284
mountains: cults, 17n2; deities, vii, 3–4, 17nn2–3, 207, 217–18, 231–32; expeditions, 78–80; holy, 140; living conditions on, 70; rituals, 218–21. *See also* sacred mountains; *and specific name of mountain*
Mountains of Southwest China, 97, 255, 257, 264
Muchi Jiacuo, 253n22
Mullen, Renée, 102, 150n2, 284
multiculturalism, statist, 202, 204, 259
museums, 57–59, 72n12

N

Napahai Prairie, *15, 208, 223, 223*
nationalism: Han, 201; Tibetan, 203
National Park Administration Office, 122–23, 127–28
national parks: administration, 121–23; constraints of, 106; designations, 142; impact on industries, 115–16; management and policy, 119–23; plans and proposals, 111–15, 118; principles of, 108; promotion of, 117, 119; resident involvement, 125–26; as tourism attractions, 105–6; U.S. model, 128n3. *See also* Meili Snow Mountains National Park; Pudacuo National Park
nation-state: boundaries, 155, 281; Chinese, viii, 59, 62, 73n16
Natural Forest Protection Program, 109, 162
natural products, 99, 101

natural sciences, 102, 148
nature: commodification of, 99, 155; culture and, 40, 56; exploitation of, 82, 212; management of, 180; as resource in potential, 99; social behaviors and, 226; urbanites and, 31; Western traditions and, 145, 151n9
Nature Conservancy (TNC): adaptive management framework, 147; China Program, 108–9, 112, 120, 132, 134, 147; conservation origins, 131; criticism of, 129–30; economic limitations, 98; Khawa Karpo conservation, 135–42; land acquisition strategy, 131–32; and local governments, 105–6, 126–27; medicinal plant conservation, 97–98; national parks initiatives, 107, 111–13, 117–25, 142; nature tourism promotion, 161; social science integration, 149–50; staff and budget, 141–42, 146–47, 284–85; use of Photovoice, 137–38, 284; Western social scientists' critiques, 130, 142–47; Yunnan Great Rivers project, 102, 108–10, 132–35
nature reserves: designations, 142, 145; locations in Yunnan and Sichuan (map), *15*; Sanjiangyuan Nature Reserve, 100–101; as tourism attractions, 106. *See also* White Horse Snow Mountain (Baimaxueshan) Nature Reserve; Yading Nature Reserve
Naturvölker, 50n1
Naxi, 34–35, 50n7, 285
Nedu Village, 220
neri, vii–viii, 4, 217–18. *See also* Khawa Karpo Mountain
New Socialist Countryside, 200
Ngawa, 48
NGOs (nongovernmental organizations): Friends of Nature, 266; funding, 98; organic agriculture promotion, 165; political pressures, 274, 276; poverty alleviation, 281; proliferation in China, 96–97; sovereignty and, 277; Tibetan, 256, 258, 267–68. *See also* Nature Conservancy (TNC)
Nishi Administrative Village, 224
nomadic people, 8, 66, 280

non-timber forest products, 101, 162, 168, 170n3
nyen, 4, 17n3, 217–18
Nyíri, Pál, 56, 58

O

Oakes, Tim, 50n7
Olympics (Beijing), 229, 273, 279
ontologies, 6, 26n4, 56, 213
"othering" process, 30
Ou Xiaokun, 134

P

pastoralism, 30, 32
pastures, 182–83
People's Republic of China (PRC): conservation strategies, 111, 132–33; domestic tourism, 24, 55–56, 77–78, 89–93; ecological modernization, 12, 14, 96, 100; environmentalists/environmental movement, 262, 267–68, 271–73, 276; environmental management in, 154–55, 157; exports, 164, 171n7; food safety, 164; miniaturizations and, 57–59; pesticide usage, 155, 164–65, 168; placemaking projects, 90–92; protected areas, 94n2, 106, 128n1; state incorporation, 11–12, 49; territory, 7, 9; tourist sites classification, 50n4
personhood, 16, 203, 207, 210, 260
pesticides, 155, 164–67, 172n18
photography practices, 77, 87–89
Photovoice, 137–38, 284–85
place, practice of, 77, 83, 88–89, 92–93
placemaking projects, 90–92, 211
political ecology: of changing landscapes, 7; of resource governance, 99, 103, 176
pollution, 5–6, 157, 164
population, 8–9, 10, 11; development and, 12; of Gannan Prefecture, 69; of western China, 13; Xiahe County, 65–66
power relations: in conservation, 141, 150, 186; landscapes and, 7, 22; in resource control, 190–91, 194–95; of villagers and outsiders, 138
property rights, 176
protected areas: categories, 128n1; for endangered species, 131; management

and regulation, 94n2, 102, 106, 110, 124–26; planning, 114–15; for tourism, 92, 106; in Yunnan, 108–10. *See also* national parks; nature reserves
protests (2008), 229, 250; across the Tibetan Plateau, 98, 201, 273
Pudacuo National Park: establishment of, 105, 116; management, 122; resident involvement, 119, 120; success of, 120; TNC retreat from, 124; tourism plan, 116–18

Q

Qinghai, 185, 236, 252n11; *zhidak* and *xiejiao* cults, 234, 239–40

R

Rebgong: annual offering festival, 252n19, 253n21; infrastructure, 253n25; *lhawa* figure in, 241, 244, 251n10, 252n18; location, *10*; mountain deity recognition, 249; *zhidak* cults, 231–32, 235–36, 239. *See also* Jima Village (pseud.)
Red Poppies (Alai), 46, 50n8
regionalism, 50nn6–7
religion: of borderland ethnic groups, 33–35; environmental protection and, 270, 272–73; rituals, 205, 216–21, 232, 238–39; space and, 207, 227n1; spirituality, 216; state regulation of, 236, 238–39; Tibetan practices, 36–37. *See also* Buddhism; cults; deities
Remote Country of Women, The (Bai Hua), 30, 32
representation-practice relationship, 88–89
Research Office of the Yunnan Provincial Government: national parks involvement, 115–16, 122–23; Nature Conservancy (TNC) and, 112–13, 126–27; Pudacuo National Park proposal, 118
resource extraction, 13, 106, 215, 229, 280
resource governance, 100, 155, 160, 179; political ecology of, 99, 103, 176. *See also* environmental governance
resource management, 101, 155, 178, 258
reterritorialization, 24, 202, 211
Return (Huigui), 29, 39–40, 44, 49

sovereignty: of NGOs, 277; over individual bodies, 201; of Sino-Tibetan borderlands, 9, 13; Tibetan, 202, 204; transnational organizations and, 267

space: of Chinese nation-state, viii; Lefebvre on, 205, 207, 227n1; miniaturizing methods and, 57, 59–60; production of, 211, 214; ritual demarcation of, 210–11; sacred, 205–7, 227

special conservation zones, 109, 111–12

special ethnic zones, 54–55, 109

Stalin, Joseph, 18n9

Stanley, Nick, 72n10

state incorporation, 11–12, 49

state-led development, 190, 229–32; education and social welfare, 251n3; infrastructure, 232–34, 250, 253n25. *See also* Great Western Development strategy

state power: governance and, 154; nature conservation and, 16, 107; in Sino-Tibetan borderlands, 13, 28

Stedman-Edwards, Pamela, 172n13

Stewart, Michelle Olsgard, 103

subject formation, environmental, 259–60, 271, 277

suicide, 202. *See also* self-immolations

Sullivan, Laurence, 228n7

Sun Baohua, 240

supernatural, the, 204, 228n7

surveillance, 96, 201, 216, 273

sustainable development, 12, 96; of animate landscapes, 213–14; of Great Western Development strategy, 203, 211

sustainable yields, 178–79

suzhi, 236, 252n12

T

Tashi Dawa, 24, 40

"tashi delek" greeting, 63–64

Tashi Nyima, 23, 29, 49; *The Eye of the Snow Mountain*, 41; poetry, 43–44

territorialization, 100, 276

theme parks, 57–58, 72n10

Three Parallel Rivers World Heritage Site, 110, 215, 286; map of area, 15

Tibetan culture: backwardness of, 45, 231, 267, 280; biodiversity conservation and, 264, 267; borderlands and, 8–9; China's nature and, 203; Chinese promotion of, 265–66; ecological knowledge and, 98–99, 257; environmental protection and, 258, 263, 266, 270–73, 276; in Labrang, 61–65, 73n17; preservation of, 37–38; reinvention of, 201; threats to, 146; tourism and, 24, 38–39

Tibetan Doctors Association, 98, 264, 267

Tibetanness: Alai's, 46, 48; of Diqing national parks, 106; Gannan Prefecture and, 68, 70; Labrang embodiment of, 61, 64–65, 69–70; tourism and, 59

Tibetan Plateau: Alai's view of, 45; climate, 178; landscapes, 29, 45; nature reserves, 106; "opening up" the, 280; pastures, 183; protests (2008), 98, 201, 273

Tominaga, Yasuto, 158

Tongren. *See* Rebgong

tourism: Chinese tourists, 24–25, 51–60, 71, 72n8; and exploration, 91–92; in Gannan Prefecture, 69, 71; independent, 78, 92, 94n4, 267; in Japan, 72n7; in Labrang, 62–65; in Langmusi, 51–54; photography practices, 87–89; in Tibetan Autonomous Region, 20–22, 25n1; Tibetan culture and, 24, 38–39; Western, 55–57, 60, 71. *See also* Great Western Development strategy; "Little Tibets"; tourism development

tourism development: highway expansion, 181, 187, 195–96; in Jiuzhaigou, 85, 92; in Northwest Yunnan, 113–15; promotion of national parks, 117; Shangrila and, 20, 91; in Sino-Tibetan borderland areas, 16, 20; in Yading, 76–78, 86–90

trade routes, 156, 169, 206

Trador, 256, 269, 271

translation, 260, 272

transnational conservation, 98; organizations, 126, 129, 264–65, 267, 277; sacred lands and, 276. *See also* Nature Conservancy (TNC) travel writing: of Alai, 29, 45–49; of Fan Wen, 33–39; frontier minority writers, 29–30; guides, 23; Han writers, 25, 27–28, 39; on landscape features, 48–49; outsider/insider relations in, 48; self-discovery in, 28–33; shangrilazation and, 23–24; of Wen Pulin, 30–33

tree planting, 269–70

tsampa, 53

tsen, 218

Tserangding, 257–58, 269

Tsering, Topgyal, 50n9

Tsing, Anna, 260, 285

U

unity: of Chinese nation, 57, 59; "interethnic" (*minzu tuanjie*), 36, 202; Tibetan, 11, 49

urbanites, 31, 38, 45, 48, 58

V

Varutti, Marizia, 57

Vasantkumar, Chris, 24

violence: law and, 201, 275; state, 275–76

Voluntary Environmental Protection Association, 263, 269–71, 274–76, 278n3

W

Washington Post, 129

Weixi, 27, 35

Wen Pulin, 23, 28, 37, 39, 48; Axu writings, 31–33

White Horse Snow Mountain (Baimaxueshan) Nature Reserve, 27, 185–87, 286; village rules, 162, 171n12

Wilcox, Emily, 73n19

wilderness, notion of, 131

wildlife: conservation, 266, 275; management, 179–80; products, 171n7, 172n15

Wilson, Ernest Henry, 82–83

Winkler, Daniel, 170n6

Wolf Totem (Jiang Rong), 30, 40

women: compared to landscapes, 38; ritual practices, 219, 221; rural, 137; Tibetan, 32

World Wide Fund for Nature (WWF), 161–62, 222, 263

X

Xiahe County: dialect, 63–64; Hui merchants, 53–54; name, 62–63; population diversity, 65–67; tourism, 62, 66–67; travel texts of, 24, 60. *See also* Labrang

Xianggelila, 280–81, 283, 285. *See also* Shangrila

xiejiao: cults, 216; legislation, 239, 252n16; as the market's Other, 240, 245, 247; state scrutiny toward, 239

Xining, 241, *242*, 245

Xu Xiake, 27–28

Y

Yading Nature Reserve: horse trekking, 86, 94n10; naming and establishment, 82–85; religious significance, 75–76; Rock's discovery of, 80–81; tourism, 24–25, 76–78, 86–90, 92–93; UNESCO designation, 92

Yan Hairong, 252n12

Yanjing, 38

Yeh, Emily, 50n3, 203–4, 285

Ying, Li-hua, 23

Yin Kaipu, 24, 81–85, 93

Yubeng Village, 4–6, 119, 161

Yúdice, George, 227n4

yullha, 3, 17n2, 216; ritual practices, 218–20

Yunnan: biodiversity, 281–83, 285; "Conservation and Development Action Plan," 108–10, 133–36, 138, 140; critiques of TNC in, 144–50; cultural revitalization in, 40–41; cultural tourism in, 161; economic change, 211; ethnic groups, 18n9, 49; Forestry Department, 121–26; matsutake production, 103, 154–55, 156, 158–59, 164–67; national parks initiatives, 102, 105–7, 111–16, 122; Shangrila designation, 90, 94n13, 281; tourism development plan, 113–15

Yunnan Great Rivers Project, 102, 108, 149, 284–85; conservation priorities, 133–34; implementation of, 135, 138; partners and funding, 110, 132

Yunnan Matsutake Association, 166–67

Yu Qingyuan, 27–28

Z

Zhang, Paul, 34

Zhang Xuezhong, 90

zhidak: agency, 249; belief in, 225; cults, 231, 234–36, 239, 243–44; description, 3, 17n2, 218; legend of Shika and Chuji, 208–10; political ecologies of, 207; protection of, 19, 246; recognition, 234; retaliation, 213–14, 226–27; ritual practices, 218–20, 248–49; sovereignty and, 203. See also *lhawa*

Zhongdian County: definition/meaning of, 39; deforestation, 219; landscapes, 38; Shangrila designation, viii, 20, 90, 212, 283

Zhongxin Town, 20–21, 159

Zinda, John, 101–2

Zomia, 9, 103, 156, 170n2; regional extent, 17n7